What Journalism Could Be

Barbie Zelizer

polity

Cues for Considering Section I, Section II, Section III © Barbie Zelizer, Jennifer Henrichsen & Natacha Yazbeck

First published in 2017 by Polity Press

Polity Press
65 Bridge Street
Cambridge CB2 1UR, UK

Polity Press
350 Main Street
Malden, MA 02148, USA

ISBN-13: 978-1-5095-0786-3
ISBN-13: 978-1-5095-0787-0 (paperback)

A catalogue record for this book is available from the British Library.

Library of Congress Cataloging-in-Publication Data
Names: Zelizer, Barbie, author.
Title: What journalism could be / Barbie Zelizer.
Description: Cambridge, UK; Malden, MA: Polity Press, 2016. | Includes bibliographical references and index.
Identifiers: LCCN 2016016611 (print) | LCCN 2016029002 (ebook) | ISBN 9781509507863 (hardcover : alk. paper) | ISBN 1509507868 (hardcover: alk. paper) | ISBN 9781509507870 (pbk. : alk. paper) | ISBN 1509507876 (pbk. : alk. paper) | ISBN 9781509507894 (mobi) | ISBN 9781509507900 (epub) Subjects: LCSH: Journalism.
Classification: LCC PN4731 .Z455 2016 (print) | LCC PN4731 (ebook) | DDC 070.4--dc23
LC record available at https://lccn.loc.gov/2016016611

Typeset in 10.5 on 12pt Times by Servis Filmsetting Ltd, Stockport, Cheshire
Printed and bound in the United Kingdom by Clays Ltd, St Ives PLC

For further information on Polity, visit our website: politybooks.com

Contents

Acknowledgments   page vii

1   Imagining Journalism   1

Beginnings   9

2   Twelve Metaphors for Journalism   11

Section I Key Tensions in Journalism   33

   Cues for Considering Key Tensions in Journalism   35
   With Jennifer Henrichsen and Natacha Yazbeck

3   "Eyewitnessing" as a Journalistic Key Word:
    Report, Role, Technology and Aura   39

4   How the Shelf Life of Democracy in Journalism Scholarship
    Hampers Coverage of the Refugee Crisis   61

5   Practice, Ethics, Scandal, Terror   84

Section II Disciplinary Matters   105

   Cues for Considering Disciplinary Matters   107
   With Jennifer Henrichsen and Natacha Yazbeck

6   Journalism and the Academy, Revisited   111

7   Journalism Still in the Service of Communication   132

8   On Journalism and Cultural Studies: When Facts, Truth
    and Reality Are God-Terms   150

Section III New Ways of Thinking About Journalistic Practice   169

Cues for Considering New Ways of Thinking About
Journalistic Practice   171
With Jennifer Henrichsen and Natacha Yazbeck

9   A Return to Journalists as Interpretive Communities   175

10   Reflecting on the Culture of Journalism   193

11   When 21st-Century War and Conflict Are Reduced
to a Photograph   212

Endings   237

12   Thinking Temporally about Journalism's Future   239

References   263
Index   317

Acknowledgments

The author would like to acknowledge the kind permission of publishers to reproduce and rework chapters (listed here under their original titles) from the following publications:

Chapter 2: Definitions of Journalism. In Kathleen Hall Jamieson and Geneva Overholser (eds.), *The Press*. Oxford University Press, 2005, 66-80. Reproduced by permission of Oxford University Press, http:// global.oup.com/academic.
Adapted from Barbie Zelizer, *Taking Journalism Seriously*. Thousand Oaks: Sage, 2004. Reproduced by permission.

Chapter 3: On "Having Been There": "Eyewitnessing" as a Journalistic Key Word. *Critical Studies in Media Communication*, 24(5), December 2007, 408–28. Reproduced by permission of Taylor and Francis.

Chapter 4: On the Shelf Life of Democracy in Journalism Scholarship. *Journalism* 14(4), June 2013, 459–73. Reproduced by permission of Sage.

Chapter 5: When Practice is Undercut by Ethics. In Nick Couldry, Mirca Madianou and Amit Pinchevsky (eds.), *Ethics of Media*. London: Palgrave Macmillan, 2013, 317–37. Reproduced by permission of Palgrave Macmillan.

Chapter 6: Journalism and the Academy. In Karin Wahl Jorgensen and Thomas Hanitzsch (eds.), *Handbook of Journalism Studies*. Mahwah, NJ: Lawrence Erlbaum, 2008, 29–41.
Adapted from Barbie Zelizer, *Taking Journalism Seriously*. Sage, 2004. Reproduced by permission.

Chapter 7: Journalism in the Service of Communication. *Journal of Communication*, February 2011, 1–27. Reproduced by permission of Wiley.

Chapter 8: When Facts, Truth, and Reality Are God-Terms: On Journalism's Uneasy Place in Cultural Studies. *Communication and Critical/Cultural Studies*, 1(1), March 2004, 100–19. Reproduced by permission of Taylor and Francis.

Chapter 9: Journalists as Interpretive Communities. *Critical Studies in Mass Communication*, 10, September 1993, 219–37. Reproduced by permission of Taylor and Francis.

Chapter 10: The Culture of Journalism. In James Curran and Michael Gurevitch (eds.), *Mass Media and Society* (4th edition). London: Edward Arnold (Bloomsbury Academic), 2005, 198–214. Reproduced by permission of Bloomsbury Academic, an imprint of Bloomsbury Publishing Ltd.

Chapter 11: When War is Reduced to a Photograph. In Stuart Allan and Barbie Zelizer (eds.), *Reporting War: Journalism in Wartime*. Abingdon, Oxon: Routledge, 2004, 115–35. Reproduced by permission of Routledge.

Chapter 12: Tools for the Future of Journalism. *Ecquid Novi: African Journalism Studies*, July 2013. Reproduced by permission of Taylor and Francis.

1

Imagining Journalism

Albert Einstein is rumored to have said that logic can take people from A to B, but imagination will take them everywhere. *What Journalism Could Be* draws from that sensibility. Imagining journalism into its margins, across its corners and beyond its limitations is an exercise that invites the accommodation of change. It calls on scholars of journalism to interrogate the commonly accepted and generally unchallenged contours of journalism's practical accomplishment and intellectual conceptualization. And it calls on journalists to consider the possibilities of novelty and transformation, while being mindful that the risks this entails may complicate an already tenuous landscape.

Why should we rethink journalism today? The change in its environment suggests that doing so might be fruitful, but not in any immediately obvious or predictable fashion. From moves into automated news copy, user-generated content, wearables and virtual reality to newspaper closures and layoffs, many presume that journalism is currently at its point of exhaustion. The lines of that reasoning, embraced by many journalists and journalism scholars alike, are clear: they rest upon stress points of many kinds that offer either spirited proclamations of how the news must move with the times or depressed lamentations of what has been irretrievably lost. One side – the enthusiasts – sees change as the omnipotent enabler of all things new, the other – the naysayers – as the elimination of a legacy gone too soon. Neither invokes an incremental understanding of change as reciprocal give and take, adjustment, modification or turn-taking. And yet each of these activities regularly comes to the fore when change is on the horizon.

This book is situated in-between the naysayers and the enthusiasts. I argue that change in journalism can be embraced by considering it as a gradual back-and-forth between positions, where journalism's practitioners, observers and analysts might imaginatively assess both what change can bring and how it resonates with where journalism has been. By accommodating new ways of understanding tensions in journalism, of thinking disciplinarily about journalism and of conceptualizing journalistic practice, this book thus charts a path toward a more textured environment through which to imagine what journalism could be.

Imagination does not inhabit journalism without qualification. A slew of factors – historical, social, cultural, economic, political, moral, ideological, technological – has separated it from most understandings of the news. An alignment with narrow understandings of modernity and reason, an identity that highlights its preoccupation with realism, an institutional neighborhood whose most proximate residents – politics or the economy – privilege truth-telling over making-up, a university environment that accommodates its relevance for the public good are some of the variables that have pushed imagination aside. Though imaginative thinking invariably slips into theories and discussions of journalism – Adam (1993, 1), for instance, defined journalism "as a product of the imagination," while Schudson (1996, 96) observed how "making [news] is not faking, not lying, but . . . it cannot be done without play and imagination" – by and large thinking about journalism in conjunction with imagination has been confined to the art of narrative storytelling (Fishkin, 1985).

And yet its relevance in journalism is practically airborne. The very essence of journalism is creating an imagined engagement with events beyond the public's reach. How that is accomplished is also imagined because journalism operates largely out of the public eye (Zelizer, 1992a). Journalists gather their information in ways and from domains that remain largely invisible. Acting much like shamans who journey to inaccessible worlds and return with some critical insight, journalists act as "stabilizing agents who solidify consensus and reinstate social order on their return" (Zelizer, 1992a, 21). What the journalist knows is valued precisely because no one else shares that knowledge, rendering it necessarily the target of public imagination. Even journalism education, wrote Keeble (2007, 2), "needs to encourage the creative spirit just as practitioners need to acknowledge and further explore its creative possibilities." There is, then, far more of a connection to imagination in journalism than just narrative craft.

The focus on imagination draws too from beyond journalism. It has long been the focus in social and cultural theory, where multiple scholars have invested efforts in understanding what imagination could bring. Often aligned with the US sociologist C. Wright Mills in his description of the discipline of sociology – as "the capacity to shift from one perspective to another . . . to range from the most impersonal and remote transformations to the most intimate features of the human self and to see the relations between the two" (Mills, 1959, 7) – or with what Anthony Giddens (2001, 699) later paraphrased as the "application of imaginative thought to the asking and answering of sociological questions [in which someone] . . . thinks oneself away" from what is already known, imagination has been invoked by scholars in wide-ranging disciplines: Benedict Anderson (1983) in history and political science, John Thompson (1984) in sociology, Arjun Appadurai (1996) in anthropology, and Charles Taylor (2002) in philosophy, among others.

More a response to concerns over a particular version of modernity than to other obstacles obstructing its fuller accommodation, the current turn toward imagination constitutes for many a redress to modernity's impacts and burdens, where it was to be disciplined via an insistence on instrumental reason and rational thought. As Theodor Adorno (1976 [1969], 51) famously said, fantasy – his word for imagination – "is only tolerated when it is reified and set in abstract opposition to reality." Imagination's current reclamation is seen instead as an enterprise that can "either be used to compensate for the shortcomings of existing realities or to produce new ones" (Schulte-Sasse, 1986, 25). With that in mind, scholars have elaborated the layers of its presumed use-value: imagination, wrote Appadurai (1996, 31), "has become an organized field of social practices, a form of work (in the sense of both labor and culturally organized practice), and a form of negotiation between sites of agency (individuals) and globally defined fields of possibility."

So it is with journalism. Though running free with the fields of possibility through which journalism itself can be conceived has always been diminished by the aforementioned obstructions to imagination's inclusion, this book makes a pitch for thinking anew about the mindset that has unwisely – and, in this view, unproductively – set reason on one side of the fence and imagination on the other. Though surveying the field is always in part reductive, we need to rethink how we can understand their relationship more productively. What has been lost in imagination's compartmentalization? What might be gained by reviving its centrality?

The chapters in this book aim to address these questions. Though extensively revised, the work assembled here has by and large made claims to imagination before, if less definitively than it does so in these pages. Offering an updated set of articles and book chapters that originally saw the light at some point over the last 25 years, this book engages vigorously with the idea of imagining journalism, focusing on how imaginative thinking – and its prevailing associated concepts and practices – fare in journalism today.

The current moment has been characterized as one of radical uncertainty, but the fields of possibility for thinking it through have been smaller than they need to be. When asked to predict developments for journalism on the eve of 2016, most responses tended to avoid the task's broader contours and chose to focus almost unilaterally on technology. Headlines such as "Technology Trends Journalists Should Watch in 2016" (Ciobanu, 2015) or "The Most Likely Media and Tech Developments in 2016" (Sutcliffe, 2015) were plentiful. While useful for hedging against technology's push forward, such efforts nonetheless suggest a paring down of imaginative thinking. Where are the people and texts of journalism? Its craft and culture? Its ideology and mindset? Its labor, workplace politics or relations with other institutions – all products of what C. Wright Mills classified as the stuff derived from the "playfulness of mind" (Mills, 1959, 211)?

Five attributes of the current moment make the essays collected here newly relevant. Because each revisits earlier arguments and applies them to different dimensions of journalism's contemporary environment, each asks us to reconsider journalism today through the prism of imaginative thinking. Each suggests new vantage points through which to reenergize the exhausted quality of much of journalism's current discussion.

A first reason to accommodate imagination has to do with craft. Because so much of journalism takes place out of the public eye, much of the initial drive toward journalistic activity has never been codified sufficiently for academics in search of repeatable results. What G. Stuart Adam (1976, 3) called "the journalistic imagination" is overloaded with individualized doses of curiosity, autonomy, improvisation, adventure and exploration that are central to newsmaking. Though other modes of thinking about journalism have been developed in academe – and are engaged in the pages that follow – the best one can hope for in understanding the idiosyncrasies of journalistic craft is to consider them against their many fields of possibility. Thus, for instance, how journalists scramble to cover politics when its contours are aggressively shifting – as seen in the US presidential race or the UK's decision to exit the European Union – or how journalists improvise the disconnect between their visions of journalistic activity and a diminishing institutional landscape for its practice are examples of journalistic craft rising to the fore. Imaginative thinking lays open the potential for assessing its relevance.

A second reason to reconsider imaginative thinking is political – the evolving nature of what journalism must necessarily address in the current political environment. Though journalism has always adapted to evolving topics of newsworthy interest, many of today's political news stories are bigger, more widespread and more broadly impactful than much of what passed as news in earlier time periods: the global refugee crisis and its diminution of human dignity in scores of nations around the world is a powerful and much more challenging follow-up to the local, regional or even national political stories of earlier times that tended to reflect more precisely the jurisdiction of conventional news outlets. Thus, an older scandal like Watergate – US-centric, involving US politics and US legacy journalism – was more directly and readily covered by journalism of the time than was the more recent scandal involving the Murdoch news empire. As the latter's authority spread in nondescript ways across institutional, generic, technological and geographic arenas, when its underside surfaced with the 2011 *News of the World* scandal, it impacted politics, the police, technology and journalism across multiple continents, revealing institutional collusion writ large. Here, too, imaginative thinking helps clarify the contours of a previously unforeseen environment.

A third element relevant to inviting imagination into considerations of journalism is technological. Data repeatedly confirm that the old/new media split is more complicated than either the naysayers or enthusiasts of change proclaim. Over half of all newspaper readers in the US retrieve their news from print only (Barthel, 2015), while social media serve as the main source of political information for the Millennial generation in a way that resembles what local TV did for Baby Boomers (Mitchell, Gottfried & Matsa, 2015). Old and new media remain mixed, mutually adaptive, with boundaries often blurred. Thus, embracing "the new" does not necessitate abandoning "the old," emblematized by a proclamation by Amazon's Jeff Bezos following his 2015 buy-out of the *Washington Post* that he intended to make it the "new paper of record" (Owen, 2015b), or Twitter's development of a feature that could accommodate tweets 10,000 characters in length (Wagner, 2016). Understanding the shape of the fusion between old and new needs more inventiveness than shown till now: while an early governmental fall-out like McCarthyism was covered in identifiable – though problematic – ways by the then-existing conventional news media, the new pan-national entity of Islamic State expertly uses a sophisticated mix of conventional *and* social media to ensure that its message is distributed successfully, regardless of who helms the controls of conventional news outlets. Imagining an amalgamation of what has long been with what is already resting ahead – more fully understanding *the bridge* of new and old media, rather than pushing one aside at the expense of the other – might force both the naysayers and enthusiasts of change to consider each other's vantage point more fully.

A fourth reason to reconsider imagination is economic. Most reports of contemporary journalism note that journalists recognize that their environment is changing and are on board to accommodate it (Picard, 2015; *State of the News Media*, 2015). Trends include an orientation toward entrepreneurial modes of newsgathering, more attention to branding techniques and greater adaptation to multi-tasking and multiple sources of part-time employment. There are surprises in this landscape: the *Philadelphia Inquirer* and its sister publications – *Philadelphia Daily News* and Philly.com – were donated in January 2016 to a newly formed non-profit media institute in a move "designed to ensure that quality journalism endures in Philadelphia for generations" (Gammage, 2016). Though it is too early to predict how much its innovative linkage of news company, media institute and foundation will impact public-interest journalism, the move nonetheless burst with imaginative ways to ease economic pressures on news outlets. But there is sobering evidence too: Nieman Journalism Labs predicts that there will soon be half as many local daily journalists as existed in 1990 (Doctor, 2015). As Rottwilm (2014, 6) observed, we are seeing "evidence of a decoupling of acts of journalism (work) and journalistic employment (labor)." Reflective of larger social transformations that favor temporary, specialized work, multi-tasking, outsourcing and a service economy, today's economic circumstances suggest a need to rethink how journalism sees itself and articulates its creed. Thus, the eyewitnessing activity that was prevalent in journalism's early days and so central to its sense of self today depends more on disembodied technology and user-generated content than on journalists per se, a development born mainly – though not exclusively – of economic pressures. A global reliance on live-streaming in covering the Paris attacks of November 2015 and the Brussels attacks of March 2016 showed how tenuous current journalistic claims to being an eyewitness have become. But applying imaginative thinking to these transforming parameters might engender more creative alternatives that continue to qualify as journalism, as the recent change in Philadelphia media owner- ship suggests.

A fifth variable that foments imaginative thinking consists of moral considerations. The twenty-first century is filled with difficult events that seem to endure forever and encompass more of the world than ever before – often in unpredictable and intertwined ways. Spanning national, racial, religious and ethnic boundaries, they raise questions of who is responsible for recurrent indignities and violence and what might be a responsible response to them, especially when they stretch across widespread territory. Though we are only a bit short of two decades into the twenty-first century, even a handful of such events is far-reaching: the first and second Intifada, 9/11, the war in Afghanistan, the 2003 Iraq War, the killing of Osama bin Laden, the Arab Spring, the Occupy and Black Lives Matter movements, the Syrian conflict and the current refugee crisis, none of which has been easily identified by burgeoning and differentiated publics as moral, or its opposite. The dif- ficulty with taking a moral position has intensified in the 2010s, as vigorous activity in the digital media environment has made clear that having just one moral stance is a thing of the past. Thus, coverage of the Black Lives Matter movement was both hailed as a Twitter Revolution and denigrated for affixing a racial prism to its ensuing activity. Videos of people about to be beheaded by Islamic State were spread across social media, but when conventional news outlets considered their display, decisions were splayed across the spectrum of possibilities. Each instance calls stridently for new, less binary, more nuanced ways of envisioning the moral charter connecting the news and its multiple publics.

Thus, on craft, political, technological, economic and moral grounds, the current environment lays bare circumstances that push journalism to accommodate change, but in a thoughtful fashion. Each of the events mentioned above inhabits the pages that follow, though not necessarily demarcated in the ways just suggested. Rather, journalism in the current landscape wrestles continuously with all of the aforementioned challenges, as different combinations of craft, politics, technology, economics and morality impact its viability. The texture of that landscape – its instability, internal contradictions and resistance to resolution – overflows with evidence that marks the need to take journalism's centrality seriously. It challenges both the naysayers and champions of change to speak to each other more so than they have done until now.

Considering journalism through its field of possibilities thus has a value-for dimension that extends to knowledge acquisition, writ large. In the ensuing chapters, I highlight multiple characteristics that align with imagination in the journalistic context – contingency, flux, noise, contradictions, the emotions, inclusiveness, interdisciplinary sharing, multiple vantage points – while urging for the reduction of those attributes that have prevented imagination from taking flight – didacticism, insularity, binaries, absolutism, linearity. While recognizing that these qualities by definition always coexist in some fashion, I argue that journalism needs imagination to survive. I also believe that journalism offers a clear harbinger of the richness that might ensue when practical and theoretical knowledge complement rather than constrain each other. Imagination is central to both.

Though many of the following chapters argue for a more fluid and unstable embrace of the categories that comprise journalism's environment, I usher us into this volume by embracing one final binary: the flip side of the exhaustion of a phenomenon is its triumph. This book makes the argument that, with journalism's exhaustion, comes the potential for journalism's height and rebirth, not as a phenomenon markedly different from earlier days but as a complex and nuanced enterprise that forces us to stretch beyond reason into the imagination so as to better understand

and appreciate its trappings. John Dewey (1929, 294) noted how "knowledge falters when imagination clips its wings or fears to use them. Every great advance in science has issued from a new audacity of the imagination." I hope that what follows resonates with that thought in mind.

Beginnings

2

Twelve Metaphors for Journalism

Metaphors for understanding journalism are direct reflections of the prisms through which newsmaking has come to be understood. Though implicit in the many notions of journalism – among them, a profession, industry, ideology and craft – is the ability to inform, individuals involved in doing or thinking about journalism take different pathways of address and thereby scatter definitional efforts in multiple directions. Naming, labeling, evaluating and critiquing journalism and journalistic practice reflect populations and their individuals, types of news work, media and technology, and the relevant historical time periods and geographical settings. No wonder, then, that the distinguished broadcast journalist Daniel Schorr noted that journalism was not only a livelihood for him but "a frame of mind" (Schorr, 1977, vii). By extension, journalism as a frame of mind varies from individual to individual. Twelve metaphors for understanding journalism prevail – seven of them among journalists, five among journalism scholars.

Thinking about Journalism

Though the fluidity and complexity implicit in imaginative work tend to largely retract when orienting to the precise nature of definitions, a particular set of terms has nonetheless given journalism its contours over time. The most frequently used terms for journalism – *news, the press, the news media, information* and *communication* – reference its different aspects and suggest subtle differences in what individuals consider "journalism" to mean and what expectations they have of journalists. Although the term *journalist* initially denoted someone who systematically kept a public record of events in a given time frame, today it is applied to individuals with a range of skills, including publishers, photographers, field producers, digital content providers, bystanders, fixers, citizen journalists and bloggers. Largely associated with journalism's craft dimensions, the term tends to reference the evolving skills, routines and conventions involved in making news. The term *news* – widely thought to have derived from the word *new* during the late sixteenth century – tends to signal a commercial aura that surrounds the ongoing provision of information about current affairs. *News media,* by contrast, and *the press* as one of its forms, came into use in association with the industrial, institutional and technological settings in which journalists began to work in the eighteenth century. More recently, a focus first on *communication* and then on *information* – drawn from, first, the ascent of academic curricula in communication that took over journalism training programs in the mid twentieth century, and then the rise of digital media that opened the journalism field to non-journalists in the twenty-first, in many cases diminishing conventional understandings of *news* – reflects the complex role that journalism can and does play as a central information provider.

None of these ways of understanding journalism provides the complete picture of what journalism is. And none of them reflects all of the expectations we might have of the news media. Instead, each underscores a search for the universal nature of what we call news work, regardless of how limited those attempts might be. For journalism is anything but universal: we need only recognize that Lester Holt, John Oliver and Perez Hilton – a professional broadcast journalist, popular television satirist and widely followed celebrity blogger – convey authoritative news of contemporary affairs to a particular public, despite the questions raised about what kind of journalism they might promote.

Thus, journalism today reflects many contradictory sets of people, dimensions, practices and functions, making it unsurprising that different terms for journalism have been unequally invoked – by journalists themselves, the journalism educators who teach students aiming to be budding reporters, the scholars who study journalism's workings and the publics which journalism is presumed to serve. Perhaps because of this, discussions of journalism tend to be reduced to one variant of practice – hard news in conventional legacy establishments. And though discourses about journalism among journalists, educators, students and scholars necessarily inform one another, by and large the stubborn dissonance between "the realities of journalism" and its "official presentation of self" (Dahlgren, 1992, 7) has grown more severe as the popular eye on journalism becomes ever more attuned to its various and often internally contradictory permutations.

How Journalists Talk about Journalism

Journalists are notorious for knowing what news is but not being able to explain it to others. More prone to talking about writing or getting the story than providing definitions of news, journalists easily trade sayings such as "News is what the editor says it is" or "News is what sells papers or drives up ratings." As one early journalistic textbook commented, "It is easier to recognize news than [to] define it" (Johnson & Harris, 1942, 19).

Nonetheless, journalists do repair to collective ideas about the news, though they do not readily discuss them. As Theodore Glasser and James Ettema (1989a, 18) argued, there remains a "widening gap between how journalists know what they know and what students are told about how journalists know what they know." Yet journalists talk about journalism in patterned ways. Revealing what the sociologist Robert Park (1940) called "synthetic knowledge" – the kind of tacit knowledge that is "embodied in habit and custom" rather than that which forms the core of a formalized knowledge system – journalists display much of how they think about journalism in journalistic guidebooks, how-to manuals, columns, autobiographies and catchphrases associated with journalistic practice. The metaphors they invoke illustrate potentially problematic, and not altogether revered, dimensions of journalistic practice, providing a venue to talk about journalism in ways that are true to experience but not necessarily respected by the journalistic community.

Seven metaphors are prominent in journalists' discussions of their craft: a sixth sense, container, mirror, story, child, service and engagement. Not all of them surface across the landscape of journalistic interventions. For instance, "journalism as a mirror" tends to be invoked most frequently by traditional journalists working in legacy media outlets, while "journalism as engagement" is widely referenced when news is discussed in social media platforms. Nonetheless, together they comprise the meaning set by those widely engaged in journalistic activity.

Journalism as a Sixth Sense

Journalists make frequent mention of what they call a "news sense," suggesting a natural, seemingly inborn, talent or skill for locating and ferreting out news. Because "news" refers to both a phenomenon out there in the world and its report, journalists who can seamlessly track it are said to have a news sense with olfactory qualities – having "a nose for news" or being able to "smell out news." As the Poynter Institute stipulates, journalists need to write with their noses: "Good reporters have a nose for news. They can sniff out a story. Smell a scandal. Give them a whiff of corruption and they'll root it out like a pig diving for truffles" (Scanlan, 2003).

Most directly associated with the idea of news as craft, the news instinct is so central to journalism that it has been referenced in journalistic textbooks, campaigns to recruit new reporters and the development of new modes of reporting and public relations strategies. "ABC Seeks

Publicity Director with a Nose for News," proclaims the typical recruitment ad (Cheung, 2011). Journalists often maintain that one is either
born with a news sense or not. Lord George Allardice Riddell, a longtime
newspaper editor in both the United Kingdom and Australia, wrote in
1932 that all "true journalists" possess an itch to communicate the news
(Riddell, 1932, 110). Having "a nose for news" was so important to the
US journalism educator Curtis MacDougall that he used the expression
to title a section in the many editions of his text *Interpretative Reporting*
(MacDougall & Reid, 1987). A nose for news also prompted former
Washington Post editor Ben Bradlee to publish Seymour Hersh's exposé
of the My Lai massacre, the 1968 massacre of unarmed civilians by
US troops during the Vietnam War. "This smells right," Bradlee was
rumored to have said (cited in Glasser & Ettema, 1989b, 25). Even the
rise of data-driven journalism is expected to perfect the news sense. In the
view of technology platform ITworld.com, big data provide journalism
with "a nose for news (via) analytics-inspired journalism" (Khan, 2012).

It thus makes sense that when journalism falls short of expectations, its failings are often blamed on a faulty development of its sixth
sense. Journalists are said to miss the scent trail of a story or to have
"underdeveloped noses" (Gibson, 1998; Overholser, 2001; Cherbonnier,
2003). And sometimes the metaphor works backward: when NBC news
anchor Brian Williams fabricated a war story in 2015, the *New York Post*
ran a February 6 cover called "A Nose for News," on which Williams
sported a Pinocchio-like snout under the headline "Lyin' Brian War
Scandal Engulfs NBC."

Journalism as a Container

Journalists talk about journalism as a phenomenon with volume, materiality, dimension and complexity. Thought "to contain" the news of a
certain time period, journalistic relays are said to hold information for
the public until it can appraise what has happened. "Containing" in this
regard has two meanings – keeping the news intact and keeping the news
within limits, or checking its untoward expansion. Journalism as a container thus facilitates access to information while putting limits on the
information that can be accessed.

Seeing journalism as a container is reflected in the idea of "journalistic
depth." Good journalism is said to go beyond the superficial and play to
the volume and complexity of information in the world. Journalism's role
is to reflect that depth by turning complex events and issues, and their
unobvious, often embedded dimensions and meanings, into understandable stories. VICE News, for instance, was created in 2013 as a way to
promote more extended engagement via YouTube with the underreported

stories associated with current affairs. Certain modes of journalistic practice – investigative journalism, muckraking, journalistic reformers, news sleuths and exposés, to name a few – are premised on the notion that journalists dig deep to find their stories. No wonder, then, that events and issues are said to be *"in* the news" and journalists *"in* the know."

Against this background, the material in the container of news is unevenly valued. Though hard news tends to be the bread and butter of most news outlets, the news world sports multiple rankings of what matters. Most longstanding news outlets continue to divide their relays by world news, national news and local news, and they further segregate information about business from that about sports, lifestyle or the arts; less space is left for topics like religion or self-improvement. The Huffington Post delineates between what it calls "Weird News" and "Good News" (in that order), while BuzzFeed offers nearly 30 sections of non-traditional content, including "Ideas," "Parents" and "DIY." Regardless of the type of news platform, the ranking of content is driven primarily by concerns over audience engagement.

Conversely, the journalistic "scoop," or the advantage gained by being first on an important news story, almost always rises to the top of the container. Made famous as the title of Evelyn Waugh's book-length lampoon of England's newspaper business during the 1930s, the "scoop" references not only the victorious activity of filing a story before anyone else but also the news items themselves, positioning them as evidence of journalistic triumph over usually adverse circumstances. Memorable scoops include the *Washington's Post*'s revelation of the Watergate Affair or the *Guardian*'s relays of both the *News of the World* phone hacking scandal and Edward Snowden's leaks of classified NSA material. Often scoops help legitimate peripheral members of the journalistic community – TMZ.com's report of Michael Jackson's death in 2009 or reports of Manti Te'o's imaginary girlfriend by Gawker Media's Deadspin in 2013.

The rush to score a scoop often engages with tenuous territory, as reflected in the criticism of erroneous information circulated by numerous news outlets after the 2013 Boston Marathon bombing. Calling CNN "the human centipede of news," comedian Jon Stewart lampooned the organization for reporting that was exclusive because it "was completely fucking wrong" (Logiurato, 2013). Scoops, argued *The American Prospect*, "are beside the point . . . Americans . . . don't care whether you got a scoop. They want to understand what happened" (Waldman, 2013). Yet the provision of scoops remains a journalistic accomplishment for many journalists, as the *Columbia Journalism Review* noted in a column titled "In Defense of Scoops" (Grueskin, 2013). Scoops help journalists stay connected with their sources, their publics and the very flow of news.

Relevant to the idea of journalism as a container is the corresponding notion of the "news hole" – the capacity of a newspaper, newscast or digital platform to deliver the news across available spaces within a given time period, whether it be a day, an hour or a 24/7 news cycle. Responding to the fact that journalists always face more information than can be processed in any given period, the news hole offers journalists cues for systematically and reliably culling that information and filling the spaces available: a large news hole suggests that journalists need to find more news; a small one indicates an inability to take new copy. Thus, one early US textbook provided novice practitioners with this advice: "'We're filling up,' the news editor warns. 'Boil hard.' The copy editor hears this warning often. There is almost always more news than space" (Neal, 1933, 27).

The relevance of the news hole has changed with today's digital environment, in which seemingly unlimited space and constant connectivity might appear to shrink the anxieties connected to the news hole. Multiple observers now claim that the news hole no longer exists. "It's never an issue on the web. The news hole is what we make it," said digital reporter Jeffrey Katz (cited in Kern, 2008). However, constraints on information processing can still be found – in algorithms, headline aggregators, feed readers and search engines that wrestle with a news user's time constraints: Twitter's "Trending Topics," Mashable's line-up of "What's Rising" and Politico's category of "Most Read" all reflect a recognition that news coverage continually experiences changes in value, and those changes foster different degrees of attention. Though limitations are more in the audience's hands than before, it is nonetheless unsurprising that anxiety over journalism's capacity to hold the news prevails in today's information environment, where mobile start-ups and social media platforms cohabit with the websites associated with traditional news outlets. Thus, the *New York Times* decided not long ago to cede control of its audience by publishing some of its stories through Facebook. At the same time, BuzzFeed accompanies its quizzes, lists and memes with a declaration that it supplies "the most shareable . . . most interesting and important stories, handpicked by our editors and reporters around the globe," and in that light it periodically revisits and revamps the available categories by which it organizes its content.

Journalism as a Mirror

Journalists see journalism as the work of observation, tantamount to gazing on reality, or the objective happenings taking place in the so-called "real world." News, in this view, is equated to an objective reflection of all that happens of importance, without additional filtering activity on the part of journalists. Journalism as a mirror is central to professional notions of objectivity, still prominent in the United States and elsewhere, and it presumes that journalists function primarily as recorders, observers and scribes, reliably taking account of events as they unfold.

A central part of existing journalistic lore, the metaphor of journalism as a mirror surfaces among some of the most highly regarded reporters. Lincoln Steffens remembered his years on the *New York Evening Post* by recounting that "reporters were to report the news as it happened, like machines, without prejudice, color, or style" (Steffens, 1931, 171). Ernie Pyle's dispatches from the foxholes of World War II were said to have a "worm's eye" point of view, and Walter Cronkite's famous nightly sign-off on CBS – "And that's the way it is" – was built on the notion of journalism as a mirror. As Daniel Schorr (1977) told it, "the word 'reporting' was always closely associated in my mind with 'reality.'"

Many journalists and news outlets use the metaphor of journalism as a mirror when promoting themselves publicly. It surfaces in catchphrases by which journalists often describe their work – providing "a lens on the world," producing "newspaper copy," compiling "journalistic relays," offering "all the news that's fit to print." MSNBC's collaborative social media website Newsvine defines itself as "an instant reflection of what the world is talking about at any given moment." Names for news outlets regularly play to the idea of journalism as a mirror of events, likening them to a sentinel, beacon, watch, post, emblem, report, scout, herald, standard, reflector or chronicle.

Seeing journalism as a mirror also has particular resonance for the visual side of journalism. Not only do catchphrases like "having an eye on the news" or relying on "the camera as reporter" crop up, but the epithet for many local television news stations – "eyewitness news" – builds on the idea that journalists are able to reflect what they see into the processing of news. The camera is said to be a reliable and objective recorder of reality, echoing noted photographer Robert Capa's maxim that "if your pictures aren't good enough, you're not close enough" (cited in Hagen, 1994, C26). As news photographer Don McCullin said of his time in Vietnam, Biafra and Lebanon, "Many people ask me, 'why do you take these pictures?' It's because I know the feeling of the people I photograph. It's not a case of 'There but for the grace of God go I'; it's a case of 'I've been there.' . . . My eyes [seem] to be the greatest benefactor I had" (McCullin, 1987, 11, 13). The ability to provide a lens on current affairs is also prominent across citizen journalism platforms, particularly when coverage involves the user-generated content and amateur footage recording warfare and human rights violations: Global Voices, Human Rights Watch and Witness (Ristovska, 2016) are three such examples.

And yet the idea of journalism as a mirror is today often critiqued as a less than viable way of explaining journalism. Its limitations are particularly problematic for news platforms whose focus on current affairs is expected to come through the prism of perspective. Examples abound: Sean Hannity is described on his show's webpage as "a gutsy talk-show host who always lands on the right side of the issues"; Democracy Now! provides "access to people and perspectives rarely heard in the US corporate-sponsored media." Digital media often provide opportunities for even the most diehard proponents of the mirror frame to voice perspective: Lasorsa, Lewis and Holton (2012), for instance, found that when microblogging online, mainstream journalists freely express opinions in ways that are counter to norms of impartiality and nonpartisanship.

In fact, however, degrees of skepticism about the viability of the mirror metaphor have been around almost as long as the metaphor itself. As Pete Hamill noted nearly 20 years ago, "Things ain't always what they seem to be. . . . If you want it to be true, it usually isn't . . . [and] in the first twenty-four hours of a big story, about half the facts are wrong" (Hamill, 1998, 89). While this hints at the understated fact that reporters have multiple opportunities to engage with a story's particulars over time, the mirror metaphor tends to prevail across all of them.

Journalism as a Story

For many journalists, journalism is reflected in notions of the "news story." The "story" – a narrative form that carries news information – describes what journalists produce when gathering and presenting news. Different kinds of news stories – items, briefs, reports, series, records, chronicles, accounts, opeds, features, vines, tweets – vie for public attention, and each draws upon different expectations about the most valuable kind of information, the style in which it is presented, the presentational position that it occupies and the role that it plays.

Journalists distinguish most frequently between the kinds of stories typical of hard and of soft news (Tuchman, 1978a), with the front pages and top items of websites, newspapers and broadcast line-ups commonly favoring the former over the latter. As Michael Schudson (1978) demonstrated in his history of American newspapers, practices of storytelling have long been central to distinctions made between journalism that informs and journalism that tells a gripping tale. Among journalists, hard news has been associated with an absence of storytelling, involving no narrative technique whatsoever, though that notion is complicated by an increasing degree of attention to what Hugh Kenner called "the plain style" – a storytelling mode that strategically involves brevity, simplicity and explicitness (Kenner, 1985; Adam, 1993). Soft news, by contrast, uses a variety of narrative techniques that produce dramatic and heartrending stories, moral lessons and compelling plotlines. Both are impacted by the generic and technological platforms used to relay the news, and they exist more often than not in blended forms, as shown by Bird's (1992) discussion of mainstream and tabloid storytelling and Carey's (1986a) study of the telegraph's impact on storytelling form.

Getting the story is the imperative of every reporter. As one editor commented, "There are so many times when I hear reporters gripe about the fact that 'there just isn't a story there.' And that 'they can't believe they have to make a story out of this; nothing happened.' And yet, there in the paper the next morning is 12 inches of informative non-story" (Awtry, 2003). Journalists aspire to producing a "top or lead story," often a "special report"; in-depth efforts secure labels of the "story behind the story" or a "news series." Ironically, good stories often come at the expense of good journalism. As National Public Radio reporter Nina Totenberg said in reference to stories that she had worked on and then thrown away, "I've had more good stories ruined by facts" (cited in Newton, 1999, 143).

Journalism is often characterized by the kinds of stories it uses: human interest news, new journalism and literary journalism commonly take on storytelling forms that diverge from default assumptions about journalistic relays. Hunter S. Thompson, credited with founding "gonzo journalism," consciously turned his writing into a blend of fact and fiction because, paraphrasing William Faulkner, "the best fiction is far more true than any kind of journalism – and the best journalists have always known this" (Thompson, 1972, 2).

The form of journalistic stories changes with the ascent of each new medium, and journalism's accommodation to digital media is no exception. New forms in part always adapt old forms: podcasting, for instance, which saw a huge rise in 2015 thanks to NPR's podcast *Serial*, played upon the growing centrality of mobile devices to update the longstanding value of audio, while a return that same year to long-form journalism was evident in the increase in audiences for magazines like *The Atlantic* and *Rolling Stone* (*State of the News Media*, 2015). Similarly, the telegraphic relays of the early 1900s are called to mind by both the brevity of tweets and the progressive layering of information in live blogging. But each new form also introduces degrees of singularity: for instance, Twitter's conventions for sharing 140-character relays on its newsfeed have produced a succinct way of telling a journalistic story, with its newest venture, Project Lightning, aiming to position short breaking-news updates at the platform's center. The dynamic nature of digital media storytelling, which incorporates interactive, hypertextual and non-linear forms, continues to change as mobile devices take the web's place of primacy. Though the questions surrounding the role of bursts of digital information vis-à-vis the larger environment are still unsettled – do they drive the public to more traditional story forms or stand on their own? – the story forms available in 2016 differ markedly from those of earlier times.

Journalism's capacity to thrive as a story is undermined, however, by various violations involving storytelling – plagiarism, fabrication and misquotation among them. The plight of journalists whose reputation was destroyed for such violations – Janet Cooke, Jayson Blair, Mike Barnicle, Stephen Glass, Sabrina Rubin Erdely – is often said to have developed on the backs of their strong storytelling skills. As the *Washington Post* said after NBC's Brian Williams fabricated accounts of his journalistic exploits, it was "the intimacy of his storytelling . . . that was at the root of his undoing" (Roig-Franzia, Higham & Grittain, 2015).

Journalism as a Child

For many journalists, the news is a child that requires careful nurturing by caretakers. Journalism is seen here not only as fragile and vulnerable – a phenomenon in need of attention, supervision and care – but also as often demanding an unreasonable and unpredictable on-call presence, which is readily offered so as to protect journalism's perceived value. No surprise, then, that journalists can and do adopt a parental stance toward the news, in which they necessarily attend to its well-being at all times. That position, which according to professional lore has been variously held responsible for journalists' fabled premature professional burnout, high divorce rates and uneven social lives, tends to figure prominently in popular cultural representations of journalists in fiction, television and cinema. From the title character of *Lou Grant* to *The Newsroom*'s Will McAvoy, journalism's tempestuous personalities owe their unsettled nature to a heartfelt and oversized devotion to the news.

Seeing journalism as a child forces on journalists the combination of a watchdog role – by which they stand guard over its shaping – and a gentler nurturing role – by which they protect it against those forces aiming to dismantle it. Catchphrases like "putting the paper to bed" (closing the press for the night), "sitting on a story" (taking care of a story until it is time for publication), and "pampering" or "coddling" a story (elaborating a "thin" or unsubstantiated story line) all build on this idea. "Feeding the beast," a reference to an always hungry journalistic impulse, describes journalists' reaction to situations in which journalism's demands are excessive and go too far, not unlike those of an overly demanding child.

The 24/7 news cycle of the digital environment complicates the capacity to nurture the news, rendering it even more akin to the unending parental duties of caring for a child. One reporter remarked on the overwhelming demands of the 24/7 news cycle thus:

> Where the news cycle used to be fueled by muckrakers and gumshoes, today those whose jobs require interpreting and offering opinions on the news of the day . . . saturate the industry. The result is a media effort drained of its ability to feed the beast with hard news stories. Don't let the 24/7 news beast fool you; we've become a culture of repeaters relying on a diminishing cadre of real reporters for our news.
>
> (Smerconish, 2010)

In one view, the drive to feed the beast in the digital era has produced an insatiable focus on page-view journalism, forcing journalists to pair stories about risky topics with sure-fire ones that will generate audience views (Foremski, 2010). In another, the 365-day news cycle leaves "little time, money, or staffers to spare to try experimental reporting methods" (Lichterman, 2014).

Seeing journalism as a child helps legitimate journalists' need to remain invested in their craft. Without journalists to organize and process the news, the assumption is that current affairs would remain unruly and incomprehensible, much like the actions of a child without guidance or care.

Journalism as a Service

Journalists think of journalism as a service in the public interest, one that is shaped with an eye toward the needs of healthy citizenship. A notion of service to both the profession and the community permeates the language that journalists use in referencing journalism – news *service*, wire *services* and news as being *in the general interest*. Journalists are said to "serve" London, Washington and Beijing. Central to the concept of the Fourth Estate, the aspiration to serve underlies notions of "good" journalism.

Serving the public surfaces frequently in journalists' discussions of their craft. Addressing journalists' isolation from the lives of poor and working-class individuals, *Columbia Journalism Review* reminded its readers that "we in the press have a responsibility to engage everyone" (Cunningham, 2004, 32). Longstanding ombudsman Michael Getler complained that the tendency of newspaper chains to "work on the cheap" shortchanges "readers and our democratic foundations" (cited in Kelliher, 2004, 49). Drawing upon the growing presence of the non-profit media, a call to launch a new news venture "Report for America" was envisaged as an enhanced service-based journalistic model that could save local journalism (Waldman, 2015). Awards – the Pulitzer Prizes,

National Magazine Awards and Dupont Awards, to name a few – are regularly given for journalistic service.

Significantly, references to serving the public rarely make explicit the specific parameters of identity that characterize and flavor the engagement. Race is a useful construct in this regard, for its unequal distribution tempers the broad contours associated with the notion of public service. On the one hand, the coverage of stories like Hurricane Katrina in 2004 or the 2015 Baltimore unrest brought to light how unequal the foregrounding of race was for the publics being served by that coverage (Zelizer, 2017 in press). On the other hand, journalists themselves provide an unrepresentative reflection of US racial distribution. As *The Atlantic* noted, with the ascent of the Black Lives Matter movement in 2015, the lack of minority journalists diminishes journalism's service aspirations. "Homogeneity," it observed, "is a big problem in an industry whose ambition is to serve and inform an increasingly diverse public" (White, 2015). Discussions of journalism serving its public tend instead to be generally void of detail about which kinds of journalists serve which kinds of publics.

Mission statements of platforms associated with current affairs regularly highlight the goal of serving the public: AlterNet notes on its front web page that its mission is to "inspire action and advocacy" on a variety of news topics; Politico proclaims a "promise of delivering nonpartisan news . . . exactly what readers and advertisers need"; and the non-profit Center for Public Integrity aims to "serve democracy by revealing abuses of power, corruption and betrayal of public trust by powerful public and private institutions, using the tools of investigative journalism."

From older platforms like PBS and NPR to newer ones like ProPublica, IowaWatch and First Look Media, news outlets regularly proclaim themselves as being "in the public interest." The idea of journalism as a service received renewed attention in the early 1990s with the ascent of the public journalism movement, which defined journalism in conjunction with its ability to serve the public. Journalists' willingness to break with old routines, a desire to reconnect with citizens, an emphasis on serious discussions as the foundation of politics, and a focus on citizens as actors rather than spectators all position journalism squarely in the service mode (Charity, 1995; Merritt, 1997; Rosen, 1999). Though the frenzy initially associated with public journalism eventually died down, its mission to serve the public energized new media start-ups. By 2014, the potential for realizing journalism as a service drew marked optimism, when a number of well-known journalists launched start-ups in that vein – producing what the *New Yorker* dubbed "the new public interest journalism" (Cassidy, 2014): examples included Glenn Greenwald's The Intercept and its focus on NSA documents, Nate Silver's statistical platform FiveThirtyEight and Bill Keller's The Marshall Project and its investment in covering the criminal justice system.

However, with the ascent of digital media's investment in news, the metaphor of service is in many cases less attuned to a notion of the public good and more to the ability to give select audiences what they want. In that regard, platforms as wide-ranging as Facebook and reddit articulate satisfying the audience as part of their mission. Yahoo News strives to "connect people to their passions, communities and the world's knowledge," while VICE News' planned foray into a daily 30-minute newscast on HBO followed its retraction of an early current affairs story – a 2013 fashion spread about female writers killing themselves, titled "Last Words" (Ip, 2015). As the *Nieman Reports* succinctly put it, "what interests the public . . . is not the same as public interest" (Tremblay, 2010).

Journalism as Engagement

Thinking about journalism as an opportunity for engagement has become increasingly prevalent in the digital environment. Journalism here is seen as a platform that can accommodate and facilitate audience investment, enabling the distribution of information accessed together with others. Offering an antidote to the focus on page views and clicks that accompanied the rise of digital news media and the ensuing uncertainty about sustaining readership, the metaphor of engagement helps connect media outlets to journalism's longstanding objective of serving the public. It also connects the news to impulses thought to engender involvement and connection across the digital environment, news and non-news platforms alike.

Seeing journalism as engagement thus helps position it more squarely in the world today. It helps foment the linkage of news users to the non-news media at journalism's side, and in doing so it allows for a wider range of story forms – lists, pictures, memes, maps, audio files, graphs, videos, tweets – than has typically been the case in traditional forms of journalistic relay. In fact, much of the last decade has been taken up with the efforts of new outlets trying to better enhance their connectivity with audiences – adding social networking functionality to websites, fostering brand loyalty and adding features that incorporate users' views (Boczkowski, 2004; Singer, 2005; Deuze & Marjoribanks, 2009; Hermida, 2010).

At the core of the engagement metaphor rests the activity of sharing, which in this view constitutes the primary act by which audiences experience the news. Though engagement is valued across new and old media, the digital environment's accommodation of social networks makes them particularly relevant to the viability of sharing. Sharing not only allows users to organize information by those whose views they find of value, but it facilitates the creation of personalized spaces where the news received coheres with already valued topics. Sharing has generated a slew of practices not usually associated with journalism – comments, followers, fans, friends, retweets, likes, reblogs, pins and favorites among them. Consequently, social media sites as varied as reddit, LinkedIn, Medium and traditional news media platforms all use what they know about their communities to feed on their information needs. Social media are particularly efficient in this regard, pulling the act of sharing into their self-definitions: Upworthy touts itself as a platform for "things that matter. Pass 'em on"; Mashable as "news, resources, inspiration and fun for the connected"; Storify as a platform that "turns social content into shareable stories." No wonder, then, that the names for many digital platforms associated with current affairs invoke the act of sharing – vine, loop, connection, coalition, interactive.

Unlike the notion of journalism as service, which implies the capacity to instill in the public a longstanding preoccupation with current affairs that can enhance rational deliberation over a wide range of issues connected to a healthy body politic, journalism as engagement tends to reference a rubric of involvement with a narrower set of issues, ones that already have presumed value and that do not necessarily point to a lasting investment in the news writ large. Though the notion of engagement was initially appended with the adjective "civic," "public" or "community" in earlier forms of journalism, today's notion of engagement does not always have that aspiration. This does not mean, however, that engaging with the news does not have value, and multiple researchers have established its worth as a social activity (Couldry, Livingstone & Markham, 2007; Singer et al., 2011; De Zuniga, Jung & Valenzuela, 2012). At the same time, it references a decidedly weaker gatekeeping function for journalists. As Hermida et al. (2012, 7) noted, "essentially a person's social circle takes on the role of news editor, deciding whether a story, video or other piece of content is important, interesting or entertaining enough to recommend."

How Scholars Talk about Journalism

Scholars borrow from various disciplinary interests in talking about journalism. Five metaphors prevail in the scholarly literature: a profession, institution, text, people and practice. These metaphors are not mutually exclusive, and just as journalists' talk of journalism often prevails in scholarly discourse, so too does scholarly discussion of journalism often surface in journalists' talk of themselves.

Journalism as a Profession

Many scholars regard journalism as a set of professional activities first and foremost, practices by which one qualifies to be called a "journalist." Historically helpful for organizing a basically disorganized group of writers in the 1900s into a consolidated group, the designation today comes with some qualification: journalists display few of the traits by which sociologists tend to identify professions – certain levels of skill, autonomy, service orientation, licensing procedures, testing of competence, organization, codes of conduct and training and educational programs (Schudson, 1978; Tuchman, 1978b; Schiller, 1981). In David Weaver and G. Cleveland Wilhoit's words, "The modern journalist is *of* a profession but not *in* one . . . The institutional forms of professionalism likely will always elude the journalist" (Weaver & Wilhoit, 1986, 145).

But other ways of understanding journalism as a profession point toward the metaphor's broader resonance. Scholars have been divided in terms of how they see its value. On the one hand, many argue that the profession provides a body of knowledge or ideological orientation about what to do and avoid in any given circumstance and that it constitutes an organizational and institutional firewall for reporters, safeguarding against change, loss of control and possible rebellion (Hughes, 1958; Larson, 1977; Freidson, 1986; Soloski, 1989). Waisbord (2013) argued for the term's revamping, noting that the normative demeanor of "professionalism" has prevented a fuller understanding of how journalists are continually redefining their conditions of labor and rules of work. On the other hand, many scholars have been critical of the connection between journalism and professionalism. Carey (1978) branded journalism's professional orientation "the great danger in modern journalism," because the client–professional relationship it implies leaves the public no real control over information and thus dependent on journalism for knowledge about the real world. Patterson (1993) explained the failure of journalists to energize a robust political sphere by pointing toward the longstanding idea that professional journalists could and should be politically neutral. Bromley (1997, 2006) argued that its invocation has diluted the attention to craft, demoralizing journalists' passion for what they care about most. Aldridge and Evetts (2003) maintained that claims to professionalism allow news executives and managers to exert discipline over low-ranking individuals.

New challenges associated with today's digital environment further complicate the notion of journalism as a profession. Many longstanding claims to professionalism have been leveled – full-time employment, affiliation with a news organization, identification with a specialized set of practices – and no longer hold. But the news landscape is adaptable:

Lowrey and Mackay (2008) showed how the practice of blogging compli-cates journalists' professional identity but still encourages an adaptation of conventional practice. Ornebring (2009) displayed how trends toward professionalization are almost always accompanied by patterns of deprofessionalization – among them a separation of newsgathering and news writing alongside patterns of convergence that impose cohabitation between journalists and non-journalists.

Nonetheless, the idea of journalism as a profession lives on, if unevenly so. Many quarters of the academy readily include the norms, values and practices associated with professionalism as part of their curriculum, and concerns over professionalism remain implicit in much of the jour-nalistic trade literature. Trade journals as wide-ranging as the *Columbia Journalism Review, American Journalism Review, Quill* and *Editor & Publisher* invoke journalistic professionalism in discussions of breaches of consensual journalistic practice and ongoing conversations about the need for stronger journalistic ethics. The outcries in 2014 and 2015 over both the *Rolling Stone* rape story and Brian Williams' fabrications of a conflict-zone helicopter ride were shaped around invocations to professionalism.

Journalism as an Institution

Scholars often regard journalism as an institutional setting, characterized by social, political, economic and cultural privilege. Journalism is seen here as a large-scale and complex phenomenon, whose primary effect is wielding power, shaping public opinion and controlling the distribution of informational or symbolic resources in society. Although the institu-tion simultaneously means the setting, the behaviors that constitute the setting and the values by which the setting is organized, including organi-zations or formal groups that work according to collective standards of action, regarding journalism as an institution by definition addresses the historical and situational contingencies through which journalism performs a range of social, cultural, economic and political tasks or functions. By this view, journalism must exist institutionally, if it is to exist at all.

In thinking about journalism as an institution, scholars tend to search for the interfaces by which it links with and is differentiated from other institutions, facilitating interchange between journalism and the gov-ernment, the market, culture, the educational system and the religious establishment. Primary here has been work devoted to the study of the intersection between journalism and economics, highlighting patterns of ownership and convergence, corporate influences, deregulation and privatization, as well as journalism's impact upon the production and distribution of material goods and wealth (Gandy, 1982; Golding &

Murdock, 1991; McManus, 1994; Bagdikian; 1997; Pickard & Torres, 2009; McChesney & Pickard, 2011). Other scholars have targeted the meeting point of journalism and politics, focusing on journalism's impact on public opinion, its blurring of public and private spheres and its role in changing conventions of citizenship (Blumler & Gurevitch, 1995; Scannell, 1996). Recognizing the melded nature of the digital environment, scholars have tracked the blending of entertainment and information platforms for addressing current affairs (Baym, 2009; Jones, 2009; Williams & Delli Carpini, 2011). An institutional lens has also generated global and comparative analyses of the news, in which institutional pressures vary as nation-states jockey for power with the interests of broader economic corporations and global concerns (Morris & Waisbord, 2001).

The first two decades of the new millennium have given journalism as an institution new life by work in "field theory" and "new institutionalism": substituting the term "institution" with that of "field," field theory has helped explain the simultaneous heterogeneity and homogeneity that exist across media outlets (Benson, 2006). Similarly, new institutionalism draws from organizational theory to argue that news outlets develop parallel practices so as to counter uncertainty, with news produced in ways that "span across news organizations to compose an institutional regime of news" (Sparrow, 1999, 146). Both, in Benson's (2006) view, make place for considering journalism as a semi-autonomous sphere that exhibits internal homogeneity, and in that vein substantive work has complicated and elaborated the parameters of journalism's institutional identity (Benson & Neveu, 2005; Yazbeck, 2015).

Though the ability to define a news institution has never been clear, it has become increasingly complicated with the ascent of digital media. Those invested in news production from an organizational or institutional vantage point now merit titles of "news platforms," "news start-ups," "media companies" and "media outlets," all of which underscore the degree to which institutional identity has become increasingly difficult to pin down. Current economic conditions helped bolster journalism's orientation toward public relations, now exemplified – and in many cases, heralded – as "brand journalism" (Lee, 2015). The *News of the World* phone hacking scandal in the UK showed how complicit and intertwined were the many institutions at the margins of journalism's environs, including the police, politicians and technological mavens (Zelizer, 2012). The current information environment promises more of the same.

Journalism as a Text

Scholars interested in the patterned relay of news see journalism as a text. Seeing journalism as a text considers the public use of words, images and sounds in patterned ways. Key here has been the evolving notion of different kinds of news styles – print versus broadcast, mainstream versus alternative, elite versus tabloid, new media versus old. The texts of journalism tend to have agreed-upon features – importance, interest, a concern with certain types of events (a fire, a summit conference, a murder), currency or timeliness and factuality. In the United States, they also tend to display less readily articulated features – an anonymous third-person author, a generally reasoned and unemotional accounting of events and an uncritical gravitation to the middle of the road on issues of contested public interest. In David Halberstam's view, such features have "required the journalist to be much dumber and more innocent than in fact he [is]" (cited in Parenti, 1986, 53).

Scholarship over decades of research – produced by Helen Hughes, Robert Darnton and Roger Fowler, to name a few – paved the way for thinking critically about the various ways in which a news text can be put together (Hughes, 1940; Darnton, 1975; Fowler, 1991; Adam, 1993), and that understanding extends to the digital age (Cotter, 2010). As the role of journalism has been claimed by an increasingly varied register of venues – the news magazine, the Internet, reality television, the comedy show – a focus on the texts they use shows how they resemble, differ from and combine with more traditional modes of reportage (Campbell, 1991; Bird, 1992; Glynn, 2000; Baym, 2009; Conboy, 2013). Seeing journalism as a text has also produced discussion both of the frames through which journalists and news outlets structure their presentation of events, using story presentation as the prism for considering the lack of neutrality in US news (Gamson, 1989; Entman, 1993; Price & Tewksbury, 1997), and of the discourses through which news language is made understandable (van Dijk, 1987; Fairclough, 2013 [1989]).

As with other metaphors for thinking about journalism, the idea of the news text has undergone substantial revision with the rise of personalized news platforms and the proliferation of tweets, instagrams, blogs and memes typical of the digital age. Live blogging, for instance, became by 2013 the "default format for covering breaking news stories" (Thurman & Walters, 2013, 82). These changes become most evident when old media orient toward digital contours: when the *Financial Times* went digital in 2014, it adopted a new digital interface – new fonts, bolder graphics, a new grid (Garcia, 2014). As one editor explained to readers in 2015 when his newspaper enhanced its digital presence: "Our redesigned website will put you, the reader, at the center, to create a fundamentally different experience for everyone. Not only will you be able to personalize your reading experience, you will also be able to tuck away articles to be enjoyed later" (Samyn, 2015).

Textual features of news stories are thus said to be more permeable, dynamic, interactive and personalized than before. Personalization reaches a high with the orientation to "structured journalism," which dissolves and customizes news texts for each reader: in the words of the *Columbia Journalism Review*, the form "challenges the supremacy of the narrative, non-interactive form that, despite an explosion of digital innovation, remains the cherished mainstay of journalism" (Gourarie, 2015). Readers read what they find most relevant and segue into related stories at their own pace. However, its spread is still restricted to those with digital access and the know-how to manipulate its textual options.

Thus, it is no surprise that scholars have not agreed about which journalistic features to analyze. Words still tend to take prominence over either images or sounds, despite the increasing orientation to video on online platforms. Nor has there been agreement about which texts to appraise – a singular digital story, all of one news outlet's feed or all existing coverage of a given event.

Journalism as People

Defining journalism through the people who work as journalists has been common since journalism's initial days of academic study. Although Walter Lippmann was first to note that "anybody can be a journalist – and usually is" (cited in Newton, 1999, v), others have offered more elaborated descriptions of the attributes of the journalistic community. In one view, journalists need:

> a knack with telephones, trains and petty officials; a good digestion and a steady head; total recall; enough idealism to inspire indignant prose (but not enough to inhibit detached professionalism); a paranoid temperament; an ability to behave passionately in second-rate projects; well-placed relatives; good luck; the willingness to betray, if not friends, acquaintances; a reluctance to understand too much too well (because *tout comprendre c'est tout pardoner* and *tout pardoner* makes dull copy); an implacable hatred of spokesmen, administrators, lawyers, public relations men and all those who would rather purvey words than policies; and the strength of character to lead a disrupted life without going absolutely haywire.
>
> (Tomalin, 1969)

Scholars have invested substantial efforts in defining the wide range of traits characterizing the people called journalists. J. W. Johnstone and his colleagues David Weaver, G. Cleveland Wilhoit and Lars Wilnat were all instrumental in conducting wide-ranging surveys of journalists in the US and other contexts, providing a comprehensive picture of who they are, where they were educated, what their values and beliefs are, and what kinds of experiences they have as journalists. Much of this work focused primarily on high-ranking individuals employed by recognized and elite legacy news institutions (see Johnstone, Slawski & Bowman, 1976; Weaver & Wilhoit, 1986; Weaver and Wilnat, 2012). Similar work developed elsewhere in the world, where variations in the ensuing picture underscored how divergent the people are who comprise journalism's multiple ranks (Hanitzsch & Mellado, 2011; Hanusch, 2013).

Degrees of residual disagreement over who is a journalist have lingered alongside the ongoing attempts to define the journalistic community. Early ambivalence over the inclusion of print setters, proofreaders and copyeditors as journalists gave way to an ambivalence directed at individuals engaged in page layout, graphic design, video-camera editing, fact checking and provision of Internet access. Today that same ambivalence targets fixers, translators, drivers and other individuals working on a freelance basis as well as news users providing user-generated content of all kinds, though some scholars now offer a more divergent picture (Al-Ghazzi, 2014; Murrell, 2015; Yazbeck, 2015). Nonetheless, a still persistent focus on the most prestigious national or global news outlets, and primarily on their top correspondents, has minimized academic attention to women, people of color, precarious labor and holders of nonmainstream political views, all of whom can be found more easily on digital platforms, in the ethnic media, in weekly journals of opinion and in local and regional media.

Moreover, many journalists today often do more than just practice journalism. Not only have opportunities for full-time journalists shrunk as a given of the contemporary work force, but many journalists engage in activities long seen as anathema to the craft – public relations, marketing and consulting, among others.

Journalism as a Practice

Scholars also envision journalism as a set of practices. How to gather, present and disseminate the news has been a key target of this metaphor for journalism, which has produced a flow of scholarly work on "getting the news," "writing the news," "breaking news," "making news," "news-making strategies" and "newsroom practices."

Thinking about journalism as a set of practices focuses on the practical and symbolic dimensions of news practice. Not only does journalism have pragmatic effects, such as information relay and agenda setting, but it is ascribed a crucial role in shaping consensus by relying upon tested routines, practices and formulas for gathering and presenting the news. Scholarship by Gaye Tuchman, Herbert Gans and Todd Gitlin, among others, was first to establish a register of features that characterize what is readily recognized as news work (Tuchman, 1978a; Gans, 1979; Gitlin, 1980). Following their lead, work by Boczkowski (2004), Paterson and Domingo (2008), Ryfe (2012), Anderson (2013) and Usher (2014) extended the ethnographic register of the earlier work into contemporary, often online environments.

As journalism has expanded into new technological frames, the set of practices involved in doing news work continues to change. Typesetting skills of the print room gave way to today's demand for general digital proficiency, and an increasingly diverse list of sources necessitates changes in news practices, making journalism a more collective operation: the work of curation, crowd-sourcing and fact-checking teams, for instance, are only some of the practices that lend newsmaking a collaborative dimension that it did not have in earlier days.

Still in need of attention are the alternative ways for thinking about journalistic practices. Today that issue focuses most directly on the practices associated with the digital age. But they have always been part of the picture of what matters as journalism. Those following the tenets of muckraking were hard-pressed to deliver their relays through wire-service briefs. Literary journalism ranked the actions of journalists differently than did investigative journalism, and that difference was made more marked by the preferences of the Anglo-American tradition, which sided with briefer, more fact-based chronicles than its French counterpart, which preferred a more elaborated prose style (Chalaby, 1996). Difference, then, needs to come more stridently to the forefront of what is considered journalistic practice.

The Usefulness of Metaphors

Journalism is a phenomenon that can be seen in many ways – as a sixth sense, a container, a mirror, a story, a child, a service, engagement, a profession, an institution, a text, people, a set of practices. Though they do not fully embrace the fluidity that imagination requires, these metaphors for thinking about journalism suggest various routes for considering the news media. They are useful here because each offers a way to think about how journalism could work better than it does today.

How much different, better, fuller, more challenging and more satisfying could journalism be? And for whom? Much is suggested by the broad range of terms through which journalism is defined here. We might remember that no one metaphor has been capable of conveying all there is to know about journalism. But, taken together, they offer a glimpse of a phenomenon that is rich, contradictory, complex and often inexplicable. Each of these attributes needs to be sustained and nurtured, for recognizing their uneasy coexistence can help us see what journalism could be. The political philosopher Thomas Paine is rumored to have said long ago that journalism helps us "see with other eyes, hear with other ears, and think with other thoughts than those we formerly used." In thinking about journalism, we might do well to heed his advice.

Section I

Key Tensions in Journalism

Cues for Considering Key Tensions in Journalism

With Jennifer Henrichsen and Natacha Yazbeck

Contrary to what most journalism scholarship implies, the news does not exist in easily identifiable, stable or predictable forms. Rather, it oscillates in and among tensions by which we determine what we want from journalism, what we think it is going to do, what we expect it to accomplish and whom we think it serves. We settle upon certain understandings of these tensions, while recognizing that they continue to exist – often more broadly, more powerfully and in more contradictory ways than we tend to readily acknowledge.

Though only partially emblematic of the impulses underlying journalism, multiple tensions inhabit the broad continuum of ideas that are frequently invoked in discussions of the news. Freedom of thought, freedom of opinion, public deliberation, civic engagement and representativeness are among the concepts that help underscore journalism's better sides. Yet each takes on a clearer identity via tensions that coax us to diminish the spaces separating journalism's optimum self from what exists in actuality.

Such tensions can be instrumental. Characteristic of a larger set of ideas by which journalism can be held accountable, they usefully project ways of combining aspiration and reality. They represent emulated objectives toward which journalism is expected to aim. They hold up the hoped-for contours of exemplary practice and coax those in journalism to ensure their relevance.

But the tensions in journalism are also problematic, for they steer journalism off its presumed track, introducing blinders and obstacles in the ensuing picture of how journalism actually unfolds. Across the board, they create subjunctive noise in the relationship between what journalism is and what journalism could be, leaving clutter that makes us focus on what we should want, often at the expense of what we could have.

This is critical, because the noise around what constitutes journalism in part stifles our ability to think productively and realistically about the news. These tensions thus have acute ramifications that repeatedly diminish the capacity to fully appraise journalism's manifestations on the ground.

Tensions of this kind surround the notions of eyewitnessing, democracy and ethics – featured in this section – so forcefully that their invocation easily gives way to discussions of fundamental questions about journalism's role, stature, authority and existence.

For instance, tensions repeat themselves over time, especially in conjunction with models of practice like eyewitnessing. Though we might turn to journalism because it offers us presence, proximity and on-site activity, that expectation is challenged by the larger question of who the public is, exacerbated by the rise of new media, data-driven journalism, user-generated content and increasingly diverse populations with tools to speak back to those reporting on them. Thus, tensions around the use-value of eyewitnessing, apparent already in sixteenth-century reports of natural disasters, reappear in more recent coverage, such as that of post-Katrina New Orleans or the Occupy movement. Because they necessarily reflect broader tensions in the surrounding culture, models of practice like eyewitnessing bring them to a head in unpredictable ways. A strong reliance on user-generated content in covering the 2015 Ferguson and Baltimore protests, for instance, tied questions about ocular objectivity – who is doing the witnessing and what the ethical parameters of journalism can and should be – to larger questions about the coverage of race in the United States. Tensions thereby have impact not only on topics of news coverage but also on the parameters of what turns out to be narrowly representative journalistic demographics. As a key term for journalism, then, eyewitnessing needs to reflect more specifically the circumstances in which it is invoked.

Similarly, although journalism and democracy have been historically linked for centuries and many democratic countries have helped to provide the space for journalists to generate news, democracy is not central to journalism. Indeed, some nominal democracies – Russia and Turkey among them – repress and harm journalists for what they write. Though at times repression gives way to activism in unorthodox ways – such as the Turkish citizen journalism platform "140journos," created in 2012 after airstrikes on the Turkey–Iraq border – by and large current conditions demonstrate that democracy is not a pre-condition for journalism. Furthermore, the relationship between them is exacerbated by the slowness with which journalism in presumably strong democracies attends to unrest in weaker ones. Uneven coverage of instability in Turkey, the recent coup attempt and subsequent recriminations is a case in point (Zelizer, 2016c).

Finally, current conditions complicate the capacity for ethical behavior among journalists. They necessitate subjecting the orientation of journalism and questions surrounding its authority to both offline and online considerations. Though the idea of journalists as ethical agents who follow standards of ethical conduct might sound nice in the laboratory, in fact journalism takes shape both in and out of the public eye, leaving us unable to discern whether or not journalists do what they say they are going to do. Such ramifications have been particularly prevalent in western journalism's multiple responses to the media displays of Islamic State. While traditional newsroom ethnographies disassembled the idea that a journalist can in fact "report from nowhere," ethics and even the core of journalistic accountability – the ombudsman – should be open to the same scrutiny. The centrality of ethics, then, might be more fully considered as a mutable and relativistic phenomenon, along the lines of the Online News Association's recent "Build Your Own Ethics" project.

It might therefore be worthwhile pulling far enough back from the subjunctive noise that guides our thinking of journalism to give voice to its tensions and multiple emergent conditions. The section that follows offers three examples of what that might look like, addressing some key tensions in journalism's eyewitnessing practices as they have stretched over time and into the first decades of the twenty-first century, in discussions of the democracy/journalism link as it has impacted western coverage of the refugee crisis, and in questions of ethics separately generated by the 2011 *News of the World* scandal and the media efforts of Islamic State.

3

"Eyewitnessing" as a Journalistic Key Word: Report, Role, Technology and Aura

Ever since journalists were first expected to provide an account of events beyond the experience of ordinary citizens, they have relied on eyewitnessing to underscore, establish and maintain their reportorial authority. That reliance has taken different forms over time: eyewitnessing logos appear as the insignia of news media outlets; evolving technologies play to certain audience senses over others; and the involvement of bystanders and citizen journalists, alongside that of conventional journalists, now makes mobile devices necessary to document presence.

No surprise, then, that the centrality of eyewitnessing has not generated consensus about what it means. Which default assumptions drive the importance of eyewitnessing in the news? How did it crystallize into a journalistic key term, and in what ways is it presently sustainable? Extending on an argument I first made in 2007, here I track the evolution of the term's invocation in news, arguing that eyewitnessing has become for many not only a synonym of good journalistic practice but more recently a sign of non-conventional journalistic and non-journalistic involvement in current affairs. In this regard, it signifies both the intensification and depletion of conventional journalistic authority.

Key Words as Markers of Culture

In *Keywords* (1983), Raymond Williams argues that certain terms evolve into markers of culture because members of a community need them. Such markers, Williams explains, are indicators of the "extra edge of consciousness" within which community members operate. Not only do key terms reflect "the vocabulary of a crucial area of social and cultural discussion" but they are "inherited within precise historical and social conditions and . . . subject to change as well as to continuity" (24). Examining a community's own terms for the practices and values by which it constitutes itself thus helps mark the shape of the culture in which that community resides.

Williams' focus on key words resonates powerfully with scholars across disciplines, who have argued both before and after him that language embodies issues of critical import for communities (Whorf, 1956; Levi-Strauss, 1966; Goodman, 1978; Lakoff & Johnson, 1980; Edelman, 1985 [1967]). Across the board of disciplinary vantage points, key terms have been seen as constitutive of the surrounding culture, central to its evolution and maintenance.

Not enough is known, however, about how communities use language to frame the practices in which they collectively engage. Here the notion of the interpretive community can be helpful. Coined initially by Fish (1982), it suggests that a collective's members develop interpretive strategies to establish what is of collective value. Applied to journalists (Zelizer, 1993a; Berkowitz, 2000; Meyers, 2002; Robinson & DeShano, 2011), the interpretive community facilitates an examination of how journalists develop shared modes of evaluating and repairing collective standards of practice. Journalists are thought to use common interpretations of key public events, shared frames of reference and other modes of informal and patterned discourse to patrol their collective boundaries. One resource for maintaining community boundaries involves the terms that accrue resonance for the collective over time. Often, though not always, these markers, akin to Williams' (1983) notion of key words, evolve in conjunction with critical incidents, whose unfolding helps to generate conventions that keep recurrent tensions or problems under control.

For journalists, eyewitnessing is such a key word. Though the act of witnessing has been addressed for its bearing on questions of perception, experience, presence and truth (Felman & Laub, 1992; Ellis, 2000; Burke, 2001; Peters, 2001), in news it has a particular meaning – the on-site presence by which journalists constitute their authority for reporting events. Eyewitnessing offers journalists a way to reference their work and create consensus on which kinds of practice are appropriate and preferred. Though long seen as an authentic core of journalistic experience, it now also reflects its diminution, as the practices surrounding user-generated content facilitate engagement in current affairs by journalists and non-journalists alike. "Having been there" has thus given way to "not being there," reflecting the term's complicated use over time.

Eyewitnessing as a Journalistic Key Word

In journalism, the words "they were there" have a special resonance. Implying a physical presence that enables reporters to accomplish news-work, these words pivot the crafting of a news story on the ability to *see* events unfold. Metaphors of sight have been recurrent descriptors of journalistic work – watchdog, revelation, discovery, insight, eyewitnesses (Hartley, 1992, 140) – and news outlets regularly enlist acts of vision in their titles: newspapers like the *Beacon*, the *Lantern* or the *Mirror*, radio programs like *See It Now*, TV broadcasts like *Eyewitness News* and digital news platforms and start-ups like Witness or Homicide Watch. From the earliest days of the modern newspaper, eyewitnessing was considered a mark of good journalism. The reporter "is the eye of the paper," wrote publisher Charles A. Dana in 1895, "there to see which is the vital fact in the story, and to produce it, tell it, write it out" (cited in Mott, 1937, 161). Journalists, then, have long favored definitions of their craft that see it as the work of "eyewitnesses, who wrote it down as soon as they saw it" (Snyder, 1962, xvii).

Eyewitnessing is not only associated with journalism. Relevant to the law, religion or the realist fiction of Tolstoy, Dickens and Zola, eyewitnessing helps establish in different domains of public expression that what one reports – either verbally or visually – is based on what one saw. Central to the act of eyewitnessing is a one-to-one correspondence between what happens and what is recorded. Although an eyewitness' ability to hear, feel or even taste helps establish on-site presence, seeing nonetheless plays a central role in offering a singular kind of proof. As the videotaped US police abuse and deaths of Eric Garner, Walter Scott, Sandra Blair and others from 2014 on attest, the importance attached to seeing things has reached new levels of salience in the contemporary moment, in which it rides on assumptions of a particular kind of authority: "Eyewitness evidence makes for authenticity," wrote the British critic John Carey; "Eyewitness accounts have the feel of truth, because they are quick, subjective and incomplete" (Carey, 1987, xxix, xxxvii). For that reason, media outlets often use eyewitnessing to cover events that cannot easily be confirmed, challenged or tested in any other way; journalism is made more credible by virtue of on-site presence. Eyewitnessing thus becomes valuable for marking journalism's credibility and authenticity, particularly when the public has no first-hand knowledge of what is being reported. And in today's environment, where bystanders are often able to witness an event before or instead of a conventional journalist, eyewitnessing becomes critical for those opting to do what was traditionally seen as primarily a journalist's job.

Eyewitnessing has also been useful to journalism's sense of self, because it is so adaptable. It encompasses, for instance, a range of individuals: Xenophon, who wrote of wars during the time of Christ; Edward R. Murrow and his World War II radio broadcasts; the amateur video camera operator who captured Rodney King's beating; and the bystander cellphone videos documenting abuse and death across the

Middle East. It also stretches to accommodate changing journalistic platforms: justifying the replacement of the anonymous relays of the late 1700s with the accounts of known individual reporters (Mathews, 1957); adapting to radio in the 1930s when it provided "a clear *word picture* of what had happened – all the more vivid because of [the reporter's] natural excitement" (Hill, 1933, 12) during a US presidential assassination attempt; accommodating the still camera with the 1937 Hindenburg disaster, and television during the hours-long footage of the O. J. Simpson police chase decades later. Today, eyewitnessing is driven by a remarkably variant environment: it includes the co-presence of conventional and non-conventional journalists alongside non-journalists; simultaneous activity on print, radio, TV and online platforms; and the use of mobile cameras, smartphones, blogs and other devices associated with user-generated content. Even when eyewitnessing itself is hard to come by – as in the 2014 disappearance of Malaysian Airlines 370 – it nonetheless constitutes an aspired standard of action which helps drive public involvement in current affairs.

But questions still persist about its value as a journalistic method. In the eyes of one commentator for the *National Review*, there is "no honest eyewitness" (Graham, 2003). Largely drawn from suspicions about eyewitnessing elsewhere – in the courtroom or in police proceedings, where "ocular proof" is seen as only partly effective in recounting reality (Loftus, 1980) – questions about its credibility, subjectivity and diminished reliability continue to prevail. Thus, a columnist for the Poynter Institute recalled seasoned advice given to cub reporters to "never trust eyewitnesses. They don't see what they think they see" (Thompkins, 2004).

How, then, has eyewitnessing maintained its salience as a journalistic key word and emerged as a cue for public involvement in current affairs? Eyewitnessing endures because its evolving aspects have functioned as uneven carriers of meaning about journalism over time. At the heart of its sustained resonance have been evolving notions of eyewitnessing as a report, role, technology and aura. Though their consideration here introduces more rhetorical structure than characterizes the messiness of eyewitnessing on the ground, it nonetheless offers a way to track the richness of the concept over time. Because these evolving notions are copresent across time but given varying primacy according to the conditions at hand, they have enabled different kinds of claims about journalistic presence and authority, even when that presence has been questionable. In its current form, eyewitnessing now extends to non-conventional journalists and non-journalists, many of whom invoke its resonance to counter and challenge conventional journalism's role in relaying current affairs.

First-Stage Eyewitnessing – Report

Early acts of eyewitnessing were defined primarily through the reports they generated, drawing upon the idea more than its implementation. Newspapers in colonial America, for instance, were operated by one or two persons under a printer's helm and so could not afford to engage in eyewitnessing as we know it today. But the transmission of news by manuscript or orally – "carried by people on the move, travelers, merchants, soldiers and other adventurers" (Conboy, 2004, 7) – made ballads, broadsheets, political treatises and commercial bulletins reliant on an implicit notion of someone having been at the site of the events being reported.

From their earliest usage, eyewitness reports were employed to describe a range of events, most sensational in nature – Pliny the Younger described the AD 79 eruption of Mount Vesuvius in letters that were discovered in 1538, while a 1592 report relayed from Saragossa, Spain, reflected public executions across Europe: "Don Juan de Luna had his head cut off from the front and Don Diego from the back, Ayerbe and Dionysio Perez merely had their throats cut, then they were laid down and left to die by inches" (cited in Stephens, 1988, 75). Used to narrate political affairs as well as explorations of the "new world," eyewitness accounts circulated in newsletters and eventually pamphlets and newsbooks, where they played a key role in legitimating news from afar. As Christopher Columbus noted in a widely disseminated account of what he saw on discovering America in 1492: "I found a great many islands populated with inhabitants beyond number [who. . .] go naked, men and women, just as their mothers bring them forth. [T]here could be no believing, without seeing, such harbors as are here, as well as the many and great rivers, and excellent waters, many of which contain gold" (cited in Stephens, 1988, 83–7).

With the arrival of the printing press, eyewitness accounts gave way to more widely and regularly disseminated modes of recounting. Mindful of an ever-larger public, newspapers began sending individuals to first local and then more distant events for eyewitnessing. Early court reporting, for example, involved sending individuals to the court for "directly observing events and composing eyewitness accounts" (Dicken-Garcia, 1989, 19). The reports they brought back tended to be signed by their authors and were printed with little intervention. Playing to the narrativizing typical of the time – elaborate wording that persisted throughout much of the nineteenth century – they reflected romantic impulses that viewed humankind as "feeling, emotional, instinctual being[s]" and reality as "primarily internal, inside human beings" (Webb, 1974, 39). Subjective in tone, they stressed the "writer's personality and emotions" (Schwarzlose, 1989, 278) and proffered lengthy and dramatic accounts of the concrete scenes being witnessed (Shaaber, 1929). Thus, the widely known *Fugger News-Letters*, which processed false rumors about the Spanish armada in Germany during the 1500s, were not expected to be accurate but to offer colorful prose (Stephens, 1988, 76). Images also bore questionable degrees of reliability and were widely mistrusted: a German broadside image from 1511 displayed the "monstrous birth" of Siamese twins (Daston, 1994, 254), while a newsbook illustration of the Seine River flooding the streets of Paris in 1579 was "the same picture that had been used back in 1480 to represent a view of the city of Venice" (Stephens, 1988, 137–8).

Although all acts of eyewitnessing depended on physical human presence, the question of who could become an eyewitness remained open. During the American Revolution, the letters and reports of private citizens and members of the legislature were printed verbatim (Mathews, 1957, 7). Military officers produced eyewitness reports, such as General George Washington's 1781 account of the Battle of Yorktown (Emery & Emery, 1996, 57), while one British business establishment listed 32 persons supplying information from 30 ports in 1792 (Wright & Fayle, 1928). Though full-time news gatherers would eventually arrive on the scene, it would take time before eyewitnessing was to be accomplished primarily by journalists.

Across much of this first stage, then, eyewitnessing was defined primarily through verbal and visual reports that were viewed with skepticism. The elaborate, subjective style of their reports, provided by different kinds of individuals, made eyewitnessing an important, but suspect, mode of journalistic relay. Significantly, many of these same attributes reappear in modified form in newsgathering of the current digital environment – specifically, a broad range of individuals providing subjective reports from unverifiable quarters. Not only does this highlight the practice's adaptability to evolving circumstances but also it underscores its cyclical nature.

Second-Stage Eyewitnessing – Report/Role

Eyewitnessing began to change from the mid-1800s, when the question of who could be an eyewitness gradually became as important as its reports. Though two journalistic styles of the time – story and information (Schudson, 1978) – produced words and images that accommodated subjectivity and realism, realism proliferated only when eyewitnessing became recognized as professional journalistic activity. At first, romanticism continued to shape eyewitnessing, producing subjective accounts and romanticized images of what was seen – Walt Whitman's response to

John Brown's 1859 execution or a *San Francisco Call* reporter's response to the 1906 earthquake. Driven by intense curiosity – "I must see it," he said – he came up short on facts: "I thought that I was observing very carefully, but I wasn't . . . It was rather unimportant detail that struck my eyes . . . in spite of what we had already seen, our power of realization was behind time as it was to be through the three days' progressive disaster" (Irwin, 1906, 760b–d). One trade discussion of earthquake pictures lamented that, despite extensive on-site presence, very few photographers "saw or realized there was a picture afforded until they viewed a portrayal of the scene made by someone else. It is the difference in the point of view" (Cohen, 1906, 187).

Such romanticism typified the war coverage of the nineteenth and early twentieth centuries that depended so strongly on eyewitnessing. The *New York Tribune* recorded a US Civil War battle by collecting details from officers and then publishing "a brilliant but entirely imaginary eyewitness report. To the chagrin of the two correspondents who had actually seen the battle, the dispatch was acclaimed . . . 'the [war's] ablest and best battle account'" (Knightley, 1975, 26). The prose in Felix Gregory de Fontaine's 1862 report of the battle at Antietam was almost poetic:

> The air was filled with the white fantastic shapes that floated away from bursting shells. Men were leaping to and fro, loading, firing and handling the artillery, and now and then a hearty yell would reach the ear, amid the tumult, that spoke of death or disaster from some well-aimed ball . . . A fierce battle ensues in the center . . . It is a hot place for us, but is hotter still for the enemy.
>
> (cited in Emery & Emery, 1996, 141)

When William Howard Russell wrote that the "the horrors of the Crimean War cannot be described" (cited in Carey, 1987, xxxiv), he was not exaggerating. From the flamboyant and often jingoistic eyewitness accounts of the Spanish American War by celebrated journalist Richard Harding Davis to the preference for fictionalized accounts of the Abyssinian War over seemingly more authentic eyewitness reports (Mathews, cited in Knightley, 1975, 185), early war reportage of this period was characterized by "sensationalism and exaggeration, outright lies, puffery, slander, faked eyewitness accounts and conjectures built on imagination" (Andrews, 1955, 640).

Images initially also had limited believability, as drawings, sketches, photographs, cartoons and maps presented subjects in allegorical, romanticized and iconographic ways. Often they foreshadowed an event's unfolding or collapsed temporal sequencing and spatial distance: drawings of the Great Chicago Fire that appeared in *Harper's Weekly* and *Leslie's* in 1871 were touted above the photographs on adjoining pages, largely because the drawings were thought to be less mechanical and to offer a more dramatic compositional setting (Barnhurst & Nerone, 2001). Respected US photographers Alexander Gardner and Mathew Brady were widely regarded to have repositioned corpses on Civil War battlefields so as secure better pictures (Goldberg, 1981). Readers did not necessarily know whether eyewitness scenes had been produced by a sketch artist or engraver, and at times artists faked their eyewitnessing: in 1863, *Harper's Weekly* carried eyewitness sketches of the Southern cavalry setting fire to Northern army trains near Chattanooga, although the artist never came closer than 20 miles (Knightley, 1975, 26).

But the growing thrust toward professionalism, consonant with the "information" mode of journalistic storytelling (Schudson, 1978), made the embrace of realism attractive for eyewitnessing activity. By the late 1870s, the *New York Tribune's* coverage of the fall of Napoleon III was provided by "special correspondents" who were stationed with the Prussian and French armies to convey first-hand battle reports. During World War I, the military's problematic track record as eyewitnesses suggested that others might be able to do the job more efficiently: British Colonel Ernest Swinton, "an officer given the assignment of satisfying the British public demand for information with weekly human interest dispatches" (Mathews, 1957, 161), was denounced by both journalists and the military and forced to place a sign in his window appealing for news (Mathews, 1957; also Jones, 1945). When the military consequently began accrediting journalists and designating certain correspondents as eyewitnesses (Carruthers, 2011), journalists readily stepped into the role, making their reports available to the press corps at the same time as they cabled them to their own media outlets. By the time of the Spanish Civil War, most reporters welcomed the development:

> These were the days in foreign reporting when personal experiences were copy, for there hadn't been a war for eighteen years, long enough for those who went through the last one to forget, and for a generation and a half who knew nothing of war to be interested. We used to call them "I" stories, and when the Spanish War ended in 1939 we were as heartily sick of writing them as the public must have been of reading them.
>
> (cited in Carey, 1987, 519–20)

Photographers also filled the eyewitness role, both taking pictures and sending in "written messages describing incidents which attended their picture-taking" (War Photographers' Stories, 1944, 13–14). There was a peculiarly autonomous sense about the process of capturing one's vision through photographs. As Margaret Bourke-White observed: "a protecting screen draws itself across my mind and makes it possible to consider focus and light values and the techniques of photography in as impersonal a way as though I were making an abstract camera composition" (cited in Goldberg, 1986, 245).

These circumstances helped push eyewitness reports toward realism. Verbal and visual accounts embraced features that could relay factuality and truth-value as well as proximity. In words, this was facilitated by the telegraph's introduction in the mid-1800s, when eyewitness reports began to arrive more quickly and regularly than in earlier years, and by the adoption of the inverted lead. Wired prose became business-like, colorless, un-opinionated and matter-of-fact, so terse that wording "strove to copy the language of official dispatches" (Mathews, 1957, 40). Tendered in the first or third person and nearly always by-lined, these highly referential accounts made little attempt to analyze, interpret or generalize. Careful, cautious language provided the most obvious details of *what reporters saw*. One report capturing journalists' admiration was John P. Dunning's eyewitness account of an 1889 Samoa hurricane, which described "the most violent and destructive hurricane ever known in the Southern Pacific" that left a fleet of ships "ground to atoms on the coral reefs in the harbor." Though his report for the Associated Press took two weeks to reach San Francisco, it came to be seen as a "masterpiece" of concrete description (Stone, 1921, 211–12).

In images, realism's conventions helped consolidate photography's role as a carrier of truth-value (Carlebach, 1992). Increasing numbers of images crafted from steel engravings and woodcuts – seen by the mid-1800s as "reliable sketches" (Root, 1864, 31) – documented events, including Philadelphia's military occupation in 1844 and an 1853 mill fire in Oswego, New York (Carlebach, 1992). Couched increasingly in terms of authenticity rather than interpretation, images drew praise by the unfolding of Antietam: *Harper's Weekly* maintained they were "a thousand-fold more impressive than any description . . . No evidence is like these pictures" (Further Proofs of Rebel Humanity, 1864, 387). By the end of the 1800s, the Victorian art historian Lady Elizabeth Eastlake claimed that photography was "the sworn witness of everything presented to view" (cited in Schwartz, 1992, 96). Often unaccredited, images introduced an eyewitnessing tool that did not require the maker's explicit mark, a point that would have bearing on eyewitness authority as time and technology moved on.

This did not mean that stepping into the role of eyewitness avoided its longstanding problems, for it remained "an illustration of reportorial variations and contradictions" (McKenzie, 1938, 5). One much-circulated story involved Reuters correspondent Alexander Graeme Clifford, who in late 1939 served as a reluctant "eye-witness" for the

British, foreign and overseas press corps (Desmond, 1984, 96): "Clifford nearly went mad trying to find something to write about, and when he did, he had the frustrating experience of seeing it chopped to pieces by the censor" (Knightley, 1975, 219). Therefore, despite the move toward a less subjective style grounded in observation, and despite an increasingly professionalized register of journalists acting as eyewitnesses, eyewitnessing was – and still is – plagued by questions about its viability as a journalistic practice.

Yet, assuming the role of eyewitness offered a platform for providing what was seen as solid professional reportage. Media outlets spoke of eyewitnessing as if it had almost a mythic status. When famed war correspondent Ernie Pyle was killed near Okinawa, the *New York Times* took pains to comment that he had gone there "to observe the advance of a well-known division, [intending] to watch front-line action" (Ernie Pyle is Killed, 1945, 1, 14). Similarly, an obituary for correspondent William Shirer called him an "unimpeachable witness," an "eyewitness to the 20th century" (Kroll, 1994, 66). The "accent," said one journalist, "was on seeing": "[A] man may know a lot about a right hook or a curve and still not know anything about foreign politics. But one thing is certain: he can write about a curve only if he *sees* it [emphasis in original]. Once [the reporter] has learned to keep his eyes open and see what's going on, it is not likely that he will ever overlook anything" (Riess, 1944, xx).

Role and report thus developed a symbiotic relationship during this period. As the eyewitness became increasingly valued as a reportorial role, the subjectivity and unreliability associated with eyewitness reports moved to the background. This second stage of eyewitnessing highlighted journalistic involvement in what was largely seen as professional activity – embodied by assuming the eyewitness role and stylistic features associated with realism.

Third-Stage Eyewitnessing – Report/Role/Technology

Gravitation toward an objective reportorial style and greater claims of professionalism facilitated a third stage of eyewitnessing – the accommodation of a wide range of technological platforms for delivering eyewitness reports. Though report and role remained relevant here, the technological expansion of the twentieth century afforded primacy to different platforms – print, radio and television – that could accommodate different combinations of words, images and sounds. Much of this evolved around war, which crystallized the capacity of both report and role to reach new heights via an expansive technological landscape.

Eyewitnessing extended across media platforms in a way unimagined by earlier generations, with technology's potential already apparent by World War II. By the 1940s, journalists were widely ensconced in eyewitness roles and realism dominated their verbal and visual reports. Synonymous with the "brief, telegraphic 'I was there'" story (Carey, 1987, xxxiv), eyewitnessing became a favored means of verbally chronicling World War II's wide-ranging battlefields – sea tragedies near Scotland, life in POW camps and aerial torpedoing. Journals like *Collier's* featured eyewitness war reports with nearly every issue, in which first-person narratives provided blow-by-blow scenes of devastation and triumph and reporters competed "with each other to see more than their rivals" (Riess, 1944, xx). Wrote Richard Tregaskis (1942): "We squatted in the wet leaves. . . . [W]e could hear machine guns, Browning automatic rifles, and the Jap artillery banging. The firing came from the left, this time." So too with images. The adoption of wire photo in the late 1930s made photographs preferable to drawings as a way to visualize on-site presence (Zelizer, 1995a). Earning the name of the "silent witness" (Meyers, 1943, 20–2), photography forced the *New York Times* to print two reports of the Nationalists' 1937 capture of Teruel during the Spanish Civil War, largely because the second had photographs and eyewitness details contradicting an earlier one (Knightley, 1975, 199). Photographs like Robert Capa's images of the Allied deployment in North Africa and the invasion of France were among the images that froze eyewitnessing in memory.

Eyewitnessing during this period was thought to be so compelling that many eyewitness reports reappeared in book or cinematic form. Richard Tregaskis' (1943) *Guadalcanal Diary* drew from his widely read 1942 newspaper accounts, and it was reprinted again as *Invasion Diary* (Tregaskis, 2004). William Shirer's (1941) *Berlin Diary* was similarly reprinted. Eyewitness accounts were made into collections of memorable war reportage (Snyder, 1962) or films: Ernie Pyle's 1943 frontline dispatches became the 1945 film *The Story of G. I. Joe.* The technological landscape was so rich that eyewitnessing could be claimed by whichever technological platform was able to provide the more forceful eyewitness report. Thus, when photographs of the concentration camps were released in April and May of 1945, enormous sections of newsprint displayed the photographic evidence (Zelizer, 1998).

The ascent of radio – hailed by *Newsweek* in 1939 for setting off "an epidemic of radio nerves" (War in the Living Room, 1939, 43) – lent an acoustic immediacy to war reportage with sounds that created the effect of an ongoing eyewitness report. At first urged by the National Union of Broadcasters to avoid sound effects and use "a minimum of production trappings" like canned sound, imported audios or taped noises (Mathews, 1957, 192), radio newscasters developed wide-ranging conventions for capturing the sounds of on-site battle, which in turn enhanced radio's truth-value claims. When the ban on canned sound was relaxed around D-Day, listeners were treated to a 36-hour delayed broadcast of reporter George Hicks recounting the downing of a German bomber. In the coverage, "radio blurted out everything. Radio's D-Day was a random, shapeless mosaic in constant motion" (McDonough, 1994, 195) – replete with technical glitches, anxiety in the broadcaster's voice, bulletins and actualities.

By the 1940s, newsreels offered yet another mode of relaying eyewitness detail, "a way of seeing Americans during the Second World War" (Doherty, 1993). The 1944 newsreel *Attack: The Battle for New Britain*, for example, was introduced with the following: "The picture you are about to see is authentic in every detail. No scenes have been reenacted or staged" (cited in Doherty, 1993, 256). One broadcast of the attack on Pearl Harbor, though it reached the US in a highly censored version two months late, was nonetheless hailed for showing "grounded, smashed planes, American capsized ships, and burning hangers – the stuff of wartime that only an eyewitness could procure" (cited in Doherty, 1993, 231). Because newsreels rarely incorporated on-site sound, they relied on canned sound to suggest combat, prompting this response to coverage of the battle over Iwo Jima: "Faulty and blurred," the recording was "the real thing; it included scraps of barely audible conversation which, compared to the glib tones of the narrator, were like actuality shots of service-men's faces compared to polished Hollywood performances of soldiers" (Short, 1985, 22–3). The irony here – a faulty audio recording seen as more authentic than a clear and focused visual glimpse of the action – underscored the peculiarities of eyewitness appeal.

In fact, the deficiencies of eyewitness reporting continued to be widely discussed. One correspondent wrote an account of the Japanese bombing of Manila but admitted "we couldn't see anything for the glare of the fire" (Gunnison, 1942, 13). Stories that never made it to broadcast surrounded NBC radio correspondent John MacVane, whose recording batteries ran down in the middle of a story on D-Day and whose relay back to London a few days later followed the wrong frequencies and was never received (MacVane, 1979). Others, caught in battle, were unable to file their reports: AP correspondent Robert St. John was trapped first in Yugoslavia and then in Greece a step ahead of the Germans, twice finding himself eyewitness to "one of the most dramatic news stories of the moment, which he was unable to file" (Voss, 1994, 17). But, as the war's events continued to demand grounded proof, the need for eyewitnessing outpaced the difficulties it generated, particularly with the liberation of the concentration camps in 1945. By that time, newspapers took to publishing letters from a wide range of eyewitnesses, their accounts peppered with reference to the activity's advantages and limitations: wrote one correspondent, "The following letter was written amidst the smells of one of the widely publicized prison camps of Europe on the day of its liberation, by one of the corporals who helped liberate it" (Woodward, 1945, 11).

Soon after World War II ended, television entered the landscape. The capacity to cover the events of the 1960s – the student movement, the Kennedy assassination, civil rights – was predicated partly on the capacity to "see for yourself" what unfolded (Gitlin, 1980; Zelizer, 1992b). What eyewitnesses saw, of course, was variable: though commonly called the "televised war" because it was the first time that a war was broadcast into one's living room (Hallin, 1986), coverage of the Vietnam War featured "very little blood" and was "far tamer than people imagine" today (Brothers, 1997, 203). The two big wars of the 1980s – the Falklands War and Grenada – were largely off the record and unseen (Morrison & Tumber, 1988), with pictures of the former taking longer to reach London than eyewitness accounts from the late 1800s (Carruthers, 2011, 120).

Yet other circumstances enhanced eyewitness value: the increasing centrality of live coverage promoted the evolution of local TV news, which hinged its worth from the 1970s onward on its provision of eyewitness activity (Kaniss, 1991). Incorporating "eyewitness" and "action news" formats as formulas for engaging with current affairs, it provided eyewitness stories that were "dramatic, breaking and live from the scene" (Lipschultz & Hilt, 2002). Its coverage of local emergencies, accidents, crime and natural disasters – all seen through an eyewitness prism – often overstated the importance of local events that could be witnessed. Yet, even as local news moved online (Anderson, 2013), it continued to rely on eyewitness activity as its main staple. Television also proved skilled at creating a sense of on-site presence even when reporters were physically distant, developing practices of conveniently placing anchorpersons to stand in for journalists who were far from the scene (Zelizer, 1990). That practice continues today, as television pushes translators, fixers and field producers into on-air slots so as to claim presence (Murrell, 2015).

One of the first platforms to clearly underscore both the value of eyewitnessing and the slipperiness of on-site presence was the Persian Gulf War of 1990–1. Coinciding with the so-called "CNN effect" – CNN's emergence as a 24/7 news channel and the consequent emphasis on "going live" in situations of crisis – "Operation Desert Storm" was said to be "orchestrated for television" and hailed for broadcasting "live from ground zero" (Weimer, 1992). Television, newly equipped with satellite distribution, made ongoing battles look like a Nintendo game, as media outlets employed "what was basically telephone/radio technology to provide . . . dramatic live reporting" (Kellner, 1992, 110–11). In fact, however, viewers during the Persian Gulf War saw little more than either helmeted television reporters hopping before cameras as they dodged live fire, or shaky TV cameras accommodating incoming SCUD missiles without visible reporters to narrate the frame (Zelizer, 1992c). Alongside what the *Washington Post* called "censorship by delay" (Getler, 1991, D1) and the AP "censorship by lack of access" (Fialka, 1991, 6), reporters were largely "cloistered in the hotel oases . . . stranded miles from the front" (Brothers, 1997, 211). Typical of later war reporting that would limit journalists' access to conflict zones – where concerns for both the protection of information and the safety of journalists were routinely interwoven into attempts to regulate journalistic activity (Tumber & Palmer, 2004) – TV adhered to a slew of conventions that limited journalists' presence, such as censorship regulations, security restrictions and embedding arrangements. These modes of controlling reporting helped pave the way for technology standing-in for individuals, pushing aside the capacity to accommodate both the role and report aspects of eyewitness activity that had been until then central to its recognition.

Eyewitnessing continued to grow in stature across the late twentieth century, with technology driving the frame. Accommodating presence came to mean primarily "rooftop journalism" – TV reporters jumping frenetically from place to place in order to stay in front of the camera. Hinging on the need for repeatedly updated live reports to fuel a 24/7 news cycle, presence here became imperative, regardless of whether or not a reporter had new information (Tumber & Webster, 2006). As Martin Bell famously pointed out: "There were days in Sarajevo when my radio colleague, who was already working for a rolling news service, had to broadcast as many as twenty-eight separate reports. Not only did he never leave the Holiday Inn, he hardly had time to pick up the phone and talk to the UN spokesman" (Bell, 1995, 28–9). As news outlets insisted on putting reporters before the camera as what were commonly called "dish monkeys," the public began to expect a reporter's face to envelop the screen, with often dismal effect: "The fact of being embedded itself became 'the story,' narrated by television journalists decked out in brand new fatigues, surrounded by men in uniform against an exotic desert backdrop. That they had rather little actual news to relate was hardly the point. *Being there* was what mattered" (Carruthers, 2011, 135).

Common metaphors for eyewitnessing – "eyewitness news," "live satellite report" and "direct broadcast," all presuming some notion of transparency – positioned journalists in the vantage point of reflecting, seemingly without intervention, on events. But while technological expansion meant that a growing number of journalists could act as eyewitnesses, and technology helped expand the platforms for presenting reports, "seeing more" did not necessarily mean providing or receiving more information. Rather, the expansion beyond print to a wide techno-logical landscape pushed eyewitnessing to new heights that often offered less reporting than ever before even as it accommodated on-site presence.

This stage of eyewitnessing thus privileged technology over human presence, with adaptation to evolving technological platforms culminat-ing in various modes of remote-controlled newsgathering that negated the need for a human body on-site. Neutralizing the human dimen-sion of the eyewitness role and minimizing the stylistic interventions of its reports, this naturalization of technology moved from reducing subjective markers to obscuring their presence, from accommodating professional journalists as eyewitnesses to disembodied live cameras transmitting seemingly unmediated information. Technology thus made it possible to promote eyewitnessing as a remotely activated set of news-gathering practices, reliant on neither report nor role.

Fourth-Stage Eyewitnessing – Report/Role/Technology/Aura

Technology's primacy in crafting versions of eyewitness activity makes embrace of the digital environment a logical progression for the twenty-first century. However, in this most recent stage of eyewitness activity, technology's centrality has blended with changes occurring inside and beyond journalism that create a different host environment. Specifically, precarious conditions for accommodating journalists as eyewitnesses coupled with a persistent public interest in current affairs and a techno-logical ability to act on that interest have crafted an alternative eyewit-ness landscape. In many ways, this stage of eyewitnessing repeats what existed in the initial phase of the activity's development, though without the richness of its evolving aspects of role and report. Technology is no longer as much an assist to journalists as a substitute for them. As one journalist noted, following the reliance on live-streaming in covering the Paris terrorist attacks in November of 2015, "where are the journalists?" (Becquet, 2015)

This disembodied frame has been a gradual development from earlier technologies. Established during the twentieth century, it plays a double function with the arrival of the twenty-first: it promises more direct public participation while minimizing conventional journalists' proportionate role in that participation.

By 2010, CNN's 24/7 orientation to live coverage had been adopted by major news outlets around the world, including BBC World, Al Jazeera, Sky News and ABC Australia. Yet simultaneous developments curtailed conventional journalistic presence in that coverage: these included fast-paced technological change that intensified multi-tasking;

personnel cuts; a focus on parachute journalism; the eradication of established geographic beats; a reliance on precarious labor; the emergence of "one person bureaus"; and ongoing attempts to censor and prohibit journalistic access. At their side, however, was an increased potential for public involvement in newsgathering, as the enhanced portability of mobile newsgathering equipment and widespread access to multiple distribution networks catered both to non-conventional journalists and to non-journalistic involvement in the news. Thus, as events have taken place worldwide that invite on-site recording – terror attacks, protests and demonstrations, wars in civilian areas, natural disasters – eyewitnessing has become simultaneously more difficult for conventional journalists to accomplish and easier for non-conventional journalists and non-journalists to achieve. The latter has included a wide range of individuals – activists, bystanders, citizen journalists – often without clear demarcation of who was which (Al-Ghazzi, 2014; Yazbeck, 2015; Ristovska, 2016). By the 2010s, a reliance on live blogging – the direct relay of commentary as an event unfolds – further enhanced a different mode of eyewitnessing practice (Thurman & Walters, 2013).

Thus, though aspects of report, role and technology still help shape eyewitnessing today, evolving circumstances are minimizing conventional journalists' capacity to act in the role. Simultaneously, the promise of non-conventional journalistic and non-journalistic eyewitnessing is valorizing its proximity, honesty, spontaneity, rawness and authenticity. The resulting environment thereby hinges upon an aura of eyewitnessing – its potential for involvement – more than the concrete dimensions of role, report or technology. That aura has prompted two new ways of dealing with eyewitness activity: historicizing and outsourcing.

Among journalists, the simultaneous relevance and challenges of eyewitnessing have shifted the attention of media outlets to less expensive or less risky formats for providing on-site coverage. One such format is the current explosion of recollections of the past – mnemonic work that encourages journalists to look backward while reporting the news. Though journalistic retrospectives have long been part of the news (Zelizer & Tenenboim-Weinblatt, 2014), many current forays into collective memory help offset journalists' diminished eyewitness role by encouraging news platforms to historicize eyewitness activity. Doing so facilitates claims of eyewitnessing despite both the absence of immediacy and a diminished linkage between when things happened and when their story is told. Valuable because they accommodate retelling, recycling and altering events of the past long after their original reportage, journalists are increasingly able to engage in "double time" to ensure that they uphold their authority for on-site activity even if it had unfolded years before (Zelizer, 1993a).

Examples proliferate. The ongoing fascination with the JFK assassination case calls on media outlets yearly to pull out their archival footage and revisit the event, as do events as varied as space shuttle explosions or race riots of the 1960s (Zelizer, 1992b; Edy & Daradanova, 2006; Maurantonio, 2012). A 50-year commemoration of D-Day tried to invent a journalistic presence missing from the original coverage, accommodating eyewitnessing after the fact: "[T]he networks, which didn't even exist when the invasion took place, have sent shock waves of reporters to swarm the French beaches at Normandy and other battle sites for the anniversary ... [While] it was newspapers, radio, and movie newsreels that brought the war home, now TV is going out for its belated shot" (Elber, 1994, 6). "Retro Report," a joint *New York Times* and Mirror/ Mirror Productions venture that bills itself as "there to pick up the story after everyone else has moved on," began in 2013 to offer video forays into the past that replace original eyewitness reporting with smooth storytelling and extensive archival retrieval. Where it took the story, however, was often to a replay of historicized eyewitness accounts (Gilewicz, 2013).

Typical of journalism's forays into collective memory, where anniversary journalism, retrospectives and other mnemonic efforts dwell on the past (Kitch, 2003; Carlson, 2006), these acts of curation often stand in for reporting while incorporating eyewitness clips from earlier times into the news flow. Cameras visually replay events like the bringing down of the Berlin Wall with little more than a journalistic voice-over narrating what viewers have seen many times over. In each case, eyewitness authority lingers long after eyewitness activity ends. At times mnemonic work even replaces the event being witnessed, as when commemorative images of September 11 showed people looking at the towers in NYC without seeing the towers themselves (Zelizer, 2002). In this regard, claims to eyewitnessing, though lodged in the past, are more important than what is being witnessed.

At the same time, media outlets are currently outsourcing much of their eyewitness activity. As eyewitnessing draws heightened interest from a public technically more able to record and distribute its own eyewitness reports than at any other time in history, scores of individuals are stepping into the vacuum created by conventional journalism's uneven capacity to fill the eyewitness role. Outsourcing has three beneficiaries: a precarious labor force comprised of freelancers, stringers, fixers and translators; activists involved professionally in eyewitnessing for non-news outlets; and private citizens, such as citizen journalists and bystanders.

Though journalism has long relied on temporary forms of labor such as freelancers and stringers, the intensification of multiple circumstances – reduced funding for foreign correspondents, continued need for

global coverage, mobile newsgathering routines and a reliance on parachute reporting – has deepened conventional journalism's reliance on a
precarious labor force (Yazbeck, 2015). As journalists remain responsible for global affairs, often in hostile circumstances involving multiple
languages and cultures about which they know little, news outlets have
begun to regularly use locally based individuals who are increasingly able
to provide eyewitness presence – fixers, stringers, drivers and translators (Murrell, 2015). Already by the 2003 Iraq War, this had produced
a "team journalism" model, whereby responsibilities for coverage were
allocated to first- and second-order teams of personnel. As Orville Schell
noted after a visit to Baghdad, "Much of the basic reporting now is done
by Iraqis and the writing and analysis is still done by Westerners" (cited
in Murrell, 2015, 154).

At the same time, the public's capacity to deliver multiple modes
of user-generated content is extensive, often to conventional journalism's chagrin. Its on-site accounts, tweets, audio recordings, live video
streams and photographs are being crafted via mobile phones, laptops
with editing capacity, digital audio recorders and digital cameras, and
distributed via social media sites, wi-fi cards, personal web pages, blogs,
wikis, bulletin boards and portable news production/distribution systems
(ENPS). Legacy media often rely on these efforts for coverage. As one
journalist said after news of the November 2015 Paris terrorist attacks
relied on live-streaming via Periscope: "The paradox is that Periscope is
being used a lot by some news groups, but from the comfort of their nice
warm offices, in a studio environment, with the mobility and spontaneity of a marketing exercise" (Bacquet, 2015). Not only are these efforts
providing plentiful detail about contemporary events, but also they keep
eyewitnessing central to current affairs coverage, even when it is not
driven by conventional newsgathering practices. Typical here are activist
human rights organizations generating eyewitnessing (Ristovska, 2016).

Thus, conventional journalists no longer necessarily determine what
counts as eyewitness activity. Instead, the proximity, authenticity,
rawness, spontaneity and immediacy provided by a precarious labor
force, activists, citizen journalists and bystanders qualify as alternative
grounds for on-site presence, without the fuller eyewitnessing craft that
had been historically integrated into the news.

The ascent of mobile technology during the 2000s was instrumental in
this regard. Local fixers and other members of a precarious labor force
became the default providers of content when journalists were hard-
pressed to accommodate the "long war" and "short attention span" of
the 2001 Afghanistan War: "Disorientation as to where and how to find
'the story' was compounded by forbidding mountainous terrain, lack of
telecommunications infrastructure, and journalists' equally non-existent

linguistic capacity in Afghanistan's main languages" (Carruthers, 2011, 214, 217). When the Iraq War began in 2003, it was accompanied by the military embedding of conventional journalists, many of whom were unable to see most of its events, and by a rising Al Jazeera network that began to show action from the "other side." In these circumstances, fixers remained "crucial to newsgathering in Baghdad," providing language skills, safe transportation and contacts (Murrell, 2015, 123). Bloggers also demonstrated that they could authoritatively and reliably document on-site activity (Allan, 2004).

At the same time, two other events – the 2004 Asian tsunami and the 2005 London subway bombing – consolidated the role of bystanders in providing multidimensional eyewitness reports (Day & Johnston, 2005; Allan, 2006). Hailing an "eruption of amateur content" that included eyewitness blogs, audio clips, videos streams and cellular images, observers celebrated their authenticity and vividness as well as the wide availability of their reports (Noguchi, 2005).

Much of this activity has been associated with conflict sites of the 2000s. When conflict broke out in Gaza in 2008/9 and then again in 2012, western journalists were denied access and the eyewitness role was filled by Palestinian journalists, freelancers, activists, citizen journalists and bystanders, who distributed reports across the conventional media as well as via Facebook, YouTube and Twitter. In 2011, when Pakistani Sohaib Athar live-tweeted his infamous "I am JUST a tweeter, awake at the time of the crash," after he realized he had relayed intricate details of the US raid on Osama bin Laden (Hill, 2011), the serendipity of private citizens witnessing public events was widely recognized as a new force in current affairs. Called "Twitter's CNN moment" (Rosoff, 2011), the incident became a harbinger of the rapid current of activity yet to come.

Perhaps nowhere has this been as much the case as with recent coverage of the protests and uprisings connected to the Arab Spring and the Occupy and Black Lives Matter movements. Not only has precarious labor helped report these developments but also the capacity to accommodate and highlight user-generated content as part of news platforms has become the rule.

Crowd-sourcing from afar through smartphones and social media, emblematized by Andy Carvin's (2013) book *Distant Witnesses*, became useful for bypassing government control in Tunisia, Egypt, Morocco and Syria, where "live blogging" offered what the *Columbia Journalism Review* called "the most trustworthy coverage of what has happened in the streets" (Su, 2014). As media outlets developed platforms to accommodate and verify user-generated content – for example, both the BBC and Al Jazeera verified eyewitnesses on Skype, authenticated regional dialects and checked photos and video against verified geocoded images (Hounshell, 2011), though often rendering information security vulnerable

(Henrichsen, Betz & Lisosky, 2015) – citizen photographs and bystander live-stream footage began to dominate the news flow. No surprise, then, that protests associated with both the Occupy and the Black Lives Matter movements were dubbed "Twitter Revolutions." Documentation of these events, however, was subject to both internal and external critique: Al-Ghazzi (2014), for instance, argued how videos from Syria challenged the western binaries used for evaluating news practice – between civic and violent intentions, across witnessing, reporting and lobbying activity, and between amateur and professional photographers. Nonetheless, the celebratory acclaim prevailed as two of the biggest stories of the most recent decade – Wikileaks and Edward Snowden's revelation of illegal NSA activity – were broken by a combination of whistleblowers and journalists: Julian Assange, Edward Snowden and Glenn Greenwald.

Due to the wide availability of small digital cameras and mobile camera phones, eyewitnessing's fourth stage now centers on visual depiction as much as on audio or verbal reports. With the *New York Times* noting that their use had increased one-hundredfold, and an explosive circuit of digital images attesting to eyewitness presence across the globe (Batty, 2011), visuals replayed the hanging of Saddam Hussein, the shooting of an Iranian protester in Tehran, the capture of Muammar Ghaddafi, the Arab Spring and Occupy protests, to say nothing of the eyewitnessing activity propagated by jihadist groups across the Middle East. Eyewitness footage has become the user-generated content most easily processed by news outlets (Pantti & Bakker, 2009, 485). At times, eyewitness scenes caught locally have migrated to the national or global stage, as was the case with soldier photographs of Abu Ghraib or bystander video of violent police arrests in the US (Mortensen, 2014). Across all of these cases, comments about the image's authenticity – "the camera shows" or "we see through the camera's lens" – are legitimating the act of eyewitnessing, even though conventional journalists are often absent.

The limitations of this most current stage of eyewitnessing are not going unnoticed. Unreliability and possible inaccuracy, a seeming lack of structure, cooptation by official forces, online feudalism, a lack of verifiability and excessive graphicness are drawing attention (Day & Johnston, 2005; Waldman, 2005, 78; Su, 2014). In 2009, while reporting the war in Syria, the *Guardian* and other news media were duped by a blogger whom they could not identify – and who turned out to be a 40-year-old US man rather than the Syrian lesbian activist they assumed (Bell & Flock, 2011). Because news stories were often relayed faster than they could be reliably processed, coverage of the 2013 Boston Marathon bombing was riddled with inaccuracies in mainstream news outlets like the AP, CNN and the *New York Post* (Manjoo, 2013; Stahl, 2013). Perhaps it is no surprise, then, that reports show a decline in press freedom in the Middle East from 2012 onward, despite the advances associated with the Arab Spring (*Freedom of the Press*, 2014).

Eyewitnessing during the start of the twenty-first century thus has been both historicized within and outsourced beyond conventional journalism. Its contemporary viability rests on a curious displacement of the longstanding linkage between journalism and eyewitnessing, with the latter existing primarily in journalism's past or in nonconventional journalistic spaces. Dependent on its aura, eyewitnessing has by and large lost connection with the activity's other constitutive features – report, role and technology – to the extent that journalism now invokes the stature of eyewitnessing without providing the conditions from which that stature grew.

Eyewitnessing, then, may have broadened its activity almost to the point of its attrition as a journalistic phenomenon. As eyewitnessing claims an aura of on-site presence more than it upholds longstanding practices of on-site coverage, questions arise about how much alternative activity is standing in for contemporary eyewitness practice, thereby chipping away at journalism's own authority.

From "Having Been There" to "Not Being There"

It was with a certain prescience that the German historian Leopold Ranke declared, "I see a time coming when new history will be built up from the reports of eyewitnesses" (cited in Riess, 1944, xiii). Today, such reports provide on-site details of crime, police brutality, war and terrorism, accidents and natural disasters, each of which constitutes the core of unfolding news.

And yet, eyewitnessing would not have persisted in news had journalism not sanctioned its status as an accounting of reality. What is most salient about eyewitnessing – its ability to convince publics of distant experience in a seemingly unmediated style – offers a stage on which to display the different contingencies for engaging with public life. Its transformation across different periods speaks to the activity's resonance and adaptability. Each period drove its own strategically relevant aspects of eyewitnessing: the early period's reliance on a romanticized and subjective eyewitness report provided by a wide range of individuals was minimized during a second period, when journalists took on the eyewitness role amidst professional aspirations that were reflected in realism. A third period was dominated by the growth of varying technologies that allowed for remote-controlled and disembodied eyewitness activity. That, in turn, ushered in a contemporary period that plays to the aura of eyewitnessing, which has lost its connection to role, report and technology and instead historicizes eyewitness activity as a regular feature of news presentation and outsources it to precarious labor, activists and non-journalists.

Across all four evolutionary periods, eyewitness activity has thus highlighted ongoing issues within journalism regarding the most effective way to craft authoritative presence. But it remains unclear to what news outlets refer when they make claims of eyewitnessing – the technology of newsgathering, the person, the report being produced or the aura generated. This slippage of terms has enabled eyewitnessing to prevail over time, regardless of how it takes shape, what it produces or what its costs might be.

Eyewitnessing thus signals the intensification and depletion of conventional journalistic authority, the presence and absence of journalism and journalists. In invoking eyewitnessing, news outlets blur the distinctions that separate the dimensions of eyewitnessing from each other and substitute that which appears most relevant to current circumstances. This occurs even when it undercuts journalism's own centrality, allowing the news media to claim that they "have been there" as witnesses of events that they have not witnessed. In persisting as a privileged term of reference for contemporary journalism, eyewitnessing thus extends journalistic authority in questionable ways. It has undoubtedly helped legitimate journalism in the popular imagination. But that legitimation has been crafted through practices which only partly bolster journalism, or which journalism only partly implements.

4

How the Shelf Life of Democracy in Journalism Scholarship Hampers Coverage of the Refugee Crisis

Scholarship on journalism has long privileged a journalistic world that is narrower than that which resides on the ground. But given the evolving circumstances in which journalism continues to find itself – via political, technological and economic changes – not all of its key terms remain as relevant to understanding journalism as they might have been at the time they were first proposed. Here I consider one such term – democracy. Surveying democracy's centrality in scholarship on journalism and assessing its relevance against the contemporary journalistic environment, primarily in the US and UK context amid coverage of the current refugee crisis, I use the metaphor of shelf life to conceptually consider whether the repair to democracy in journalism scholarship has over-extended its use-value and what might be gained by enabling its retirement.

The Shelf Life of Ideas

Shelf life is popularly defined as the length of time that goods can be stored until they become unsuitable for use and turn bad, undermined or neutralized by ground conditions (American Heritage Dictionary, 2000). Measured by the passage of time, sunlight, heat and other kinds of destabilizing influences, the expiration of shelf life has to do with the unfolding of challenging conditions that reduce or diminish the expected optimum performance of goods.

The shelf life of scholarly ideas has long been relevant to intellectual inquiry, even if it has not been labeled as such. Thomas Kuhn (1962) was among the first to argue that knowledge takes shape gradually, occurring only after the development of shared paradigms which name and label problems and procedures in ways that generate consensus. Playing to the lowest common denominator – the known, familiar, proven and, over time, broadly predictable – the dissemination of knowledge tends to be inherently unstable and accommodates change begrudgingly: it either adds slowly and discreetly to what has already been established or it wears out, grows old and diminishes in relevance. Knowledge dissemination thereby follows patterns of durability and ephemerality relevant to the shelf life of material goods – food, technical devices and other products.

Four strategies are associated with the expiration of shelf life. First, users adopt commonsensical notions about how long shelf life is supposed to last – milk for two or three days, print cartridges for 18 months – that help control circumstances that might interfere with use. An idea's shelf life is shaped by the internal and external deadlines surrounding its germination and development, as well as the prominence and affiliation of those proposing it. Second, users often prematurely shorten shelf life so as to ensure that value remains high until the end of use. Much like marketing trends in fashion create short-term fads that stifle the durability of clothes even before the majority of users recognize their value, academics too frequently jump to post-isms – post-modernism, post-feminism, post-racism, post-journalism – before the ideas that preceded them may have exhausted their worth. Third, users can extend shelf life often surprisingly or unintentionally, putting slipcovers on worn furniture or reselling used clothing in trendy second-hand shops. Ideas like freedom, fairness, love and happiness might be given a critical bypass, as users embrace them as universally relevant across time and space; notions of ethics or morality might be deemed newly relevant because existing theories have not sufficiently addressed them; ideas like capitalism might build a second-stage appeal in new locations. Fourth, users tend to appraise material goods and ideas unevenly, earmarking only certain dimensions with an early shelf life: car models may last generations while an unpopular color or repeated mechanical design flaw is retired early. In a like fashion, the idea of culture moved from referencing upper-class edification in the field of aesthetics to being a key term for the popular arts in cultural studies.

Like material goods, then, ideas are subject to patterned action on the part of people who support and challenge them. Drawing from one's interactions with the environment, the reactions of others and the long-term regard that builds for or against an idea in the public imagination, they "do not float freely" (Risse-Kappen, 1994). Instead, they act like "switchmen [determining] the tracks along which action has been pushed by the dynamic of interest" (Weber, 1958 [1913], 280). Taking on the form of hooks, weapons, road maps, flashlights, or combinations thereof (Krasner, 1993; McNamara, 1998; Berman, 2001), they are always, like material goods, dependent on strategies that shape them at any given point in time.

Shelf Life and the Democracy/Journalism Nexus

The application of shelf life – and its implicit invocation of a temporal lifeline – has particular relevance to scholarship on journalism. By definition, journalism involves newswork that is valued for its temporal dimensions (Schudson, 1986). Not only are notions of newsworthiness and topicality among the earmarks rendering journalism distinct from other modes of public discourse, but journalists develop intricate routines for time-management as part of their newswork. Popularly labeled the "first draft of history," journalism is expected to turn its efforts elsewhere once historians are ready and available to account for recently occurring events (Zelizer, 1993b). As discussions of journalism's value, role and function wrestle continuously with the expectations that circumstances change rapidly and that today's news remains in constant danger of going stale or losing value (Jones, 2009; McChesney & Pickard, 2011), the news has thus always been associated in some form with a relatively short shelf life.

In today's digital information environment, the abbreviated timeline against which journalism is appraised has shrunk further, which in turn magnifies attentiveness to shelf life. Not only do new media alter what is meant by topicality, but the involvement of citizen journalists, bystanders, activists and producers of user-generated content decentralizes and speeds up the process of dissemination, complicating the ability to generate agreement about what is news. Journalism scholars, then, like journalists themselves, need to consider time's heightened centrality in newsmaking. Tenenboim-Weinblatt and Neiger (2015), for instance, noted a surprising tilt toward the past in online relays. As news technologies become progressively faster and enable more immediate information relay, the question of timeliness becomes only more complicated. Conducting scholarship on a phenomenon that is certain to exist in different forms at different points in time thus requires continual adjustment of journalism's own expected shelf life as well as that of the various notions associated with journalism's understanding. It is within this context that the lifeline of the nexus between journalism and democracy can be fruitfully considered.

The regard for journalism and democracy as necessary props for each other derives from the earliest normative theories of journalism, which saw a free press as necessary for democracy and prescribed parameters that the news was expected to follow in democratic regimes. Though this linkage differs by geographic context, its appropriation in the West, and specifically the United States, has favored narrow definitions of each side of the relationship. With journalism commonly seen as the provision of information through news media outlets and democracy commonly seen as a system of governance that privileges liberty, equality and well-being for all, a long host of complicating factors – new media and the Internet, corporatization, public indifference, involvement of elites, among others – tend to be left out of the conversation. Instead, much of the regard for journalism in the West has been narrowly refracted through a vested interest in the political world, with journalism thought to possess the most value when it is used to enhance democracy (Zelizer, 2004b). Drawing from a broader connection between journalism and politics, this connection has been more presumed than debated and challenged. Its naturalization reflects what Sheri Berman (2001, 238) has referred to as a process of institutionalization: "Ideas become embedded in organizations, patterns of discourse, and collective identities and manage to outlast the original conditions that gave rise to them. Once institutionalized, ideas can separate from the factors that helped bring them to prominence and act as truly independent variables." Following the rationale implicit in this process, the nexus between journalism and democracy thus persists as a largely unquestioned given in much western journalism scholarship.

How Journalism Became Necessary for Democracy

The link between journalism and democracy is not a recent supposition. Outlined here in broad strokes, hints of journalism's instrumentality for democracy are embedded in the story of the establishment of the American republic and in many European writings that inspired its evolution over time. Founding father Thomas Jefferson's oft-cited dictum that "information is the currency of democracy" offered a formulaic way of seeing journalism's relevance. It suggested a view that put journalism in democracy's service, tasking journalism with providing a common ground from which a democratic public could thrive.

Western political philosophers have long argued for the connection of democracy with journalism. Journalism featured in John Stuart Mill's (2008 [1869]) ruminations on democracy, which he considered reliant on the free exchange of ideas that journalism could make available (2008 [1869]). Promoting the need for mediated interaction in democracies, Immanuel Kant defined public reason as that disseminated by "addressing the entire reading public" (1885, 55), while Georg Hegel famously likened "reading a morning newspaper" in the early 1800s to "the realist's morning prayer" (cited in Buck-Morss, 2009, 49). By the end of the nineteenth century, journalism was being likened to a Fourth Estate, with the press seen as a guardian of democracy and defender of the public interest (Carlyle, 1974 [1905]). Alexis de Tocqueville (1900) was among the first to specifically outline journalism's effect on public opinion in both France and America. Gabriel Tarde (1969 [1901]) and Ferdinand Tönnies (1971 [1923]) soon thereafter delineated different versions of an intersection connecting journalism, the public and polity, seen as central to democratic functioning.

The journalism/democracy nexus that prevailed was consonant with a certain version of modernity. It underscored an association with rationality, certainty, consent, reasoned thought, order, objectivity, progress and universal values – all of which journalism was expected to promote in order to create the conditions needed for an optimum public life (Giddens, 1991a; Thompson, 1996; Tomlinson, 1999). In this view, journalism was seen as a unifier, an enabler of understanding and reasoned deliberation, a provider of common reference and informed decision-making, a warning light and promoter of reconciliation, a facilitator of conversation.

Such expectations shaped twentieth-century thinking in the United States. By the 1920s, journalism was regularly interwoven into ongoing conversations about the requisite circumstances for democracy. One of the most noted was the so-called "Dewey–Lippmann" debate, in which American philosopher John Dewey (1954 [1927]) and journalist Walter Lippmann (1914, 1925) considered the relevance of journalism to democracy – though not necessarily together (Schudson, 2008) – arguing for different roles of the press but echoing the connection's centrality. Lippmann (1960 [1922], 31–2), in particular, saw the crisis of modern democracy as a crisis of journalism: "The problem of the press is confused," he noted, "because the critics and the apologists expect the press to . . . make up for all that was not foreseen in the theory of democracy."

To be sure, journalism's role for democracy was also defined in more nuanced ways. Habermas (1974) theorized the public sphere as working alongside a normative, self-regulating journalistic system that would defend pluralist ideals, though in some views he continued to "understate and undertheorize the potential pro-active role of the media in the public sphere" (Benson, 2009, 182), and in others he minimized its exclusionary nature in a way that obscured the unequal access it afforded (Fraser, 1990). According to Muhlmann (2010, 187), journalism's unifying task itself went beyond creating consensus from the very beginning, for it involved the "act of unification through a test, that is, in conflict." In optimum circumstances, she noted, "The reporter shows that something 'is not right' and that the political community must fight this otherness which prevents it from being wholly itself. The idea of a test assumes a conflictuality that is guided and orchestrated by the report, culminating in the clear designation of an 'other' and the recentering of the political community" (195). Regardless of the degree of complexity associated with the tie between journalism and democracy, however, expectations by and large saw journalism and democracy as woven together.

This linkage was bolstered in World War II, which threw into relief what could happen when different governing systems collided. Intensifying expectations of the role that democracy could play in facilitating world stability, journalism came to be regarded – for US citizens, in particular – as a precondition for democracy to flourish, largely because it could disseminate – implicitly and explicitly – the western values of free expression and civil society around the world (Hallin & Mancini, 2004). By the middle of the war, a free-press crusade was under way in the US, with proponents seeking to export the First Amendment guarantee of press freedom to the rest of the world (Blanchard, 1986). Excitement for the idea was widespread, prompting one newspaper editor to write at the time that "our obligation is to extend freedom of the press to the entire world . . . if we fail, then all fail" (Hoyt, 1943, 9).

The linkage was relevant too across the academic voices that became invested in administrative research during the same time period, reaching new heights during the Cold War. As the United States intensified its investment in the project of democracy-building, journalism became widely regarded as the lifeblood of democratic theory beyond the West. Part of this was connected to the development of academic disciplines that saw democracy as the best possible outcome for world politics. US political science departments, for instance, developed curricula that delineated the mechanisms for determining, in Hans J. Morgenthau's words (1985 [1948]), the "nature, accumulation, distribution, exercise, and control of power on all levels of social interaction, with special emphasis on the role of the state," where, as a choice among alternatives, democracy was uppermost and journalism was central to its workings. The rise of administrative research in the US, whose prescriptions for what was considered "good journalism" were exemplified most explicitly in the *Four Theories of the Press* (Siebert, Peterson and Schramm, 1956), further cemented the usefulness of the democracy/journalism link, setting out how the news "ought" to operate under optimum political conditions. The book – later critiqued as ideological and optimistic rather than scientific and realistic, affected unilaterally by World War II and its aftermath (Merrill & Nerone, 2002) – offered a detailed template for how the journalism/democracy nexus might look and provided concrete markers by which it might be identified and evaluated. The insistence on wedding notions of journalism and democracy became so central that years later US scholars would label the news "the connective tissue of democracy" (Gunther & Mughan, 2000), asking why the academy did not "call journalists political actors" (Cook, 1998, 1) and "whether the media [should] govern" (Iyengar & Reeves, 1997). Though it could be argued that democratic theorists, rather than journalism scholars, might be the ones to consider reshaping their thinking on the journalism/democracy linkage, its prevalence now often figures as an automatic given when discussing the journalistic environment.

Though the relevance of journalism to democracy was addressed differently by academe in other countries – surfacing in departments of sociology in the UK, for instance, as a challenge to notions of pluralism (Morrison & Tumber, 1988), or in the Middle East through the lens of international relations (Mowlana, 1996) – its fundamental appeal as a conceptual linkage remained. Generating terms and phrases later that succinctly captured the tenor of the intersection – "mediated political realities" (Nimmo & Combs, 1983), "media politics" (Bennett, 1988), "mediacracy" (Taylor, 1990) and "mediated democracy" (McNair, 2000), among them – the idea remained sufficiently resonant for some to see its two interlinked terms as interchangeable: James W. Carey (1995) famously noted that both "journalism" and "democracy" were names for the same act of making society intelligible. Even today, lamentations over the future of newspapers are easily framed as concerns over the "future of democracy-sustaining journalism" (Pickard & Torres, 2009).

Yet multiple dimensions of the linkage between media and governing systems complicate these expectations. Democracy, for instance, has not thrived as forcefully around the world as its proponents hoped. While much of the force driving the democracy/journalism nexus has rested on an assurance that democracy can prevail in some aspired form, various compromised types of democracy exist – democracies labeled partial, low-intensity, defective, empty or illiberal. Newer democracies look different from older ones, and a spectrum of different kinds of relationships connects the institutions of journalism and democracy (McConnell & Becker, 2002). As Jebril, Stetka and Loveless (2013, 16) observed, "Unlike the established democracies of the West in which media studies originated, the countries and regions of democratization have a varying level of comparability with each other. As such there is an unsurprising and resultant lack of coherence in approach."

The fact that emerging democracies develop unique types of media systems whose journalistic conventions reflect the wider context suggests that there emerge "several – and larger – gaps between the 'ideal' and the reality of journalism than in established democracies" (Jebril, Stetka & Loveless, 2013, 6). Additionally, the causality of journalism over government has not been established. Examples of the frequently argued axiom – that liberalized media and democracies exist in a mutually causal relationship – have, in Price and Rozumilowicz' (2002, 254) view, proven "elusive":

How can we tell whether, as is so widely assumed, media reform is a necessary condition of democratization, or rather, whether free and independent media are merely attractive, superb and even justifying products of an already liberalized society? Does media reform promote democratization or is the existence of healthy and independent media merely a consequence or sign of a society that is already on the way toward greater democratic practice?

All of this diminishes the assuredness with which the link between democracy and journalism can be argued. Different kinds of democracies develop different kinds of journalisms, and they in turn produce different kinds of links between the two institutions.

Many more individuals, arguments and details fill the spaces in this trajectory than have been outlined here. But even the cursory shape of this tale suggests that, since the early days of the American republic, journalism has been widely expected to foster the conditions necessary for democracy to thrive. It is no wonder, then, that western scholarship on journalism, itself largely driven by US thinkers, has tended to adopt the journalism/democracy nexus as a naturalized part of understanding what journalism is for.

Why Democracy is Not Central for Journalism

While one might argue that journalism has been historically necessary for democracy, the opposite assertion does not hold to the same degree. In fact, circumstances show that democracy has not been necessary for journalism, and the idea that democracy is the lifeline of journalism has not been supported on the ground. This does not negate the fact that being a journalist in democratic societies can be less hazardous than being one in non-democratic regimes. But it does suggest that journalism in some form has flourished in places where democracy has not.

Though here too the applicability of this assertion differs by geographic region, the West – led by the United States – has played a central role in positioning the link as a naturalized given in global understandings of journalism. As US scholarly work on journalism has accompanied the export of US models of journalistic practice around the world, the aspiration that journalism would fuel the democratic polity has been widely echoed, if unevenly practiced. But the opposite assertion – that democracy would fuel journalism – has not generated similar acclaim, even if the space for practicing journalism in democracies was a safer one than in non-democracies. The relevance of the journalism/democracy linkage has been instead undermined by two wide-ranging but inter-related complications – one theoretical, the other practical.

The theoretical shortcomings of the journalism/democracy nexus draw first from the version of modernity to which many political philosophers repaired. Western in geographical orientation and narrow in applicability, the mindset they invoked is modern primarily from a certain geographical and cultural perspective, and it assumes conditions related to safety, transparency and ease of information flow, among others, that are not part of the default settings elsewhere. This means that the nexus between journalism and democracy rests on circumstances that are not wholly representative of conditions beyond the West, where, as Garcia-Canclini (1995) argued over 20 years ago, different modes of entering and leaving modernity have become widely prevalent.

This has lent a sense of moral uprightness to the possibility of democracy's spread, where internationalization and the sharing of scholarship across geographic regions often mean making sure that "they" (those from the East or the Global South) practice "our" precepts (those largely from the industrialized regions of the West or Global North). As one observer noted, "a free press is needed everywhere, no less in developing countries than in advanced industrial societies" (Ungar, 1990, 369). This logic continues to link journalism repeatedly with democracy, refracting understanding of the kinds of resulting journalisms more through the lens of the aspired project being imagined than through the realities that exist. The idea of journalism that has resulted is more stable, more morally unambiguous, less contingent, more socially useful, less corrupt and, most importantly, more aligned with western notions of democracy than it ever could be on the ground.

A second complication that has undermined the journalism/democracy nexus is practical in nature. As suggested above, multiple aspects of the conceptual democracy/journalism nexus do not reflect conditions in practice. Historically, journalism has taken on many forms, which are both more and less connected to democracy: journalism has been more partial, biased and conflicted and unevenly related to different types of governance than models of journalism aligning it with one notion of democratic process have assumed (Schudson, 1978; Curran & Seaton, 1985; Chalaby, 1996). For instance, Americans involved in the free-press crusade of the 1940s found a marked degree of resistance to their version of the democracy/journalism link when allies in France and Great Britain favored press controls more extensive than they were willing to entertain (Britannia Waves the Rules, 1946; Perlman, 1946). Similarly, the US-mediated landscape that engaged with McCarthyism a decade later displayed the underside of journalism's rigid adherence to balance and impartiality, when journalism failed to clearly assess and sufficiently oppose the Red Scare because of its loyalty to then-prevalent conceptions of how journalists were supposed to act in democratic regimes (Zelizer, 1993a). More recently, the present period of partisan news in the United States undermines the picture of rational discourse that has long supported the democracy/journalism nexus, suggesting instead that so-called "objective journalism," so central to western notions of democracy, modernity and civil society, is an anomaly. The major US and UK journalism scandals of the past decade – WikiLeaks and the phone hacking at the *News of the World* – as well as the NSA leaks by Edward Snowden and current governmental pull-back in response to issues of national security reveal problematic aspects of journalistic practice in countries that have been heavily invested in promoting the conventional view of the interconnection between journalism and democracy.

Beyond the West, the link between journalism and democracy has become even more tenuous. The debate over the New World Information and Communication Order from the 1970s to 1990s was touted as a discussion about the free flow of information, but it remained at heart a conversation about how free one's journalists could be or what their freedom actually meant. Its assumptions – normative ideas that only one kind of journalism should prevail, the kind most relevant to western democracies – have not disappeared, but rather continue to be replayed in debates over the censorship of Google searches in China or responses to threats against the physical safety of journalists in multiple places around the world. Certain privileged forms of journalism – the very notion of a free and independent press, the idea of a Fourth Estate or the public's right to know, the embrace of neutrality or facticity – have never been the practice in much of the world, even in those regions aspiring to some form of democratic polity (Waisbord, 2000; Jacubowicz, 2007). And in nearly every region of the world, journalism has regularly operated in conditions in which modernity is tied to repression and a respect for order, consensus and authority, rather than freedom of expression. Journalism is central in transitional states with high degrees of self-censorship, irresolution and noise; in cultures characterized by new modes of identity like hybridity and marginality; in regimes bearing odd mixes of colonialism and post-colonialism; in states of soft authoritarianism which offer little hope of developing civil society; in circumstances affected by tensions between the nation-state and pan-regionalism; in states which support information suppression, terror and the persecution of journalists; and in multiple situations of contingency with no clear beginning, end or obvious trajectory (Zelizer, 2011a). As Josephi (2009, 47) noted, "the outdated dichotomous view of a world split into countries in which journalism and journalism education is either free or fully controlled is giving way to the recognition that countries may [control in ways other than] suppression and that the freedom of the media in democratic countries can come with commercial and ideological strings attached."

The tenuous link between journalism and democracy is borne out powerfully in current conditions. Reliance on democracy has left current news outlets wondering what to do next as multiple challenges to the democracy/journalism link surface, many of them from unexpected quarters. How, for instance, is one to evaluate journalism's role given the current back-sliding against the 1990 democratic reforms in much of Central and Eastern Europe? What should be the media response of democracies to the current manipulation of journalistic conventions in the West by Islamic State?

All of this is exacerbated by the variable technological circumstances that underscore democracy's marginality in thinking about how journalism works. Though multiple historic examples show how democracy only sometimes or in part motivated journalism's operation – the radio broadcasts of US government-supported agencies during the Cold War, for instance – the contemporary digital environment complicates the journalism/democracy nexus in new ways. Its decentralization, anonymity, wide-ranging access to both production and consumption, rapidity and accommodation of endless vantage points make certain claims to a kind of newswork that may be more democratic than that exhibited by the conventional news media, but that fly in the face of broader, longstanding assertions about journalism's capacity to support the so-called "democratic objectives" of civil society, reasoned discourse, progress and universal values. In the Middle East, for instance, the online environment promotes multiple, simultaneous discordant conversations which pull as much toward dissensus as toward agreement (Khamis & Sisler, 2010). Though this certainly underscores an access to discourse, it hardly reflects the ideals of reasoned engagement and civility on which democracy rests.

Thus, powerful qualifications modify the notion that journalism and democracy need each other to thrive. What is evident is that journalism prospers in multiple ways that bear little relevance to the neighboring presence of democracy.

The Refugee Crisis and the Journalism/Democracy Link

Limitations on the interdependence between journalism and democracy can be found in recent coverage of the global refugee crisis. Though the current refugee crisis arguably ranks among the most newsworthy examples of circumstances deserving widespread journalistic coverage in democracies – 2015 earned the label "Year of the Refugee" on one progressive news site, for instance (Yu-Hsi Lee, 2015) – such coverage has not been readily forthcoming in the West, particularly not in the two democracies most central to its imaginary, the US and the UK.

Reasons for a lack of coverage are multiple in nature. They include diminishing available revenues for news outlets, diminishing staff with knowledge of the story or the region in which it takes place, a tendency toward pack journalism, a lack of physical safety for journalists, difficult access to refugees and competition with non-journalistic postings on digital media outlets. This has produced coverage that by and large has been less in quantity and quality than the nexus between democracy and journalism might presume.

To be sure, coverage in the West has had multiple high points. An early focus on numbers as a way to understand the crisis' proportions gave way in many outlets by the end of 2015 to an engagement with the story's human aspects. Coverage was often "laced with humanity, empathy and a focus on the suffering of those involved" (White, 2015, 2). By year's end, both the *Washington Post* and the *New York Times* produced intricately focused stories not seen elsewhere, such as how Hungary's Muslim community became actively involved in hosting the refugees (Samuels, 2015), or how the extended family of Aylan Kurdi fared months later (Barnard, 2015), as well as bringing audiences into the refugee crisis via virtual reality. VICE News ran a multi-episode documentary called *Europe or Die* (2015), which unfolded the complicated circumstances under which refugees live.

Yet there have also been problematic patterns of coverage. As the UK-based watchdog Ethical Journalism Network noted in its examination of coverage from fourteen countries, the story oscillated between two themes – numbers and emotions – neither of which were able alone to sustain public involvement: "The conclusions from many different parts of the world are remarkably similar: Journalism under pressure from a weakening media economy; political bias and opportunism that drives the news agenda; the dangers of hate speech, stereotyping and social exclusion of refugees and migrants" (Cooke & White, 2015, 6). No wonder, then, that polls around the world showed low percentages of people interested in coverage of the crisis. In August 2015, half of the British public was unconcerned about migration (cited in Suffee, 2015, 42). In November 2015, most US citizens did not want the US to accommodate additional Syrian refugees (Talev, 2015).

Three distinct patterns are relevant here: in some cases, western news outlets delayed or have not yet taken up the difficult challenge of more fully covering the story. In other cases, news outlets addressed the story with prejudicial limitation – an excess of stereotypy or reporting that was reactive to political discourse. And in yet other cases, western journalism depended on members of a precarious labor force, as well as on a melding of activists, citizen journalists and bystanders, to provide coverage, many of them non-western individuals reporting under conditions of authoritarianism in crisis zones. Each of these circumstances raises a different challenge to the viability of the notion that journalism needs democracy to survive. As Jan Egeland, Secretary-General of the Norwegian Refugee Council, noted: "It is not just a lack of humanity on the news agenda or a matter of luck or a matter of caring more about some people at the expense of others. We need a broader lens to see what really is going on" (cited in White, 2015). Nowhere did he mention democracy.

Delayed Coverage

With more than a million refugees crossing into Europe alone in a single year and an estimated 19 million individuals currently claiming refugee status, the fact that news outlets in democracies delayed or have not yet addressed the refugee crisis suggests that journalism operating in democratic political systems does not always act on behalf of democratic values. This underscores the possibility that democracy's aspirational aims are falling short worldwide.

The most egregious aspect of western coverage of the crisis has been its delay: the refugee crisis only became a major news story for the West in late 2015, though Turkey, Lebanon and Jordan had already been deep in crisis for years. Once the story reached Europe's shores, it did not receive automatic coverage. One journalist in Brussels said that the story "was there to be told, but media failed to alert their audiences or to challenge the readiness of the European Union and its member states" (Bunyan, 2015, 11). Coverage escalated in the West in early September 2015 with the photograph of Aylan Kurdi (Demir, 2015), a Syrian toddler who drowned off the shores of Turkey with his mother and brother. Images of the child were reportedly seen by 20 million individuals over 12 hours (Withnall, 2015), and coverage ballooned immediately after the photo appeared: according to an eight-nation study undertaken by the European Journalism Observatory, humanitarian stories in Germany, Italy and Portugal increased threefold; in the UK, twofold (EJO Research, 2015). As UK news outlets switched from scare-mongering to a plea for hospitality, they displayed a schizophrenic reaction to migration – "fearful on the one hand, fearless on the other" (Suffee, 2015, 41). At the same time, most news outlets in Eastern Europe and the Baltic States did not publish the images and "barely covered the story" (Greenslade, 2015). Even at its height of global public attention, then, the refugee story was differently covered, and those differences had little to do with whether or not democracies were part of the picture.

Most importantly, journalism's investment in the story was short-lived. With the claims of long-term effect emblematizing a facile understanding of what a specific photo could do (Zelizer, 2015b), already within a month of the drowning and circulation of its photograph news outlets returned to their old normal regarding the refugee crisis (Greenslade, 2015). News outlets returned to an equally negative or more negative stance on migration after one month than they had shown before the child's death (EJO Research, 2015). US web searches related to "refugee" dropped sharply in the same time period (Yu-Hsi Lee, 2015). Stories on the refugee crisis reverted to their pre-photo levels, and there was "a return to media coverage focused on refugee numbers rather than human interest" (Bunyan, 2015, 13), and little attention to the complexities of refugee experience (Halabi, 2016).

Moreover, those aspects of the crisis that secured coverage remained smaller than the crisis itself. Much coverage focused on refugees from Syria, Iraq and Afghanistan – in that order – arriving in Europe. The second-largest current humanitarian crisis – that of Yemen – received little attention, while crises in South Sudan, Myanmar and Bangladesh were mentioned almost not at all (Egeland, cited in White, 2015, 1–2), to say nothing of invisible ongoing humanitarian disasters elsewhere. Refugees arriving in Australia, detained in Papua New Guinea and Nauru, were denied journalistic access – and hence coverage – altogether, while internal migrations in China, India and Brazil, no less violating than the Syrian, Iraqi or Afghan exodus, remained basically unreported (White, 2015).

What this suggests is that even an issue in undebatable need of journalistic attention in democracies receives neither uniform nor predictable coverage. Additionally, coverage often veers from that assured by the proclaimed link between journalism and democracy.

Prejudicial Coverage

News outlets that picked up the story and then splayed it with stereotypes, sensationalist reporting and biases imported from policymakers have created other problems. By and large, these news outlets saw refugees through the prism of domestic politics: "There is a tendency, both among politicians and in sections of the mainstream media, to lump migrants together and present them as a seemingly endless tide of people who will steal jobs, become a burden on the state and ultimately threaten the native way of life" (Cooke & White, 2015, 7). Described in pejorative language – labeled as a "swarm," "flood" or "invasion" – or favoring terms of reference – such as "migrants" – despite their articulated problems, refugees were seen as a threat to domestic stability.

Though finding a stable and coherent narrative of what was transpiring was difficult, western news outlets were generally stingy with the space they offered to accommodate the story or reimagine its terms of reference. This was exemplified by the ongoing fracas over whether to use "migrants," "refugees" or "asylum seekers" – or, in Italy, "criminals" or "migrant-terrorists" (*Border News*, 2015) – as descriptive terms for those fleeing their homelands. As Al Jazeera commented in August 2015: "There is no 'migrant' crisis. There is a very large number of refugees fleeing unimaginable misery and danger" (Malone, 2015).

When the Ethical Journalism Network produced its report at the end of 2015 (White, 2015), its focus on UK and US news outlets was particularly damning. The report criticized journalism in both places for politicizing coverage. Though they each practiced democracy of the order imagined by political theorists, and developed media in conjunction with stable political systems, each failed to deliver the story of the refugee crisis in non-prejudicial ways.

From the UK side, the report was unsparing in criticism. Observing that reporting "remains framed through an old fashioned perspective which for some people has an imperial if not colonial tone," it lambasted the unthoughtful use of racist and xenophobic rhetoric (Suffee, 2015, 43). Exemplified by the *Sun* labeling migrants "cockroaches" in April 2015, and its subsequent rebuke from the UN High Commissioner on Human Rights, the report noted that immigration had turned into a "highly charged, volatile and polemical" debate (39). Though criticism targeted the tabloid news outlets – the *Sun* received over 300,000 online protests and the newly established Independent Press Standards Organization (IPSO) more than 300 complaints – the incident stood for "media inspired hatred": "Why does Britain appear to be the only settled democracy in Europe where the problem of hate-speech is generated less from outside the newsroom – by extremist political or religious leaders – than from within, where it flourishes amidst a mix of editorial stereotypes, political bias and commercial self-interest?" (39–40).

The anti-migrant agenda was not new. In 2013, the Leveson Report that followed the *News of the World* phone hacking scandal had singled out UK migration coverage for generating fabricated and discriminatory stories, a negative reportorial tone and careless reporting. Additional reports – by the Media Standards Trust (Moore, 2015) and the campaign group Hacked Off (Failure of IPSO, 2015) – made similar claims in early 2015. Ironically, the newly established IPSO said it could not intervene, because the complaints did not come from the refugees themselves – more evidence that "too little attention [is being] given to the failure of the political system to deal with a humanitarian situation" (Suffee, 2015, 43).

From the US side, the report was no less critical. It assailed news outlets for eclipsing the refugee story within coverage of domestic political affairs, making it an "utterly domestic debate about the legal status of millions of immigrants who have been peaceably settled in the country for years" [with] the "refugee crisis across the Atlantic and in more distant parts [left as] distant sideshows . . . a foreign story." There was "little initial reporting on the US role or responsibility in the origins of the crisis, or as a potential safe haven for those fleeing turmoil and often savage cruelty" (Orme, 2015, 101).

Because political reporters were assigned to coverage, not beat specialists who understood immigration, it is no surprise that the economic and political dimensions of immigration stood out. Their centrality fostered divisive partisan debate, facilitating the perpetuation of negative stereotyping by politicians eager to secure public support. Subsequently, the "most pressing ethical question was how much newsprint and air time to devote to a single presidential candidate whose campaign strategy was the use of virulent attacks on immigrants as a device to secure more of this media coverage" (Orme, 2015, 101).

Thus, it was Donald Trump's inflammatory rhetoric and harsh criticism of immigration generally – Mexican, in particular – that became the launch pad for discussions of the global refugee crisis. US news outlets were faulted for facilitating the unchecked distribution of unfounded right-wing political claims about the refugees. Ironically, Trump's declaration "that he had singlehandedly put immigration at the center of US political debate and media coverage for the first time in years" was one of his "few objectively accurate claims" (Orme, 2015, 102).

US news outlets did not actively wrest the story from Trump for some time. Because his bombastic rhetoric "seemed to many to be deliberately, almost tauntingly devoid of any factual foundation," few rushed to fact-check what he said (Orme, 2015, 102), But, even as polls began to show that the public was accepting his claims as fact (Lauter, 2015), journalists were slow to act. The most prominent attempt came in August 2015 by Spanish-language Univision reporter Jorge Ramos. Attending a Trump press conference in Iowa, Ramos was first insulted by Trump and removed from the event before posing his questions with the aid of other reporters. The incident both prompted other journalists to examine Trump's many erroneous assertions and earned Ramos criticism from some US news outlets: Fox News chided him for having asked a question before called upon and for having expressed an opinion while doing so, and Tucker Carlson called him "an editorialist, an activist" (Fox's Tucker Carlson, 2015).

What this suggests is that journalism in the most well-established democracies has not always fostered reasoned understanding of the crisis. Instead, journalism has been prejudicial, offering information that is often subordinated to other platforms undermining democratic aims – partisan debate, racist discourse or blind adherence to political and/or commercial agendas.

Delegated Coverage

A third challenge to the democracy/journalism nexus can be found in the voices of individuals in non-democracies who provide much of the crisis' coverage. This has included both precarious members of the labor force operating in crisis zones on behalf of conventional news outlets from stable democracies, and individuals using personal social media accounts and digital tools to share information from those same crisis zones. The investment of local citizen journalists, bystanders, fixers, stringers, drivers, translators, feelancers and activists – few of whom are necessarily or even willingly part of the ideological mechanisms that drive journalism in democratic systems – provided much of the West's coverage. Said one observer: "If the mainstream media were largely ignoring the gathering storm, social media and civil society reported and forecast what we were to witness in 2015" (Bunyan, 2015, 11).

The impact of these efforts was variable. Some "flooded the debate with opinion over fact, pushing freedom of expression into hate-speech and prejudice," while the involvement of digital outlets and their various operators "opened the door for more opportunities for critical journalism" (Suffee, 2015, 40). Results aligned more with the latter when journalistic efforts involved former refugees or activists on their behalf as well as local citizen journalists, fixers, freelancers and stringers who were invested in providing reliable content and context. The Ethical Journalism Network found more balanced and in-depth reporting in alternative media and smaller media outlets – mentioning MediaDiversified, Open Democracy! and Ceasefire Map as examples – than in larger, more conventional ones. Said to neither "toe the government line" nor "reduce the argument to slogans" (43), they offered a useful corrective to the reporting not always easily or readily accomplished by more conventional outlets.

At the same time, individual bystanders took up much of the slack in covering the crisis. As the story moved with the refugees, fewer journalists remained to cover the beginnings of their journeys. In reporter Zaina Erhaim's view, in Syria "there are no actual journalists, within the traditional definition. There are none left" (cited in Berkhead, 2015). Thus, enterprises like the Institute for War and Peace Reporting (IWPR) and Global Voices helped to train local individuals in basic journalistic skills and to provide reporting from places otherwise missed in global coverage.

Central to the ability to provide delegated coverage of the crisis were both technological know-how and physical safety. Periscope, Snapchat and live stream video were among the digital tools that facilitated the provision of what one news outlet called "a day by day documentary" (Scott, 2015). Though they were used by full-time employees of western news outlets as well as by local individuals, the latter's access to technology often constituted the last resort for securing coverage. Even selfies – self-portraits taken by bystanders with camera phones – helped craft a sense of what was transpiring: with smartphones instrumental for refugees' contacts with others, their "nonprofessional snapshots document the bad – overcrowded refugee camps, miles of travel on foot – but also the good – the joy of overcoming an obstacle or reaching a final destination" (Selfies, 2015). Connected here was the fact that those providing delegated coverage tended to endure the greatest risks in covering the crisis. When Islamic State began seizing journalists, it went first to local individuals. When two British VICE News reporters were seized in late August 2015 in Turkey along with their local fixer, the British nationals were released days later but the fixer remained in late December in Turkish custody (Buchanan, 2015).

A marked degree of adaptability, crafted in accordance with the singularity of much delegated coverage, was also instrumental. Multiple websites used by the precarious labor force helped organize access, including The World Fixer Community, hostwriter and Journohub. Though immersive journalism remained of value, coverage itself was wide-ranging – from the humanitarian efforts of Witness and Human Rights Watch to websites for sharing refugee stories, such as Multeci.net, and visualizing refugee journeys, such as The Refugee Project. The photographic series *Humans of New York* – which, under the acronym, HONY used social media to share the stories of Syrian refugees as they made their way to the US – promoted itself as "filling the gaps that most news coverage has missed about Syria." Other platforms combined the efforts of journalists with those of activists, policymakers, developers, designers and refugees to service the common aim of diminishing the crisis: for instance, The 19 Million Project put journalism in the service of the refugee community by utilizing the efforts of local personnel.

While it can be argued that the individuals involved in delegated coverage did so in order to widely share information and spark civic awareness about the crisis, a goal supported avidly by democracies, such efforts took place not necessarily within the embrace of democracy or even necessarily in support of democracy, but despite the proximity of authoritarianism. This raises the question as to whether or not the journalism/democracy nexus works most effectively in conflict situations when individuals under authoritarian reign risk their lives for so-called "free information" elsewhere.

Refugees, Democracy and Journalism

The lagtime that western news outlets displayed in lending coverage to the crisis, the zigzagging over whether to name the affected individuals refugees or migrants, the pandering to racist rhetoric or political debates are data that attest to some of the fundamental shortcomings of the democracy/journalism link. These data offer a sobering practical note, for, without media attention, "humanitarian crises, with their horrifying impacts, will continue to be learned by the outside world too late" (Egeland, cited in White, 2015, 2). Though journalists can take steps to improve coverage, and recommendations have been lobbied to that effect across multiple global forums – including employing reporters who are specialists in immigration; providing in-house training on migration; improving links with migrant and refugee groups; and employing refugees, as already exemplified by *The Road*, a magazine written by journalists living in the Zaatari refugee camp in Syria (White, 2015) – the data are sobering conceptually too.

For, given what has been discussed here, it is troubling how much assumptions of the linkage between journalism and democracy persist as an inevitable condition everywhere. Such a linkage is far from describing the whole picture of journalism. Perhaps it is in response to its persistence that the first media summit of the BRICS nations resolved in December 2015 to find a way to "strengthen multilateral and bilateral cooperation in reporting, so that we may come together and tell stories that truthfully reflect BRICS' cooperation" (Full Text, 2015). Democracy was mentioned nowhere in its declaration.

Why, then, has democracy retained its centrality in so much western academic theorizing about journalism, despite the fact that multiple sources of evidence – historical, geographical, economic, political and cultural – suggest that it is not? Why has the shelf life of democracy been given immunity from expiration? And why does this immunity in journalism scholarship continue despite the multiple conditions that have destabilized, challenged, reduced and diminished democracy's optimum performance?

The Immunity of Democracy's Shelf Life

Though democracy's long life in discussions of journalism draws from many intervening political, social and economic variables, academic scholarship about journalism is in part responsible. Because much of the scholarly world in the West – and specifically the US – depends directly or indirectly on the presumption of democracy and its accouterments, the notion has been slow to fade.

Whole academic fields, communication and its longstanding study of journalism among them (Simpson, 1999; Glander, 2000), surfaced from tensions that had positioned democratic regimes on one side of the continuum and varying kinds of authoritarian polities on the other. Classes on democratic governance, on journalists' interactions with official bureaucracy and even on sourcing practices in the free flow of information regularly populate curricula at all levels of academic expertise. This has lent an either/or demeanor to the sharing of academic knowledge in the West, a demeanor that over time has naturalized the polarization of attributes on both sides of the continuum. An implicit or explicit separation between the West and the rest, the center and periphery, the Global North and Global South, the First World and Third World, or the BRICS and the non-BRICS has metaphorically spatialized distinctions between camps for a wide range of intellectual projects, such as the field of international relations (Downing, 1996) or theories of development (Escobar, 1995). Though not the only naturalized given underlying journalism – Vos (2012), for instance, offers a useful discussion of journalism education and the naturalized status of objectivity – the ties binding journalism and democracy shed a particular light on the ways in which academic inquiry and public life draw from each other in western university settings and on the ways in which they disseminate across the global environment.

Democracy's immunity from shelf life reflects the fact that it remains a western-driven and universal standard of subjunctive action, regardless of the degree both to which it can or cannot be achieved and through which it ultimately impacts the various kinds of journalism prevalent in the world. Academic theorizing has played a critical role in keeping this mindset afloat. Democracy has no date by which it needs to be used, no deadline for necessary discarding, no built-in recognition of the affairs or states of being that call for its dismantlement. Instead, notions of democracy flourish as naturalized givens in a range of academic fields that in turn impact the practical applications of the knowledge they disseminate. Journalism thus remains central to democracy's well-being, even if disseminated knowledge about journalism does not fully reflect journalistic practice.

In large part, this has to do with the flow of ideas, writ large. The stubborn durability of democracy's invocation in journalism scholarship reflects what has been widely argued in ideational analysis – that "the greater the uncertainty (in the environment), the more influential is the role of ideas" (Jacobsen, 1995, 293). Moreover, ideas themselves have attributes, "properties that may lend to their selection . . . their institutionalization and their perpetuation" (Garret and Weingast, 1993, 178). It may be that the attributes of democracy – continuity, stability, progress, optimism for the future, institutional centrality – are important for the academy. In this sense, invoking democracy helps it wrestle with its own practical and existential problems, echoing the oft-cited formulations of Ann Swidler (1986), who maintained that cultures or belief systems – the ideas held about the world – are like tool kits used to drive action. Even when ideas change – and they do, as they encounter challenges, conflicts and necessary compromises – they continue to play a role in shaping what ensues.

But democracy also endures as a reference term for journalism, because maintaining its centrality is consonant with existing patterns of knowledge acquisition in the West. As Arjun Appadurai (1996) argued, western research is decidedly collective, conformist and uniform. This is the case not in the sense that people huddle together and think aloud, but that, following Kuhn (1962), new knowledge necessarily builds on that which has already been approved. Ideas can be easily and successfully disseminated when they discreetly pass the familiar and expected threshold rather than overtly challenge, minimize or make irrelevant longstanding parts of the canon.

Democracy has thus settled in for the long haul of journalism scholarship in part because so much existing institutionalized knowledge depends on its presence. Once the idea of democracy passed the threshold as a necessary part of the intellectual frame for understanding journalism, it generated its own cheerleading squad, a squad that has proliferated over time. On the road from old to new paradigms reside multiple scholars, programs, departments, research trajectories and careers that have invested in it as an originary idea for thinking about journalism. In part, this is commonsensical: as in other disciplines (Zelizer, 2016a), journalism researchers have protected a commitment, to no small degree, to keeping scholarship as is, largely because so much of their existing work depends on what has already gone into the canon (Zelizer, 2004b).

The nexus between journalism and democracy has occupied a significant part of that canon. The acts of unlearning and relearning it pose risks to those who have staked their intellectual reputations on certain kinds of knowledge. The upshot here is that, by reducing, relativizing, particularizing or eliminating democracy as a given for understanding journalism, scholars would need to fight an uphill battle in generating a different understanding of its role and centrality.

This is problematic in the present, but it becomes more so as time moves on. For, as Paul Connerton (2009) has noted more broadly of memory and modernity, settings that align their evolution with notions of progress, reason and democracy also exhibit a particular affinity with practices of forgetting. Forgetting, in this regard, becomes a useful mnemonic practice for those attempting to narrow understanding of what matters.

The effects of a narrowed intellectual prism are already evident: in retaining the centrality of democracy in thinking about journalism, the reasons for journalism's existence have become aligned more with the political world beyond the news than with reflecting the workings of journalism itself. The rhetoric for legitimating journalism promotes a vision smaller than the world that journalism inhabits, primarily because its presumed conditions of operation reside beyond journalism. Instead, its nexus with the political environment has foregrounded a set of externally imposed subjunctive aspirations which make the call about journalism's parameters of study. Significantly, that same set of aspirations remains oblivious to journalism's own welfare.

No wonder, then, that much journalism scholarship constantly fends off critiques about its narrow intellectual base. Paraphrasing Appadurai (1996), all intellectual projects have different points of origin and completion, speeds and axes of development and links with institutional structures. This suggests that positing democracy as a necessarily progressive, reasoned and universal phenomenon, as a particular form of modernity coaxes scholars to do, is unworkable because it disregards the conditions by which journalism keeps itself afloat. The dissonance that ensues – between what exists in the head and what exists on the ground – is becoming more rather than less the case, as disparities continue to grow not only between the Global North and Global South but between North and North, and South and South.

Enabling Retirement

Retiring the exclusive and exclusionary relationship that democracy is presumed to have with journalism thus may be overdue. This is not only because the centrality of democracy has generated undemocratic journalism scholarship, by which those kinds of journalism most germane to the core of democratic theory have been privileged over those which are not. It is also because the idea of democracy has created and maintained blinders about all the other variations by which some premise of a governing body might be linked with journalism. Misunderstanding, then, both the key terms in the journalism/democracy nexus – journalism and democracy – undermines the capacity of journalism scholars to speak reliably about the world of journalism practice. Instead, many existing discussions of journalism have become insular, static, exclusionary, marginalizing, disconnected, elitist, unrepresentative and historically and geographically myopic.

Admittedly, the centrality of the United States – in both journalism and scholarship – makes this argument more geographically specific than it might otherwise be. But those in the United States bear a special responsibility for the direction that conversations about journalism and democracy have taken in the West. And while their role in the global spread of knowledge deserves further analysis in its own right, there is no question that US centrality has set the stage for thinking about both democracy and journalism across the global environment.

Though much work has been done on the ascent of new ideas to prominence and their embedding in institutional memory (Jacobsen, 1995; Berman, 2001), less is known about what it takes to remove long-standing ideas from use. Research on professional knowledge acquisition maintains that knowledge tends to have a shelf life of five or six years (Brandsma, 1998). This means that the retirement of democracy as a key term for journalism scholarship would not come easily.

But retiring the concept of democracy in the study of journalism might force scholars to recognize that democracies are not as clear-cut as theories would have them be, that democracies are not as integrated with journalism as has been assumed, that space for other kinds of governing structures needs to be crafted alongside the news, and that, as the power of the nation-state wavers, the real nexus between government and journalism may lie elsewhere. We need to be thinking more forcefully about the effect of other systems that go beyond government per se, such as religious fundamentalism or capitalism.

Doing so might help offset the exceptionalism that democracy has introduced into existing academic discussions of journalism. At the same time, it might open those same discussions to new voices on the horizons of journalistic practice, to the less shiny goods that may be more relevant to journalism than democracy ever could be.

5

Practice, Ethics, Scandal, Terror

We live in an age where the issue of ethics seems to be up for grabs, debated as fervently by those engaging in a given activity as by those observing it. But who decides which ethics matter? Where do the boundaries of decision-making lie? And how does one determine who falls in line, in which way and by which agenda?

Two seemingly disparate events offer platforms on which to consider these questions: the 2011 scandal surrounding the *News of the World*, and the media responses five-odd years later to pictures of people facing death that were displayed by Islamic State. Though striking for what appears to be a dissonant comparison, these events show how fluid are the vantage points from which ethics in the news media tend to be discussed. They also show that journalistic practice – as it takes shape in newsgathering, presentation and distribution – defies the establishment of meaningful ethical standards, revealing how untenable a workable journalism ethics remains. Using both events as examples, I will show how ethical standards, as they are realized by codes of ethics, cut short the potential for ethical practice on the ground.

The Problem of Ethics

Journalism ethics are regularly touted as offering important standards of action to which journalists can and should aspire in practice. Ranging across a panoply of subjunctive earmarks for action – truthfulness, accuracy, fairness, integrity, service to the public good, impartiality and accountability – ethical standards, following what Aristotle labeled "phronesis" or practical wisdom, provide what is thought to be an instrumental high ground of journalistic practice. But such standards are aired far more regularly and supported far more stridently by academics than by journalists, who tend to eschew and deride their presence, exhibiting what one columnist called an "instinctive journalistic aversion to official codes of conduct" (Marcus, 2011). This general journalistic disregard for abstractions is exacerbated by "a busy newsroom . . . impatient of any form of reflection which doesn't contribute to a result or which may slow things down" (Brock, 2010, 19).

Ethics, by and large realized in journalism via codes of ethics, have always presented a multidimensional quandary for journalists. As conceptual projects, ethics and journalism are built upon a different directional understanding of the relationship between thought and action. Drawing from philosophy, ethics tend to work from the top down to establish stable codes of action that negotiate universal and particular means and ends; while earlier invocations tended toward universal standards, more recent ones orient toward situated particularity. By contrast, journalism tends to work from the bottom up, its practitioners needing to negotiate and renegotiate around constantly shifting sources of contingency in practice. That difference has, to no small degree, driven negativity amongst most journalists toward codes of ethics. They see dominant approaches to ethics as simplifying, restricting or ignoring the various circumstances in which the news is crafted. In the eyes of the editor of the *Australian Journalism Review*, it is possible in many places around the globe to "practice as a journalist for years and never so much as look at an ethics code" (Richards, 2009). Or, as a UK non-profit devoted to journalism ethics observed, "the proscriptions on journalistic behavior are many and obvious, but they all have one thing in common: they are not worth the paper they are written on" (Norris, 2000, 574).

The problem of ethics in journalism derives in large part from the multiple vagaries of action with which journalists must wrestle as part of doing work, and the difficulty that ensues in establishing standards for mutable practice. For that reason, each evolving practice in journalism tends to promote hand-wringing over the ethical quandaries it raises. For instance, just one week in July 2015 produced calls for ethics codes in journalism on multiple fronts: the hacking of the casual sex website Ashley Madison highlighted the issue of whether to use hacked documents in the news (Bradshaw, 2015), while a discussion of the ethics of outing followed the resignation of two leading Gawker editors over their intervention in an article that identified a married Conde Nast executive as a closeted gay man (Greenhouse, 2015). Even the cinematic release of the Amy Schumer film *Trainwreck* prompted the *Wall Street Journal* to consider the ethics of journalists who sleep with their subjects (Steinberg, 2015).

The first ethics codes in journalism came into being in the US during the late nineteenth and early twentieth centuries, aligned with the ascent of professionalism and a particular notion of modernity. Richly implicated in the quest for truth, that mindset saw rationality, objectivity, impartiality and reason as the modes of engagement which journalists could offer those needing information about the world (Zelizer, 2011a), and the ethics codes that resulted reflected its values. Mirroring a transformation in journalists' affiliations from reigning work models of partisanship to those of objectivity, they were used to justify those hoping to promote journalism as more of a profession than an occupation. Ethics codes thus set in place a prism for evaluating journalistic practice that was aligned with particular expectations of professionalism in a particular kind of modern context.

In the US the first use of the word "ethics" in a journalistic context surfaced in a 1889 essay on press criticism, written after the *Philadelphia Public Ledger* attempted during the 1860s to set new rules of fairness and accuracy for covering the American Civil War (Lilly, 1889). Sensationalist coverage of the Spanish–American War helped to prompt the adoption of the first code of ethical behavior, established in 1922 by the American Society of Newspaper Editors and embraced four years later by the Society of Professional Journalists, Sigma Delta Chi (SPJ). Repairing to a broadly scoped notion of serving the larger good that grounded the authority of professional-minded journalists in a modern age, the notions of ethical conduct it forwarded were seen as offering journalists protection from growing rates of corporatism in the surrounding culture, intensifying political attacks and public disillusionment with the press. Codes remained more or less stable until after World War II, when the famed Hutchins Commission offered a more socially scientific rationale for journalistic responsibility (Dicken-Garcia, 1989; Christians, Ferre & Fackler, 2003; Wilkins & Brennen, 2004; Rodgers, 2007).

Since then, many news outlets have tried to buttress ethics codes by implementing self-regulating news councils such as the UK Press Complaints Commission or the Independent Press Standards Organization (IPSO) that replaced it, or by setting up in-house public editors or ombudsmen. They experimented with different kinds of situated ethics that were more primed to accommodate change and presumed to shift with new technologies, new journalistic practices and changing economic and political conditions. For instance, Ward (2010, 2015) investigated how the digital environment has changed longstanding notions of ethics, including when to report tweets and how to fashion online presence. Perhaps the most eloquent defense of ethics came from Theodore Glasser and James Ettema, who sidestepped many of the pitfalls associated with rigid ethics codes by narrowing the act of "being ethical" to that of "being accountable" (Glasser & Ettema, 2008). In 2011, Aidan White launched the Ethical Journalism Network, a platform designed to reflect ethics initiatives begun by journalists rather than news outlets. And in 2015, recognizing that no ethics code could pertain to all news outlets, the Online News Association (ONA) began its Build Your Own Ethics Code project, designed to offer multiple solutions to ethical problems raised by user-generated content, social media, graphic visuals, privacy and hate speech, among others.

Though such efforts have moved increasingly toward instituting codes that anticipate the changing nature of journalism's environment, by and large most journalistic ethics codes still continue to fall short of reflecting the range of circumstances undergirding journalism. Beyond offering a generalized edict to "do the right thing," they tend to twin universal principles with levels of specificity that have insufficient bearing on the ever-changing grounds of journalistic practice.

This is exacerbated by the array of practices that constitute contemporary newsmaking. Journalism has always taken shape in situations largely beyond the control of journalists, where rapidly unfolding circumstances, high stakes, a marked degree of risk and inherent unpredictability are all part of the ground that journalists must navigate on their way to making news. Today, however, journalism is complicated by additional factors – a 24/7 news cycle, multi-tasking, falling revenues, corporatism, privatization, sensationalism, convergence and high doses of user-generated content. As conventional journalists, members of a precarious labor force, citizen journalists, activists and bystanders all engage in covering the same story, journalistic practice both eludes standardization and is often controlled by others. This makes the project of ethics in journalism – of inspiring shared rules of conduct that distinguish right from wrong, good from bad – both irrelevant and untenable. Moreover, as global journalism becomes increasingly the rule of coverage, even the most situated code of ethics becomes problematic: how does one determine "conflict of interest" in areas where journalists are so poorly paid that they need to take more than one job? What does "truth" look like when overshadowed by the threat of punitive action or persecution? What does "public interest" or "civil society" mean in regions where public institutions are corrupt? Can "impartiality" exist in locations with no tradition of civil society? How does one determine lexical choices for persecuted groups when ethical alternatives are already corrupted?

Journalism is thus more porous, more unstable, more variegated and less authoritative than might be assumed. Though it may be relatively easy to delineate one's ethical aspirations as a journalist, it is far more difficult to translate those aspirations into practice across the range of situations that constitute newsmaking. These include the temporal, geographic, institutional and technological parameters of newswork, each of which presents additional challenges to the idea of a shared ethics.

Perhaps nowhere is this as easily seen as with the two events considered here: the 2011 *News of the World* scandal and the display of pictures of people about to die by Islamic State from 2014 on. Coverage of both events showed how a blending of time, space, institutional cultures and technology complicate the imposition of relevant ethics codes for journalism. The first event occurred in the Global North, exhibiting a symbiotic melding of institutional boundaries in which technology helped showcase the underside of modernity's aspirations. The second event occurred in the Global South, displaying a temporal/geographic blend of what was labeled "new-media savvy and medieval savagery" (Sella, 2014). Both events dominated the global news agenda for considerable periods of time and triggered extensive discussion of the ethics of journalistic practice in odd and disjointed ways.

Complicit activity against the public good constitutes a central earmark when considering journalism and ethical behavior. The widespread assumption that journalism works – or should work – for the public good is rent asunder when public scandals reveal untoward behavior. The *News of the World* scandal is one such moment. It unfolded in the UK atop a panoply of unethical practices – illegally hacking the phones of celebrities, public figures and murder victims; illegal pay offs across institutions; corruption; conspiracy to pervert justice – committed by members of the news media, the police and the political establishment, generating intense public discourse over which ethical course to take in recovery from the damage wrought. Topping the list was the practice of journalists paying sources for information – a "decades-old principle [that] stems from the belief that the tawdry practice corrupts the authenticity of information" (McBride, 2015). Though most held the news media – and, in a more narrow form, tabloid journalism – primarily responsible for what ensued, the calls for accountability splashed across the wide spread of institutional settings and involved a long list of ethical violations, extensive navel-gazing and public hand-wringing (Zelizer, 2012).

News images of impending death offer a different kind of litmus test for thinking about ethics. Repeatedly positioned as the target of various appeals to "decency," "privacy," "taste," "appropriateness," "sensitivity" and the so-called "cereal test" of journalistic depiction, about-to-die images are by no means certain candidates for display in journalism (Zelizer, 2010). Debates over what to show, how to show it, where and when it can be seen are rampant, particularly regarding depictions that involve contentious circumstances. The question of which images surface in the news airs so regularly – prompted by politicians, news executives, human rights workers, members of militias and bereaved parents – that much of journalism has backed itself into self-censorship and the improbable position of showing less while forcing the public to imagine more. How often are pictures of vital public events – war, terrorism and corruption – pushed from public display? Against these circumstances, Islamic State's decision from 2014 on to take and circulate videos and photographs of countless captives about to die enraged a western public, which saw the gruesome display as unethical. Missing from their discussions was the larger question of how images of this type regularly play across journalism's landscape.

Taken together, the incidents inhabit a broad continuum on which the issues of "what is" and "what should be" repeatedly collide. On its own, each incident was challenged by fundamental uncertainty concerning whether and how to address the ensuing ethical violations that made coverage possible. What that means in a 24/7 news cycle shaped by multiple, often contradictory forces in and beyond journalism becomes clearer when considering the aforementioned dimensions of practice as they relate to ethics – temporality, geography, institutional culture and technology.

Temporality and Ethics

Temporally, journalism exhibits a remarkable affinity with what came before, with journalists tending to repeat behavior across time. For that reason, and despite repeated declarations of their egregious status, the same ethical violations are often committed again and again across the landscape of journalism's many pasts and presents. Plagiarism, trading favors for financial gain, fabrication and violating the line between public and private are among those practices that tend to repeatedly visit journalism's environs. So too is the explicit display of news images, where standards of acceptable pictures vary with the current political, cultural, moral, economic and technological climates.

Why is this so? Journalists do what they can to secure coverage, while the bedposts securing that coverage have systematically floundered, buckled and often disappeared. Much of journalism today is improvisory, exhibiting a "can do" approach to shrinking odds. For instance, journalists remain less able than ever before to protect their sources, due to the digital compromises necessitated by a reliance on metadata. All of this creates a necessarily elastic affinity between news practice and abstract codes of action, which reveals how marginal ethics codes have been in changing action on the ground and how stubbornly consistent most aberrant news practice has been across time.

Thus, it is no surprise that many of the unethical practices critiqued in both the *News of the World* scandal and Islamic State's visual displays of impending death are longstanding. It is also no surprise that interpretive responses of their egregiousness have been cyclical. In the former case, using deception and impersonation to secure information, cozying up to officials and disregarding privacy concerns have gone through waves of legitimation. They were exhibited as early as the penny press and yellow press by the 1800s, buttressed by muckraking and investigative journalism, neutralized in an era that valorized objectivity and reified in new journalism's narrative imagination. Journalists paying sources for information, commonly called checkbook journalism, captured the public imagination when the *New York Times* famously paid $1,000 in 1912 to speak with the surviving wireless operator aboard the *Titanic*, and it reached new heights when TV personality David Frost paid former US President Richard Nixon $600,000 in 1972 for an interview (Peters, 2011). At its core, the practice secured news outlets scoops of seemingly hefty importance.

In the case of Islamic State, the ethical problems with showing people on the cusp of death date back to the earliest uses of images in the news. Inspired by early depictions of the crucifixion, about-to-die scenes appeared already as hand-drawn pictures of suicide in police bulletins of the 1870s, used to set the boundaries of the social order (Suicide, 1872). Over time they came to be increasingly associated with persuasion and propaganda in contentious circumstances – the image of the Warsaw Ghetto Boy, the My Lai massacre, the Tiananmen Tank Man, the Gazan child of the Intifada, and more recently two US journalists gunned down on live television in Virginia. With each display came intense debate over the ethics of showing an individual or group en route to death, and where the debate ended was driven less by images and more by the moral, political and cultural contours that affected the ethics of the time: thus, pictures of people falling from buildings earned news photographers a Pulitzer Prize in the 1930s and 1940s but similar photos in the 2000s and 2010s, labeled "distasteful" and "sickening," were decried as major violations of privacy and decency (Hardy, 1946; Schwartz, 2004).

Much of the *News of the World* scandal evolved around the problematic dimensions of checkbook journalism, at least in the West. In then-ABC anchor Chris Cuomo's (2011) view, "the commercial exigencies of the business reach into every aspect of reporting . . . It's the state of play right now." Though paying for information tends to be discredited primarily as a tabloid practice, where it is thought to "taint" the value of the information being secured, it has in fact surfaced across much of journalism, used by almost all of the major US TV news programs, where it has often been instrumental in generating the relay of important information, often under the guise of "memoir fees" or "licensing fees." In 1963, *Life* magazine paid $150,000 to dressmaker Abraham Zapruder for his filmed sequence of the assassination of US President John F. Kennedy; in 1970,

Esquire magazine paid $20,000 to US Lt. William Calley for his version of the story of the My Lai massacre; in 2009, CNN paid $10,000 for an interview with a Dutch citizen who had overpowered the so-called "Christmas Day bomber" midair on a transatlantic flight; in 2014, multiple Canadian news outlets disclosed that they had paid for information about Toronto mayor Rob Ford's substance abuse; and Wikileaks stunned news outlets in 2015 when it issued a call for a $100,000 bounty on the text of a multinational trade agreement, the Trans-Pacific Partnership pact. Given the questionable ethical nature of the means used to obtain information, should any of these news stories not have come to light? Without a clear rank-ordering of ethical violations – by which ethics codes might establish that serving the public good trumps other wrongs in journalism – the unethical nature of newsgathering in each case might have denied the public fuller information critical to its functioning as a body politic. Furthermore, ethics codes obscure a sliding scale of evaluation: if paying for information was acceptable in these cases, who is to say where its appropriateness ends?

And yet, despite evidence of its instrumentality and its intensification over time, paying for information has been vilified by nearly every existing ethics code in conventional journalism, including those of the *New York Times*, *Washington Post* and *Los Angeles Times*. The SPJ, for example, maintains that journalists should never pay for information, under any circumstances. No wonder that then-US presidential candidate Herman Cain pulled out the SPJ's code of ethics when he was charged with sexual harassment (Cain Offers, 2011), suggesting that the *code* had become more useful for those looking to scapegoat the media than for those needing behavioral guidance. Displaced here are a number of relevant questions, including how to assess the ethics of news flow when unethical practice generates coverage by reputable news outlets; how to account for journalists who remain with a source for long periods of time; and how to assist journalists with long-term involvement in a story when certain aspects require remuneration.

In the *News of the World* scandal, the practice of paying for information was widely critiqued. In Britain, wrote the *New York Times*, "public tolerance seems to have reached its limit with revelations that journalists working for Rupert Murdoch's *News of the World* routinely paid the police for information" (Peters, 2011). The *Columbia Journalism Review* observed that "Murdoch just never bought into . . . the ethical edifice that journalism as an institution built up over the last half a century or so . . . It's like Gresham's Law, where bad money drives out the good" (Chittum, 2012). Called sleazy, opportunistic and dishonest, the practice was seen as derivative of British tabloids, thought to threaten the integrity of journalism writ large. But, as befit the pattern, the frenzy had no effect and gave way to further scandals involving similar practices in 2015: "Despite all the hoopla, nothing substantial changed" (Naughton, 2015). As the *Guardian* later noted, the "phone hacking trial was officially about crime; in reality it was about power . . . the power of the play-ground bully: he has only to beat up one or two children for all of them to start trying to placate him" (Davies, 2014).

In like fashion, Islamic State's visual practices followed a long line of activity made conventional by the western media. They included playing to an emotional past, varying the exposure to gruesome images depend-ent on the purpose at hand, regularly melding fictitious and factual tech-niques of presentation and, in particular, showing people on the cusp of death. Western journalism had long shown people in such a way – facing bullet fire in the Spanish Civil War, Vietnam War or Intifada; falling to their death from the World Trade Center; being swallowed by tidal waves in the 2004 Asian tsunami (Zelizer, 2010). Lest the argument be made that such pictures differed because they had not been taken by those who perpetrated the violence, one need only consider a two-step legacy of image display over the past century: first, military trophy pictures from locations like the Nazi concentration camps, Khmer Rouge outposts, Abu Ghraib and Afghanistan; and, second, the camerawork of non-state actors like Boko Haram and Mexican drug cartels, organizations which, in the view of The Committee to Protect Journalists, "are not merely producing videos; they are acting as competitive media outlets" (Simon & Libby, 2015).

Responses to the ethical nature of these images wavered with the climate at hand, with decisions for and against showing graphicness varying according to moral, political and social considerations: for instance, the visual depictions of the victims of Nazi concentration camps in 1945 were displayed with a graphicness, frequency, primacy and salience that was not repeated in other mass atrocities that followed in Rwanda, Bosnia and Sudan, among others (Zelizer, 1998). As US White House Press Secretary Jim Carney famously said when the Obama administration in 2011 decided to depart from tradition and prohibit the release of photos of Osama bin Laden after his death, "It's not in our national security interests to allow those images . . . to become icons to rally opinion against the United States" (cited in Montopoli, 2011).

Thus, when Islamic State displayed images of captives about to be beheaded, thrown off buildings, set ablaze or dismembered, it brought into relief western journalism's own complicity with a long line of similar display practices in the news media. The stylistic aspects of these visuals drew from a longstanding aesthetic template: invoking the middle-ground of photography, where intervention was presumed to be minimal, the images featured a balanced, uncluttered compositional shot, with the victim featured saliently in the center frame and unselfconsciously facing the camera (Zelizer, 2010).

But despite the visual trope's persistence over time, and wide – though variant – usage in western journalism, when Islamic State began showing pictures of people about to die, it shocked western sensibilities. The challenge, said the Associated Press' Santiago Lyon, was "to show reality without succumbing to propaganda" (cited in Simon & Libby, 2015). Western media outlets immediately criticized the practice as inconsistent with standards of decency. Islamic State's activity violated the SPJ's ethical code to "minimize harm," it was said (Harper, 2014), and one ethics website listed it among its media ethics issues of 2014 (Smith, 2014). Media commentators disparaged the images, calling them inhumane, cruel, shocking, propagandistic and immoral. Fox News' decision to embed a full video of Islamic State's burning of Jordanian pilot Moaz al-Kasasbeh drew widespread criticism from other media outlets, with NBC's Brian Williams tweeting, "We're not going to air one bit of that on air." Some news outlets showed parts of the images, with verbal rejoinders cautioning viewers not to look. While some commentators, mostly associated with non-conventional news platforms like VICE News and Vox, discussed their eerie resemblance to the past – orange jumpsuits mnemonically cueing to Guantánamo Bay, an animated black-and-white banner recalling the eighth-century Black Standard of Islam, a cinematic style of martial triumphalism reminiscent of Nazi filmmaker Leni Riefenstahl – other news outlets substituted the about-to-die images with pictures of happier times, showing photos of already dead individuals drinking beer or chatting with family and friends (Alan Henning "Killed by Islamic State," 2014). Yet still other news outlets blocked the images altogether: removing the pictures from its October 5, 2014 front cover, the *Independent* proudly noted, "The media finally stop playing the terrorists' tune . . . here is the news, not the propaganda." Even coverage of Islamic State was distrusted, as suggested by the *Atlantic Monthly*'s story, "Is VICE's Documentary on ISIS Illegal?" (March, 2014). Though lone voices protested – such as an opinion piece titled "The Only Way is Ethics: To Censor the Atrocities of ISIS Would Dishonor James Foley and His Work" (Gore, 2014) – they were rare. After journalist James Foley's beheading, Twitter suspended the accounts of those sharing or reposting the pictures, and Twitter users crafted the hashtag #ISISMediaBlackout to prevent further sharing on the platform (Franceschi-Bicchierai, 2014).

Temporally speaking, then, codes of ethics in journalism have not done much to eradicate unethical behavior. They have done an even less impressive job of clarifying what to do when decidedly unethical practices produce an ethical public engagement with the news.

Geography and Ethics

Geographically, the range of circumstances in which journalism is practiced worldwide is testament to the inability to prescribe either one standard for all or any standard for some. Ethics codes in journalism are largely an invention of the industrialized democracies of the West and Global North, where the usually voluntary issuance of guidelines offers a set of best practices without an accompanying official or legal mechanism for enforcement, pre-emptively "ward[ing] off any potential government interference with the freedom of the press" (Meyer, 2011). Certain privileged forms of journalism – the notion of a free and independent press; the idea of a Fourth Estate or the public's right to know; the embrace of neutrality, facticity and objectivity – are central and uncritically positioned in ethics codes. But they have never been the practice in countries where soft authoritarianism, transitional governance, government-owned media, odd mixes of colonialism and post-colonialism, blends of secular and religious authorities, self-censorship and government interference are prevalent, and this is to say nothing of the mix of perspectives that ensues when North and South unevenly converge on a news story (Zelizer, 2016c). Thus, ethics codes bear a particularly tenuous relationship with the geographic spread of journalism. Often driven by a different kind of modernity – one connected as much with repression, social order and authority as with hopes of free expression – the aspiration to standards of action commonly espoused in the West and Global North shrinks in relevance for many practicing journalists.

The *News of the World* scandal bears this out. Though much of the outrage was driven by the exchange of information for money, beyond the West and Global North the efficacy of paying for information is so engrained that in many places it has spawned systematic responses to rampant institutional corruption. Multiple examples exist of officials and journalists regularly exchanging pay and information: China's *hongbao* or "red envelope journalism," Africa's "brown envelope journalism," Russia's *zakazukha* practices or "paying for favorable coverage" (Zhao, 1998; Skjerdal, 2010; Tsetsura & Kruckeberg, 2014). Seen as necessary for information to readily flow, despite the unethical nature of the practices that produce it, such interchanges are requisite to securing information both locally and in the global flow of news. In other words, ethical violations regularly undergird news-stories gathered beyond the West and Global North, and they thereby often remain in the background of stories about those regions that are distributed globally.

It is understandable, therefore, that coverage of the scandal beyond the West and Global North made little fuss over its aberrant activity. "Unlike Britain," wrote the Delhi-based *Asian Age*, "in India top journalists have got away lightly for getting mixed up with the undesirable actions of corporate lobbies and some politicians" (UK Phone Hacking Scandal, 2011). State-run Iran TV reported on the scandal by noting that it had "this week caused concern and distress among the people of Britain and topped their economic concerns" ("News of the World" Closes, 2011). Calling the scandal a "typical case in which many of Western media and society's problems can be seen," the Chinese news agency Xinhua saw the infringements as representative outgrowths of the western notion of freedom of the press (Chinese Journalists Criticize, 2011).

Similarly, coverage of Islamic State's visual displays differed in and beyond the West and Global North. Though certain tenets tend to emblematize the display of individuals and death wherever they are – distant over proximate, other-caused over self-caused, victimized over perpetrated – slight differences across cultures and shifts within cultures vary the degrees of visual graphicness that are accepted as appropriate. Thus, when individuals jumped or fell from the World Trade Center on 9/11, US news outlets scrambled to remove the visual display of their actions but they continued to appear in media outlets in the Middle East, South America and much of Europe (Zelizer, 2002). But when individuals were killed not long after by the Asian tsunami, US news platforms featured close-ups of local individuals dying or already dead, prompting one Indian newspaper to lament the graphic display and complain that "Asia's tsunami was open season ... every American network's Disneyland party" (Malik, 2004).

Geographic responses to Islamic State's visuals varied in a similar fashion. While in the West and Global North the images were lambasted widely, elsewhere condemnation tended to be contextualized within discussions of the peace-loving nature of Islam (Anees, 2015) or to surface when individuals with local connections were affected – in Ethiopia, Algeria, Kuwait or Libya (Has ISIS Found a Base, 2015). When Islamic State burned alive a Jordanian pilot in 2015 and a full-length video of his death went viral, public sentiment hardened in much of the Arab world. The event unified Jordanians against Islamic State, as "even skeptical Jordanians [began] rallying around their government's position and denouncing the extremists," with many who had maintained "it's not our war" changing their minds (Nordland, 2015). One Jordanian editorial went as far as comparing execution styles, noting that the "other recently filmed executions carried out by the group – being 'mere' beheadings – were much more merciful than the tragic, abhorrent fate the group doled out to the Jordanian pilot" (Boycott ISIS's Videos, 2015).

It comes as no surprise, then, that when considered geographically, ethical standards take on many faces. It has been widely argued that "promoting ethical standards in journalism cannot be separated from the advancement of human rights and welfare in general" (Meyer, 2011). Though ethics may be seen as having abstract value, their positioning in local contexts can render them redundant, troublesome and even the source of institutional adaptation or political danger.

Institutional Culture and Ethics

Institutionally, the challenges in establishing ethical standards have been no less strident. Journalism today exists as part of a broad institutional culture, in which politics, economics, social welfare, education, security, religion, the military and other institutional settings regularly impede on what might be thought of as autonomous newsmaking. These institutions exist in a complicated symbiosis with the news media, revealing in some places entrenched attributes of a widely shared institutional culture and shedding doubt on the workability of any ethics that target only some of those responsible for their shaping. Contemporary institutional culture, particularly as it has evolved in the West and Global North, often involves widespread institutional corruption, a concentration of media ownership, a culture of promotionalism, extensive kowtowing to power, inter-institutional dependency, corporatism, a gravitation toward impunity and cover-up, a resistance to change, opposition to transparency, an entrenched sharing of power, placing commercial profit above all and a revolving door of personnel. In the Global South, many of those same characteristics are joined by the punitive measures and restrictions typical of authoritarian intervention in newsmaking. Because the parameters necessitated by other institutional settings can easily intrude on what might be thought ethically correct for journalists, institutional culture raises the question of how viable ethics can be when the news includes journalism as only one of its many drivers.

Such was certainly the backdrop to the *News of the World* scandal, where much of the unethical behavior at the heart of the affair involved a complicated interweaving of three supposedly separate institutions – journalism, politics and the police service. As one observer for the Poynter Institute noted of the inter-institutional collusion that surfaced, "this should've been the fifth season of *The Wire*" (Myers, 2011). A larger ethos of competition, strident in an era of shaky economics, meant that when other news outlets, high and low, regularly paid for information, it became easier to see doing so as a necessary condition for journalists to remain in the game. At the same time, as adjacent institutions paid for information – lawyers pay expert witnesses, police services pay informants – the unethical nature of the practice became relativized. Because the blurring of institutional domains was not controlled by journalists, the ethical nature of activity was in part situated beyond their purview. Much of the hacking was outsourced to private investigators, who were paid for information they provided and in turn subsequently paid the police and other officials for theirs. While observers were keen to pinpoint which narrow part of the larger institutional context was most culpable, generally assigning blame to UK tabloid journalism – the *Columbia Journalism Review* carefully positioned "paying for news . . . at the root of News Corp.'s hacking and bribery scandals" while contending that "the tabloids *are* the dominant newsgathering culture in the UK, at least in print" (Chittum, 2012) – it was not at all clear whether the disconnect between journalism writ large and its non-journalistic institutional neighbors was deserved. In fact, the intimacy across institutions – widely labeled "too cozy" and "incestuous" – merits as close attention as that paid to the interiors of the *News of the World* (Zelizer, 2012). As the *Washington Post* noted, the scandal pointed to a deeply engrained system, involving the "long failure of authorities, the legal system and news outlets in Britain to come to grips with a broad array of illicit newsgathering that went far beyond *News of the World*" (Faiola, 2011).

Institutional culture of a different sort drove Islamic State's display of pictures. Its authoritarian rule made religious precepts, as embodied by the institution of the Caliphate, the default setting from which all news content would ensue. Reflecting an amalgamation of values deemed relevant by its unified authority, a top-down assertion of control made content provision highly strategic, repetitive and formulaic, capable of projecting messages that could be easily accessed and understood by multiple external institutional settings – military and security forces, governments, potential recruits and censors, among others. Because Islamic State regularly bypassed conventional media outlets – "ISIS fighters," said one news executive, "do not give interviews. They speak directly into the camera" (cited in Simon & Libby, 2015) – and the West lacked a reliable, independent journalistic enterprise in the territories under its control, the western media were by and large denied access to Islamic State in any venue other than through its produced content, making its institutional culture all the more pronounced.

The lack of institutional congruence had many effects. It complicated understanding Islamic State on its own terms of reference, a prism reflected in coverage. For instance, most news outlets focused on the regime's brutality while sidestepping accounts of its state-like functions, like collecting taxes, maintaining order or running hospitals. Only in late July 2015 did the *New York Times* report on its state-building, despite the fact that it had been in effect for months (Arango, 2015). The resulting emphasis on spectacle undermined the capacity to understand its powerful spread (Zelizer, 2016d). It also created an institutional reliance on an evolving journalistic labor force – the precariate. Fixers, minders, translators and other members of this precarious labor force provided much of the news coverage, despite the fact that institutional settings tend to be unresponsive to the realities under which they work (Yazbeck, 2015). Associated both with and against Islamic State, they offered western news outlets little way of distinguishing between the two: British journalist Anthony Lloyd reported being captured and shot by the man he had trusted as his fixer in northern Syria (Williams, 2014). Nor did institutional settings accommodate the ambiguous circumstances that arose around the precariate: for instance, Yosef Aboubaker, the fixer who was captured by Islamic State together with US journalist Steven Sotloff, was never interviewed by US officials or security personnel about the events leading up to the journalist's beheading (Martinez, 2014). The effect of all of this on ethics codes should be clear: what would be the value of introducing ethics standards into a situation where practice is beyond conventional journalism's control or, at times, understanding? Not only did this render the insistence for ethical journalistic action at the bottom of any media outlet's wish-list, but it reduced much of western journalism to second-hand observation and a state of perpetual reactiveness over a show staged by Islamic State.

Thus, both cases reveal unethical action in certain quarters alongside attempts to keep institutions afloat, raising fundamental questions about which ethics matter and to whom. In fact, given the widespread scope of institutional intimacy, in the first case, and the stark lack of institutional interchange, in the second, it is probable that action of all kinds violates some notion of ethics somewhere. A journalist's most routine questions might push sources to betray confidence or to commit brutality. Audience imperatives – pleasing sponsors or political authorities, keeping ratings high or subscriptions up, attracting recruits – often displace the ethical limitations of privacy, while educational cues – a desire to shield children from negativity and brutality or to harden them to its occurrence – can censor the ethical insistence on the public's right to know in different ways. Whose ethics should remain at the core of debates between, on the one hand, bereaved parents, who do not want details of their dead child aired, and, on the other, politicians who feel that covering the death has instructive civic value or jihadists who use it for persuasive/propagandistic aims? These circumstances underscore that whoever is responsible for producing ethically correct coverage does not necessarily make ethical decisions about the news. Intervention instead comes from multiple institutional settings, each of which makes its own call about what topics news should address and in which ways – in journalism's name but not always with journalism's sanction.

Institutionally, then, ethics codes in journalism project a simplified understanding of the complicated contexts in which journalists work.

They tend to apportion blame to only some of those committing ethical violations, while leaving the broader institutional culture and its offending institutions largely intact. In circumstances that have either extensive institutional affinity or no affinity at all, ethics codes offer a weak corrective to unethical behavior.

Technology and Ethics

The digital environment poses additional challenges to journalism's ethical codes, particularly around the questions of who and what constitute journalists and journalism. The cohabitation of conventional and non-conventional journalists, as well as non-journalists, in the available maze of digital spaces complicates the contours of an ethics that could be applied to the practitioners and practices therein. Not only are newsgathering operations more visible and varied than ever before, but the import of practices of crowd-sourcing, tweets and online postings by individuals from a variety of political, military, religious, economic and cultural vantage points undercuts the establishment of shared or standardized behavior of any kind. The question of what it might mean to be a responsible journalist depends in no small part on an understanding of ethical behavior that is consonant with practice on the ground. Multiple questions thus arise about the viability of ethics codes and technology, which, given the rapidity of technological diffusion, promise to be out of date almost as soon as they surface (Buttry, 2011). For instance, most existing ethics codes in journalism mention the accountability and/or transparency of those doing the reporting. And yet the anonymity associated with many online postings, particularly visual ones from conflict zones, renders those objectives unattainable and often unsafe (Henrichsen, Betz & Lisosky, 2015). Left unclear are the ways in which news outlets must balance the public good against their inability to display accountability and/or transparency.

At the same time, technology has complicated particular practices in particular ways, and the ethics of paying for information, emblematized by the *News of the World* scandal, constituted one of them. The digital environment intensified competition in ways that made unmanageable the kinds of checks and balances necessary for optimum journalism – corroborating information, piecing together fragments of a larger story, contextualizing incongruent information – and by the time the scandal broke, coverage of multiple stories had capitalized on the gains associated with checkbook journalism. For instance, from its inception Gawker's repeated and much publicized payment for stories – a sexting story about former NFL player Brett Favre or the leak of a prototype for the iPhone 4 – relied on digital immediacy, and the outlet was upfront about the value of paying for information (Cook, 2009). But though such stories brought attention to Gawker, they were also subsequently picked up by conventional news outlets with no problem running news that had been gathered unethically. Technology's underside, then, highlighted the value of paying it forward, where paying for information at one point in the news flow could then be used as the basis of presumably ethical news reports down the line. Thus, though the *Washington Post* noted that "journalism's Thou-Shalt-Not-Pay commandment has lately been taking a beating" at the time of the Gawker incidents (Farhi, 2010), other stories brought media observers more in line with the practice. By the time that Wikileaks issued its 2015 "cash-for-leaks" venture, Poynter Institute executive Kelly McBride was calling for "new codes of ethics that embrace the best of the Internet's potential for citizen journalism and information sharing" (McBride, 2015).

No surprise, then, that the potential, scale, permeability, immediacy and widespread availability of technology fueled the *News of the World* scandal. The activity preceding the scandal – journalists accessing the private phone and email accounts of countless individuals on the basis of information tips provided by the police in exchange for cash – was crafted around what was widely decried as the illegal usage of technology. The frenzy following the disclosure of multiple acts – impersonating users and obtaining passwords, "pretexting," "blagging," "pinging," using hand signals in the newsroom to indicate hacking as an information source – reached new intensity when it became clear that the police had provided tips that made possible the phone hacking of victims of the London subway terror attack and relatives of deceased UK soldiers. In particular, the hacking of the phone of dead schoolgirl Milly Dowler turned the scandal "from a local irritant to an international catastrophe" (Mirkinson, 2012). The very technological capacity that drove the scandal thus in effect displayed technology's underside.

When details of the hacking became public, observers were outraged. Widely referenced as journalism's "dark arts," the phone hacking produced what the *Guardian* called a "rotten empire" (Murdoch's Malign Influence, 2011). The *Washington Post* labeled the journalism behind the scandal as so "corrosive [that] in the name of the masses anything goes" (Ignatius, 2011), while US journalism executive Rem Rieder, writing for the BBC, opined that *News of the World* was "off the charts in the sleeze department . . . the sheer gall of listening to the phone messages of missing teenage girls and relatives of terrorism victims – and deleting some of them – has shocked even the most jaded media critics and consumers" (Rieder, 2011).

A similar coupling of technological potential and the unethical behavior it fostered cluttered the landscape around Islamic State's visual display. On the one hand, Islamic State's power was tied to technology: parlaying a knowledgeable and energetic engagement with social media that involved tweeting via 46,000 Twitter accounts (Berger & Morgan, 2015), the group exhibited a sophisticated reliance on branding, an information wing called al-Hayyat Media Center and a social media guru who enhanced its message. Using a vast and growing repertoire of platforms – Twitter, Tumblr, YouTube, Facebook, Instagram, WhatsApp, Kik, Soundcloud and Ask.fm, among others – the audiovisual content it produced firmly situated Islamic State in a media-savvy world. Rendering its high production values distinct from the grainy footage circulated earlier of jihadist beheadings in Chechnya, Pakistan or Iraq, its techniques involved two and sometimes three cameras, seamless editing, adept camera work with cut-aways, voice-overs, music and sound effects, slow motion and instant video retrieval, earning the group the label of "the cinematic caliphate" (Sakka, 2015). Conjuring up familiar new and old media forms, its content displayed a highly stylized aesthetic that borrowed from fictional action movies, horror films and video games, interweaving *Natural Born Killers* with *Grand Theft Auto*, *The Evil Dead* with *Call of Duty*. As the *Guardian* noted, "Islamic State might have outlawed music, singing, smoking and drinking alcohol, but it clearly embraces Final Cut Pro" (Rose, 2014).

On the other hand, that technological potential was decried for the messages it contained and effects it wrought. What NPR (ISIS Runs a Dark Media Campaign, 2014) called a "dark media campaign on social media" was widely critiqued for its technological savvy. As the *Washington Post* noted, Islamic State left technology platforms "torn between free speech and security": the question remained "how to preserve global platforms that offer forums for expression while preventing groups such as the Islamic State from exploiting those free-speech principles to advance their terrorist campaign" (Higham & Nakashima, 2015). Media outlets sided in varying degrees on the question: Facebook generally exhibited a no-tolerance policy, banning terror-related content from the 2000s on, while Twitter alternated between supporting diverse perspectives and closing down suspicious accounts. By the end of 2015, the online protest movement Anonymous had taken on the shuttering of suspect social media accounts.

In short, journalistic ethics codes cannot operate today as if they are separate from the ethics practiced by those beyond journalism. Current technological platforms blend the two populations. When ethics discussions continue to repair to outdated notions – such as an insistence on clear boundaries around privacy – they do not sufficiently take heed of how difficult it is to establish and police such conditions given today's technological landscape. Some news outlets have begun to offer guidelines to their employees on mining the Internet – the BBC, National Public Radio and the *Washington Post*, for example – but many still act as if journalists exist in a professional ghetto, where the newer presence of digital and social media is not necessarily part of the picture and where ethical standards for journalists are far from reflecting what unfolds on the ground. What hope, then, can journalism ethics codes have of changing the landscape of unethical practice if many of journalism's non-journalistic collaborators and competitors and their practices reside there too?

A technological view of journalism's codes of ethics thus underscores the gaps in practice currently not addressed by ethics codes. Not only are such gaps instrumental in understanding journalism in today's online environment but they obscure the unfolding of unethical action that finds its way back into conventional news.

On the Impossibility of Journalism Ethics

I have argued here that collective ethical standards are close to impossible to achieve in journalism and that even codes of situated ethics do not come close to reflecting all that journalism constitutes. I have also maintained that ethics codes may fall short in what they can offer journalists, where collectivity – so central to maintaining ethical standards – is regularly undermined by the temporal, geographic, institutional and technological settings that journalists must navigate. Without such collectivity, the possibility of realizing shared standards of ethical action remains in peril.

It is unclear, then, under which conditions ethics codes can be imagined in journalism in any viable fashion. This is not to say that journalists should not aspire to be ethical insofar as that means "doing the right thing." But in their present encapsulation as collective codes of action, ethics tend to be the least worried over, debated and enacted by those whose behavior remains the most targeted by the magnifying glasses of others. In fact, ethics in journalism tend to draw the most attention when an ethical code is egregiously broken, as in the *News of the World* scandal or the display of about-to-die pictures by Islamic State, and such attention tends to come from outside journalism as fervently as from inside. These circumstances are hardly a propitious way of determining ethical standards for journalists.

The difficulties with establishing ethics codes in journalism are multiple and systemic. Such codes presume a collective that may not exist; draw from a clarity of purpose and authority of decision-making that are more aspired to than real; pay little heed to the intrusion of multiple quarters in deciding what counts; and fail to raise the question of whose ethics are at stake and for what purpose. Until they can spark productive disagreements that have a fuller connection with practice, ethics, as conceptualized since the days of Aristotle, may be more improbable in journalism than we think.

This is not new. Decades ago, Jay Black and Ralph Barney laid out the principles that made media codes of ethics unviable in their eyes. Among other things, they argued that ethics codes helped the regulators more than those who were being regulated, regulated the neophytes more than the established practitioners and satisfied those lured by the promise of ethical behavior more than those tracking its implementation (Black & Barney, 1985). In other words, "codes arise in response to public demand but they are framed to cause the least commotion" (Black & Whitney, 1983).

Why, then, do we continue to insist that some kind of ethics code must be applicable to journalism? Part of the reason may rest in ambivalence about all of the circumstances that allow journalism seemingly untouchable authority: its reliance on practices that unfold largely behind closed doors; its insistence on power without commensurate degrees of accountability; its ballooning public stature when things go right; and its easy access to tools and platforms of self-enhancement. Part, too, may derive from ambivalence about the certain kind of modernity with which journalism often aligns. As we ponder modernity's historical myopia, mechanically shifting centers, overt confidence about the future and blinding belief in rational reasoning, journalism's status as one of its high achievements comes to the fore. Ethics, at some primal level, offer a step back into simpler, more certain times. In conjuring up a pre-modern moment, one replete with value and aspiration and good, we cling to it perhaps because it lessens our own existential ambivalence. But it does not solve the problems we face living in today's world.

Journalism regularly addresses the space between what we read, see and hear versus what we know and understand. A call for collective ethical standards, as embodied in ethics codes, may thus undo what should be most ethical about journalism – providing the information necessary for a public to engage on ethical grounds. Rather, a call for collective standards undermines the principles of full and complete journalistic relay: it reifies ethics even when ethical standards may be at cross-purposes with critical news coverage; it justifies the universal at the expense of understanding the particular; and it allows for the intrusion of others to make the call about which news to address. Why, then, are we concerned with a workable journalism ethics without first considering more fully what we want – and need – from journalism?

Section II

Disciplinary Matters

Cues for Considering Disciplinary Matters

With Jennifer Henrichsen and Natacha Yazbeck

Disciplinary matters shape the understanding of journalism. When the academy engages with the news, it faces a number of deficits typical of the more general linkage between conceptual and practical worlds. In journalism's case, each makes it difficult for academic scholarship to encompass all that journalism is.

Academic engagement wrestles centrally with a temporal deficit. Because journalism changes more quickly and with more variation than do academic disciplines, any intervention that ensues consequently operates at a temporal lag. Scholarship builds gradually on what is already known, magnifying the challenge of accounting for novelty in real-time. With journalism primarily defined through real-time practice that is always changing, academic interventions are often reduced to playing catch-up. This pairing of essentially different kinds of temporal pacing – one associated with journalistic craft, the other with knowledge transfer – means that academic interventions about journalism work most effectively when they can simultaneously reflect both rapidly changing journalistic practice and incrementally changing journalism scholarship.

But there are multiple aspects of journalism that do not readily cohere to available recipes for twinning academe and journalism. The stubborn question of journalism's relevance, for instance – which changes frenetically in conjunction with whomever journalism's audiences and publics are thought to be at a particular point in time – confounds the capacity of scholars and practitioners to have a ready meeting of minds. Even at one point in time, journalists' recognition of particular communities as visible and relevant may not resemble the orientation held by journalism scholars or even by publics themselves.

Changing technologies play a role in this scenario. They can both extend journalists' abilities to reach audiences – exemplified by the recent partnering of several news outlets with Facebook and by journalism's widespread reliance on user-generated content – and enable communities historically underrepresented in the news to voice their experiences of implicit and explicit invisibility, marginalization and stigmatization. Black Twitter, for instance, gives voice today to perspectives that have been overlooked for too long in the news.

The evolving nature of diverse publics also exacerbates the uneasy match of journalism and academe. While an increasing recognition of a plurality of publics bolsters journalism's relevance through the popularity of newer journalistic forms, such as BuzzFeed listicles and virtual reality, today's post-broadcast era favors news that represents the lived experiences of more diverse communities than conventionally assumed. Transphobia and Islamophobia are but two examples of lived realities that are entering certain – but not all – public lexicons of which experiences count.

Despite these changes on the ground, journalism scholarship – which by and large espouses a narrow view of what constitutes journalism and its publics, who qualifies as a journalist and what qualifies as news – has been ill suited for recognizing the transformations that regularly occur in journalism. Even the notion of "ethnic media" assumes the ancillary existence of news outlets that are not rooted in nor aimed at a community of one particular race, religion, sexual orientation, gender identification or ethnicity. Thus, it is no surprise that in Syria, where the media were once dependent on the military for news from the front lines, journalism finds itself today reliant on activists, bystanders and stringers (Yazbeck, 2015). A fuller accommodation of change, then, might undergird current conversations about journalism's relevance, both scholarly and practical.

Among the challenges facing journalism and its study is the critical question of which intellectual vantage point to privilege in its discussion. It is worth remembering that evolving fields continue to complicate the dissonance underscored here. One such field – engineering – is worth noting in particular because it has been so absent from traditional academic discussions of journalism yet looms centrally in present and future-oriented conversations about what journalism could be. With journalists and news outlets increasingly relying on technological systems and tools to create, publish and disseminate news, journalism's over-reliance on free or low-cost technology platforms needs to be further considered: it runs the risk of both reducing autonomy from economic and political pressures and creating security challenges for journalists (Henrichsen, Betz & Lisosky, 2015).

For instance, at this point in time many journalists regularly use their Gmail accounts to communicate with sources, find new sources to communicate with via Facebook and Twitter, send files via Dropbox, take notes on Evernote and record interviews on their iPhones. But these free or generally low-cost closed-source services in turn often collect detailed information, sometimes without the user's full knowledge. If compelled for legal reasons, journalists' information could be shared with third parties, such as governments, without their knowledge or immediate notification. The ensuing chilling effect on source availability could be so devastating that some observers have begun to wonder whether promises of confidentiality are no longer sustainable.

Yet if journalists and scholars deepened their connections with the engineering field, they might be able to create tools that put software more directly in journalism's service. In fact, many such tools already exist: at the time of this writing, security-conscious journalists can use a combination of encrypted platforms such as GPG when sending emails, Cryptocat when chatting online and Signal when calling someone from a mobile phone. But though they help ensure the confidentiality of the journalist–source link, they need further development that can only occur via ongoing dialogue between journalists and scholars.

Journalism's strength for the sharing of intellectual knowledge is that it lies everywhere in the academy. But its pervasiveness can also be its weakness. For in being everywhere, it is nowhere. In order to make academe and practice more relevant to each other moving forward, a more concerted effort to talk and listen to each other's perspectives needs to occur.

This section contemplates such an environment. It includes an overview of some of the major disciplines that have addressed journalism; consideration of one field of study – communication – that is well suited to embrace journalism as one of its main practical arms; and discussion of one academic arena – cultural studies – that has faltered in accommodating the relevance of journalism. Across the board, these interventions underscore the importance of linking journalism and academe more fully.

6

Journalism and the Academy, Revisited

The placement of journalism in the academy is complicated. As journalism's forms change dimension to accommodate the circumstances in which it exists, expanding beyond conventional considerations of news, the question of journalism's study has developed along an uneven route dotted with isolated pockets of disciplinary knowledge. There is thus little consensus about the two key terms at the focus of attention, with only marginal agreement about what journalism is and about what the academy's relationship with it should be. Following an argument first advanced in 2004, here I consider the various sources of existential uncertainty that continue to underlie journalism's coexistence with the academy. Recognizing that the environment has not radically changed over the past decade, I offer a number of suggestions – now inflected by increased public involvement in newsmaking – to make their uneven and often symbiotic relationship more mutually aware and fruitful.

The Shape of Journalism and Its Study

In an era when journalism stretches from tweets to satirical late-night television and its study appears in places as diverse as communication, literature, business and computer science, considering journalism's place in the academy from anew might seem like generating unnecessary alarm about the future viability of a phenomenon that seems to be everywhere. However, in being everywhere, journalism and its study continue to be nowhere. Not only has journalism's development produced a long line of repetitive and unresolved laments over which form, practice or convention might be best suited to qualify as newsmaking, but the study of journalism has not kept step with the wide-ranging and often unanticipated nature of its evolution over time.

Though much of this draws from the unfortunate fact that many scholars of journalism do not speak enough to journalists themselves, the dissonance between journalism and the academy echoes a broader dis-junction characterizing journalism's uneven and spotty existence with the world. When George Orwell added newspaper quotations to his first book, critics accused him of "turning what might have been a good book into journalism" (Orwell, 1946, cited in Bromley, 2003), and his collected works were compiled decades later under the unambivalent title *Smothered under Journalism: 1946* (Orwell, 1999 [1946]). Similar stories dot the journalistic backgrounds of literary giants like Charles Dickens, Samuel Johnson, John Dos Passos, André Malraux, Dylan Thomas and John Hersey. Reactions like these proliferate despite a profound reliance on journalism not only to situate individuals vis-à-vis the larger collective but to use that positioning as a starting point for more elaborated ways of understanding the world.

In other words, much of our situated knowledge rests in part on jour-nalism. Where would history be without journalism? What would litera-ture look like? How could we understand the workings of the polity? As a phenomenon, journalism stretches in various forms across all of the ways in which we come together as a collective, and yet the "it's just journal-ism" rejoinder persists.

Journalism's coexistence with the academy rests on various sources of existential uncertainty that build from this tension. The most obvious uncertainty stems from the pragmatic questions that underlie journal-ism's practice, by which its very definition and ensuing academic discus-sion are tweaked each time supposed interlopers – user-generated content, bystanders, citizen journalists, late-night TV comedians or reality televi-sion – come close to its imagined borders. A second source of uncertainty draws from the pedagogic dimensions surrounding journalism and the academy. How we teach what we think we know and to whom, and how and whether it matters, are questions with a litany of answers, particu-larly as journalism's contours change. In an age of big data, for instance, should the discipline of engineering not play a more active part in consid-ering journalism's viability? And yet those who teach what does and does not seem to count as journalistic practice and convention have tended to be behind rather than ahead of its rapidly altering parameters. Finally, one of the most significant sources of uncertainty surrounds the concep-tual dimensions of the relationship – what we study when we think about journalism. Because academics have invoked a variety of prisms over the years through which to consider journalism – among them its craft, effect, performance, ideology and technology – they have not yet produced a scholarly picture of journalism that combines all of these prisms into a coherent reflection of all that journalism is and could be. Instead, the study of journalism remains incomplete, partial and divided, leaving its practitioners, educators, scholars and students uncertain about what it means to think conceptually about journalism writ large.

Here I address these sources of uncertainty and in so doing think through some important challenges that continue to face the study of journalism, particularly as they take shape in today's environment. I argue for a space of reflection about the backdrop status of journalism's practice and study and its default assumptions. What about journalism and its study has been privileged, and what has been sidestepped? These questions are particularly critical when thinking about journalism studies in its global context, where variation has not been accommodated or even recognized as much as it exists on the ground.

Interpretive Communities and Journalism's Study

What academics think relies upon how they think and with whom, and perhaps nowhere has this been as developed as in the sociology of knowledge. Kuhn (1962) was most directly associated with the now somewhat fundamental notion that inquiry depends on consensus building, on developing shared paradigms that name and characterize problems and procedures in ways that are recognized by the collective. On the way to establishing consensus, some but not all individuals favoring competing insights battle over definitions, terms of reference and boundaries of inclusion and exclusion. Once consensus is established, new phenomena tend to be classified by already proven lines. In other words, what we think has a predetermined shape and lifeline, which privileges community, solidarity and power.

This notion extends beyond Kuhn's work, and it has been implicated in scholarship by Durkheim (1965 [1912]), Park (1940), Foucault (1972), Berger and Luckmann (1966) and Goodman (1978) – all of whom maintained in different ways that the social group is critical to establishing ways of knowing the world. The idea of interpretive communities, originally suggested by Fish (1982) and developed in conjunction with journalism by Zelizer (1993a), Berkowitz (2000), Lewis and Carlson (2015) and others, helps situate the strategies that go into sharing knowledge as integral to the knowledge that results. Recognizing that groups with shared ways of interpreting evidence shed light on the way that questions of value are settled and resettled, the persons, organizations, institutions and fields of inquiry engaged in journalism's analysis become central to understanding what journalism is. As the anthropologist Mary Douglas (1986, 8) argued, "true solidarity is only possible to the extent that individuals share the categories of their thought." Inquiry, then, is not just an intellectual act but a social one too.

What this suggests for journalism's study is an invitation to think about the forces involved in giving it shape. In this sense, no one voice in journalism's study is better or more authoritative than the others; nor is there any one unitary vision of journalism to be found. Rather, different voices offer more – and more complete – ways to understand what journalism is, each having evolved in conjunction with its own set of premises about what matters and in which ways.

As an area of inquiry, journalism's study has always been somewhat untenable. Primarily negotiated across five interrelated populations – journalists, journalism educators, journalism students, publics and journalism scholars – the shared concern for journalism that has been independently central to each group has not remained at the forefront of their collective endeavors. Rather, journalism's centrality and viability have been waylaid amidst lamentations that not everyone understands what is most important about the news: journalists say the others have no business airing their dirty laundry; journalism scholars say the others are not theoretical enough; journalism educators say journalists have their heads in the sand and journalism scholars have their heads in the clouds. As each has fixated on who will be best heard above the din of competing voices, the concern for journalism has often been shunted to the side. This weighs particularly heavily on journalism students, whose enthusiasm about their future is dimmed when they do not receive a clear picture about the community they aim to join. It also weighs on the public, which in its many forms regularly articulates what it thinks journalism should be. As the boundaries of journalism are tweaked by members of the public engaged in their own forms of newsmaking, social media teaming up with legacy news outlets foster ongoing public involvement in the news. Underlying the ability to speak about journalism, then, have been tensions about which of these groups can mobilize the right to speak over others and which is best positioned to maintain that right.

Each of these groups – journalists, journalism educators and students, publics and journalism scholars – constitutes an interpretive community of sorts. Each has defined journalism according to its own aims and then has set strategies for how to think about it in conjunction with those aims.

Journalists

Journalists are individuals who engage in a broad range of activities associated with newsmaking, including, in Adam's (1993, 12) view, "reporting, criticism, editorializing and the conferral of judgment on the shape of things." Journalism's importance has been undeniable, and while it has been the target of ongoing discourse in both support and critique of its performance, few existing conversations suggest its irrelevance. Rather, contemporary conditions orient toward journalism's centrality and the crucial role it can play in helping people make sense both of their daily lives and of the ways in which they connect to multiple body politics and publics. The public imagined by the *Los Angeles Times'* Black Twitter beat is a case in point.

However, not all of journalism's potential has borne out in practice. Today's journalism inhabits rugged and often unpredictable territory, with audiences for news sectors in the United States alone exhibiting decidedly uneven trends: podcasting and radio are markedly up; local and network TV oscillate yearly, though presently they are slightly up; cable news, magazines and newspapers are generally down, but long-form journalism is up (*State of the News Media*, 2015). Digital news start-ups are simultaneously growing with seeming abandon – VICE News, BuzzFeed, Vox, Politico – or shutting down abruptly and hitting rough patches – Giacom, NewRepublic, First Look Media. No wonder, then, that conventional journalists feel like they remain under siege.

Practical conditions bear this out in today's news landscape. First, journalists live in an economic environment seeping with uncertainty. The falling revenues, convergence, corporatization, fragmentation, branding and bottom-line pressures that kept forcing the news to act as a shaky for-profit enterprise a decade ago have now given way to a precarious labor force often necessarily over-burdened with personal branding and entrepreneurship, a hard-hit newspaper industry, part-time or unavailable employment and uneven profits in television and digital revenues that still remain "largely on the wish list" (Picard, 2015). Though today's journalism comprises a larger number of news outlets than ever before, these outlets have not necessarily produced a broader scope of coverage. Many journalists – those on journalism's "front lines" more than its higher-ranked executives – have taken to multi-tasking the same story in ways that previous generations would not recognize. As *New York Times* reporter David Carr noted of what he called the "hidden cost" of today's media environment: "What the editor wants to know is, 'Can they crank? Can they crank on a variety of platforms? Can she get on the camera without projectile vomiting, can she type in full sentences, does she have a Twitter following?'" (cited in Russell, 2012). Mindful of these economic constraints, some news outlets simply aggregate or recycle what has been reported elsewhere. And much of the social "buzz" taken to signify engagement with the news at times becomes little more than regurgitation across social networks, with periodic dips and rises in the numbers of those paying heed (Rottwilm, 2014).

Second, journalists regularly come under political attack from both the left and right, which argue for different definitions of so-called "journalistic performance" in a political environment that undercuts the journalist's capacity to function in old ways. While the competing and contradictory expectations from left and right paralyze aspects of journalism's performance in more stable political systems, the demise of the nation-state in many areas of the world raises additional questions regarding journalism's optimum operation. As journalists remain caught in various kinds of questionable embraces with government, local interests and the military, many have gravitated toward coverage that plays to "safe" political spaces, producing news that already a decade ago revealed partisanship, heightened localism, personalization and oversimplification (*State of the News Media*, 2007). Today, digital trends toward inclusiveness, engagement and collaboration complicate further the ability to maintain autonomous political boundaries (Rottwilm, 2014). Journalists have consequently learned to follow various models of practice – not always thoughtfully – and none of which are fully suited to the complexities of today's global political environments.

Third, journalists face new technical challenges from all sectors of the digital environment – the blogosphere, technical skills associated with computing, manipulating big data and data analytics, accommodating the increasing reliance on video, ascendance of chat and messaging apps – which make the very accomplishment of newswork tenuous. According to the World Press Trends Report (WAN-IFRA, 2015), today's newsrooms are systematically incorporating new convergence modes like virtual reality and wearables, wrestling with automated news formats, accommodating the popularity of podcasting and chat apps and utilizing data metrics for analyzing audiences. Technological platforms are eager to wade into journalists' territory: just in 2015 Google introduced Google News Lab, Accelerated Mobile Pages and Google Cardboard, and teamed up with outlets like the *New York Times*, while Facebook's Instant Articles, designed to support engagement on social media via "shares" and "likes," were for the first time shared more than conventional links (Owen, 2015a). With journalists now expected to multiskill in unprecedented ways, how they cover the news often fades in importance alongside the fact of coverage, regardless of its source.

Competition over coverage is further intensified by the rising involvement of citizen journalists, producers of user-generated content and bystanders, which challenges journalism's primacy at its core. At the same time, an enhanced interest in news with a view has helped shape public engagement. Across US venues like John Oliver's monologues in *Last Week Tonight*, Stephen Colbert's SuperPac and Amy Schumer's "comedy with a message" (Nussbaum, 2015), contemporary issues like police shootings, terrorism, court decisions and political races are being given comedic, ironic and satirical attention. Already a decade ago, traditional notions of journalism were becoming a "smaller part of people's information mix," with viewers of sites like Comedy Central's *The Daily Show* thought to be better informed about public events than those who watched conventional news (*State of the News Media*, 2007). Nearly ten years later, these early attempts have been enhanced by a roster of comedians who act as "truth-tellers – as intellectual and moral guides through the cultural debates of the moment," which used to be journalists' purview (Garber, 2015). Moreover, Facebook, YouTube, Twitter and other social media sites have become for many the delivery platform of choice (*State of the News Media*, 2015).

Lastly, moral scandals involving journalists abound. The *Rolling Stone* rape story of 2014 was among the most discussed journalism scandals of recent times, but it followed upon similar incidents involving key US journalistic figures like Brian Williams, Dan Rather, Jack Kelly, Rick Bragg and Jayson Blair. The 2011 *News of the World* scandal opened up gaping holes about ethical journalistic behavior that reverberated beyond the UK to the US, Australia, and other locations where Rupert Murdoch had a hold. This activity raised fundamental questions about the moral fiber of journalists that helped push journalistic tasks into the hands of private citizens. When the *Columbia Journalism Review* asked in 2015 whether scandals did "lasting damage to journalism," it responded that the damage was an incremental and cumulative blight on journalism's reputation (Editors, 2015). No surprise, then, that confidence in US journalism has gone down repeatedly, dipping in the United States to a low of 40 percent in 2014 (McCarthy, 2014).

All of this suggests that journalists have not been as effective as they might have been in communicating to the world journalism's centrality and importance. Questions persist about changing definitions of who is a journalist and what are bona fide instruments of newsmaking: where, for instance, is one to position Facebook, security cameras, private smartphones, messaging apps and drones?

Thus, it is not surprising that the fundamental question of what journalism is for has no clear answer. Is its function to only provide information or to more aggressively meld community and public citizenship? Journalism's different functioning in different parts of the world – as in the distinctions separating the developmental journalism prevalent in parts of Asia from the partisan models popular in Southern Europe – makes the question more difficult to answer. As Guo (2010, 16) wrote of journalists in China: "Images most readily invoked by the term *journalism* typically slant toward idealistic principles rather than realistic practices, toward beliefs of diversity rather than monopoly, and toward ideas of romanticized excitement rather than routinized operation." And as a sense of crisis, erroneously perceived as unitary, continues to pervade journalism's imaginary (Zelizer, 2015a), finding an answer that resonates with current conditions becomes urgent.

The tumultuous nature of these circumstances derives in part from the competing visions at the core of journalism's self-definition. Is it a craft, a profession, a set of practices, a collection of individuals, an industry, an institution, a business or a mindset? In that it is probably a bit of each, we need to better figure out how they work off, and sometimes against, each other. This is critical, for even basic questions about journalistic tools have never been really addressed and journalism's tools have not been equally valued. Images in particular are one aspect of news that has been unevenly executed, with pictures regularly appearing without captions, without credits and with no identifiable relation to the texts at their side (Zelizer, 1998). Yet the turn to images in times of crisis – when there are more images, more prominent images, bolder images and larger images – has been poorly matched to the uneven conventions by which images act as news relays. Following both the terror attacks of September 11 and the launching of the 2003 US war on Iraq, the *New York Times* featured two and a half times the number of photos in its front sections than it regularly featured in peacetime (Zelizer, 2004a). It is fair to assume that similar patterns surfaced after the Boston Marathon bombing of 2013, the Malaysian air disasters of 2014, the Paris terrorist attacks of 2015 and the Brussels attacks of 2016. The lack of a clear development of standards, then, is problematic, because visuals have taken over the forefront of journalism's relays even if they have not been sufficiently clarified. Moreover, because the image's so-called "correct usage" has not been figured out, its display has become an open field, with people crying foul every time journalism's pictures grate their nerves.

All of this renders journalists a group somewhat out of touch with itself, its critics and its publics. Givens that do not readily play into settled expectations of the news – such as the changing circumstances of newsmaking or the inspiration and creativity that comprise journalistic craft – remain relatively unaddressed. It is no surprise, then, that in the US journalists rank at the bottom of nearly every opinion poll of those whom the public trusts (Dugan, 2014).

Journalism Educators and Students

Journalism educators typically coalesce around a strong need to educate novices into the craft of journalism, though the relevance of this is regularly challenged by those who argue that journalists are better educated in non-journalistic specialties. Although vernacular education has differed across locations, it exhibits a certain shared aim regardless of specific locale – to prepare journalism students and novices for the exigencies of the craft. How that is considered best done, however, differs dramatically.

In the United States, universities have been key. Teaching a vernacular craft began in the humanities around 1900, when newswriting and the history of journalism moved from English departments into the beginnings of a journalism education that eventually expanded into ethics and the law. Other efforts developed in the late 1920s in the social sciences, when the impulse to establish a science of journalism positioned craft – commonly called "skills" courses – as one quarter of a curriculum offering courses in economics, psychology, public opinion and survey research. Journalism educators were thus caught in the tensions between the humanities and social sciences as to which type of inquiry could best teach journalists to be journalists. For many this split still proliferates, reflected in the so-called "qualitative/quantitative distinction" in scholarly approaches to news. Despite this legacy, the typical US journalist today does not take a college degree in journalism (Weaver et al., 2007).

In the United Kingdom, journalism education was set against a long-standing tradition of learning through apprenticeship and a prevalent view that journalism's "technical elements" were "lacking in academic rigor" (Bromley, 1997, 334). Practical journalism did not appear on the curriculum until 1937 but only became a setting worthy of academic investigation once sociology and political science, largely through the work of Jeremy Tunstall (1970, 1971), arrived in the late 1960s. From then onward, journalism education blossomed, simultaneously involving institutes of higher learning, dedicated journalism programs and university graduates (Bromley, 2009b, 606). However, a theory/practice division, heightened by the digital environment, continues (Tumber & Prentoulis, 2005, 66, 70), and many journalism students tend to learn part of the picture, not its broader contours.

In the countries of Northern Europe, in-house training set the stage early on, with the German *Zeitungswissenschaft* offering a model that targeted journalism's study alongside vocational courses. Thriving at the University of Leipzig from 1916, it was restructured by the Nazis and then went dormant during World War II. Journalism education took flight anew in the 1960s, expanding over the decades that followed (Frohlich & Holtz-Bacha, 2009). As both the media themselves expanded and the recognition of professionalism increased, countries across the region – Germany, Sweden, Denmark, Norway, Switzerland, Austria, Finland, Iceland and Luxembourg – began to develop different kinds of vernacular education, hosting programs sponsored by media outlets, universities and political organizations, and – in the case of The Netherlands and Belgium – religious organizations as well (Weibull, 2009).

In Latin America, vernacular education took on singular forms in different countries. Both Argentina and Brazil established journalism schools that rejected US communication models and followed French scholarship (Mattelart, 2006). The first lasting journalism school in Brazil, hosted by a Sao Paulo newspaper, and the first university journalism course arrived roughly together in the late 1940s. But significant growth in journalism education did not occur until the 1970s and then again in the 2000s (Lago & Romancini, 2010). While early university courses primarily followed a European pedagogical model and were academic in character, later ones took on a hybrid nature that more directly reflected Brazil's more participatory needs (Marques de Melo, 2009). Thus, a university degree in journalism is currently mandatory for Brazilian journalists (Moreira & Helal, 2009). It remains controversial: begun in 1970 and overturned in 2009, it was reinstated in 2012, largely due to intense lobbying by the National Federation of Journalists.

This underscores that journalism education rarely exists in a pure or unidimensional form, for changes in media systems generate changes in journalism education (Josephi, 2009). Thus, Chinese journalism education has moved "gradually towards the market without seriously violating traditional norms of propaganda" (Yu, Chu & Guo, 2000), while journalism education in Oman tends to fuel public relations jobs in government organizations more than it feeds news outlets themselves (Al-Hasani, 2010, 112).

In each case, the academic interest among educators helped link journalists to the outside world, but it also did enormous damage to the craft, leveling it to what James W. Carey (2000, 21) called a "signaling system." At first offering an old-fashioned apprenticeship, journalism educators over time came to address journalism by dividing it into technologies of production, separating newspapers, magazines, television and radio from each other. Lost in this was a place where all of journalism could be thought of as a whole with many disparate parts. The resulting curriculum, again in Carey's view, in many cases came to lack "historical understanding, criticism or self-consciousness" (13). In this regard, journalism education generated dissonance across the larger university curriculum: in the humanities it came to be seen as part of "the vernacular, the vulgate" (22); in the social sciences, as a tool for channeling public opinion, but not important in and of itself.

Thus, it is no surprise that basic questions remain about the value and relevance of journalism education and its embrace by students. Does education even matter? And if it does, which education – journalism, political science, literature, languages – matters most? To that end, when multiple foundations – the Carnegie-Knight Initiative on the Future of Journalism Education, the American Press Institute, the Knight Foundation – undertook separate analyses of US journalism education during the 2000s, few emerged with common suggestions. This is significant, especially in the so-called "liberal" model, in which current journalism education tends to require university training, though not in journalism necessarily, and remains "chiefly concerned with the unproblematic reproduction of the existing labor force" (Bromley, 2009a, 29).

All of this suggests that the resonant tension between practical and critical skills – which gives way to a larger distinction between journalism and the academy – has its roots in journalism education.

Publics

Though not the most obvious sector engaged in thinking about journalism, the idea of the public constitutes a central platform for articulating when journalism oversteps its boundaries or under-delivers on expectations. In particular, the repositioning of multiple publics "from news recipients to news sources, with journalists using posts, statuses and comments on social media as a means of information gathering" (Rottwilm, 2014), has made their relevance to newsgathering greater than ever before. A direct and ongoing connection between journalists and private citizens – exemplified by feedback loops, content preferences and what Robinson (2011) saw as a move from "journalism as product" to "journalism as process" – is now the norm, not the exception.

Shifting news habits have played a large part in engineering this change. What the *State of the News Media* (2015) called the "mobile majority" has helped entrench social media to such an extent that many individuals now find their news there, shrinking the centrality of TV news and newspapers that had long been central to conventional journalism's sense of self. This trend, in which members of different publics are at odds with journalism's self-appraisal, has been exacerbated by the news habits of US millennials (persons reaching adulthood around the year 2000), who rely on Facebook for their news over other sources, are less familiar with a broad range of conventional news sources and are less interested in politics than older generations (*State of the News Media*, 2015). It has also intensified with the increasing recognition of multiple publics coalescing around different needs and cohabiting what used to be seen as a unidimensional public space.

The relevance of public involvement in the news draws from many points of origin – a lingering distrust of journalists, the increasing accessibility of news platforms and the engagement they foster, a tailored environment toward news one can use. For all of these reasons, the idea of the public plays a more vocal role than ever before in articulating what about journalism matters. In the best of times, this promotes a seemingly more democratic, egalitarian news environment. It also facilitates the recognition of multiple communities giving voice to issues relevant to their formation. In the worst of cases, it provides a platform to views, issues and events that fall short on the qualities long thought to inspire journalistic involvement.

Journalism Scholars

All of these groups – journalists, journalism educators, journalism students and publics – are important to an additional population of interest, that of journalism scholars. Scholars are strongly positioned to make sense of the conflicting tendencies awash in the news environment. And yet, despite an enormous body of literature dealing with the values, practices and impact of journalism, they still have not produced a coherent picture of what journalism is.

Journalism can be found literally across the university curriculum. It inhabits academic platforms in communication, media studies and journalism schools, as well as the less obvious targets of composition sequences, history, sociology, urban studies, political science, economics and business. What this means is that much of what has been missed thus far in creating a distinctive interpretive community has been exacerbated within the academy. Because academics tend to function within the boundaries of disciplinary communities, what they study often takes on the shape of the perspectives set forth by those communities. These disciplines, themselves akin to interpretive communities, help determine what counts as evidence and in which ways. Similarly, they make judgment calls about which kinds of research do not count.

How has journalism fared across the academic curriculum? It continues to be approached in pockets, each of which isolates aspects of its environment from others. Such compartmentalization works against a clarification of what journalism is, examining partial workings rather than its whole. The result remains a terrain of journalism study at war with itself, with journalism educators separated from journalism scholars, humanistic journalism scholars separated from scholars trained in the social sciences, and a slew of independent academic efforts taking place in a variety of disciplines without the shared knowledge crucial to academic inquiry. Even when journalists working on journalist-related issues join journalism scholars, they often end up talking past each other. Alongside these efforts, journalists have long resisted the attempts to microscopically examine their work environment.

Within the academy, there have been five main types of inquiry into journalism – sociology, history, language studies, political science and cultural analysis. Suggested largely as a heuristic classification that implies more mutual exclusivity than exists in real practice, these are not the only disciplines that have addressed journalism. Computer science, economics, law and political economy are among the areas of study not addressed here. But the perspectives tracked in these pages offer a glimpse of a central range of alternatives through which journalism is often conceptualized. The underlying assumptions that each frame imposes on its examination of the journalistic world say much about how different prisms on journalism create a picture that is at best partial.

Each frame offers a different way to address the question of why journalism matters: sociology has addressed how journalism matters; history, how it used to matter; language studies, through which verbal and visual tools it matters; political science, how it ought to matter; and cultural analysis, how it matters differently. Lost here, or at least dropped into the backdrop of the research setting, is how each of these answers comes to bear on the larger question of why academics should be addressing journalism to begin with.

Sociology and Journalism

Sociology historically constituted the default setting for thinking academically about how journalism works, and it continues to occupy that position. Largely built upon a memorable body of work called the ethnographies of news, or the newsroom studies of the 1970s (Tuchman, 1978a; Gans, 1979; Fishman, 1980), sociological inquiry has by and large created a picture of journalism that focuses on people rather than documents, on relationships, work routines and other formulaic interactions across members of the community who are involved in gathering and presenting news.

Sociology established the ideas that journalists function as sociological beings, with norms, practices and routines (Tunstall, 1971; Weaver & Wilhoit, 1986; Waisbord, 2013), that they exist in organizational, institutional and structural settings (Breed, 1955; Epstein, 1973; McManus, 1994; McChesney & Pickard, 2011), that they invoke something akin to ideology in their newswork (Glasgow University Media Group, 1976; Gitlin, 1980), and that their activities have effects (Park, 1940; Lang & Lang, 1953). In that sociology largely favors the study of dominant practices over deviant ones and frozen moments within the newsmaking process for analysis rather than the whole phenomenon, it created a picture of journalism from which much other inquiry proceeded. The emphasis here on behavior and effect more than meaning, on pattern more than violation, on the collective more than the individual, helped advance a view of journalists as professionals, albeit not very successful ones (Henningham, 1985; Ornebring, 2009; Lewis, 2012; Waisbord, 2013). Moreover, this work was primarily structured within the confines of US sociology, and its analyses of primarily mainstream news organizations in the United States projected what purported to be a universal picture of journalism. For much of its evolution, then, this work remained captured by a US-centric picture, taken from journalism's past.

This has changed since the mid 2000s, as scholars have revisited many of the premises laid down by the early newsroom studies. Addressing contemporary states of digitalization, conglomeratization, corporatization, participation and convergence, this work now offers nuanced updates of the detailed pictures of newsmaking from the 1970s. Primary here has been work in Actor Network theory, where scholars have largely focused on the new social configurations emanating from the digital environment, establishing both the continuity and diversion of practices related to collective authority and decision-making (Boczkowski, 2004; Paterson & Domingo, 2008; Domingo & Paterson, 2011; Anderson, 2013). Others have addressed the blended institutional environment in which journalism increasingly finds itself (Lewis, 2012; Peters & Broersma, 2012), often using anthropological insights to renew considerations of ethnographic method (Pedelty, 1995; Cottle, 2000a; Hannerz, 2004). Still others apply contemporary sociological theory to the news, blending Bourdieu's notion of field theory and new institutionalism into a productive venue for rethinking newswork (Benson & Neveu, 2005; Benson, 2006; Ryfe, 2012).

History and Journalism
Historical inquiry into the nature of news evolved largely from the earliest expansions of journalistic academic curricula. Central in establishing the longevity of journalism and journalistic practice, the history of news has offered academics a way to use the past – its lessons, triumphs and tragedies – to understand contemporary journalism. Within this frame, what drew academic attention tended to be whatever persisted. However, the picture was often a narrowly drawn one.

Largely dependent on documents rather than people, historical inquiry has produced three kinds of intellectual engagements with the past – journalism history writ small, as in memoirs, biographies and organizational histories (Gates, 1978); history writ midway, organized around temporal periods, themes and events, like "the penny press" (Schudson, 1978; Nerone, 1994); and history writ large, which primarily addressed the linkage between the nation-state and the news media (Curran & Seaton, 1985). Missing from early studies was a conscious twinning of the role that writing history played for both journalists and the academy: for instance, the histories of journalistic practice published primarily in US journalism schools with the aim of legitimating journalism as a field of inquiry did not reflect the generalized, so-called "objective histories" that followed the model of German historicism, and not enough effort was invested in figuring out how to better combine the two (Carey, 1974; Scannell, 2002). In the United States, where the core of historical journalism scholarship originated, the focus on largely US history (and its progressive bias) bypassed the extremely rich and varied evolution of journalistic practice elsewhere in the world. Not surprisingly, assumptions about the historical record differed markedly by the country being considered, as work from other locations suggests (Mayer, 1964; Kuhn, 1995).

Much of this scholarship has more recently had to wrestle with the question of who can lay claim to the past, and this has had recent ramifications around the issue of "whose journalism history?" Directly targeted in the ensuing scholarship on collective memory and the news, which surfaced at a point in which the historical record was assumed to reflect the bias of whomever authored it, this scholarship has tracked the ways in which different voices made the past matter differently in accordance with present-day aims. Drawing initially from analyses of critical events of the past which journalism was responsible for covering – such as the liberation of the World War II concentration camps, the Kennedy assassination, Watergate and 9/11 (Schudson, 1992, 1995; Zelizer, 1992b, 1998, 2001; Edy, 1999, 2006; Kitch, 2005, 2006; Volkmer, 2006) – work on collective memory and the news in part has offset the ownership of history that had been implicit in many of the earlier works. Across a wide span of scholarship, this work establishes the multiple ways in which the past intrudes upon contemporary newsmaking (Meyers, 2002; Carlson, 2006; Meyers, Neiger & Zandberg, 2011; Zelizer & Tenenboim-Weinblatt, 2014).

Recent scholarship has also built upon earlier work to proffer a more specific tale about journalism's pasts, elaborating particular historical contexts against which certain kinds of journalism can be seen. Hardt and Brennen (1995), Barnhurst and Nerone (2001), Hamilton (2011) and Nerone (2015) are among those who have taken closer looks at the internal contradictions of journalistic performance over time – between craft and labor, word and image, domestic and foreign, journalist and public – while the 1940s wrestling match between policymakers and the media received nuanced attention from Pickard (2014). Taken together, these glimpses of the past have unraveled the temporal tapestry of journalism's multiple contexts, an achievement with ramifications for the study of journalism writ large, as Nerone (2013) noted in an article titled "Why Journalism History Matters to Journalism Studies."

Language Studies and Journalism
The study of journalism's languages has assumed that journalists' messages are neither transparent nor simplistic but the result of constructed activity on the part of speakers. Developed primarily from the 1980s onward, this area of inquiry is markedly European and Australian in origin (Van Dijk, 1987; Fairclough, 2013 [1989]; Bell, 1991; Wodak & Meyer, 2002). The combination of formal features of language – grammar, syntax and word choice – with less formal ones – storytelling frames, textual patterns and narratives – has offered a rich template for later addressing not only verbal language but also sounds, photographs,

video and patterns of interactivity (Kress & Van Leeuwen, 1996; Conboy, 2013). More recently, for instance, journalism's pictures received marked attention from scholars employing various conceptual and methodological approaches (Huxford, 2001; Wardle, 2007; Grabe & Bucy, 2009; Zelizer, 2010; Anden-Papadopoulos & Pantti, 2011).

Three kinds of language study consider journalism: its informal study, exemplified by content analysis and semiology, uses language as a backdrop without examining extensively its linguistic features (Schramm, 1959; Hartley, 1982; Gunter, 2003); its formal study – embodied in sociolinguistics, discourse analysis and critical linguistics – provides a systematic analysis of language features in connection with associated activity (Greatbatch, 1988; Fowler, 1991; Richardson, 2007; Cotter, 2010). The study of pragmatics focuses on patterns of language use as shaped either by rhetorical, narrative and storytelling conventions, often in alternative forms such as tabloids, newzines or reality television (Campbell, 1991; Bird, 1992; Glynn, 2000), or by framing, usually in conjunction with the political aspects of news language (Gamson, 1989; Reese, Gandy & Grant, 2001; D'Angelo & Kuypers, 2010).

Stressing not only the shape of language itself but also its role in larger social and cultural life, this largely microanalytic work has continued to suffer by and large from a lack of recognition by other kinds of inquiry. At the same time, its fundamental premise that language is ideological continues to challenge both conventional news scholarship and journalistic claims that the news is a reflection of the real. In particular, the rise of discourse studies and the evolving recognition of discourse as a rich parameter of the workings of power promises a more welcoming reception to the study of language than was evident in its earlier years.

Political Science and Journalism
Political science is by and large normative in nature, and political scientists have thus tended to concern themselves with journalism's optimum workings. An assumption of interdependency between politics and journalism motivates this inquiry, which examines journalism through its vested interest in the political world. Thus, many scholars have clarified how journalism can better serve its publics.

Political science inquiry has typically ranged from broad considerations of the media's role in different types of political systems, such as the classic *Four Theories of the Press* (Siebert, Peterson & Schramm, 1956) to studies of political campaign behavior, journalistic models and roles (Graber, McQuail & Norris, 1998; Hallin & Mancini, 2004). The sourcing patterns of reporters and officials, an interaction which stands as the most contained reflection of the larger journalism/politics nexus, has spawned an entire literature that elucidates how the two institutions work together (Sigal, 1973), with scholarship reconsidering initial assumptions about the interchange from different temporal, geographic and technological vantage points (Berkowitz & TerKeurst, 1999; Carlson, 2011; Kuhn & Nielsen, 2013).

In fact, the current environment in which journalism operates has forced a reconsideration of much of the early scholarship here. In particular, the rise of digital media, the accelerated news cycle and a fragmented but highly participatory audience has changed much of the terrain. Thus, Nerone (1995) challenged the *Four Theories* on its fortieth anniversary, delineating the particularities of its vantage point, while Nielsen (2012) accounted for the impact of digital communication on political campaign strategies. As the digital environment has made boundaries less stable, much scholarship has also focused on the blurred genres that import impulses into news alongside civic engagement – the blurring of news and entertainment, for instance (Jones, 2009; Baym, 2009; Williams & Delli-Carpini, 2011), or of producer and audience (Bruns & Highfield, 2012; Chouliaraki, 2012).

Still largely US in focus – although some parallel work has been done by scholars of government and politics in Latin America and Europe (Fox, 1988; Splichal & Sparks, 1994; Schlesinger & Tumber, 1995) – this work continues to consider journalism's larger "political" role in making news, foregrounding journalism at its highest echelons – the publishers, boards of directors, managing editors – over its low-ranking individual journalists. Many of these studies remain motivated by normative impulses and conclude on notes of recuperation, which suggest that journalism is and should be in tune with more general political impulses in the society at large.

Cultural Analysis and Journalism
Finally, the cultural analysis of journalism still tends to see itself as the "bad boy" in the neighborhood. Querying the givens behind journalism's own sense of self, it seeks to examine what is important to journalists themselves and explores the cultural symbol systems by which reporters make sense of their craft. In assuming a lack of unity within journalism – in newsgathering routines, norms, values, technologies and assumptions about what is important, appropriate and preferred – and in its research perspective, which uses various conceptual tools to explain journalism, much of this inquiry still follows two strains, largely paralleling those evident in models of US and British cultural studies. The former, in part following the work of James Carey (1969, 1986a, 1986b, 1995), continues to focus on problems of meaning, group identity and social change (Pauly, 1988; Bird, 1992; Steiner, 1992; Ettema & Glasser, 1998; Allan, 1999; Barnhurst, 2011), while the latter targets journalism's intersection with power and patterns of domination (Hall, 1973; Hardt, 1990; Hartley, 1992).

This work continues to look at much of what has not been addressed in other areas of inquiry – worldviews, breaches, forms, representations and audiences – but all with an eye to figuring out how journalism takes on meaning. Across the board, this has necessitated some consideration of the blurred lines between different kinds of newswork: between tabloid and legacy (Dahlgren & Sparks, 1992; Ehrlich, 1997; Lumby, 1999; Sparks & Tulloch, 2000); across evolving media forms (Campbell, 1991; Allan, 2006); between newswork and the non-news world (Eason, 1984; Manoff & Schudson, 1986; Bird, 2009).

Though the value of some of this work has been diminished by the field's own ambivalence about journalism's reverence for facts, truth and reality, all of which have been objects of negotiation and relativization when seen from a cultural lens, the cultural analysis of news has been particularly welcoming to new venues of newsmaking. Thus, much of the early work on the popular press and pictures came from this vantage point (Hall, 1972, 1973; Hartley, 1992, 1996). It has also helped to engender work on reality television (Ouellette, 2002; Sender, 2012), on news and entertainment (Baym, 2009; Jones, 2009) and on news in the digital environment (Deuze, 2005, 2007).

Blended Inquiry and Future Correctives

Each frame for studying journalism constitutes a singular and particular prism on the news, sustaining a longstanding need for more explicit and comprehensive sharing across frames. Not only would such sharing help generate an appreciation for journalism at the moment of its creation, but it would offset the nearsightedness with which much scholarship on journalism continues to be set in place. How scholars tend to conceptualize news, newsmaking, journalism, journalists and the news media, which explanatory frames they use to explore these issues, and from which fields of inquiry they borrow in shaping their assumptions are all questions in need of further clarity. Adopting multiple views is necessary not only because journalism scholarship has not produced a body of scholarly material that reflects all of journalism, but also because it has still not produced a body of scholars who are familiar with what is being done across the board of scholarly inquiry. Everett Dennis (1984) called for such an initiative over 30 years ago, and yet there is still insufficient agreement about journalism and about the academy that studies it. The result, then, is an existential uncertainty that continues to draw from pragmatic, pedagogic and conceptual dimensions of the relationship between journalism and the academy.

This existential uncertainty continues to have direct effect on what gets considered as news. One such effect has had to do with narrowing the varieties of news. In that scholars have not yet produced a body of material that reflects all of journalism, they primarily define it in ways that drive a specific form of hard news over the alternatives at its side, such as lifestyle or celebrity news, financial news, essays or long-form journalism. This metonymic bias drives a still persistent gap between what Dahlgren (1992, 7) called "the realities of journalism and its official presentation of self." Missing from discussion for long periods of time have been copy-editors, graphic designers, proofreaders, journals of opinion, fixers, camera operators and translators, to say nothing of tabloids, comedians, online content providers, fact-checkers, citizen journalists or satirical late-night TV shows. Even photojournalists have been considered less fully than their verbal counterparts. In other words, the academy continues to emphasize certain focal points in thinking about journalism that do not account for the broad world of what journalism is. The diversity of news has for the most part disappeared from academic scholarship.

A similar destiny has met the craft of journalism. The academy's move to professionalize journalists – largely driven by its sociological inquiry – tells journalists that they are professionals, whether or not they want to be, and this raises the stakes involved in being a journalist, often to the detriment of those practicing the craft. Not only does this continue to suggest that we need a re-embrace of the pre-professionalized form of the profession, but also that the ramifications here have been tangible, with traditional notions of craft going under in many circumstances. For instance, imposing codified rules of entry and exclusion has produced an anti-professionalization position among many European journalists: in the UK, this has resulted in an inability to accommodate the growing number of newly educated journalists (Bromley, 1997); in France, journalists have developed a singularly aggressive style of investigative reporting (Neveu, 1998). As longtime British correspondent James Cameron (1997 [1967], 170) put it, "it is fatuous to compensate for our insecurity by calling ourselves members of a profession; it is both pretentious and disabling; we are at our best craftsmen." And yet craft, itself the defining feature of journalism, has faded to the background of what is necessary to know.

The same narrow fate has met diverse international forms of journalism. Though the practice of journalism has taken on unique shapes in the various regions in which it has been practiced, the greatest part of scholarship continues to focus on journalism in its US venues. US-centered research thus stands in as a very limited but honorific gold standard for a wide range of journalistic practices implemented around the world. It leaves unaddressed both those kinds of journalism practiced beyond journalism's western core and the many questions about journalism that dot the global horizon (Gunaratne, 1998; Zhao, 1998; Hallin & Mancini, 2004; Thussu, 2007; Wasserman, 2010).

Equally important, though much of journalism's history has been wrapped up in the history of the nation-state, in today's global age we are hard pressed to argue that that linkage works anymore in the same way. Though one of globalization's key effects has been to undermine the nation-state's centrality, what kind of alternative impulse should be behind the journalistic apparatus it creates instead? Examples here are the contrary cases of capitalism and religious fundamentalism, both of which have created new boundaries of inclusion and exclusion, thereby adjusting the answer of what journalism is for by gravitating toward modes of journalistic practice awry with the impulses associated with free information relay. The recent media displays of Islamic State are an example in point.

What all of these circumstances suggest is that journalism scholars have still not done enough to tend the ties that bind them back to journalism in all of its forms. This remains of critical importance, in that there has developed a body of knowledge about journalism that largely preaches to the converted but does little to create a shared frame of reference about how journalism works or what journalism is for. Numerous correctives could help resolve these circumstances: positioning journalism as the core of a mix of academic perspectives from which it can more fruitfully prosper; recognizing journalism as an act of expression that links directly with the humanities, in much the same way that recognizing journalism's impact links directly with the social sciences; keeping craft, education and research together in the curriculum; and keeping inquiry porous – so that it is possible to examine not only what many of us know about journalism, but how we have agreed on what we know. In this regard, journalism studies is about making a setting to include different kinds of engagement with journalism – for those who practice journalism, those who teach others to practice journalism, those who use journalism and those who craft pathways for thinking critically about what journalism means.

Certain activity has already begun to move in this direction: its logic permeates both the Carnegie–Knight Initiative on the Future of Journalism Education and the European Erasmus Mundus program in journalism and media. The founding of two parallel academic journals in the late 1990s – *Journalism: Theory, Practice and Criticism* and *Journalism Studies* – and the more recent addition of journals like *Journalism Practice* and *Digital Journalism* reflect significant movement toward tweaking the foundation of journalism's study. A Journalism Studies Interest Group (now Division) was established in 2004 at the International Communication Association (ICA), with the intention of bringing together journalism theory, research and education. In all cases, these efforts have provided a corrective to the limitations of journalism's inquiry in its existing frameworks.

Thus, a continued investment at making journalism simultaneously more of the world while keeping it at the forefront of our imagination is in order. Finding a more inclusive template for the mutual engagement of journalism and the academy depends on scholars being ahead of journalism's development – on anticipating where it needs to go and why, and on envisioning broad and creative ways in which it might go there.

7

Journalism Still in the Service of Communication

How did communication take on a disciplinary identity? Which impulses helped shape that identity, and what happened to them over time? The codification of knowledge into disciplines works in systematic but curious ways, and the evolution of communication into a recognized field of study reveals as much about what has been strategically important to the field's development as about what has been overlooked.

The study of journalism offers a useful platform on which to trace the development of the field of communication. Because journalism, so central to communication's inception, diminished in importance as the field matured over time, it constitutes a useful prototype for other similarly overlooked parts of the field and raises critical questions about the disciplinary development of communication. I maintain here that the story of journalism's study, argued first in 2011, continues to help shed light on how scholars make sense of their origins in the academy and what they often lose in developing consensual narratives about their journeys from then to now, there to here.

Reconsidering the Establishment of the Field of Communication

Disciplines evolve in an incremental fashion, spurring and halting knowledge's codification around unexpected issues. Although disciplines can provide continuity, imply stability and offer a recognizable venue for sharing knowledge, they can also diminish innovation, offset a sense of discovery and reify the familiar as canonical, overstating those subfields or areas of research that prove strategically useful to the discipline's maturation.

The field of communication is no exception to these trends, and its historiography has generated multiple waves of reevaluation in the years since the field first developed. As communication studies aged and gained legitimacy, its history increasingly occupied the attention of its scholars, who produced scores of books and articles debating its proper legacy, timing, development, priorities and impact (Czitrom, 1982; Delia, 1987; Robinson, 1988; Hardt, 1992; Rogers, 1994; Dennis & Wartella, 1996; Schiller, 1996). The separate works of Simpson (1999) and Glander (2000), for instance, drove a rethinking of the givens in US communication historiography by linking the field's development to the Cold War, with Glander (2000, ix) suggesting a "deliberate obfuscation about the origins of the field." The widely accepted "four founders" narrative, commonly applied to the evolution of US mass communication scholarship, only later came to be "understood for what it was: A strategic vision for developing media research rather than a faithful rendering of its history" (Curry Jansen, 2010, 127). In many areas of interest and geographic regions, the field developed earlier and in more diverse ways than had been generally assumed (Wahl-Jorgensen, 2004). In Peters' (1986, 537) view, such repeated looks backward, and the interpretations they engendered, reflected larger anxieties associated with legitimating the study of communication and its transformation from "an intellectual to an institutional entity." Over time, the same anxieties – rent asunder by ascending economic and political pressures in many parts of the world – generated additional attention as the field's legitimation continued apace (Park & Pooley, 2008; Simonson, 2010).

The study of collective memory modifies the authority of historiography by asserting that tales of the past are routinely and systematically altered to fit the agendas of those recycling them into the present. Halbwachs (1992 [1925]) first argued that a fundamental reordering of the past underlies all projects of the present: In Lang's articulation, "Not only do we forget the past but we manage to see a past that fits our preoccupations" (Lang, 1996, 3). In this regard, the historiographic accounts developed by members of a discipline, seen here as a community of memory favoring shared interpretations of the past, reflect the sentiments of those who are particularly invested in shaping certain versions of the community's past.

Such an "invention of tradition" (Hobsbawm & Ranger, 1985) gains legitimacy over time by being repeatedly recycled by members of the community. Privileging particular accounts of the past through acts of both remembering and forgetting, collective memories give the community both a "history of" the discipline, delineating its past, and a "history for" the discipline, articulating how it should develop. In crafting tales of the past for the purpose of consolidating group identity across time, they thus involve the work of reconstruction, not recall, foregrounding the issues, events, personalities and impulses that resonate with the greatest number of influential members of a discipline and allowing those of least concern to fade into the background. Perhaps nowhere is this as evident as in the current debate over journalism's history.

Although communication studies, in its contemporary form over half a century old, remains temporally out of synch with the earlier institutionalization of many more traditional academic fields of inquiry (Zelizer, 2011b), it has been subject to the broader mnemonic strategies at stake in stabilizing a disciplinary past. While the field's still-relative youth, disagreements over its canonical literature and degrees of intellectual incoherence (Peters, 1986; Park & Pooley, 2008) have complicated the historiographer's task, much else has obstructed the move toward a clearer origin narrative. This has involved which tales prevailed about communication's development as a disciplinary field, why, and at what cost to the discipline's multiple subfields and research areas. As key members of the field have voiced and acted on particular notions of what the field needed to look like and what kind of past was necessary to support their vision, it is no wonder that today communication studies "needs memory more than it wants history" (Pooley & Park, 2008, 5).

These developments and the role of journalism as it has been remembered and misremembered in the service of communication's evolution are worth considering. Four related topics are relevant: how the study of journalism played in the establishment of the field of communication, where it went over time in some of communication's key subfields, how the global variations of journalism today force a rethinking of some of the longstanding assumptions about communication, and why there is a need to reposition the study of journalism – critically and urgently – in the service of communication.

How Journalism Helped to Establish the Field of Communication

The centrality of journalism to communication – its practice, personnel, management, organization, ownership, impact and effects – is embedded in the very origin narratives by which the field came to be. Remarkably, this is the case wherever the study of communication positioned itself on the academic landscape. This is not to say that the main strokes of its affinity are not offset by a number of interpretive sidelines: for instance, some of communication's roots date back thousands of years to rhetoric; multiple subfields of communication, such as interpersonal communication or organizational communication, developed alongside journalism without any discernible interaction between them; and by and large journalism positioned itself more squarely within the embrace of mass communication than alongside other disciplinary subfields. But, those qualifications notwithstanding, an alliance between the study of journalism and communication was for the most part initially a given, providing a critical developmental foothold for communication studies.

What did that alliance look like? In practice and study, both projects had many attributes that endeared them to the other. Both were born in and of a certain kind of modernity: journalism, invested in the quest for truth, saw rationality, objectivity, impartiality and reason as the modes of engagement that it could offer those wanting to know more about the larger world, in much the same way that communication provided a set of reasoned and predictable operations by which the drums of free choice, consent, progress, science, democracy and individualism could best stifle those of inequality, ignorance and injustice (Downing, 1996; McQuail, 2000). All of this occurred alongside an idealized understanding of social order and standardized conditions of knowledge and production (Kumar, 1995). Journalism, like other areas of practice-oriented scholarship – marketing and advertising, public relations, organizational communication, among others – could thus offer the field of communication a place in the real world and a reminder of why its scholarship mattered, with the media in particular seen as a useful vehicle for modernity's dissemination. This meant that, even if the set of assumptions that fueled an association between journalism and communication envisioned only a particular kind of modernity, it proliferated nonetheless.

Thus, it was no surprise that, in nearly every place that communication research took hold, journalism lurked somewhere nearby – in humanities curricula focusing on writing, language and history; in social science inquiry about political, economic and social effects; and in apprenticeships drawn from journalism education. Helping to shape communication's disciplinary objectives – "to define the field's boundaries, legitimate its authority, identify its problems and influence its paradigmatic assumptions" (Curry Jansen, 2010, 127) – the field and its core alliance with journalism worked in a symbiotic fashion.

Narratives of that initial alliance differed by place, as details were shaped differently by surrounding assumptions about the field's development in various geographic regions. In the United States, journalism's study took shape at first at the turn of the twentieth century in the humanities, but as political and social developments – first during World War I and then during World War II – drew public attention to the social sciences, the news became an instrumental setting across the curriculum for considering the making of public sentiment (Glander, 2000). As observers discerned the negative and positive workings and effects of the mass media, seen as propaganda in unfriendly regimes and as persuasion and development in friendly ones, this period, largely seen as the ascent of US communication study, relied largely on journalists and journalism.

This reliance had multiple sightings in the US academy. Initially, the Bleyer tradition of early journalism education was said to have made possible the hospitable welcome that journalism schools gave communication (Rogers & Chaffee, 1994), and some saw the field's early forefathers as firmly ensconced within journalism. Simonson (2010), for instance, identified Walt Whitman and David Sarnoff, both of whom worked in journalism – one as a reporter and editor, the other as a radio telegrapher – among the field's originators. Journalism also dominated the early days of the Chicago School of Sociology, whose early work highlighted journalism as a necessary ingredient of urban life (Carey, 1996; Wahl-Jorgensen, 2000, 2004). Largely under the helm of former reporter Robert Park, ethnography was likened to journalistic practice, and the ill-fated but creatively conceived organ *Thought News* tried to outfit journalism in academic clothes. Encouraged by journalist Franklin Ford to address the social dimensions of news, Park followed Ford's lead in rendering the world of newsmaking academic. Dewey, writing to William James in 1891, characterized Ford as driven "by his newspaper experience to study as a practical question the social bearings of intelligence and its distribution" (cited in Perry, 1935, 518). The administrative model of inquiry that came to dominate the field mid-century, and its adjacent governmental settings also relied on journalists and journalism, with the Committee for Public Information, set up during World War I, depending so heavily on its Division of News that John Dewey (1918, 216) wondered after the war whether the "word 'news' [was] not destined to be replaced by the word 'propaganda.'" Former journalists – such as Lippmann, Schramm and Casey (Rogers, 1994) – and those who studied them – such as Lazarsfeld and Lasswell, who himself became a journalist for a time after he left the University of Chicago (Rogers, 1994) – filled the landscape. Lippman was consulted for advice in setting up the Social Science Research Council around issues related to journalism (Curry Jansen, 2010), whereas Schramm, the oft-proclaimed originator of the field, required many of his doctoral students to have had practical experience in the media, preferably the press (Rogers, 1994).

The history of mass communication in the United States is thus filled with anecdotal and associative information about journalism – that it was central, that it connected practice and theory, that it spanned the humanities and social sciences and that it provided the case studies for theories about media effects, organizations, production and institutions (Dennis & Wartella, 1996). In each case, the development of communication studies took cues from journalism. No wonder, then, that in the United States many schools, departments, an association and its journal continue to bear the name journalism and mass communication.

It is too simple, however, to claim the US master narrative for communication's development as a field. Although Hardt (2002) argued that both international communication research and critical media studies developed in the United States from the journalistic efforts of Lippmann and Merz on coverage of the Russian Revolution, elsewhere journalism proved as central to the field but in different ways. In Europe, scholars in sociology and political science developed concepts straight from observing journalism that would only later in the twentieth century prove central to the nascent field of communication.

In Germany and Austria, thinkers such as Marx, Weber, Kracauer, Schaeffle, Buecher and Loebl had journalistic experience, whereas others such as Salomon and Toennies used the news to address the structure of the press and public opinion (Lang, 1996). The first academic institute to study the press was established already by 1916 – the so-called "newspaper science" or *Zeitungswissenschaft* – and Weber detailed the parameters of its study to the first meeting of the German Sociological Society in 1924 (Lang, 1996; Frohlich & Holtz-Bacha, 2003). Although that study was halted during the Third Reich, it was reignited in the decades following the war, by then newly incorporated into schools of communication (Pietila, 2008). In France, the work of de Tocqueville and Tarde demanded journalism's recognition early on so as to understand political and public life, although journalism itself only emerged in the curriculum later in the century (Charon, 2003; Mattelart, 2006). Countries of the then-Soviet bloc established institutes for journalism's study mid-century, developing a so-called "press science" combining journalism theory and history, but once the Berlin Wall came down, the same countries followed different modes of incorporating the study of journalism into communication (Hiebert & Gross, 2003; Jacubowicz, 2007). In the United Kingdom, numbers of journalism apprenticeships remained high and journalism schools robust throughout the latter half of the twentieth century, while first sociology and then media studies programs adopted journalism as a laboratory for theory development (Bromley, 2006). At the same time, programs bridging communication and journalism – largely along the political dimensions of the topics they highlighted – were set up in The Netherlands, Belgium and Scandinavia (Meerbach, 2003). Thus, although taking varied paths, journalism in Europe was connected to communication in multiple ways – as an early testing ground for theories; as an empirical and historical venue for addressing social, economic, political and cultural life; and as a source of content about public issues and sentiment.

Beyond Europe, communication's development drew squarely from journalism training programs. Australia followed close on the British apprenticeship model, although a subsequent battle over the academic territory related to the media, loosely called "the media wars," later separated those who studied journalism from those who practiced it (Henningham, 1985; Turner, 2000). In East Asia, particularly South Korea, China, Hong Kong and Japan, journalism education was key.

Journalism departments had already been set up in China and Hong Kong in the 1920s, and in South Korea in the 1950s, later offering a rich and hospitable venue from which to launch communication research (Kang, 1991; Wu, 2006). The link was symbiotic: journalism grounded communication theories, while communication pushed "reform in journalism research, education and industry" (Zhang, 2006, 105). In Latin America, the establishment of journalism schools in both Argentina and Brazil by 1934 was accompanied by a rejection of US communication models and a turn to those of the French (Mattelart, 2006). Largely initiated by Freire and followed up by Bordenave, this turn led Chilean journalist Fernando Reyes Matta and others to resist conventional understandings of journalism and develop instead a participatory model of alternative communication. It resulted in rural cassette forums in Uruguay, a so-called "prensa nanica" – or midget press – in Brazil, and radio broadcasts and mediated distance education in Mexico, Peru and Ecuador (Beltran, 2004 [1993]). In Africa, where journalism remained relevant to the on-site challenges of nation building and familiarizing publics accustomed to colonialism and authoritarianism with transitional regimes, journalism also lent a support beam for communication research. In some sites, journalism remained the core of communication curricula (Tomaselli, 2003; Barratt & Berger, 2007), whereas in others it paved the way for the development of African communication research by local scholars, replacing the so-called "parachute" field workers from Europe and America (Boafo & George, 1992; Eribo & Tanjong, 2002, vii).

In each region, the fact that journalism study preceded communication studies gave the latter a launching pad from which to develop. Significantly, these different early positions of journalism required some navigation across the humanities and social sciences in addressing communication studies' emergence, and in retrospect they highlighted the signal blending of the two in consolidating communication as a disciplinary field. In France, the importance of interpretive inquiry, structural linguistics and semiotics kept the humanities primary in linking journalism to the emerging communication field (Charon, 2003; Mattelart, 2006). In the United States, journalism study's emergence in the humanities gave way over time to communication's ascent in the social sciences (Czitrom, 1982). Although early research was primarily humanities-driven, already by the late 1950s Schramm (1957) pointed to an equal number of research projects on journalism drawing from both parts of the curriculum, and over the following years that percentage weighed heavily toward the social sciences. A similar pattern emerged in China, Hong Kong and Africa (Leung, Kenny & Lee, 2006; Wu, 2006). Tensions across the humanities and social sciences were prescient because they underscored how journalism and communication could be seen from across the curriculum. But they also heralded a cautionary note. As communication in many places became more aligned with the social sciences over time, journalism was thrown increasingly to the background.

Journalism thus had a use value that forecast some of communication's most enduring traits as its own field – a real-world relevance; a setting that repeatedly and systematically engaged with other environments such as politics, economics, culture, religion and the law; a set of patterned and somewhat predictable routines for analysis; a phenomenon that combined language and people, practices, values and mindsets related to public expression and discovery; organizational structures and institutions of power and authority. Those attributes are worth remembering, for they populated the various subfields that did not yet exist but that later came to internally mark the field of communication and subdivide it from itself. In this regard, journalism could be seen across the field's own distinctions among interpersonal, group, organizational and institutional modes of interaction, across the humanities and social sciences, across quantitative and qualitative methodologies and across empirical and critical schools of thought. As publishers participated in the field's development in varying ways – funding journalism and communication schools, creating jobs and shaping recruitment, among them – journalism was thought to underscore that connection to a certain kind of modernity and related notions of rationality and progress, consent, freedom of information, democracy and civil society. As an impetus for communication research, then, journalism promised to be useful to the field in multiple ways.

Where Did Journalism Go Over Time?

Where, however, did journalism go over time? Journalism shrank in importance and centrality, and, in some places, it disappeared altogether from the discipline. It is telling that, even in the ICA, it was for many years subsumed by one of the association's largest divisions – mass communication – in which a primary focus on effects and institutions drove a certain take on journalism's use value that did not push the recognition of all the traits mentioned above. Only after nearly a half-century of ICA's existence was an interest group devoted to journalism studies introduced onto the association's landscape.

Three kinds of scholarship within the field of communication are useful in illuminating how the marginalization of journalism took shape, because they exemplify the range of the problematic being identified here. They include scholarship on politics, scholarship on technology and scholarship on culture, and each shows how knowledge that proved useful to the discipline's maturation over time pushed aside that which was perceived as less useful. Although not necessarily more responsible for journalism's shrinkage than other scholarly subfields, in each of these three cases journalism's diminishment can be seen as an exercise in collective memory, whereby a past was created that was most valuable to the field moving forward. Each subfield within communication study thus acted as a separate interpretive community of memory and pulled from the past those aspects that fit its present-day interests (Zelizer, 1993a, 2004b). The result is that each subfield developed a limited but highly strategic and internally useful accounting of what mattered about journalism – and hence communication – over time.

Politics and Journalism

The subfield of political communication has long been motivated by normativity in its approach to journalism, querying how the news "ought" to operate under optimum conditions (i.e., Entman, 1989). Assuming that journalism has a vested interest in the political world, usually one involving a western notion of democracy and civil society, much work in this subfield sees politics and journalism as interdependent, with the conditions for journalism to better serve its publics and the polity remaining front and center (i.e., Cook, 1998; Hallin & Mancini, 2004). Emblematized by the *Four Theories of the Press* (Siebert, Peterson & Schramm, 1956), the interdependency between government and the news media has been postulated so often that it has become a naturalized dimension of this subfield of inquiry.

The emphasis on the linkage between politics and journalism minimizes those aspects of journalism that do not fit that assumption. For instance, although the debate over the New World Information and Communication Order from the 1970s to 1990s was touted as a debate about the free flow of information, it remained at heart a conversation about how free one's journalists could be or what their freedom actually meant. Resting on a distinction between first an East/West and then a North/South struggle, its response to normative assumptions about political communication suggested that one kind of journalism could and should prevail. Not surprisingly, these same assumptions have since been replayed in debates over the censorship of Google searches in China, the viability of "true press freedom" in Myanmar, and the public response to the Snowden leaks of classified information.

Other examples populate the landscape, with Frances Fukuyama's (1992) stunningly erroneous claim that liberal democracy constituted the "end of history" offering perhaps the most cited example of what amounted to missing the trees for the forest. For instance, the present period of partisan news offers clear indicators of how much journalism on the ground complicates the picture that political communication and political science tried to draw about journalism. It suggests, despite claims to the contrary (i.e., Zaller, 1992), that so-called "objective journalism" – central to western notions of democracy, modernity and civil society – is an anomaly. Rather, political communication's push for largely one version of the desired and subjunctive – the normatively hoped for – dissipated much of the focus on the multiple journalisms evident on the ground. They became denigrated, relativized and reduced in value alongside aspirations for something better. Those aspirations, often US in origin, are made even less satisfying because political priorities differ in different regions (Waisbord, 2000; Jacubowicz, 2007), and because even across the United States these aspirations cannot always be met.

Technology and Journalism

Technology studies within communication have been similarly myopic about journalism. In the push for the faster, more mobile, easier to access and more personalized, multiple dimensions of journalism have been outsourced, generalized and made incidental. Although consonant with the project of a certain kind of modernity, the growing focus on technology within communication studies, and particularly an orientation toward technological determinism, have made it difficult to remember the social relations and systems of power underlying technology's use in journalism, the historical contexts by which it gets accepted (or not) and the craft dimensions of journalism that distinguish the news from other modes of public expression.

Instead a race toward technology is creating a bias toward those modes of journalism that jump on the bandwagon of "faster is better," with resulting scholarship pushing the new and fast over the old and slow (Gillmor, 2006; Shirky, 2008, 2009). This has had many ramifications: it sidesteps the conflicts that can arise when journalists increasingly rely on technology companies to do their work, to the degree that the development of software platforms associated with work flow, work product or the dissemination of news can become uncritically integrated into the fundamental structure of a news outlet. Moreover, the overly enthusiastic embrace of technology can be used to support dire – and often overly simplistic – predictions about the death of journalism, particularly in its print form (Zelizer, 2015a).

Although the technological crisis facing journalism is a necessary part of any appraisal of its future, there is also a need to be mindful of the various ways in which new and old, slow and fast come together in today's multiplatform information environment. As Marvin (1988) established years ago, new technologies tend to coexist with older ones, not wipe their antecedents from existence. It is no surprise, then, that grounded conditions around the world still display a multiplicity of relations to news technology (Atton, 2002; Deuze, 2007; Thussu, 2007; Boczkowski, 2010; Wasserman, 2010). Even in the United States, where a "mobile majority" prevails (*State of the Media*, 2015), a variety of technological platforms inhabit the landscape: in 2014, the audiences for network and local news broadcasts were up 5% and 3% over the previous year, for podcasting they were up 41% and digital ad revenue grew 18%, while newspapers and cable news declined in audience size (*State of the Media*, 2015). In 2015, 15% of US citizens continued to avoid the Internet altogether, though the offline population is shrinking yearly (Anderson & Perrin, 2015). Moreover, although an emphasis on technology suits a larger interest in globalization because it suggests that distant individuals can be better connected, the state of technological development differs by locale, priority and context. Print journalism continues to flourish in many places around the globe, due to the digital divide, as in India, and due to state-imposed access, as in China. And the range of communication technologies – not just the Internet – helps people challenge repression in the Global South, Asia, the Middle East and elsewhere (Romano & Bromley, 2005; Khiabany, 2010).

Moreover, the digital environment is still evolving and thus remains open to multiple trajectories. It is useful to remember how much uncertainty accompanied journalism 25 years into radio or television, when the spectrum of practices yet to evolve in each case was far from clear. Predictions about the demise of certain forms of journalism thus seem not only premature but decidedly western.

Culture and Journalism

Cultural scholarship in communication has displayed much of the same narrowed understanding of journalism. Although journalism offered the original impulses for much of the development of cultural research in communication, with the early work by much of the Birmingham Centre for Contemporary Cultural Studies a case in point (Hall, 1973; Hall et al., 1978), it is almost nowhere to be found today in a shape that recalls that early centrality. The cultural analysis of journalism has tended to focus on the sides of journalism left unaddressed elsewhere. Although this scholarship usefully addresses problems of meaning, group identity, power and patterns of domination and marginalization (Hartley, 1982, 1992; Dahlgren & Sparks, 1992), its broader embrace of relativity, subjectivity and engagement has produced too a fundamental ambivalence about journalism's reverence for facts, truth and reality.

In this light, much cultural scholarship in communication pushes for the odd, outrageous, different and marginal (Lumby, 1999), leaving relatively unaddressed the central, more conventional venues of journalism. For instance, the *New York Times* and the BBC do not merit as much attention from culturally inclined scholars as do Comedy Central, reality television or the plethora of forums associated with user-generated content. This is problematic, for journalism has always embraced both the curious and the mainstream (Schudson, 1978; Carey, 1986a), and today it continues to do so in inventive ways (Williams & Delli-Carpini, 2011). Although, by definition, work in this area broadens the Eurocentric lens that remains prominent elsewhere, voices from the Global South remind culturalists too of a soft westernism in their research (Stratton & Ang, 1996).

In each of these three cases, journalism has survived in communication studies but primarily in ways that match the contemporary interests of the subfield invoking it. Such sub-disciplinary nearsightedness means that political studies of journalism diminish what we have for what we hope for, technological studies offset the old and slow with the new and fast, and cultural studies sidestep the mainstream and mundane so as to engage the odd and outrageous. As Adorno (Horkheimer & Adorno, 1972, 230) noted long ago, "all reification is a forgetting." This means not only that the field of communication has lost part of its ground, but that no one subfield reflects anymore what all of journalism is. Admittedly, this has taken shape in different ways in different regions, but the trend toward shrunken conceptualization, despite journalism's own robust presence, prevails across the board.

How Journalism Challenges Assumptions about Communication

The subdisciplinary nearsightedness of communication studies is exacerbated by the fact that it is paralleled by a geographic nearsightedness. In much the same way that conceptual subfields provide only part of the picture, so too does the discipline's geographic spread constitute only part of the environments in which scholars tackle communication.

Globalization has made it easier to connect quickly, widely and across vast distances, and so has played a part in broadening the field in fundamental ways. As various scholars have argued – with Giddens (1991a), Thompson (1996) and Tomlinson (1999) leading the way – globalization itself was built through modernity. Although communication as a field now boasts researchers in every continent – ICA alone has 5,000-odd members from over 80 countries – it has also facilitated an either/or stance among those trying to address who succeeds in shaping the field's origin narrative moving forward. Claims of intellectual imperialism,

Eurocentrism, Orientalism, academic dependency – and then as a response Occidentalism, Asiacentrism (Miike, 2006), Afrocentrism (Asante, 2005), Islamicism (Ayish, 2003) and other regionally exceptionalist responses from numerous non-Eurocentric positions – have created an as yet unresolved and unsustainable foundation for the field to realize the full dimensions of its global spread. This regional myopia, noted separately decades ago by Murdock (1993), Escobar (1995) and Downing (1996), is fundamentally counterproductive for multiple reasons.

The uneven exchange of academic knowledge, which tends time and again to privilege the haves over the have-nots, has created two very real camps, whose distance from each other is often reflected in some spatial or geographic metaphor – between the West and the rest, the center and periphery, the Global North and Global South, and the First World and Third World. As noted earlier, there is a history to these either/or positions, and it draws from the field's very linkage with a particular form of modernity and its associated concepts.

But the gravitation toward western-driven universals and an uneven recognition of what complicates them is far flung. For example, the notion of the "Ivory Tower" has persevered as a metaphor for thinking about university engagement globally despite the fact, as Jelin (2011) argued, that its decidedly western tenor presupposes a model of disengagement that was never the grounded practice for academic life in Latin America. Similarly, McQuail (2000) noted that a lack of specificity about what was meant by "non-western" has produced a fundamental deficiency of inquiry for the field writ large, which has yet to be corrected.

Multiple scholars – among them Lee (2001), Chen (2006) and Wang (2010) – have argued for strategies to move beyond the either/or dichotomy, noting that the discipline of communication is undermined by scholars focusing too stridently on its internal geographic divide. They maintain that in the struggle to clarify the distinction between the West and the rest, the variation that exists within each of those two camps has been lost. Although globalization has helped spread communication, it has also simultaneously pushed the recognition of certain kinds of difference while rendering invisible other differences that reside within the so-called "accepted" commonalities. Curran and Park (2000) were among the first to anthologize the impacts of such errors, whereas Murdock (2010) stipulated that the West/rest distinction blinded people to the ramifications of consumerism, religious and national fundamentalism and new forms of citizenship. On the other side of the global continuum, Khiabany (2007, 119) noted that the responding move to set forth an Islamic theory of communication pays little heed to the "struggle for control for interpretation of culture, for communication resources and for the system of social stratification."

This geographic nearsightedness is crucial, because scholarship in collective memory stipulates that, when variation disappears in the narratives that ensue, it is difficult to reinstate it (Halbwachs, 1992 [1925]; Nora, 1996). Additionally, as Connerton (2009) noted more specifically of memory and modernity, settings that align their evolution with notions of progress, reason and democracy also exhibit a particular affinity with practices of forgetting. Forgetting, in this regard, is a useful mnemonic practice for those attempting to narrow the past to what they think matters.

It is here that journalism has a role to play, for it provides a fruitful starting point for remembering differently the evolution of communication studies. Suggesting that communication scholars might have been misguided in their initial attempts to align the disciplinary ethos with a particular form of modernity, journalism demonstrates how necessarily divergent and internally contradictory the ground of communication must continue to be. Although locale-specific studies are important in offsetting the academic dependency on the West, a focus on journalism could spark the creation of an alternative mnemonic narrative.

Why and how is journalism useful in this regard? It provides a litmus test for thinking about how to move beyond the divides that separate parts of the field from each other. Although certain privileged forms of journalism – the very notion of a free and independent press, the idea of a Fourth Estate or the public's right to know, and the embrace of neutrality, facticity and objectivity – were never the practice in much of the world, their wide and somewhat uncritical adoption as the broad ground for communication studies has meant, to extend the words of Jelin (2011), that "specialized expertise (at times under the cover of 'neutral' technical skills) has [had] to share and establish a dialogue with broad politicized intellectual concerns." That affiliation has not always been a happy endeavor. Unlike early perspectives on journalism that insisted on its relationship with a certain kind of modernity, universalism, rationality and progress, today multiple modes of journalistic practice underscore how divergent and open-ended the field needs to remain, how sensitive to different and often contradictory cores, values and contingencies, how relative and particularistic.

Examples abound. In India, for instance, the coming of modernity was mediated by caste and communal affiliations that themselves formed the journalisms of the time into a kind of print communalism and petition journalism, operating in direct and voluntary engagement with the state (Udupa, 2015). Similar circumstances characterize much of South America, where an orientation to state over market, elimination of basic democratic rights, tradition of terrorism and military juntas, strict control of newsrooms and persecution of journalists all continue to challenge Eurocentric notions of what modern journalism should look like (Waisbord, 2000). The possibility of adhering to universal journalistic principles in East Africa is offset by media intimidation, conventions of paying for information, information suppression and government propaganda, all further exacerbated by low literacy rates, high poverty and transitional governmental structures (Kalyango & Eckler, 2010), so much so that "the more African journalism strives to implant liberal democracy, the less the successes it has had to report" (Nyamnjoh, 2005, 1; Wasserman, 2010). The former Soviet bloc displays a transition from totalitarian to democratic societies that rests on journalism, which began to take shape a full 20 years ago but still does not readily offer a full or coherent picture of what those regimes or their media look like (Jacubowicz, 2007; Krasnoboka, 2010). In Russia, journalists are being murdered from left and right, while other nations labor with degrees of democratization and a gravitation toward pre-Communist totalitarian modes of information relay (Hiebert & Gross, 2003). In Iran, despotism and a journalism rigidly linked to the state reflect little of the much-expressed hopes in the West for a civil society in that country (Khiabany, 2010). Today's multiple modes of journalism in Asia do not provide the same expected – and desired – connectors to individualism, democracy and freedom as defined in the West (Lee, 2000; Gunaratne, 2005; Han, 2016), and in various places modernity (from which contemporary journalism was presumably born) has instead been tied to repression and a respect for consensus, order and authority that comes at the expense of freedom of expression.

In each of these locations, journalism is not marginal to the developments noted above, and even when satiric or ironic venues such as Comedy Central or The Onion allow the public to be "in" on the joke, violations of western expectations continue to occur. The question is whether the discipline of communication can afford to leave journalism as a sideshow. As Garcia-Canclini (1995) noted, modernity invites multiple routes to and through engagement, various strategies for "entering and leaving." But instead of recognizing them all as alternatives, western expectations repeatedly cut short the ability to see fully what lies on the ground because an aspect of what surfaces ruffles the default disciplinary sensibility. An array of cultural and political situational particularities is seen instead as a barrier to the mindset on which the field was set in place.

Can the field of communication not do better than its default tale of the past has embraced thus far? The list of what much of the field is missing in maintaining its either/or positions – on both sides of the continuum – is breathtaking. Journalism today exists in multiple situations of contingency with no clear beginning, end or obvious trajectory: they provide ample evidence of soft authoritarianism, odd mixes of colonialism and post-colonialism, multiple kinds of neo-authoritarian systems and their altered journalistic values, increased self-censorship and government interference, collectivism, new modes of identity such as hybridity or marginality, tensions between the nation-state and pan-regionalism, corruption, transitional governments with no obvious or consensual before and after points, and spaces intertwining local and global, traditional and modern, religious and political in complicated and nonlinear ways. This is an instructive list for the field, for embracing primarily western expectations that engender more projects similar to "themselves" fails to address the situated nature of communication in non-western environments. It also obscures the fact that communication has at its core – and at its origin – multiple journalisms. Those journalisms could be used to rethink existing theories from anew, rather than positioning scholars in enclaves across from those who think differently, and could facilitate an updating of the notions that communication originally put in place as part of its own disciplinary ground.

Journalism @ the Center of Communication

In an era when disciplines and the university face perhaps greater economic and political challenges than ever before, it is useful to remind ourselves that scholars in communication, like those inhabiting other disciplinary fields in the academy, have shared their past in certain ways because doing so has helped keep the field consonant with larger notions of self-presentation. In such a light, the field has been likened to a Rorschach test: "It is whatever you see in it and make of it," its poorly defined disciplinary boundaries ensuring that "the choices we make . . . are profoundly political" (Wahl-Jorgensen, 2000, 94).

I have argued here that in the discipline's memory, journalism has become shorthand for a very constrained set of practices among communication scholars who no longer recognize how strategically localized and narrow those practices remain. This is critical because journalism remains a valuable platform for thinking about the grounded parameters of communication study. The world includes populations less free than desired, journalisms more repressed than existing models have allowed for, governments and media systems invested in different ways of piecing together the puzzle from those expected, and communication environments that are unable to access the tools, research methods or technologies that underpin the very logic of existing thought processes in places that have more.

The conceptual and geographic foundationalism discussed thus far – by which scholars reduce those who are different or think differently to simplified versions of who they are – is an error which the discipline of communication cannot afford. Although here I have focused on journalism, journalism is not the only room in the house of communication to have been closed off. Other formerly central venues – speech, rhetoric, performance and visuality come to mind (Benson, 1985; Sproule, 2008) – have been detoured around on the way to cementing a unified epistemological vision. The fundamentalism evident here thus challenges the field in its broadest strokes to redirect where communication studies is going by reacquainting itself more fully with where the field has been.

It is no accident that journalism exists in some form everywhere in the world, including those places where communication strives to make its disciplinary name. Bringing journalism back to its former centrality and recognizing it as a useful ground for thinking about communication writ large depends on a fuller consideration of the different terrains of that ground. The data that result – of diversity, discontinuity, noise, instability, tentativeness, transversality, multiple universalisms, fluidity and globalizing influences – underscore the possibility that journalism can again reflect the multiple ways in which communication as a discipline matters, even if many earlier expectations connected to the field's evolution go unrequited. This is possible, however, only if that multiplicity of pathways is brought together within one shared academic conversation, in which contemporary scholars in the field of communication can together build a collective memory anew, tweaking and adjusting the notions that initial thinkers in the field seem to have gotten wrong over half a century ago.

For communication to survive as a disciplinary field, it needs a better way of navigating difference. Although the institutionalization of communication studies requires setting aside differences so as to embrace commonalities, as Peters (1986, 1999), Craig (1989, 1999) and Wahl-Jorgensen (2000, 2004) have separately shown, it is possible that the latter has taken place at the expense of the former. It is journalism's multiple attributes, so useful in the field's early days, that make it a rich candidate for retweaking its collective memory. I have suggested here that remembering and reinstating its centrality can do much to stead communication into its future. Doing so involves recognizing that journalism lays bare the limited value of an attachment to a certain form of modernity, rationalism, universalism and progress. Journalism can remind the field of its disciplinary attachment not only to ideas but to the ground – to the messiness of practice, the hesitations of the real world and the inconsistencies and brutalities of social, economic, political, cultural and public life. Most importantly, using journalism to guide the future of communication studies suggests that it is still possible to imagine a field of communication without a center.

This is not to suggest that such a path forward is free of complications. Rather, the opportunities it raises outweigh them. As members of a discipline that repeatedly faces questions from the outside about its viability, we might do well to reassess how our disciplinary identity might look through a different prism. Not only might this help us more equitably recognize many rooms in the house of communication, but also it might help us understand how and in which ways varied approaches to normativity might coexist within the field, and how the variation that grounds communication studies might model different disciplinary contours for the academy at large (Zelizer, 2016a).

The relationship between communication studies and journalism was a given when the field of communication first evolved. Such a linkage can reclaim its place on the disciplinary mantle – with new moves, new inhabitants, new directions and new understandings. Reflecting the wide breadth and diversity that characterize its on-site practice can help make communication distinct from other disciplines with no such ground, offering the hope that the house of communication might become more of a home for all of its members, not just the few who strategically guided the field at some point in its past.

8

On Journalism and Cultural Studies: When Facts, Truth and Reality Are God-Terms

Journalism prides itself on a respect for the facts, truth and reality. Yet what happens when these god-terms for the practice of most kinds of journalism become the focus of inquiry that insists on their relativity, reflexivity, construction, subjectivity and engagement? Here I consider the odd twinning of cultural studies inquiry with the study of journalism, showing how originary premises in both arenas have rendered the two uneasy bedfellows, despite the fact that each has much to profit from a more solid and fruitful convergence.

As I argued first in 2004, I maintain here that little has changed. Four separate but related questions, derived from different historical moments in the evolution of journalism's inquiry, motivate the question posed above:

- What does it mean to study journalism from a cultural perspective?
- How and why has cultural studies both enriched and neglected the cultural analysis of journalism?
- What can we expect from the future of cultural studies and journalism?

Considering each of these questions can help determine why the linkage matters.

On Journalism from a Cultural Perspective

Although it has not always been termed as such, the cultural analysis of journalism has flourished for as long as journalism has been a target of intellectual endeavor (Zelizer, 2004a). Given a wide range of labels – including the collective knowledge journalists need to function as journalists, the culturological dimensions of the news and the examination of journalism as popular culture – this type of inquiry has produced a fruitful line of scholarship that links the untidy and textured *materiel* of journalism – its symbols, ideologies, rituals, conventions and stories – with the larger world in which journalism takes shape (Park, 1940; Schudson, 1991; Dahlgren, 1992). Approached as more than just reporters' professional codes of action or the social arrangements of reporters and editors, the cultural analysis of journalism sees the world of news as offering up a complex and multidimensional lattice of meanings for all those involved in journalism, "a tool kit of symbols, stories, rituals and world views, which people use in varying configurations to solve different kinds of problems" (Swidler, 1986, 273). With the category of those involved in journalism itself changing – reporters on the "Twitter beat" now sit alongside traditional reporters in many news outlets, while non-affiliated bloggers, bystanders, activists and citizen journalists speak to the same issues from other platforms – cultural analysis embraces them all.

Pronouncedly interdisciplinary and self-reflexive, cultural inquiry addresses journalism by traversing an analytical track with two somewhat incompatible edges. It both sees journalism through journalists' own eyes – tracking how being part of the community comes to have meaning for them – and queries the self-presentations that journalists provide. Emphasizing "the constraining force of broad cultural symbol systems regardless of the details of organizational and occupational routines," the cultural analysis of journalism moves decidedly in tandem with, but in opposition to, the pronounced and conventional understandings of how journalism works (Schudson, 1991, 143). Undercutting the pronounced sense of self that journalists have long set forth regarding their practices and position in the world, cultural inquiry assumes that journalists employ collective knowledge to become members of the group, even when it is more imagined than real, and to maintain their membership over time. At the same time, it presumes that what is explicit and articulated as that knowledge may not reflect the whole picture of what journalism is and tries to be (Goodenough, 1981). Cultural inquiry thus travels the uneven road of reading journalism against its own grain, while giving that grain extended attention.

Analysis here considers the meanings, symbols and symbolic systems, ideologies, rituals and conventions by which journalists maintain their cultural authority as the voice of events in the public domain. The inspiration for such work comes from developments elsewhere in the academy, particularly during the 1970s and 1980s: an expansion of research on the sociology of culture; philosophy's interest in constructivism; a turn in anthropology and folklore toward the analysis of symbols and symbolic forms; linguistics' orientation toward ethnography; and growing scholarship in cultural history and cultural criticism. During the same time period, cultural studies grew in both the UK and the

US, bringing different analytical tools to the foreground. In Britain, a blend of neo-Marxism, psychoanalysis, feminist studies, critical theory, literary theory, semiotics and ethnography that constituted early British cultural studies complemented a US interest in pragmatism, symbolic interactionism, cultural anthropology and cultural sociology. Although the unitary character of both British and US cultural studies has been much challenged (Stratton & Ang, 1996; Saldivar, 1997; Miller, 2006), the distinction is maintained here so as both to differentiate the treatment accorded journalism by both schools of thought and to show how culture became a productive analytical locus for considering journalism's cultural dimensions. While these dimensions were noticed by other disciplinary approaches to journalism, specific issues about journalism became necessary and constitutive from the perspective of cultural studies – its subjectivity of expression, the relativity and reflexivity that accompany action, the constructed nature of its meanings for events, the centrality of public engagement, the politics of its identity-building and the grounding and limitations of each of these premises in practice.

These tenets offer a wide-ranging analytical perspective that presumes that journalism works differently from the understanding favored by many of the more traditional academic approaches to it. First, cultural givens are thought to unite journalists in patterned ways with non-journalists, all similarly involved in diverse modes of cultural argumentation, expression, representation and production, suggesting as a starting point commonalities rather than differences between journalists and others like filmmakers, novelists and politicians. Second, variables used elsewhere in the academy to keep the centers of journalism distinct from its margins – rendering, for instance, journalism distinct from fiction, mainstream journalism distinct from tabloid journalism, journalists' verbal reports distinct from the visual images they use – are here repositioned as bridges connecting difference, consequently positioning journalism as a whole of disparate, often contradictory, impulses. The different tools of journalism, different kinds of journalisms and similarities between journalism and the world outside are brought together to illuminate the nuanced and textured character of journalism in more of its possibilities. And third, the cultural analysis of journalism views journalists not only as conveyors of information but as producers of culture, who impart preference statements about what is good and bad, moral and amoral, appropriate and inappropriate. Their positioning as the creators and conveyors of worldviews about how things work is linked with that of multiple publics, who make sense of the news in ways that reflect different identity formations.

It is no surprise, then, that this orientation facilitates the examination of facets of journalism that have not been examined readily in other scholarly perspectives. These include a worldview that underpins making sense of the world in certain ways, the inherent connections and disconnects between form and content, the often strategic but always changing relation between "facts" and symbols, the ways in which journalists work themselves into the news they provide, and the uneven and often unpredictable function of images, ideologies, collective memories and journalistic stereotypes. Even journalists' "vague" renderings of how they know news when they see it take on a decidedly nuanced flavor when seen as part of the larger constraints of meanings and symbols available beyond journalism. At the same time, those larger constraints do not figure into journalists' own presentations of self as much as do many analytical categories employed by other disciplinary perspectives. This is because the insistence here on meaning-making as a primary activity explicitly challenges two aspects of journalism's inquiry – the normative biases of much of existing journalism research and the professional aspirations and biases of journalists themselves. By definition, then, a cultural consideration of journalism negates the worldview that underpins much of traditional journalism research, journalists' professional ideology and the claim to exclusive status on which both are based.

The cultural inquiry of journalism thereby creates and proceeds from its own strategic dissonance. Conventional givens about journalism are intentionally suspended so as to address the practices, values and attitudes that go beyond those deemed relevant by either much of existing journalism research or reporters with professional aspirations. Productive examples might include the activity of reported.ly, Andy Carvin's crowd-sourced social media platform for covering breaking news in real time, or the development of speak2tweet in Egypt as a facilitator for public connectedness when the Internet was shut down. Cultural inquiry forces an examination of the tensions between how journalism likes to see itself and how it looks in the eyes of others, while adopting a view of journalistic conventions, routines and practices as dynamic and contingent on situational and historical circumstance. In the current digital moment – in which non-journalists and non-conventional journalists are treading on legacy journalists' longstanding territory and by and large receiving an unwelcoming reception – a fuller understanding of journalists' activity as dynamic and contingent could be particularly fruitful.

All of this suggests that the cultural study of journalism strategically and pronouncedly interrogates the articulated foundations for studying journalism and journalistic practice that seem to have been taken for granted elsewhere in the academy, offsetting the near-sightedness of journalism's inquiry. It moves beyond the presumption that journalism plays a "role everyone knows" of "afflicting the powerful . . . while comforting the afflicted" because it "severely limits . . . what sorts of questions can be asked about the news media in our society" (Allan, 1999, 2–3). It cuts through a false unity about journalism, regarding "what it is, what it ideally should be and the purposes it has in society" (Dahlgren, 1992, 1). Dissipating the information bias that has taken entertainment and pleasure as information's opposite and broadening journalism beyond the particular loci in which it has traditionally been examined, in much of this research scholars work against a narrow, "metonymic" conception of journalism that, in Dahlgren's view, has long accounted "for only a small portion of that which in a practical, empirical sense constitutes contemporary journalism" (Dahlgren, 1992, 7). In this regard, the cultural inquiry of journalism has done much to keep journalism's study in step with some of the more contemporary developments in the news, which have expanded without regard to the slower pace of change in journalism's study. This is particularly the case today, as the digital environment makes public engagement with the news as important as the information it provides. Thinking about news and journalism through the lens of culture is thereby valuable because it displays a pronounced interest in the transmutations by which journalists act as journalists, including the most recent challenges posed by the digital landscape.

And yet journalism remains fundamentally different from other sites of cultural analysis due to the fundaments of its own self-presentation – its predilection for facts, truth and reality, rather than subjectivity, relativity, engagement, construction and reflexivity. Journalism's presumed legitimacy depends on its declared ability to provide an indexical and referential presentation of the world at hand. Insisting on the centrality of reality, and on facts as its carrier, for maintaining a clear distinction between itself and other domains of public discourse, journalists claim a capacity to narrativize events in the real world that distinguishes them from other cultural voices, retaining an attentiveness to how things "really" happened as the premise by which journalism makes its name. Moreover, against this template rests a preoccupation with something called "truth." Although public recognition of journalists' capacity to reproduce truth has diminished in the contemporary era at the same time as platforms like Gawker and Storify are closing the gap between truth and experience by orienting more explicitly toward storytelling rather than some version of truth, the predilection for making truth claims still perseveres. This means that journalism's practices, conventions, breaches and standards – indeed, the very gauges by which its growth and stultification are measured – rest on the originary status of facts, truth and reality.

This reliance creates problems for journalism's cultural analysis, which by definition subjects these very phenomena – facts, truth and reality – to the sliding rules of relativity, reflexivity, construction, subjectivity and engagement. The complications surrounding journalism's reverence for facts, truth and reality extend too to germane aspects of its internal mindset. Journalists' professional ideology is offset by an insistence, common in cultural analysis, that the production of knowledge is always accomplished in the interests of either those who hold power or those who contest that hold. The current orientation toward multiple publics as a corrective to journalism's deficiencies, facilitated by the digital environment, is consonant with cultural studies, but it conflicts with a still-persistent assumption among journalists that journalism takes shape among journalists, not beyond them. Because much of cultural analysis privileges that which came before or that which rests outside a phenomenon as the explanatory impulse for examining the phenomenon itself, the indifference to contextual factors among most journalists and many journalism scholars undermines much of its cultural study. "Nothing disables journalism more than thinking that current practice is somehow in the nature of things," wrote Carey (1997b, 331), and there remains reluctance about drawing on contexts – historical, economic, ethical, moral, political – to explain journalism's internal trappings. As Glasser and Ettema (1989b, 20–1) contended long ago, "among journalists . . . news is not a theoretical construct but a practical accomplishment." Or, as Carey (1997b, 331) put it almost ten years later, "journalists do not live in a world of disembodied ideals; they live in a world of practices. These practices not only make the world, they make the journalist. Journalists are constituted in practice. So, the appropriate question is not only what kind of world journalists make but also what kinds of journalists are made in the process."

Thus, journalism poses a special challenge for cultural analysis. Unlike the modes of cultural argumentation favored by playwrights or the clergy, unlike the patterns of cultural production displayed on reality television or talk shows, and unlike the cultural similarities that bring together zombie films and romance novels, journalism remains constrained by its somewhat reified but nonetheless instrumental respect for facts, truth and reality. Criticized for remaining a bastion of positivism when relativity, subjectivity, construction, reflexivity and engagement have become in many quarters the more endearing tropes for understanding public expression, journalism's adherence to the facts, both real and strategic, and related reverence for the truth and some version of reality render it sorely outdated and out of step with academic inquiry of a cultural bent. And yet, were it to loosen its adherence to these foundational tenets, journalism would lose its distinctiveness from the other modes of cultural expression, argumentation, representation and production which frequently comprise the targets of cultural analysis.

How, then, is it possible to yoke the cultural study of journalism with a pronounced and explicit insistence on facts, truth and reality as part of journalism's own raison d'être? Is journalism simply an antiquated position of how to think about the world or does it reflect the limitations of cultural inquiry? More importantly, is there something that can be done within cultural studies so as to accommodate journalism's fuller study across more of its dimensions?

Cultural Studies and Journalism

The uneasiness with which cultural analysis encounters journalism's predilection for facts, truth and reality has been reflected in an ambivalence displayed toward journalism in cultural studies. That unevenness has been differently exhibited by the two main strains – US and British – of cultural studies scholarship, themselves loosely connected to the US and British experiences.

The long revolution by which cultural studies turned from an idiosyncratic, uneven study of culture in various academic disciplines into a recognizable and identifiable program with its own journals, departments and key figures has long been heralded as the birth narrative of cultural studies in both the US and the UK. Though not always articulated as such, within that birth narrative British cultural studies took over the helm of much of what came to be recognized as the default setting for cultural studies as it spread more globally (Hartley, 2003; Turner, 2011). Within the drive to legitimate cultural studies across time and space, stress points emerged and took hold, while emphases that were initially secondary or adjunct by nature blossomed gradually into semi-autonomous subfields: audience studies and ideology studies, for instance, were initially both integral parts of the field that took on independent status. With their development, complaints about the absence of recognition became a concern over recognition being shared with others, delaying a more complete recognition of the field as a legitimate arena of inquiry on its own terms (Nelson & Gaonkar, 1996). And thus, alongside its formidable growth, lingering points of neglect, misunderstanding and omission became embedded within the newly broadened default setting.

On the US side, journalism remained a fairly consistent area of inquiry. The invocation of early visionaries – Dewey, Park and Veblen, among others – led the way to the development of a strand of cultural studies concerned with problems of meaning, group identity and social change (Jensen & Pauly, 1997). Largely fashioned as what came to be called the "Illinois strand of cultural studies" led by James W. Carey, this school of thought saw a resident evil in social science's positioning as the preferred mode of knowledge in the American academy, identifying the critique of positivism as the charge for American cultural studies. Eschewing Marxism as the central problematic through which society was to be examined, the scholarship that developed here positioned the news media as conveyors of experience and shapers of broadly defined cultural systems. Journalism emerged as a key strain of resonance for thinking about how culture worked.

The work of Carey was central to weaving discussions of journalism into the larger social and cultural fabric, including concerns about politics, technology and the public. Carey's argument for the recovery of journalism as a cultural form rather than as a profession was mounted in numerous contexts, each of which demonstrated the complex nature of journalism's cultural world (Carey, 1969, 1986a, 1986b, 1989a, 2000). In Carey's (1997a, 11) view, a dialogic and normative side to journalism's cultural life "required a mode of understanding actions and motives, not in terms of psychological dispositions or sociological conditions but as a manifestation of a basic cultural disposition to cast up experience in symbolic forms that are at once immediately pleasing and conceptually plausible, thus supplying the basis for felt identities and meaningfully apprehended realities." Others at Illinois followed in Carey's path, such as Kreiling (1993), who already in the early 1970s used the African American press to address the shaping of middle-class identities. A second generation – comprising Carey's students such as Marvin (1983), Sims (1984), Mander (1987), Jensen (1990) and Connery (1992), among others – produced a substantial body of material in the 1980s and 1990s emphasizing journalism's meaning-making capacities. The work of Pauly (1988) and Steiner (1992) extended Carey's sensitivity to the internal view of journalistic practice to show how phenomena as varied as journalistic handbooks and discourse about key journalistic personalities served as boundary markers for the group.

This strain of cultural studies was implicit elsewhere in the academy. One early attempt to adopt a wide-ranging notion of journalism as culture, though it did not make the claim explicitly, was Manoff and Schudson's (1986) edited volume *Reading the News*. Marketed as a "Pantheon Guide to Popular Culture," the volume made clear that the professional prism of most journalists required tweaking, and it organized its discussion of culture's intrusion into news by adapting the fundaments of "doing a news story" – the "who, what, when, where, why and how" of public events – into categories for analyzing journalism's performance. Elsewhere, Schudson (1982, 1988, 1996, 2002) prodded open many givens of journalism scholarship by insisting on the cultural nuances of journalistic work, using narrative form as a reflection of identity or journalistic autobiographies to expose mindsets from different temporal eras. Eason (1984, 1986) elaborated how journalists shaped public events by focusing on the internal breaches within the journalistic community. Scholars such as Adam (1989, 1993), Reese (1990), Campbell

(1991), Bird (1992), Glasser and Ettema (1993, 1998), Zelizer (1993b), Hardt and Brennen (1995), Eliasoph (1988) and Barnhurst and Nerone (2001) all concentrated on the contingencies involved in newsmaking and on the fact that news was relative to the givens of those who engaged in its production. As time moved on, the list of scholars doing work with an eye turned to journalism's cultural dimensions continued to grow (Ehrlich, 1997; Meyers, 2002; Wahl-Jorgensen, 2002; Tenenboim-Weinblatt, 2008; Meltzer, 2010; Gilewicz, 2015; Han, 2016).

At the same time, this strain of cultural studies was not always recognized as such, particularly when compared to the spread of British cultural studies. Although the adoption of British cultural studies elsewhere was uneven, its potential recognition as a global field of inquiry was far more assured than that of its US counterpart, which at times was shunted from the conversation altogether (Stratton & Ang, 1996; Mariscal, 2001; Yudice, 2001). To wit: one 2003 discussion characterized US cultural scholars Carey, Katz and Marvin as distanced from the field, noting that "few would have identified themselves as practitioners of cultural studies" (Hartley, 2003, 102). Similarly, one much-cited mapping of the various geographic trajectories of cultural studies scholarship mentioned Carey and his progeny not at all (Maxwell, 2000, cited in Miller, 2006). The lack of recognition, despite the consistently vocal role that Carey and others took in identifying cultural studies as a field at least partially consonant with their own interests, marks a dissonance between the two strains of cultural studies (Carey, 1989b). Its persistence, discussed independently by Hardt (1986), Grossberg (1997) and Erni (2001), exacerbated journalism's precarious positioning in the larger domain of cultural study.

From the British side, the interest in journalism was not as steadfast. In the early days of British cultural studies, journalism and the workings of news were a key focus for work in the early 1970s from the Centre for Contemporary Cultural Studies (CCCS) in Birmingham, UK, and much of the groundbreaking work from the CCCS at that time explicitly involved journalism, usually in its hard news form. As British cultural studies emerged as a response to the formalism of Marxism and its resonance in literary theory, British scholars took as their mandate the elucidation of the conditions of the British working class.

Within this rubric, many of the early classic British texts on cultural studies based their groundwork on the news. CCCS director Stuart Hall was an early editor of the *New Left Review* and a frequent contributor to *New Times*, making it no surprise that his seminal essay "Encoding/Decoding" dealt with news as a stand-in for other modes of cultural production (Hall, 1980). Heralded as "a turning point in British cultural studies," the essay came to be widely regarded as the classic cultural studies formulation of the production–audience intersection, and its offering of audience decoding positions set the bar for considering different audiences for different content (Fiske, 1992a, 292). A similar generalizability greeted Hall's (1973) equally celebrated invocation of Barthes' (1967) work on the rhetoric of the image in his "The Determination of News Photographs." Both works, firmly situated in the analysis of journalism, were extrapolated to refer to a whole range of non-news texts; – for example, Brunsdon and Morley's classic study of *Nationwide* news audiences extended Hall's scholarship to become the primary initial text for thinking about a range of audience responses to different kinds of mediated messages (Brunsdon & Morley, 1978; Morley, 1980). This emphasis on the link between audiences and production can be seen as a precursor to later scholarship on the news that drew from cultural analysis but not necessarily cultural studies (Boczkowski, 2010; Anderson, 2013).

Other early work followed in this vein (Hall, 1972; Hall, Connell & Curti, 1976). Cohen and Young's *The Manufacture of News* (1973), labeled the "earliest 'standard' critical work on the media's construction of reality" (Turner, 1990), drew attention to symbolic construction by considering the patterns underlying journalism's treatment of crime and deviance and developing an understanding of the media's role in moral panics. *Policing the Crisis* and Hebdige's work on subcultural style all used the news as a background arrangement for thinking about more generalized modes of cultural production and the distribution of social and cultural power (Hall et al., 1978; Hebidge, 1979, 1988). It is no surprise, then, that one key initial text on the evolution of British cultural studies, Graeme Turner's *British Cultural Studies: An Introduction* (1990), used press photographs of Oliver North and Ferdinand Marcos to illustrate culture's broad workings. In one view, much of this scholarship was in effect "a defense of the importance of journalism" because, for one of the first times in British academe, it took the news media seriously (Hartley, 1999, 23).

A default regard for journalism was further echoed as British cultural studies extended to institutions other than Birmingham. A split in the English department at Cardiff University in Wales, UK (then University College Cardiff), created a new alliance that was tellingly titled the new school of "Journalism, Media and Cultural Studies." Under the auspices of its first head – former journalist Tom Hopkinson, also former editor of the *Picture Post* and the first journalism professor in the UK – the school produced celebrated cultural work on journalism by the mid-1970s. Coming from the Polytechnic of Wales, Fiske and Hartley (1978) were particularly renowned for advancing semiology as a way to read television and the news, invoking journalism as the default case for understanding cultural power, cultural production and the impact of culture and the media on audiences. The 1966 opening of the Centre for Mass Communication Research at the University of Leicester led to a groundbreaking study of the media's coverage of political demonstrations, which set the analytical parameters for thinking about journalism's role in shaping public events (Halloran, 1970). Even Philip Schlesinger's *Putting Reality Together* (1987), though not strictly aligned with cultural studies, followed the field's tenets in detailing the ideological constraints of news production. In one view, alliances of this sort constituted a "migration away from the imaginative system of modernity (literature) towards its realist textual system (journalism)," establishing what seemed to some as the obvious natural connection between cultural studies and journalism (Hartley, 2003, 49).

The recognition of journalism as a way of thinking about culture continued along a trajectory of culturally oriented scholarship. The early interest in journalism's cultural nuances, displayed in the work of Fiske and Hartley (1978), became for both scholars an ongoing address over the 1980s and 1990s to journalism's more populist dimensions (Fiske, 1988, 1992a, 1992b, 1996; Hartley, 1982, 1992, 1996). At the same time, others joined in: Dahlgren and Sparks, together and separately, twinned a consideration of journalism's cultural dimensions with those of citizenship (Dahlgren, 1992, 1995; Sparks, 1992; Dahlgren & Sparks, 1992), while the Glasgow University Media Group (1976, 1980) tackled the various image/text coordinates that made their way into the news. A long list of scholars during this time period – Cottle (1993, 1997), Schlesinger and Tumber (1995), Bromley and O'Malley (1997), Bromley and Stephenson (1998), Carter, Branston and Allan (1998) – investigated the intersection between journalism and inequities of class, gender, race and other indices of cultural identity. In each case, journalism was offered as a default case for understanding cultural power, cultural production and public engagement. Seen as "definite, if unlikely, bedfellows," the two remained inextricably aligned (Wark, 1997, 111, 179–85; Hartley, 1999).

This early linkage between journalism and cultural studies made sense, evolving from a certain shared commitment to the real world. While cultural studies tended to be fueled by political commitment, journalism's commitment tried to account for real-life events in a way that enhanced public understanding of the key institutional processes at work in everyday life – government, economics, education. Born of a lingering dissatisfaction with existing explanations for culture as it impacted on the real world, cultural studies tried to simultaneously mark life in and beyond the academy, and journalism offered valuable terrain on which to gauge its shape. The emphasis on power and discourse made journalism a natural setting for probing many of the issues relevant to cultural studies. In Hartley's (2003, 137–8) view, the disciplinary gaze of journalism and cultural studies was similar, licensing both to "explore the full range of the social, describe other people's lives, generalize specialist knowledge for general readers, interrogate decisions and actions on behalf of 'governmental' discourses of appropriate behavior (legal and ethical) and manageability (decision-making, policy), textualize the world in order to know it and communicate by appropriate idiom to target demographics."

Furthermore, the interest in citizenship and the rights and responsibilities of an informed citizenry rested at the foundation of both fields. As Turner (2000, 362) argued, both pursued "a common ethical project aimed at reinforcing the principles of citizenship and the development of the skills of critical literacy which underpin the ideals of a democratic press and a democratic readership." Hartley (2003, 138) pushed the point even further, noting that "journalism and cultural studies were in fact competitors in the social production of knowledge about everyday life," sharing an attraction to "the negatives of human life, the human cost of progress."

Yet as British cultural studies grew to embrace broader and more varied forms of cultural production in and out of the UK, journalism's attractiveness as an analytical venue of choice waned. In fact, journalism began to disappear from much of the work in British cultural studies published over the following decades. A brief overview of some of the key lexicons and central texts then published bears this out.

While the publication of lexicons denoting the key words or key concepts of cultural analysis took off from the late 1980s onward, the terms "journalism" and "news" rarely appeared in their indices (O'Sullivan et al., 1983; Brooker, 1999; Edgar & Sedgwick, 2007 [2002]; Bennett, Grossberg & Morris, 2005; Mikula, 2008). Some of the fattest cultural studies anthologies of the time – by Nelson and Grossberg (1988), During (1993), Baker, Diawara and Lindeborg (1996) and Shiach (1999) – did not mention news or journalism anywhere prominently. One anthology thoughtfully tracked the disciplinary intersections relevant to cultural studies (Miller, 2006, 12), but its long list of connections with what it called "an array of knowledges" – including sociology, anthropology, law, philosophy and archaeology – neglected to include journalism as a site of relevance. The reader by Grossberg, Nelson and Treichler (1992) offered sixteen thematic headings for the study of culture, none of which mentioned journalism, while Ferguson and Golding's *Cultural Studies in Question* (1997), heralded as the "most aggressive attack" on the field (Erni, 2001), also excluded journalism from its discussion. Even introductory texts attempting to lay the field's ground discussed journalism nowhere prominently (Brantlinger, 1990; McGuigan, 1992; Storey, 1993; Giles & Middleton, 1999; Tudor, 1999; Oswell, 2006). Some of these works did eclipse mention of journalism under discussions of the media writ large, but as Carey (1997b, 332) noted, "to confuse journalism with the media or communications is to confuse the fish story with the fish."

The uneven attention paid journalism has had its effect on journalism's cultural inquiry. On the one hand, scholarship migrated to those dimensions of journalism that were most distant from its pronounced sense of self – the tabloid, alternative newspapers, online relay, and over time reality television, comedians, satirists and user-generated content producers. To be sure, journalism's sense of self has never remained stable, and many journalists even today exclude certain platforms, like Gawker or *The Daily Show*, from the journalistic community. But though researchers produced a wealth of important scholarship on the kinds of journalistic engagement seen as antithetical to journalism's core – consider Langer (1998), Lumby (1999), Sparks and Tulloch (2000), Andrejevich (2003), Baym (2009), Jones (2009), Jarvis (2011) – they nonetheless reproduced a different kind of narrowness, providing a vision of journalism that was drawn on alternative lines which tended to eschew the conventional dimensions of news most closely promoted by journalists. In other words, while offering a valuable addition to journalism scholarship, this research unwittingly furthered the separation between conventional news and news of a different order – alternative, tabloid, oppositional and, after a time, collaborative, user-generated, satirical and comedic. Lost were the nuances that legitimated both as part of one world.

When articles on conventional news did appear, they were couched as if journalism were but one choice of many background settings aligned with "the media." Thus positioned, journalism lost its singular features, hidden as the uneven and often unarticulated target of discussions of gender representation, government censorship, or democracy and the public sphere. Accordingly, this view of journalism rendered it more similar to than different from other cultural platforms like cinema, TV and novels. While this premise had initially motivated journalism's cultural inquiry, it may have been too much of a good thing, for left relatively unexamined were the peculiarities connected to cultural authority that pertained exclusively or primarily to journalism, particularly its reverence for facts, truth and reality. Moreover, as other kinds of cultural texts – like soap operas, James Bond films or gaming – became available for analysis on the hitherto-disregarded margins of cultural production, journalistic settings began to look less interesting as platforms of an explicitly cultural nature.

All of this is not to say that journalism professionals themselves have welcomed the attention of cultural studies, as uneven as it has been. Problems between the two fields remain. When cultural studies targeted journalism as a viable analytical venue, it did so with the express aim of contextualizing its power and recognizing that journalism played an instrumental role in circulating powerful ideas about how the world worked. Thus, the scholarship that developed often had more to say about culture and cultural power, in general, rather than offering valuable insights with which journalists could continue to work as journalists. Particularly in areas where journalism's inquiry promoted turf wars over insufficient resources, the antipathy between the two camps was strident, as witnessed by the very public dispute between Australian journalism educators and cultural studies scholars during the late 1990s (Windshuttle, 1998; Hartley, 1999; Turner, 2000). The disaffection between the two areas became so pronounced that one South African scholar (Tomaselli, 2000), critically paraphrasing journalism educators, observed that cultural studies was "the central disorganizing principle in journalism education."

The uneven interest in journalism among cultural studies scholars seems to have come from numerous sources. In part, it derives from a critique of Enlightenment thinking and the lack of confidence in the emancipatory power of reason that increasingly underpinned much of cultural studies' mandate for looking at the real world. Journalism's persistent loyalty to modernism and to what Miller (1998) called "technologies of truth" kept it at odds with that worldview, with cultural studies scholars increasingly regarding journalism as unthinkingly supporting facts, truth and reality. In other words, journalism's god-terms were themselves seen by cultural studies scholars as troubling evidence of a somewhat blind devotion to a deity gone rotten.

The uneven interest also derives from journalism's powerful institutional status, now waning, which encouraged the examination of certain aspects important for critique – its establishment bias, its collusion with political and economic powers, its failure to provide ongoing independent investigation. Once these dimensions were identified, however, journalism as a whole tended to be abandoned by much of cultural studies as a worthwhile target of analysis. The less obvious – and seemingly less fruitful – routes for studying journalism's power and authority, such as the profoundly conflicted performances that emerge when power and authority begin to break down while a belief in facts and truth perseveres, drew less energized interest from many cultural scholars. Their reluctance to break apart the institutional presence of journalism persisted both because the power associated with that presence offered a rich target of analysis and because the picture that emerged when institutional presence dissipated was not as compelling for cultural studies.

Finally, the uneven interest in journalism also reflects fundamental differences over what counted as evidence. The positivism of journalism's inquiry and the concomitant attention to notions of facts, truth and reality all seemed to be at odds with cultural studies' examination of culture via its historical, social, political and economic contingencies.

Cultural studies' insistence on constructivism, reflexivity, engagement, subjectivity and relativity was ill matched to journalists' proclaimed invocations of distance, accuracy, balance and objectivity. Some of this may have derived from the problems associated with applying British cultural studies to the US context. As Hardt (1986) already warned in the mid-1980s, the appropriation of British cultural studies by US scholars facilitated the loss of its original political commitments because it modeled itself on circumstances different from those in the United States. Perhaps nowhere was this seen more clearly than in journalism's subsequent reduction to a world of marginal practices, popular auras and generalized otherness.

When combined, all of this made journalism, particularly its conventional dimensions, uninteresting for much of British cultural studies in its global spread. And yet we need to ask whether cultural studies took its subject of inquiry too much at face value. In defining journalism and its study on its own terms – that is, in adopting journalism's own self-presentation as indicative of what journalism is or could be – the nuances of journalism's own workings were simply left out of analysis. Rather than tackle the unpronounced, illogical and dissonant sides of journalism – the contingencies and contradictions involved in the constant, often tiresome and frequently fruitless negotiations to yoke popular and official, private and public, lay and professional, dishonest and truthful, and biased and balanced impulses – cultural studies scholars closed their eyes. They catered to official journalism's pronounced sense of itself, which articulated an adherence to each of the latter choices and disavowal of each of the former, and thereby consolidated a reason for largely dismissing the study of journalism as a whole. The uneven response in cultural studies toward journalism played to the modernist bias of its official self-presentation, a presentation that promoted the informative, civic and rational sides of its practices over its pleasure-inducing, entertaining or simply affective ones. Playing to this side of journalism, however, recognized only part of what it was.

For much of cultural studies, then, conventional journalism was examined through the near-sighted eyes adopted by much of the academy. In many of its forms, journalism became codified as an extension of the sciences and the scientific model of knowledge production, oppositionally positioned to cultural studies' dominant scholarly stance of criticism and sometimes parody. Cultural studies reduced the impact of positivistic knowledge about journalism to a whisper and missed the nuances of the journalistic world, failing to realize that in so doing it neglected to examine much of what contradicted journalists' own parameters of professional practice. Yet these nuances were worth addressing precisely because they rested underneath the articulated core of how journalism saw itself.

It is not surprising that this tendency generated divergent interpretations, which echoed the differences between British and US cultural studies: some saw it as representative of a mode of knowledge that sought "nothing less than to rethink received truths and remake inherited frameworks of explanation," becoming a "symptom of widespread doubt and disillusion about the contriving ability of inherited truths to command assent" (Hartley, 2003, 2). Others saw it as buying into "a moral and political vocabulary that [was], if not anti-democratic, at least insufficiently sensitive to the ways in which valued political practices intertwine with certain intellectual habits" (Carey, 1989b).

Thus, the originary premises of journalism and much of cultural studies positioned them at odds with each other. One believed in truth, reality and facts; the other in construction, reflexivity, engagement, subjectivity and relativity. Though some scholarship tried to bridge the two arenas – notably Epstein (1973), Tuchman (1978a) and Gitlin (1980) – a fundamental difference remained. Driven by different notions of what counted as the compilation and interpretation of evidence, it concretized a broader dissonance in journalism's cultural study that underscored the difficulty, if not impossibility, of figuring out *how* to study the cultural dimensions of a phenomenon that made claim to an indexical and referential presentation of the world at hand.

What has been the effect of such unevenness? The erratic interest of cultural studies in journalism de facto encouraged its gradual transformation into material that looked more like the stuff of contemporary journalism education and echoed the aspirations toward journalistic professionalism, resembling less a set of practices of symbolic expression in the public domain and more a narrowly conceived intersection of political and economic interests. The insects of positivism – reality, truth and facts – were exterminated from analysis with a kind of self-righteous zeal. For a time, and in considerable scholarship, journalism retreated to the territory from which it had originally come – the largely atheoretical world of journalism education, training and professionalization, and a valorization of its capacity to account for the true, real and factual. The centrality of "facts" and a migration toward positivistic knowledge as a way of tamping a fundamental self-doubt about journalism as a profession became obstructions to cultural studies' interest in journalism, and journalism's claims to the real – invoking objectivity, balance, accuracy, distance – muted the capacity of many cultural scholars to consider the nuances of journalistic practice. Largely unrecognized as a cultural form in itself, it became positioned as "the other," codified by much of British cultural studies as uninteresting territory and resembling in growing degree what had originally been claimed of it by journalism educators. This meant that, despite auspicious beginnings, scholarship on journalism in much of cultural studies came to look less like other kinds of cultural phenomena and more like the material in which cultural analysis had no interest. In other words, many cultural studies scholars led the way of those who took journalists and journalism educators too much at their word, reducing the cultural inquiry of journalism to a marginal interest, a sideshow.

Admittedly, there have been exceptions to this trend, and they have happily grown over time, facilitated in part by a digital environment that values the subjectivity, reflexivity, relativity, construction and engagement which cultural studies had long championed: Storey devoted a chapter to the press and magazines in his overview of the field, *Cultural Studies and the Study of Popular Culture* (1996), and, in *Inventing Popular Culture* (2003), began his discussion of globalization with a consideration of television news. Lacey (1998) used a text from the *News At Ten* to illustrate institutional analysis in his reader on media studies and visual culture. Pearson and Hartley (2000) opened their volume *American Cultural Studies: A Reader*, with reprints of politically progressive journalistic articles and followed them up with a chapter specifically addressing journalism. Durham and Kellner (2001) addressed the status of newspapers in different cultural contexts, while Brants, Hermes and van Zoonen (1998) dedicated an entire section to "the ethics of popular journalism." Hartley's (2002) key concept reader, *Communication, Cultural and Media Studies*, included terms relevant to news and journalism, and his *A Short History of Cultural Studies* (2003) tracked the status of journalism alongside an interest in larger questions of cultural power. Updated versions of popular readers and introductory texts expanded their discussion of journalism (O'Sullivan et al., 1994; Barker, 2000; Stokes, 2012; Burgett & Hendler, 2014). Both Lewis (2002) and Rodman (2014) wove journalism and news into their discussions of cultural studies. By the 2000s and 2010s, then, journalism had a sturdier footing in cultural studies texts. It is in keeping with this trend that new introductory texts to the field now often use journalism as a primer from which to consider the contours of ideology (Ryan, 2010).

No less important, the cultural work that did address journalism has helped to broaden its inquiry in ways that now impact the very core of journalism's study, extending the parameters of what is now recognized as news. This includes forms of news that remain distant from its pronounced conventional core – talk shows, reality television, guerrilla television, video activism, user-generated content, collaborative forums, satire and comedy (Boyle, 1992; Shattuc, 1997; Rowe, 1999; Friedman, 2002; Andrejevich, 2003; Allan, 2006; Baym, 2009; Jones, 2009; Ristovska, 2016). It also includes work on the intersection of journalism and various indices of identity, including race, class, gender, sexual orientation and ethnicity (Gabriel, 1998; Ainley, 1998; Gross, 2002; Stabile, 2006; Meyers, 2013; Yazbeck, 2016), as well as work on the variegated practices that emerge from the intersection between journalism and different institutional settings (Waisbord, 2000; Ouellette, 2002; Fox & Waisbord, 2002; Deuze, 2007; Williams & Delli-Carpini, 2011; Sender, 2012). This suggests that even if the attention has been uneven, it has still made its presence felt.

On the Future of Journalism and Cultural Studies

The epistemological uneasiness at the core of journalism and cultural studies' coexistence is one that asserts itself whenever dissimilar areas of inquiry come into close contact. The question remains how to engage that uneasiness in a way that maintains the integrity of both journalism and cultural studies.

Since the mid-1990s, we have heard repeated calls to reinvigorate the charter of cultural studies, in both its British and US forms (Frow, 1995; Stratton & Ang, 1996; Wright, 1998; Bennett, 1998; Striphas, 1998; Couldry, 2000; Berube, 2009). They have been accompanied by bids to better address the merger of cultural studies and journalism (Hartley, 1999; Turner, 2000, 2011; Tomaselli, 2002; Deuze, 2005; Harrington, 2012). While, by and large, I have not addressed the lingering problems in journalism education and resistance among journalists aspiring to professionalism regarding the value of a cultural perspective on the news, the trajectory I trace here suggests that journalism continues to offer a litmus test of sorts regarding the future of cultural studies. Repositioning journalism at the forefront of cultural studies inquiry could help cultural studies on its own road to academic maturation, by which cultural studies might become more of a full-fledged discipline of knowledge, rather than one positioned in opposition to surrounding fields of study.

Nearly thirty years have passed since Meaghan Morris (1988) first voiced her concerns about the banality of cultural studies. Her prediction – that cultural studies would find it hard to resist making similar pronouncements about dissimilar cultural objects simply because the existing analytical template worked so well – seems to have been borne out when thinking about journalism's neglect. Journalism remains one area of study that can help cultural studies navigate its own middle age with grace and generosity. A re-examination of the tenets of cultural studies might not only accommodate journalism more fully but also serve the mission of cultural studies more effectively.

More than just a difference of perspective keeps journalism and cultural studies at an uncomfortable distance from each other. Cultural studies' capacity to instantiate itself as a field of knowledge secure in its own claims and in what counts as evidence is key here. Its maturation into a field with sufficient self-knowledge to grow depends on its capacity to expand and include a phenomenon like journalism rather than shrink to keep it outside. There is enough evidence to suggest that it can do so. Even if journalism partly challenges some of cultural studies' own claims, it also displays an often reluctant recognition of the need to broaden its own boundaries.

It is possible that cultural studies has neglected incorporating journalism at its core because doing so would necessitate a close look at the limitations of cultural inquiry. It may be time, then, for cultural studies to confront the problems embodied by journalism and the limitations such problems suggest for the study of any longstanding inquiry into the real. Recognizing that there is a reality out there and that, in certain quarters, truth and facts have currency does not mean letting go of relativity, subjectivity, reflexivity, engagement and construction. In fact, the current focus within journalism on user-generated content and digitization highlights the need to embrace both. It merely suggests yoking a regard for them with an increased cognizance of the outside world.

Section III

New Ways of Thinking About Journalistic Practice

Cues for Considering New Ways of Thinking About Journalistic Practice

With Jennifer Henrichsen and Natacha Yazbeck

The complexity and constant change that mark journalism require an understanding that accommodates its flux as notions about journalism are themselves transforming. Because any conceptualization of journalism, no matter how comprehensive, is always delimited by existing knowledge, those invested in thinking about the news need to keep one ear to the ground in order to track change as it occurs.

Any attempt, though, to expand the boundaries of what qualifies as journalism is inevitably impacted by largely unarticulated but strictly observed hierarchies of what matters. In a manner befitting an environment that came of age alongside modernity, a long string of binary opposites structures much intellectual engagement with the news. Driving the high ground of aspirations concerning what journalism should be, it forefronts a set of impulses about the large contours of journalistic work that tend to be positioned in oppositional ways to each other – certainty/ambivalence, information/expression, dispassion/engagement, impartiality/perspective, professional standard / cultural mindset. Expected largely to come at the expense of each other rather than exist in continual and often messy negotiation, such impulses are given black-and-white contours that sidestep the more blended hues of everyday life. They set up parameters for thinking about journalism in ways that play to its exceptionalism, positioning the news as more separate from the world than derivative of it.

The binary opposites for thinking about the news haunt those who practice journalism. Splitting journalism's populations and practices into more and less valuable categories, they often unknowingly penetrate the default assumptions that drive the most intricate details of journalism's workings by creating unnecessary and often erroneous dichotomies. The tools and settings of newsgathering are differently assessed – hard/soft news, mainstream/tabloid, opinion/fact, word/image, old/new media. Similarly, the demographics of journalistic labor are delegated into categories – executive/staffer, male/female, white / person of color, senior/

junior, full-time/freelancer – while the platforms for journalistic work are differently privileged – traditional/digital, single/multiple issue, neutral/ partisan. Some topics of news are seen as automatically worthy of coverage while others require discussion – crisis/calm, race/gender orientation, politics/style, blue collar / white collar crime. As problematic as these dichotomies are on their own, they are additionally at issue because they fuel public expectations of the news more generally.

Not surprisingly, then, these binaries extend to environments beyond journalism that are tasked with helping to shape its intersection with the world. They privilege expectations of which platform is responsible for overseeing journalism – nation-state/global overseer, political/military, commercial/regulatory – and they fashion journalistic linkages with politics – consensual/dissident, left/right, liberal/conservative. They forefront the important notion of journalistic protection but not necessarily across the board – some/all journalists, established correspondent / local fixer, legacy journalist / user-generated content provider, bylined reporter / translator.

Writings on late modernity suggest that such demarcations are ill equipped to address current conditions. A predilection for binaries in thinking about what kind of news works most effectively renders journalism increasingly unresponsive to the world. Rather, a more fluid, less linear, less steady set of impulses drives change in journalism, and in so doing it unsettles the insistence on binaries that make us favor stability and permanence even as conditions necessarily change on the ground.

The 2003 war coverage of Iraq, for instance, stands both as a construct of what journalism is, or can be, and as an exemplar of the inter-institutional dependence that has long masqueraded as an autonomous institution. Embedded reporting ended up highlighting the perils of too much proximity to the troops, while unembedded journalists lacked physical protection and access to military personnel. The either/or dichotomy of embeds versus unilaterals manifested in different coverage and consequences on the ground.

At the same time, external forces regularly shape what we think we know about journalism by supplying evolving definitions that involve, protect and constrain those in the field. Though the UN had long labeled journalism a profession, more currently it sees journalism as a function: the UN Human Rights Committee said in its General Comment No. 34 that journalism is "a function shared by a wide range of actors." Yet, despite evolving proclamations of the belief that journalism plays a special role in society – providing the public with information to allow for the exchange of ideas, opinions and information – a climate of impunity continues to flourish for those who harm journalists worldwide. Alongside well-articulated aims of protection, often violence and censorship prevail, including self-censorship by journalists who wish to live unharmed. This sustains journalists as a test case in an environment invested in freedom of expression and the plurality of ideas – as exemplified by UN Resolution 1738, which recognized that the issue of protecting journalists in armed conflict is urgent and important.

This section draws from the belief that the either/or categorizations within much longstanding scholarship on journalism are insufficient to fully articulate the internal and external contours of journalistic practice. The section argues that journalism exists as part of the world on which it reports, drawing on recognizable cultural forms and tropes and on broader modes of expression, representation and interpretation. It thus forwards a number of alternative prisms for thinking about journalistic practice, few of which have been typically part of the prescribed sense of self among journalists. Included here is an embrace of interpretive community over profession, of culture over impact, and of image over word. Considered against events as wide-ranging as Watergate, McCarthyism and 21st-century combat – touching upon the first Intifada, 9/11, the war in Afghanistan, the 2003 Iraq War, the killing of Osama bin Laden, the Arab Spring and the current Syrian conflict – it raises the possibility that thinking anew about the news necessarily involves first thinking anew about its changing landscape of practice.

9

A Return to Journalists as Interpretive Communities

What does it take to make a community? Since American journalists were first identified as an upwardly mobile group, the academy has looked at reporters as members of a professional collective. Seeing journalism as a profession, however, has restricted our understanding of journalistic practice, causing us to examine only those dimensions of journalism emphasized by the frame through which we have chosen to view them.

Here I return to an alternative way to conceptualize community, other than through the profession. As I first articulated in 1993, I argue here that journalistic discourse, informal contacts, narrative and storytelling are all important dimensions of journalistic practice that are eclipsed by general discussions of professions. Yet each of these domains helps to unite journalists, and together they point to the need for an alternative frame through which to examine why they act as they do. By accounting for different dimensions of journalistic practice, this frame suggests that we consider journalism not only as a profession but as an interpretive community, united through its shared discourse and collective interpretations of key public events.

Seeing journalists as an interpretive community calls for examining the proliferation of journalistic discourse around key moments in the history of newsgathering as a means of understanding the shared past through which journalists make their work meaningful. Applying this frame to two central events in American journalism – Watergate and McCarthyism – helps us to consider how journalists have productively used discourse about both to generate meaning about journalism and address elements of practice overlooked by the formalized cues of the profession.

The Dominant Frame: Journalists as Professionals

Seeing journalism as a profession has long helped us to understand its trappings, but what being professional means has never been clear.

Sociologists view occupational groups as "professional" when they show certain combinations of skill, autonomy, training and education, organization, codes of conduct, licensing and service orientation (Moore, 1970). "The profession" also provides a body of knowledge that instructs individuals what to do and what to avoid in any given circumstance (Larson, 1977; Gouldner, 1979; Freidson, 1986). Journalists are thought to gain status through their work by acting professionally, exhibiting predefined traits of a "professional" community and generating an ideological orientation toward the production of work that journalists view as necessary to maintain their communal boundaries (Janowitz, 1975; Larson, 1977; Johnson, 1977; Freidson, 1986). As such, the commonality of journalists is determined by a shared frame of reference for approaching work-related tasks, even if it sways across space and time. As Waisbord (2013, 3–4) notes, professions eclipse clear definitions. The result of ongoing "semantic squabbles," professionalism is at once a "conceptual category, a normative ideal, a narrative that reveals how journalism intersects with economic, political, social and cultural forces that shape media systems."

How does journalism benefit from its affiliation with professions? Since the early 1900s, when a scattered and disorganized group of writers was able to consolidate via agreed-upon standards of action (Schudson, 1978; Schiller, 1981), the notion of a profession has been used to give reporters a sense of control over work conditions, wages and tasks. Journalists' ability to decide what is news, often in conjunction with non-journalists in upper management, has been regarded as the expertise that distinguishes them from non-reporters. Already by the 1920s, then, "media professionals had themselves adopted the notion that professionals are more qualified than their audience to determine the audience's own interests and needs" (Tuchman, 1978b, 108).

This idea has been used within news outlets to safeguard against change, loss of control and possible rebellion (Soloski, 1989), rendering the ideological orientation behind determining such expertise part of journalism's claims to authority. Making claims to professionalism not only generates an aura of authoritativeness based on a specific attitude toward accomplishing work, but it also suggests that reporters ought to approach reporting in certain ways – as objective, neutral, balanced chroniclers (Schiller, 1981). Historically, adopting that stance helped to offset the dangers inherent in the subjectivity of reporting and to secure protection from legal and public backlash, at the same time as it allowed journalists to call themselves professionals (Tuchman, 1972; Schudson, 1978).

Although contemporary academics tend to evaluate journalism through the frame of the profession, it is in fact unevenly realized in practice. Various types of journalistic activity, for example, are not addressed in most formal discussions of journalism as a profession, which, in Waisbord's (2013, 6) terms, are "grounded in the constant blending of occupational and normative definitions." For instance, practicing reporters rarely admit their *usage of constructions of reality*, seen among critical observers as a common way of presenting the news (Tuchman, 1978a; Schiller, 1981; Goldstein, 1985). They instead stress their adherence to notions of objectivity and balance, both of which are upheld by professional codes (Gans, 1979). How and why journalists use professionalism as a way to conceal the constructed nature of their activities thus remains under the radar, as do the ways in which "being professional" becomes a codeword for hiding the elaborate mechanisms by which reality is constructed. The failure to address this common part of newswork has allowed it to flourish uncritically.

The *informal networking* among reporters has been similarly overlooked in formal discussions of journalism. Sociologists argue that journalists work via a distinct sense of their own collectivity (Tunstall, 1971; Roshco, 1975; Tuchman, 1978b; Gans, 1979; Fishman, 1980; Roeh, et al., 1980), favoring horizontal over vertical management, and collegial over hierarchical authority (Blau & Meyer, 1956; Tuchman, 1978a; Gans, 1979; Fishman, 1980). So-called "pack journalism," media pools, briefings, membership in social clubs and other ways that reporters absorb rules, boundaries and a sense of appropriateness about their actions without ever actually being informed of them by superiors are more the rule than the exception, and suggest that informal networking may be as responsible for consolidating journalists into communities as the highly standardized cues promoted by notions of professional practice. Yet acting in ways that build upon informal collectivity does not figure in discussions of journalism as a profession, leaving multiple questions unanswered. How, for instance, does journalistic community emerge through cultural discussion? How do journalists accomplish work by negotiating, discussing and challenging other journalists? What role does consulting regularly with one's colleagues about story ideas or modes of presentation play? How do journalists benefit by recycling stories across media? And how do journalists navigate their depended-on explanations provided by members of other institutions – legal, medical and military, among others?

Practices of *narrative and storytelling* among reporters have been similarly overlooked for their power to coalesce community. Though journalists tend to discuss among themselves issues connected with narrative and storytelling – the craft of "how to tell a news story," how to mark fact from fiction or how to accommodate the different stylistic conventions of news presentation (Berryhill, 1983; Evans, 1991; Farhi, 2007; Truong, 2015) – admitting to non-reporters a dependence on narrative practice seems to imply a lack of professionalism. Despite extensive and continuing scholarly work produced on precisely this issue (Darnton, 1975; Schudson, 1982; Carey, 1986a; Campbell, 1991; Johnson-Cartee, 2004; Fulton, Husiman & Murphet, 2006), the general premise persists that good storytellers make for bad journalists (Bird & Dardenne, 1988).

And yet, ignoring narrative in discussions of journalism comes to no good effect, for doing so generates, among other things, ambivalence over narrative practice that produces outrage over the fact–fiction distinction. Though related scandals on the topic go back far in time, most recently they involved *Rolling Stone*'s gang rape story of 2014 and NBC anchor Brian Williams' fabricated tale in 2015 of his helicopter being brought down by fire years earlier in Iraq. Williams was subsequently put on unpaid leave and demoted, yet brought back to revive one of NBC's less successful platforms. Journalism's unevenness in dealing with the issue – in one irate observer's eyes, Williams "broke the first tenet of journalistic ethics by trampling the truth . . . and yet all he suffers is indignity and a pay-cut" (Hallock, 2015) – underscores the degree to which existing frames for understanding journalism have not clarified the impact of storytelling practices. And yet how journalists ascribe to themselves the power of interpretation, how certain favored narratives of events are adopted across news outlets and how narrative helps reporters neutralize less powerful or cohesive versions of the same event are worth considering. A narrative's repetition in the news may have as much to do with connecting journalists with each other as it does with audience comprehension or message relay (Zelizer, 1992b).

And, finally, journalism simply does not require all of the *trappings of professionalism.* Unlike classically defined professions such as medicine or law, in which professionals legitimate their actions via socially recognized paths of training, education and licensing, these trappings have only limited relevance for practitioners. Journalists tend to avoid journalism textbooks, journalism schools and training programs, and codes of journalistic behavior (Johnstone, Slawski & Bowman, 1976; Weaver & Wilhoit, 1986; Becker, Fruit & Caudill, 1987). Training is considered instead a "combination of osmosis and fiat," with largely irrelevant codes of ethics and a routine rejection of licensing procedures (Goldstein, 1985, 165), and media credentials have limited value, functioning, in Halberstam's view, like a "social credit card" (cited in Rubin, 1978, 16). Journalists also are unattracted to professional associations, with the largest – the SPJ – claiming only 9,000 members nationally in 2015. The trappings of professionalism, then, have not generated a coherent picture of journalism,

No surprise, then, that the journalistic community does not fare well when seen as a profession. In some cases, in tending to ignore, downplay or at best remain ambivalent about its trappings, reporters run the risk of being labeled "unsuccessful professionals" and are faulted for promoting "trained incapacity" (Tuchman, 1978b, 111). As one research team suggested, in a much-repeated refrain, "the modern journalist is *of* a profession but not *in* one . . . [T]he institutional forms of professionalism likely will always elude the journalist" (Weaver & Wilhoit, 1986, 145). Existing discussions of journalism as a profession thereby offer a restrictive way of explaining journalistic practice and community, with the organization of journalists into professional collectives providing an incomplete picture of how and why journalism works.

This does not mean that the collectivity represented by the profession does not exist among journalists. For we know that journalists function as a community, even if they do not organize solely along lines of the profession: "The boys in the bus" or "the eyes in the gallery," for instance, both signal a shared frame of reference. It does suggest, however, that we need another approach to account for shared practice, other than formalized professional cues. We need a frame that might explain journalism by focusing on how journalists shape meaning about themselves.

The Alternative Frame: Journalists as an Interpretive Community

An alternative way of conceptualizing journalistic community can be found by looking beyond journalism and media studies to anthropology, folklore and literary studies, to the idea of the "interpretive community." Hymes (1980, 2) defines the interpretive community as a group united by its shared interpretations of reality. For Fish (1982, 171) in literary studies, interpretive communities produce texts and "determine the shape of what is read." Members of interpretive communities display certain patterns of authority, communication and memory in their dealings with each other (Degh, 1972). They establish conventions that are largely tacit and negotiable as to how community members can "recognize, create, experience and talk about texts" (Coyle & Lindlof, 1988, 2). In some cases, they act as "communities of memory," groups that use shared interpretations over time (Bellah et al., 1985). These views suggest that communities arise less through rigid indicators of training or education – as indicated by the frame of the profession – and more through the informal associations that build up around shared interpretations.

While the idea of the interpretive community has been most avidly invoked in audience studies, where local understandings of a given text are arrived at differently by different communities (Morley, 1980; Radway, 1984; Lindlof, 1987), communicators themselves can be examined as an interpretive community (Zelizer, 1992b, 1993a). Journalistic reliance on some sort of collective knowledge has long been implicit in journalism studies: Park's (1940) view of news as a form of knowledge, Carey's (1975) definition of communication as ritual and a shared frame for understanding, O'Brien's (1983) ideas about news as a pseudo-environment, Schudson's (1988, 1992) studies of how journalists construct knowledge about themselves. Like these studies, a view of journalists as an interpretive community locates unity in discourse, which becomes a marker of how journalists see themselves.

Examining journalists in this way addresses their legitimation through channels other than the cues provided by the profession. Journalists come together by creating stories about their past that they routinely and informally circulate to each other – stories that contain certain constructions of reality, kinds of narratives and engagement in informal practice. Through channels like informal talks, professional and trade reviews, professional meetings, autobiographies and memoirs, interviews on talk shows and media retrospectives, they create a community through discourse. Viewing journalism as an interpretive community thus depends on different cues than do assumptions that journalism is a profession: cues that are central to journalists themselves. In particular, the shared past through which journalists discursively set up and negotiate preferred standards of action – the work of collective memory – hinges on the recycling of stories about certain key events. Journalists become involved in an ongoing process by which they create a repertoire of events of critical importance from the past that is used as a standard for judging contemporary action. By relying on shared mnemonic interpretations, they build authority for practices not necessarily recognized by views of journalism as a profession.

While journalists consolidate themselves as an interpretive community when discussing everyday work, the value of the interpretive community as an analytical frame can best be seen by examining journalistic discourse about key incidents in the annals of journalism. Such targets of interpretation, through which journalists mark their authority, constitute critical incidents, or what Levi-Strauss (1966, 259) called "hot moments" – phenomena or events through which a society or culture assesses its own significance. These critical incidents do not necessarily exist "objectively," but, following de Certeau (1978), are projections of the individuals and groups who give them meaning in discourse, selected as a platform on which to air, challenge and negotiate boundaries of practice. For instance, wartime reportage might be viewed against that of earlier wars, as when the 1991 Persian Gulf War was judged against reporting of World War II and Vietnam (Reporting a New Kind of War, 1991; Valeriani, 1991; Zelizer, 1992b). Discourse about critical incidents offers a way to address concerns at issue for the journalistic community through collective memory, and professional consciousness emerges at least in part around ruptures where the borders of appropriate practice need renegotiation. For contemporary reporters, such discourse creates standards of professional behavior against which to evaluate daily newswork.

Discourse thus tends to proliferate when unresolved dimensions of everyday newswork need redress. One such set of practices surrounds the journalist's relation to time. Journalists are constituted (or need to be) in what might be called "double-time" (Bhabha, 1990, 297). Journalists constitute themselves not only as the objects of the accounts they give but also as the subjects of other accounts that elaborate on their earlier reportage. Thus, while traditional scholarship examines journalists largely on the basis of their original reportage and not its shared recollection years later, viewing journalism as an interpretive community accommodates double-time positioning as a necessary given. It offers a way to analyze journalists' authority for critical incidents through the simultaneous accommodation of two temporal positions, thereby enlarging the boundaries of their collective authority and the community it engenders. These narrativized interpretations of double-time operate in both local and durational modes.

Local Mode of Interpretation

Reporters establish themselves as qualified to discuss a critical incident through what I call the local mode of interpretation. Here reporters discuss the importance of one target of interpretation from a localized and identified contemporaneous temporal viewpoint. Critical for providing reporters with discursive markers that uphold their own professional ideology, journalists' authority is assumed to derive from their presence at events and the ideology of eyewitness authenticity (Zelizer, 2007). In producing metaphors like "eyewitnessing," "watchdogs," "being there," practices of discovery or "being on the spot," reporters establish markers that not only set up their presence but also uphold its ideological importance. To borrow from Bhabha (1990, 297), reporters assume the role of "pedagogical objects" – "giving the discourse an authority that is based on the pre-given historical event."

The local mode of discourse can be either positive or negative, but rarely both. Although journalists might discuss initially the pros and cons of any given change in standards of practice, they quickly reach consensus about what it means. Already at the time of occurrence, then, a critical incident is filtered for its value in setting up and maintaining standards of action. In cases of professional accomplishment, highly laudatory discourse gives reporters the opportunity to discuss the incident across news

formats, copy the practice it embodies and emulate the reporters responsible. Awards and prizes abound. References to the incident appear in
trade magazines and become the topic of professional meetings, as journalists become highly strategic about consolidating associations with it.
In cases of professional failure, the local mode of discourse displays less
of these imitative practices, and there are no prizes or awards. But this
does not mean that the critical incident is ignored. Rather, reporters set
themselves up in a mitigated association with it, sometimes emphasizing
how they observed but did not participate, referencing other journalists who were involved or simply marking their own membership in the
community. The incident is discussed at professional meetings and trade
reviews, but not as a marker of positive accomplishment.

Regardless of how positively or negatively a critical incident is initially
encoded, the local mode of discourse displays an initial tightness of interpretation. Because it is predictable and in keeping with journalists' explicit
claims about practice, the local mode of discourse helps consolidate the
boundaries of journalists as an interpretive community. Association,
presence and "being there" are instrumental in making larger authoritative claims that stretch across time. For this reason, change – as embodied
by the incident – is either embraced and accepted, or denied and rejected,
but treated discursively in a unitary fashion. Thus, as a critical incident
unfolds, journalists tend to interpret it unidimensionally because they see
it collectively moving the community in one way or another.

We need only consider how often journalism provides meta-discourse
that evaluates how its coverage of a particular event or issue is faring.
From US presidential election reporting to coverage of Brexit in 2016,
publics have been treated to ongoing commentary about how well
journalism was doing. This reliance on local modes of interpretation
underscores the instrumentality of discourse in maintaining collective
boundaries.

Durational Mode of Interpretation

What is not yet explicit is how journalists use the authority of local discourse to transport themselves to a second interpretive mode – the durational. Journalists extend their cultural authority by invoking a second
temporal position that allows them to compensate for not being there.
In assessing incidents that occurred many years preceding their incor-
poration into discourse, they position the critical incident in collective
memory. Here we see reporters as recollectors or historians. Often they
use the authority culled from their local placement within an incident to
expound on its more general significance. Thus, they create their own

history of journalism by making critical incidents representative of some greater journalistic dilemma or practice.

In this view, covering the Kennedy assassination becomes a platform to consider problems associated with live televised journalism (Zelizer, 1992b). The reporting of Vietnam becomes part of a larger discourse about war reportage, while the coverage of Hurricane Katrina stands in for the reportage of natural disaster. More recently, *Rolling Stone* revisited the ramifications of falsifying news after scandal was associated with the magazine, while multiple US news outlets looked back upon their coverage of the Syrian conflict as emblematic of new terrain for news coverage. Reporters use durational discourse to generate a continuum of contemporary reportorial work against which they can situate themselves. They discuss a given incident as a marker in this continuum by connecting it to other incidents that both preceded and followed it. The journalist becomes, to use Bhabha's (1990) terminology, a performative subject engaging in a process of signification that uses the past as data to generate contemporary accounts. *Washington Post* reporter David Broder (1987, 15), for instance, defined his journalistic career as stretching from "the Watergate case, which banished the President from government, to the Janet Cooke case, which tarnished the reputation of journalism's highest prize." James Reston (1991, ix) talked about a stretch of time – "from Pearl Harbor in 1941 to the Gulf War in 1991" – as years that for him "didn't always make sense but always made news."

Because journalists are involved in making their own history and reference its sequencing in books, films and talk shows, the incident becomes a marker about journalism. Reporter Sam Donaldson (1987, 68) framed his book on TV news around the Vietnam War and Watergate, because "these two events . . . convinced many of us that we should adopt a new way of looking at our responsibilities." At issue here is a larger durational continuum into which journalists can place an incident and against which the whole of journalism can be appraised. Starting one's overview of reporting with the Teapot Dome scandal or with Vietnam, for instance, suggests highly different views of what is relevant to the community at large in determining contemporary standards of action.

Unlike in local discourse, journalists in durational discourse tend to differentially associate themselves with a critical incident, loosening the tight interpretations initially accorded it. If journalists at first praised the incident, some might continue to do so but through different technological lenses. Thus, television reporters might interpret Vietnam or the Kennedy assassination differently from radio reporters, while online platforms would evaluate their coverage of Middle East conflict in the 2000s differently from newspapers. In cases of professional failure, journalists might appreciate the incident's pedagogical value even if at the time it occurred they found it problematic. Though changing one's vantage point across time may have less value in pronouncedly partisan news environments, these broad subcultures of interpretation within the larger community – subcultures that allow for the systematic tailoring of a key incident over time – suggest that more than one mnemonic interpretive community may evolve. Interpretation as it unfolds therefore becomes an index of a wider networking of forces, interests and capabilities, and when discourse is examined, its complexity presents itself for analysis. The view of journalism as a profession highlights the local mode of discourse at the expense of the durational. But the uncritical way in which the latter has flourished as the work of collective memory raises important questions about its role in maintaining community for journalists.

Watergate and McCarthyism

The interplay between local and durational modes of interpretation plays itself out systematically across negative and positive markers of journalistic accomplishment. Watergate and McCarthyism offer two examples whose interpretations have collectively changed over time, and in both cases these changes enabled journalists to shape their recollections so as to address larger discourses about the then-existing state of American journalism.

Consider Watergate. From a local perspective, Watergate appeared to be a glaring success, one that reporter Peter Arnett called "a glorious chapter in American journalism," alongside one of the "darkest in American history" (Newsmen Hailed Over Watergate, 1973, 28). Observers experienced a "Watergate honeymoon" (Adamo, 1973, 152). Reporters talked of Watergate in professional meetings and media columns, as numerous prizes and awards marked what seemed to be a turning point for journalism, earning the *Washington Post* a Pulitzer Prize and Daniel Schorr three Emmy Awards. Inspired by the lore of Deep Throat, professional forums, like the Freedom of Information Committee at the Associated Press, vigorously debated the journalistic issue made most relevant – how to protect sources (Ayres, 1972, 42). Guidelines appeared on how best to use anonymous sources (Pincus, 1973), and journalists celebrated what appeared to be a marked rise in their employment (Newsmen Hailed Over Watergate, 1973). News outlets initiated programs that utilized extensive sourcing techniques, such as ABC News' *Closeup* – begun in September of 1973, it coincided with the expansion of investigative staffs in news platforms (Sesser, 1973). Though many of these issues remain unresolved even today, growth and confidence were everywhere. It was, in reporter Mary McGrory's (1973, 437) view, a "time not to be away."

Central to it all were the *Washington Post*'s Carl Bernstein and Bob Woodward. In 1973 they earned nearly every award available to journalists, including the Sigma Delta Chi Award, the Worth Bingham Prize, the Newspaper Guild's Heyman Broun Award, the Drew Pearson Prize and the George Polk Memorial Award. Bernstein secured his own listing in the periodical guides under the entry "journalists," and one trade story on Walter Cronkite introduced the piece by apologizing "with all due respect to the *Washington Post*'s Bob Woodward and Carl Bernstein" (Powers, 1973, 1). CBS executive William Small predicted that the story, as Woodward and Bernstein had reported it, would become "the story of the decade," and he applauded the rare circumstances that had propelled the two reporters "so clearly ahead of the rest of us in covering that story" (cited in Bernstein, 1973, 45). As Dan Rather commented, no one "in journalism can applaud themselves [for their coverage] but Woodward and Bernstein" (cited in Sesser, 1973, 15). The "heroics of Woodward and Bernstein," he observed (Rather, 1977, 340), turned journalism into a "glamour profession."

Yet Woodward and Bernstein's names also persisted beyond the local interpretive mode. During the 1970s they wrote two best-selling books on Watergate (Woodward & Bernstein, 1974, 1976) and appeared as the focus of the popular movie *All the President's Men*. The story of the journalistic coup began to displace the story of the nation's electoral and judicial processes: one commemoration was titled "All the President's Men – and Two of Journalism's Finest" (All the President's Men, 1976). Stories about reporting Watergate became a regular part of stories about Watergate itself: typical in this regard was one retrospective of Watergate, the political scandal, that was accompanied by a smaller piece about Watergate, the journalistic story (Martz, 1992). By 1977, half of all the Watergate listings in the periodical guides concerned Woodward and Bernstein. Dan Rather (1977, 296), who devoted some 50 pages of his autobiography to the topic, argued that Watergate was in effect a story of the televised hearings – hearings that "said volumes about the Congress. And about television. Both systems worked." Through these two reporters, then, the story of Watergate was moved from a particularistic discussion of sourcing techniques to a discourse about journalism in its broadest contours. Tellingly, this durational story often bore little resemblance to the event as it had unfolded.

Investigative journalism became the pivotal point of the durational discourse that ensued. Defined by the late 1970s as a craft with "Watergate popularity" (Behrens, 1977, xix), investigative journalism topped the list of desired journalistic practices, and discussions centered on anecdotes about Deep Throat and *All the President's Men* (Leslie, 1986; Mauro, 1987). The narrative had enduring appeal over the decades that followed. Marvin Kalb maintained that the reporting represented "a milestone of American journalism" (cited in Feldstein, 2004). As recently as 2012, the *Guardian* ran an article about investigative journalism under the telling title "Journalism Once Had Woodward and Bernstein: Now It's Guns for Hire" (Preston, 2012). Even in cases where Watergate's effect on practice was questionable, editors and reporters altered the narrative to fit the recollection: Schudson (1992, 110) relayed how the *Atlantic Monthly* framed an article about journalism education as upholding the Watergate myth, even though the article's author had not intended the connection.

From a durational perspective, then, the event was reframed so as to acknowledge a broader temporal perspective on journalism. Reporters saw Watergate not only as suggesting new practices of sourcing or newsgathering but as broadly instrumental for setting up standards of investigative reporting (Armstrong, 1990; Banker, 1991; Langley & Levine, 1988; Rather, 1977, 238–96). Called "the most crucial event in the rise of investigative reporting" (Broder, 1987, 141), the "most intense story I've ever covered" (Donaldson, 1987, 61), and a marker of a "new degree of respectability" for the anonymous source (Schorr, 1977, 179), journalists were lavish with their praise. All of this made it easy to claim that Watergate remained a "proud moment in the history of American journalism" (Broder, 1987, 365), even though evidence now suggests it was Vietnam, not Watergate, which pushed reporters to be more aggressive in their reporting (Schudson, 1992).

As befits durational discourse, however, there was also a critical side to the collective interpretations that prevailed. With time, the appeal of the narrative dimmed for many. Journalists wondered whether Watergate had actually changed journalism or had just highlighted the atypicality of Woodward and Bernstein (cited in Schudson, 1992). While early warnings to that effect had been relegated to side-bars – one reader's letter in 1973 had called the *Quill*'s adulation of Watergate "excessive" (Watergate Bacchanal, 1973, 6) – reporters began increasingly to question the association between journalism and the scandal (Sesser, 1973). Journalists were criticized for having uncovered little of the story on their own (Epstein, 1974). Watergate's impact was challenged, as exemplified by an *Esquire* article entitled "Gagging on Deep Throat" (Branch, 1976). By the late 1980s, even Bernstein admitted that Watergate had not had the hoped-for effect on journalism (cited in Schudson, 1992, 121).

Implicit here were concerns as to whether the incident had introduced new standards of action that were unattainable. One *ASNE Bulletin* (Press After Nixon, 1974, 9) in late 1974 predicted that Watergate would demonstrate that "the American press oversold itself on its adversary role." That same year the *Columbia Journalism Review* warned that the press would overreach "in the pride, or even arrogance, that may come with power. In the self-congratulation about Watergate, there has been perhaps too much assertion that only journalists know what is best for journalists" (Press and Watergate, 1974, 1).

David Broder (1987) complained that reporters at Washington briefings had adopted an overly prosecutorial style to their questions. Anxiety over the inability to meet so-called "Watergate standards," which involved renegotiating the boundaries of investigative journalism within the more general parameters of "good" reporting, continued to be reflected in the coverage of numerous other scandals: one 1990 trade headline proclaimed: "Iran-Contra: Was the Press Any Match For All the President's Men?" (Armstrong, 1990, 27). Over the following decades, invoking "gate" as a suffix to denote scandal saw widespread usage: Billygate, Iraqgate, Troopergate, Donutgate, Gamergate, Closetgate and Murdochgate are but a few of the more salient examples. Invested in evaluating the broader impact of Watergate on practice, this interpretive work complicated the initial unidimensional surge of interest in Watergate at the time it was taking place. And even today, the skepticism over its narrative entrenchment has continued, where it was called "one of the most highly mythologized episodes in the history of journalism" (Cook, 2012; Himmelman, 2012).

These patterns of recollection suggest that, years after the event, journalism was better able to appraise Watergate, both positively and negatively. Doing so made it possible to position Watergate within a continuum of journalistic practice that rendered it, regardless of its accountability to real-life events, a representative incident of the heights and limitations surrounding investigative reporting. This was not accomplished through a local mode of interpretation, but required the durational mode to mnemonically position the critical incident in place.

Do similar distinctions between local and durational discourse exist surrounding a negative critical incident – McCarthyism? In 1986, some 30-odd years after the event, the *Columbia Journalism Review* defined coverage of McCarthy as a "journalistic failure" because journalists had remained more "accomplice than adversary" (Boylan, 1986, 31). It was, recalled Broder (1987, 137), a time when reporters felt "personally and professionally debauched by the experience."

But this was not how McCarthyism was appraised initially. At first, reporters almost seemed to humor McCarthy and his cronies. Headlines like "Busy Man" (1951, 26) or "Dipsy-doodle Ball" (1951, 21) suggested that they did not take him as seriously as they might have. Once developments became more than just a humorous side-bar, reporters generally wanted no part of the incident and acted like it was a non-story. Framed as a "battle of the files" rather than a battle with the press, only a near fist-fight between McCarthy and Drew Pearson won widespread coverage in 1950 (Battle of the Files, 1950, 16). There were no prizes, no awards, no emulation of the practices used to cover the Wisconsin senator. Rather, McCarthyism served to mark the vulnerability of objective reporting. As Ronald May of the *New Republic* wrote in 1953, "For decades the American press has worshipped the god of objectivity. This seemed to keep voters informed until the invention . . . of the big lie [which by current reportorial standards] . . . will be reported straight" (May, 1953, 10–12). Almost no mention was made of McCarthy in the professional and trade literature, and one of the first indications that he had become a force to be considered in journalism came at the end of 1951, when the main organ of the American Society of Newspaper Editors, the ASNE *Bulletin* (Should Tass Reporters, 1951) debated whether Tass reporters in the US should be curbed. Even more telling, in 1955 the ASNE voted McCarthy the second most overplayed story of 1954 (Second-Guessing, 1955, 1). All of this suggests that journalists were slow to recognize the impact this story would have on American journalism.

This is curious given the debates about interpretive reporting that pro-liferated at the time. In numerous trade columns and professional meet-ings, reporters fell on both sides of the fence, preaching "objectivity" or "interpretation" to each other (Christopherson, 1953; Lindstrom, 1953; Hamilton, 1954). Oddly enough, McCarthy was not initially mentioned; only one article obliquely referenced him as "Senator McThing" (Markel, 1953, 1). Instead, the value of interpretive reporting was linked to reporting the Korean War. And while journalists sporadically addressed the incident – Edward R. Murrow's exposes in 1954, Drew Pearson's increasingly biting columns, Herblock's cartoons – their voices joined the fray too infrequently and too late to have a lasting influence. As James Reston (1991, 227) recalled, "it wasn't until 1954 . . . that I was able, along with many other colleagues in the press, to take a stiffer line." Few journal-ists made McCarthyism a story about journalism, at least not at the time.

This changed, however, in durational discourse, when journalism itself became a fundamental part of the McCarthy story. There, reporters embedded tales of the period within a larger discourse about interpre-tive reporting. Within that discourse, reporters underscored the value of having experienced McCarthyism, even if they had not personally done so. Comments were often apologetic, as in James Reston's (1991, 222) comment that "no journalistic memoir would be complete without an attempt to explain, however painful, the role of the press during McCarthy's anti-Communist crusade." Recalling that the McCarthy era had given him his "first test as an editor," a test that he "didn't handle well," he remembered being stunned when the "best congressional reporter we had" was attacked by McCarthy, who screamed in the Senate that the newspaper was employing a former member of the Young Communist League (Reston, 1991, 225–6). It was no accident that Reston turned his narrative recounting of that incident into a moral lesson for the larger community, for the damage inflicted by McCarthy in this case was contextualized via the larger threat to the authority and well-being of journalism.

In durational discourse, journalists did not view the reporting of McCarthy positively, but they offered various justifications of their relationship to the incident. Needing to frame what had happened in a way that would allow for the change demanded by journalistic failure, journalists tended to mitigate their association with the incident after the fact – quoting other reporters rather than themselves, positioning them-selves as representative of whole cadres of reporters, emphasizing instruc-tional value regardless of negative impact. For instance, David Broder (1987, 138) framed his recollections against the words of United Press International (UPI) correspondent John Steele, who said "there was very little opportunity in those days to break out of the role of being a record-ing device for Joe," and of Charles Seid of the *Washington Star*, who said "he felt trapped by our techniques. If [McCarthy] said it, we wrote it." James Reston (1991, 227–8) admitted how "intimidated (the press corps felt) much of the time . . . with the exception of Ed Murrow every-body came out of the McCarthy period feeling vaguely guilty." Richard Rovere (1984, 100) remembered that he was "one of the first writers in Washington to discover what in time became known as McCarthyism."

Durational discourse, then, was differentiated by a range of mitigated associations with the incident, associations once removed from respon-sibility. Positioning themselves as distanced observers and colleagues to the entrapped – journalists born from the experience but not of it – was instrumental because it cemented an association with a different kind of post-McCarthy reporting: in contrast to the objective recounting that had ensnared reporters covering McCarthy, the interpretive report-ing that arose following the McCarthy era was seen as desired practice (Bayley, 1981, 219). McCarthyism provided an example of what *not* to do as a reporter. Its value, then, by definition, needed to emerge in dis-course – not at the time of McCarthyism's unfolding but at the time of its retelling.

In other words, journalists reframed the incident within a continuum of journalistic practice that stressed the value of interpretive report-ing. David Broder (1987, 137–9) held McCarthy responsible for setting up the limits of so-called "objective" reporting and starting an era of interpretive reporting. McCarthy forced the "leading journalists of the time and their colleagues to reexamine how they were operating, the codes that guided their work" (Broder, 1987, 139). Eric Sevareid complained that covering McCarthy's "exposés" of American Communists revealed the insufficiency of "our flat, one dimensional handling of news" (cited in Broder, 1987, 138). One former journalist claimed that "covering McCarthy produced lasting changes in journalism," in that it took "a performance [that] spectacular . . . to move the guardians of objectivity to admit that the meaning of an event is as important as the facts" (Bayley, 1981, 85). Others saw the incident for its technological value: Daniel Schorr (1977, 2) claimed that it taught him about television's impact. Here again, journalists utilized the incident as a marker in durational discourse that often had little to do with the initial discussion of what had happened. Moreover, it often obscured journalists' own susceptibility to McCarthy, exacerbated by considerable participation in the anticommunist Cold War consensus (Bayley, 1981). In a sense, then, the value of McCarthyism increased over time, fulfilling a pedagogic function for journalists who invoked it in their discourse years later. It was transformed from an uncomfortable experience into a lesson well learned, again regardless of its accountability to real-life events. This narrative perseveres even today, echoed most recently in discussions of the coverage given Donald Trump, 2016 Republican contender for US president: "McCarthy's rise was abetted," journalist Lou Cannon (2015) observed, "as Trump's has been, by press coverage that took outrageous claims at face value." As became clear once the race for presumptive US presidential nominees intensified in the US electoral campaign (Zelizer, 2016b), US journalism had been there before.

What does this suggest? Thanks to the two modes of interpretation, journalists are able to consolidate authoritative evaluations of critical incidents in the news by valorizing them, regardless of how problematic they might have been initially. As Schudson (1992) demonstrated in his study of Watergate, the event's impact has more to do with the carrying power of the recollection than with the definitive changes it brings about in practice. In the best of cases, reporters can celebrate an incident because it upholds the professional ideology of eyewitnessing. But when it does not meet expectations at the local mode of interpretation, journalists have a second chance at making things meaningful. This leap into collective memory means that they are able to employ a temporal perspective that evaluates events differently from how they first transpired.

This second chance at interpretation that is afforded by the work of collective memory suggests that journalistic discourse extends the authority of the journalistic community beyond that suggested by the frame of the profession. Through durational discourse, reporters are able to compensate for their own dual temporal positioning, despite the fact that their professional ideology accounts for their presence only at the time of an incident's unfolding. In establishing authoritative views of what happened long after it took place, they generate contemporary standards of action for other members of the interpretive community.

The forcefulness of these two interpretive modes surrounding journalists' relation to time raises critical questions about the far-reaching ability of reporters to establish themselves as interpretive authorities, both past and present. It points to the possibility that journalists exercise similar license in building authority for and through other practices not accounted for by traditional views of journalism. Equally important, it underscores the bias of understanding journalism only in terms offered by the profession. For without a frame that validates the examination of discourse unfolding over time – in informal exchange, memoirs, news-clippings, social clubs and the proceedings of professional forums – a fundamental platform by which journalists create community eclipses attention. These pages suggest that discourse is critical in this regard for it helps journalists structure recollection according to evolving agendas and sets up ever-changing standards of action by which journalists can conduct themselves.

Discourse and the Interpretive Community

It is a well-known truism among reporters that journalism is but a first rough draft of history. That assumption suggests that journalism ends where history begins, and that as time passes reporters yield to historians in taking over authority for the message. But this examination of journalists' discourse suggests that in fact reporters do not necessarily yield their interpretive authority to historians, and that journalists regularly engage in collective memory, using multiple temporal points in discourse to maintain themselves in double-time. Examples abound. The very practices of updating news stories online or as events unfold in real time constitute a temporal return to the event after its first unfolding. Similarly, institutional attempts to reappraise earlier foibles or understatements – reconsiderations of journalism in a post-Snowden moment or recaps of the coverage of terror in an age dominated by Islamic State – are productive reminders of how double-time allows journalists to claim discursive authority even when they missed doing so the first time around.

What does this suggest about journalistic community? The swells of journalistic discourse around each target of interpretation underscore the centrality of discourse for journalists. The proliferation of discourse about Watergate and McCarthyism shows that reporters regularly use conversation to generate meaning about journalistic work, and through that discourse they set standards of evaluation to appraise journalistic coverage writ large. Discourse is particularly instrumental when it challenges the reigning consensus surrounding journalistic practice, and in this way it facilitates journalistic adaptation to changing technologies, changing circumstances and the changing stature of newswork. While these are not the only critical incidents relevant to US reporters – reporters today might cite events like the Weapons of Mass Destruction debacle, the Snowden information leaks or the Drone Papers on The Intercept – the centrality of discourse here points to the consolidation of journalists not only into a profession but also into an interpretive community. They come together not only through training sessions or formal meetings, but also through stories that are informally repeated and altered as circumstances facing the community change. The collective discourse from which such a community emerges may thus be as important in understanding journalism as the formalized cues through which journalists have traditionally been appraised. This does not mean that other professional communities, such as doctors or lawyers, do not do the same. Nor does it mean that the journalistic community is not concerned with professional codes – only that it works through much of its response to newsmaking through collective discourse.

Daniel Schorr (1977, vii) once offered the view that reporting is "not only a livelihood, but a frame of mind." This discussion has addressed how that frame of mind is set and kept in place. Recognizing journalists as an interpretive community depends on the proliferation of discourse about events and circumstances that are instrumental in establishing standards of appropriate practice. This view suggests that journalism does not need to be coded as overly folkish or unprofessional. Rather, it is the profession as a dominating frame that makes it appear so. By viewing journalists also as an interpretive community, such folkishness might be coded equally as a tool of empowerment or as an indicator of untrained incapacity. And understanding that empowerment may help us better understand how and why journalists create their own history of journalism, and how and why they use that history in the relay of news.

10

Reflecting on the Culture of Journalism

Journalism is a world of contradiction and flux, held in place by those with central access and stature while challenged by those on its margins. Since journalism's beginnings, it has been shaped by outliers. A long list of luminaries, including Charles Dickens, Samuel Johnson, George Orwell, Ernest Hemingway, André Malraux, Martha Gellhorn and Joan Didion in the West, all made clear that who is a journalist and what constitutes journalism remain categories to be challenged on craft, professional, moral, political, economic and technological grounds. Today, the challenge has been taken up by individuals assumed to have even less traditional credentials, primarily because the challenge they pose is too close to be considered with perspective: from blogger/journalist Glenn Greenwald and data guru Nate Silver to Julian Assange of Wikileaks, a list of "as ifs" in the world of journalism shows yet again that we still have not found a way to embrace all of journalism's internal messiness and flexible contours. Embarrassingly, hundreds of years into its consideration, we still reference journalism in ways that are limited, narrow and by definition incomplete, preferring instead what Peter Dahlgren (1992) long ago critiqued as a metonymic grasp of the phenomenon. Much about this situation, suggested first in 2004, remains the same. As news scholars, we can do better.

Seeing journalism through the lens of culture offers one way to do that. The construct of culture offers a mode of repairing the longstanding neglect of journalism's contradictions while attending to the flux of its territory. Had there been a more productive way to account for the culture of journalism, the journalistic work of Dickens and his long list of cronies, arguably among the more interesting journalistic personalities, might have expanded the boundaries of what counts – or not – as journalism. Previously and presently considered outliers such as political cartoonists, tabloid reporters, satirists, photojournalists, fixers, stringers and bloggers might all have been given at least qualified membership in the club at the time of their emergence. For recognizing journalism as a culture – a complex web of meanings, rituals, conventions and symbol systems – and seeing journalists, who provide different kinds of discourse about public events, as its facilitators offers a way to think about the phenomenon by accounting for its changing, often contradictory, dimensions. By definition, then, the culture of journalism provides a mode of thinking about journalism more broadly by following the contours of its internal variations.

Culture as a Construct

Thinking about journalism through the construct of culture is a notion derived from various academic focal points. They include the sociology of culture, constructivism, the analysis of symbols and symbolic forms, ethnography and scholarship in cultural history, cultural criticism and cultural studies, all of which orient to culture as a beginning point for understanding complex phenomena. In different ways, each arena has drawn scholars toward culture as an analytical locus – by extension making journalism one of its venues.

An emphasis on culture invites the consideration of different sides of the journalistic world from those common to conventional news scholarship. Key here are the collective codes of knowledge and the belief systems by which journalists are presumed to make sense of the world, in an approach which has its roots in early work in humanistic sociology (Park, 1925, 1940; Berger, 1963), symbolic interactionism (Blumer, 1969) and cultural anthropology (Geertz, 1973; Lukes, 1975). Each points to the utility of using culture as a way to understand a phenomenon like journalism, both as a frame of mind and as patterned conduct. Work on Marxism and cultural criticism (Williams, 1978, 1982; Eagleton, 1995), combined with the two separate strains of cultural studies in the UK and the US (Hall, 1973; Hartley, 1982; Carey, 1986a), lends a pragmatic focal point to journalism's study, making central the grounding of subjective expression, constructed meanings, identity building and public engagement.

Implicit in what Park (1940) identified as the collective knowledge that journalists need to function as journalists, the prism of culture has over the last few decades begun to surface in an increasing number of scholarly considerations about how journalism works (Schudson, 1991; Dahlgren & Sparks, 1992; Allan, 1999; Barnhurst & Nerone, 2001; Hannerz, 2004; Hanitzsch, 2007; Mellado et al., 2012; Hanusch, 2014). That scholarship links the complex symbols, rituals, conventions and stories that drive journalists with the larger world in which journalism takes shape, and it surfaces in productive ways when journalism operates less effectively than hoped for. When journalism must navigate internal and external tensions simultaneously, it becomes particularly attuned to articulating, debating and often renegotiating the contours of its collective identity.

But culture has not been the most obvious prism through which journalism can be understood. Instead, four other constructs have inhabited the foreground of journalism's understanding – journalism as a profession, an industry, an institution and a craft. Each has brought with it particular vantage points that emphasize some aspects of journalism and minimize or fail to notice others.

Seeing journalism as a profession, for example, targets the learned values, beliefs and practices by which journalists are constituted as professional beings. Professionalism – its standards and cues for appropriate and inappropriate activity – provides a normative and occupational terrain against which the everyday performance of journalists can be judged (Waisbord, 2013), and it laces those evaluations with subjunctive aspiration. Alternatively, invoking the culture of journalism as a prism for understanding that same activity takes it on more indicative, grounded terms that are internally negotiated by and among journalists. It presupposes a wide range of internal and external conventions that identify practices as journalistic but without the honorific aura attached to "being professional." By definition, this opens journalism's contours to activities that go under professionalism's radar – venues such as activism or alternative media like Indymedia, opinion-driven formats like political satire, blogs and cartoons as well as forums on journalism's margins like late-night comedy and reality television.

The industrial prism for thinking about journalism targets the large-scale mechanistic, bureaucratic and technical processes by which the news is set in place. This perspective often focuses on efficiency, where it considers the problems generated by failing newspapers, an eroding and ageing audience, media concentration and convergence or dwindling economic profit (Picard, 2002). Seeing journalism as culture considers those same largely economic impulses while addressing the dimensions of journalistic practice that they often realign. By focusing on those aspects of work that have little to do ostensibly with the workability of the news industry, the prism of culture directs attention to the viability and integrity of journalistic activity, which comes to the forefront regardless of whether or not it has impact on the survival of either a specific news outlet or the industry as a whole. The very persistence of pack journalism, for instance, is a journalistic convention that rarely works for the good of the industry but it helps journalists do their work.

Seeing journalism as an institution focuses on its role in the large-scale rendering of power in society. In particular, the prism of journalistic institutions tends to consider the larger institutional environment, addressing how adjacent institutional settings of the market and government help shape that of journalism (McChesney & Nichols, 2010). Invoking the prism of culture, in contrast, targets how journalistic practices, routines and conventions take on meaning internally for and among journalists who live in institutional settings. In this view, seeing journalism as culture considers practices that are good for journalists but potentially prob-lematic for their institutional setting – sourcing routines, for example, or practices related to securing an individual reporter's physical safety.

Finally, focusing on the craft of journalism tracks the skills and quali-ties inherent in doing journalism that are most relevant to journalists themselves – writing well, exploring, being autonomous, developing a news-sense (Adam, 1993). The culture prism embraces these aspects of craft while situating them in a larger context that accounts for external exigencies as well. Doing so facilitates connections between internal mind-sets about how the world works and the external arrangements by which social life is set in place. The institutional routines produced to accommodate the lore of having a "nose for news" is one example.

The prism of culture thus takes shape by bridging centers and margins. Variables that traditionally keep certain aspects or types of journalism distinct – hard news versus soft, editorial versus fact, feature versus report – are here repositioned as links across difference. Differences in journalistic tools, practices and kinds of journalism, as well as differences and similarities between journalism and the external world, are brought together here in an attempt to illuminate more about the phenomenon than accomplished thus far. This consequently positions journalism as a whole that embraces multiple dynamic and often self-contradictory impulses.

Three givens about journalism as culture are worth considering. They all revolve around fundamental, though not mutually exclusive, ques-tions of definition:

- What is the culture of journalism?
- Who inhabits the culture of journalism?
- What is the culture of journalism for?

Such questions come to the fore particularly when journalism is situated in crisis. It is then that thinking about journalism through the construct of culture becomes particularly valuable.

The first phase of the 2003 war in Iraq offers a productive context for considering these questions. Then-prevalent public discourse about the US media and the war concentrated on how and why journalistic cov-erage fell short, not only in contesting the dominant narrative of entry into the war but in aspects of its coverage. In large part, such appraisals were framed by invoking the four foregrounded constructs mentioned above – journalism as a profession, industry, institution and craft. Thinking about US journalism through the prism of culture, however, can provide a more nuanced understanding of what happened and of how news typically unfolds during the first stages of war.

What is the Culture of Journalism?

More than just reporters' professional codes of action or the social arrangement of reporters and editors, the culture of journalism references a complex and multidimensional lattice of meanings for all those involved, "a tool kit of symbols, stories, rituals and world views, which people use in varying configurations to solve different kinds of problems" (Swidler, 1986, 273). Allowing for a wide expanse of journalistic activity, the culture of journalism by definition embraces impulses that can be counter-productive, contradictory and contrary to the supposed aims of what journalism is for: its inability to remain impartial, its problems with authority, its unexpected lapses into satire or irony. Culture recognizes journalism's various moments of creation and revision, with all of their problems, limitations, contradictions and anomalies, giving equal credence to the informal and formal, high and low, unarticulated and articulated, implicit and explicit, and contradictory and coherent. In effect, this means that seeing journalism through a cultural lens strategically and pronouncedly interrogates the articulated foundations for journalism and journalistic practice that may be taken for granted elsewhere in the academy.

The culture of journalism travels the uneven road of reading journalism against its own grain while giving that grain extended attention. It both sees journalism through journalists' own eyes, tracking how being part of the community comes to have meaning for them, and queries the self-presentations that journalists provide. Emphasizing "the constraining force of broad cultural symbol systems regardless of the details of organizational and occupational routines" (Schudson, 1991, 143), the culture of journalism moves decidedly in tandem with, but in opposition to, the pronounced and conventional understandings of how journalism works. Undercutting the sense of self that conventional understandings of journalism have eschewed regarding news practitioners and their position in the world, culture assumes that journalists employ collective, often tacit knowledge to become members of the group and maintain their membership over time (Goodenough, 1981). Drawing from what Robert Park (1940) called "synthetic knowledge" – the kind of tacit knowledge that is "embodied in habit and custom" rather than that which forms the core of formalized knowledge systems – this forces attention to the cues by which journalists think about journalism and the world. It also presumes that what is explicit and articulated as that knowledge may not reflect the whole picture of what journalism is and tries to be. In particular, seeing journalism as culture allows for a wide range of attributes not included in other longstanding constructs for thinking about the phenomenon.

And yet many aspects of this textured frame for understanding journalism are not reflected in assessments of how journalism operates. Perhaps nowhere was this as obvious as in the beginning of the 2003 war in Iraq, when much of the first draft of US journalistic coverage of Iraq was evaluated instead in line with notions of journalism as a profession, industry, institution and craft. These views, which primarily reflected normative and subjunctive aspirations of what journalism should be doing, did not engage enough with what unfolded on the ground. The professional lens primarily concentrated on the degree to which journalists had or had not been able to do their job impartially, accurately and with balance. The industrial lens tended to track the degree to which news outlets successfully met the logistical and organizational challenges of covering war. The institutional lens largely justified the close tracking of national sentiment among US reporters. And the craft lens focused in large part on embedding practices. Nowhere, however, were these prisms brought together in an attempt to more fully consider how journalism changes in the early stages of war in conjunction with unfolding circumstances.

This is key, for changes and adaptations centrally shaped journalism during the early stages of the war. It is in this sense that seeing journalism as culture – as a setting that operates through shared reliance on meanings, rituals, conventions, symbol systems and consensual understandings – enables much of the early coverage of the Iraq war to be understood.

By and large, journalists struggled to make sense of the war in ways not consonant with prevailing sentiments about newsmaking. This was particularly evident when the primarily mainstream US news corps was impacted by the political margins on both sides of the political spectrum. On the one hand, the voice of the political right was magnified. As the war proceeded, Fox News surpassed CNN as the top-rated cable news channel, raising questions about what kind of journalism much of the US public wanted. Although many journalists distanced themselves from its kind of news, labeling it derisively "the Fox effect" or the "Fox formula" and ridiculing its "opinionated news with an America-first flair" (Rutenberg, 2003a, B9), its popularity lingered nonetheless. Already during the war's early days, Fox News provided twice as much coverage as did any of the US broadcast networks (Media Monitor, 2003) and was watched avidly by a marked percentage of the US public. By mid-2004, its still-high popularity left an unepleasant taste for many journalists who had to navigate its increasingly mainstreamed voice.

On the other hand, the political left also forced journalism to rethink definitions of its own culture. The ascent of Al Jazeera, a satellite network then based in Qatar, not only created a presence that drew journalistic attention to aspects of the story not usually covered by western news, but also broadened the repertoire of practices by which US war coverage would be implemented. Multiple practices, begun at Al Jazeera, were adopted for US media use as the war pushed on, despite the fact that they initially raised concerns about violating codes of professional behavior.

First among these were Al Jazeera's initially contested displays of video footage of wounded US POWs and dead bodies of coalition forces. Critiqued widely in March of 2003, by late 2004 similar images were being shown regularly across western news media. Similarly, the display of pre-taped videos by key figures on the Iraqi side, a practice largely begun by Al Jazeera during the war in Afghanistan when it showed video tapes of Osama bin Laden to wide-ranging critique, also became a far more widespread practice during the coverage of the Iraq War. Finally, by mid-2004, beheading videos from Iraq, parts of which were shown first on Al Jazeera, were later picked up and displayed by the western news media. In each case, practice migrated from the so-called "margins" to the center, affording a different answer to the question: what is the culture of journalism? Dismissing them as unprofessional was an unsatisfactory response to what was transpiring, as the practices' widespread adoption attested.

Technology also drove new questions about the culture of journalism during the war. At the forefront of the available prisms for considering journalism because it was unrealistically glorified by the news industry, technology drove predictions that the war would become online journalism's breakthrough event (Outing, 2003; Walker, 2003). Web-based news coverage, wrote one observer, "could define how future wars are covered" (Swartz, 2003). With the US TV networks engaged in "an 'armaments race' of their own" in challenging CNN's superiority in battlefield reporting capability (Biernatzki, 2003, 13), the availability of video satellite phones with compression technology made it possible for nearly every reporter to transmit stories first-hand. Baghdad alone sported close to 300 phone links and a dozen video links (Blumenthal and Rutenberg, 2003).

This technological race for the immediate and ongoing on-site relay drove the ratings for 24-hour news skyward. CNN's audience went up by some 393 percent compared with the same week the previous year, and Fox News rose 379 percent (Deans, 2003; Allan and Zelizer, 2004, 7). News executives praised a technology that was "lighter, cheaper, easier to transport and sturdier" (Grossman, 2003, 6). Disputing reports that the new technologies incurred long-term losses for the news industry, former

NBC head Lawrence K. Grossman noted that war reporting might be the most efficient way a news division could spend its money, because "so much of what the money is spent on gets on the air" (Grossman, 2003, 6).

But these primarily industrial celebrations of technology overlooked the fact that in many instances technology overshadowed news content. Many images and stories that technology provided "in the end didn't amount to anything" (Doward, 2003). Longstanding problems of "uneven translators, brutal deadlines, the difficulty of finding sources in an unfamiliar environment" (Beckerman, 2004, 41) remained, and the technological mastery over immediacy only made them more evident. Moreover, in addition to safety needs, "making frequent live transmissions . . . forced [reporters] to spend a great deal of time on logistics and technology – time that could not be spent on gathering pictures and information for more complete stories. It turned out the technology was not quite ready for this war" (Friedman, 2003, 30). The immediacy of the web and video phones thus made time into "the enemy" (Sandler, 2003). Newspapers bucked the celebratory discourse as they pondered an audience compelled by the quickest relay (and consequently downwardly spiraling advertisements) (Moses, 2003).

In fact, the technological parameters for covering the war were problematic for multiple reasons. The memorable One-Man Mobile Uplink – caricatured during the late 1980s by Al Franken teetering under a massive satellite dish on *Saturday Night Live* – was reflected in Iraq when the reliance on extended technology rendered many front-line reporters unable to move freely. Embedded reporters offered hushed, somewhat frenzied accounts of the war that showed little more than the reporter's torso and offered on-site detail severely curtailed by military restrictions, sandstorms and other uncontrollable circumstances. Though NBC correspondent David Bloom's much-heralded "Bloommobile" was equipped with high-quality, high-tech cameras that made "other broadcasters drool with envy" (Friedman, 2003, 29), it was there that he met his death. Moreover, his reports often provided little more than what the troops were eating or offering soldiers a chance to send regards home (Embedded Reporters, 2003).

While such accomplishments were hailed for using some of the newest mobile technology in the industry, from the onset it was clear that certain kinds of reporting were being compromised. Telling news rather than collecting it became the motto of the day, a shortcoming of the US media more generally, as pointed out in a view of the industry at the time (*State of the News Media*, 2004). In Iraq it underscored the degree to which the "toys" of journalism were displacing those who operated them. Split screens, continual if static cameras and an insistence on their use irrespective of what was being shown demonstrated, as the Project for Excellence in Journalism put it, "a tendency to use [technology] regardless of the news" it brings (Embedded Reporters, 2003).

Finally, unpredictable and non-routine circumstances also tweaked definitions of the craft of journalism, forcing an adaptation of long-held journalistic beliefs, conventions and routines. Missed stories, erroneous interpretations and a loyalty to misleading sources all revealed situations in which reporters had "their hands full trying to cover a bewildering, determined urgency" (CJR Comment, 2004, 6; Mooney, 2004).

Examples abound. The uncritical reportage regarding claims of weapons of mass destruction forced the New York Times to publish an unprecedented mea culpa (The Times and Iraq, 2004; A Pause for Hindsight, 2004), while other misjudgments produced additional scurrying to set the story right: tracking Ahmed Chalaby's strategically erroneous leads (McCollam, 2004), embodied most directly but not limited to New York Times reporter Judith Miller, highlighted the limitations of the source–reporter dyad. Elaborated stories about bioweapons laboratories, the Jessica Lynch rescue story, the defection of Tariq Aziz and uprisings in the south of Iraq, many of which were contested by Al Jazeera at the time of their reporting, were later found to be false, rendering "figuring out Iraqi sentiment one of the most complex journalistic endeavors in years" (Beckerman, 2004, 40). The media's initial reticence in pursuing the Abu Ghraib story turned the focus onto troubling journalistic activity, which exacerbated with reports of reporters missing the story, Dan Rather's thin justification of CBS' two-week delay of its airing and Chelsea Manning's leaking of information to Wikileaks rather than to a conventional news outlet (Mitchell, 2004).

Each instance fomented excessive critiques of the war's coverage, which was found to be fundamentally problematic. For instance, the erroneous initial reports of widespread looting of the Iraqi National Museum were later blamed on "the difficult and imperfect nature of [war] reporting" (Lawler, 2003, 68). It was no surprise that, as late as July 2004, observers wondered whether journalists even knew how to cover battlefields that were overrun with terrorist activity (Eisendorf, 2004). According to longstanding prisms on journalism, then, journalists did not always get the story fully right because they did not follow cues provided by the profession, industry, institution or craft.

But absent from this discourse was an understanding of what changed in journalism that was not covered by these prisms. Missing, for instance, was the little discussed backdrop to journalistic activity: grassroots information relays, for instance, or the informal networking with NGOs and aid workers. Though they were not readily available during the early stages of the war, their absence was rarely commented on because the foregrounded prisms for evaluating journalism saw little value in such activity. Missing too was the heightened role of the precarious labor force, with fixers and translators becoming flawed but indispensable tools for journalists to cover the war. Thinking about journalism as a culture accommodates both more fully. Because the culture of journalism references action taken in accordance with conventional understandings that guide journalists to act in collective ways, the prism necessarily reflects the resources journalists draw upon to coordinate their activities. By recognizing that journalism's record of the war took shape as much through improvisation, adaptation, trial and error and informal discussion as through more frequently discussed journalistic cues, journalism as culture helps explain how shifts on the ground forced the continual re-tweaking of journalistic practice, an inevitable state of affairs in wartime.

Who Inhabits the Culture of Journalism?

Who journalists are – or, to frame the question more explicitly, who is included within the community of journalists – is key to thinking about journalism as culture. Derived from a sociological perspective that sees culture as a phenomenon produced by people instead of an anthropological view that sees culture as antecedent to people (Becker, 1986), the culture of journalism is given shape by the people who inhabit its terrain. Journalists to a large extent shape the news.

But who is a journalist? Traditionally this question has been addressed by attending to the activities that journalists are expected to fulfill: a journalist expresses "a judgment on the importance of an item, engages in reporting, adapts words and metaphors, solves a narrative puzzle, assesses and interprets" (Adam, 1993, 73). And yet the people who inhabit journalism are not equally regarded; nor are they given equal credence. While tensions over the boundaries of who was a journalist in Iraq stretched from the inclusion of field producers in UN Security Resolution 1738 to freelance photographers being taken into Iraqi custody, differences persist more broadly. Even as UNESCO's definition of who is a journalist has become increasingly inclusive, persistent distinctions between the central and peripheral roles associated with professional groups engaged in creative activity (Becker, 1984) reflect a fundamental and longstanding ambivalence over who "gets" to be called a journalist.

To be sure, the exclusionary nature of the journalistic field is longstanding. Tabloid journalists have been long denied legitimacy by mainstream reporters, while those who report from alternative streams, use less central technologies or cohabit journalism part-time have tended to be excluded from journalism's "who's who." Photojournalists, for instance, only became ranking members of journalistic professional associations in the 1940s, a full 80 years after images made their way into news, and only 50 years later did they take on leadership positions (Zelizer, 1998). And so it continues today, with the journalistic field during the Iraq War failing to include the unilaterals – those invested in remaining outside the prism in order to stake out the story without institutional support or interference – and the precarious working force that were both central to providing coverage.

Much of the tension over who is a journalist derives from the prevailing prisms for thinking about journalism. When seen as a profession, those who do not ascribe to norms of professional behavior are kept outside of the community. In this regard, citizen journalists and human rights workers were among those who received little media attention. Seeing journalism as a craft, however, is no more inclusive, for those who did not perform pre-defined requisite skills remained positioned beyond the boundary, as was evident in the then-prevalent discussions in the trade media about whether online reporters were journalists (Singer, 2003). The prism of the institution tends to embrace those employed full-time in conventional news outlets, thus precluding both members of the precarious labor force and unilaterals. And when seen as an industry, journalists tend to get categorized through lists of "relevant personnel" that are demarcated by division, such as broadcast TV, radio or newspapers, hiding the fact that many journalists then – and nearly all today – worked at more than one task simultaneously (Cottle, 2000a). It thus stands to reason that when operating increasingly from a financial point of view, US news outlets made decisions about personnel that at times undermined journalism's newsgathering function.

By contrast, seeing journalism as a culture offsets the boundary-marking that tends to exclude certain reporters or kinds of reporters from the community. Cultural conventions offer a way to unite journalists in patterned ways with people who are regularly excluded, including non-journalists who are situated beyond the boundaries of journalism – film-makers, satirists, comedians, playwrights, poets and politicians. Similarly involved in diverse modes of cultural argumentation, expression, representation and production, these individuals can be seen as inhabiting the margins of the culture of journalism. They thus broaden the journalistic field precisely in ways that challenge the territorial boundaries set in place by conventional scholarship.

This way of thinking has particular resonance when addressing the first draft of reporting the war. Early discussions about embedded reporters displayed a "gee whiz quality" through which journalism's impending war coverage was initially appraised (Friedman, 2003, 29). Amidst expectations of journalism that rose to "what may be a historic high" (Fisher, 2004, 2), professional organizations such as the Project for Excellence in Journalism organized responses to what was largely seen as a relatively novel reporting arrangement (Embedded Reporters, 2003; Fisher, 2004). Though embedding in effect constituted a return of the practice of pooling correspondents, used widely in World War II, its surfacing in 2003 was hailed for giving reporters what was widely considered unprecedented access to battle.

But all of this set those who were embedded apart from those who were not. The few hundred who accepted the arrangement received assistance with rations, medical attention, fuel and communications and were subject to over 50 contractual conditions (Boyd-Barrett, 2004, 31). The embedded reporters' work was subsidized by the Pentagon and overseen by public relations experts; none were assigned to Iraqi families, humanitarian agencies or anti-war groups (Schechter, 2003). Limited to a three-week ground war, embedding provided access to a narrow swathe of activities, even though the frame had been explicitly delineated for journalism by a separate institution.

That proximity, however, obscured the ramifications of embedding for the larger picture of US journalism during the war. Its ensuing problems – a lack of reflection or skepticism, excessive empathy with the troops and unrepresentative or narrowly focused stories and visuals – diminished embedding's glitter as the war continued. CNN reporter Christiane Amanpour, for instance, noted that embedding failed to give "a concise and broader context. [The network thinks] 'live' brings more spontaneity, 'keep it moving' is what they tell us" (cited in Lowry & Jensen, 2003, E1). The persistent focus on a very small percentage of journalists who became embeds created a narrow understanding of who journalists were.

Central here was the fact that a large group of less institutionally supported individuals worked from a different vantage point. Called unilaterals, scores of reporters from many countries went to cover the war from non-embedded positions, excluded from military transports and often paying their own way. Some chose not to be embedded so as to preserve freedom of movement; many were young and inexperienced, and several died in the first days of the war. And yet, as Michael Massing commented, "the US military believed that only reporters who were officially embedded had the right to protection," even though it was sometimes offered begrudgingly (Massing, 2003, 33–5). Caught in the middle, the unilaterals were resented by the US military and had to sneak into Iraq across an officially closed border. They did, however, secure stories of civilian casualties, a broader context and other complications of the war in a way that embeds, who offered mostly on-site detail, did not (Donvan, 2003). How these reporters fared was as much a part of the journalistic community as the experiences of their more protected colleagues. In many views, "embedding did not live up to advance billing" (Friedman,

2003, 29) And, if nothing else, the contrast between the embedded and non-embedded reporters underscored the degree to which different kinds of journalists always make the news.

Within the recognized media corps too, observers critiqued some of its more marginal members. Early snafus surrounded Peter Arnett, whose interview with Iraqi TV lost him his job on MSNBC and landed him an alternative position with the British *Daily Mirror*, and Geraldo Rivera, whose drawing of a map in the sand pulled him away from the troops and repositioned him in Kuwait. Jokes circulated freely about MSNBC reporter Ashleigh Banfield, whose changing hair color and designer sunglasses were topics of discussion in the Afghanistan War but whose criticism of US war reporting in Iraq generated extensive name-calling by both other journalists and the public (Rutenberg, 2003b). Some pondered the inclusion of "reporters" for *People* magazine or MTV: called "inexperienced," their coverage was said to be "checkered," "chancy" and "super slick" (Sims, 2003). Mainstream journalists continued to be rattled by online websites (Singer, 2003), in a way that seems anachronistic today. In this regard, it is no wonder that, by mid-summer of 2004, documentary films such as *Fahrenheit 911*, *Control Room* and *Outfoxed*, or theatrical productions like *Embedded*, rang a popular chord with the US public. They dared to address some of the issues left unaddressed by much of US journalism.

Relevant too was the precarious labor force that inhabited journalism's underside increasingly throughout the war. Important for language skills, knowledge and familiarity of location, contacts and ability to blend in with the local population, a subset of journalistic practitioners – stringers, fixers, minders, translators and drivers – became more and more central to the war's reportage as it continued. Though at first they were hired on an ad hoc basis, as security needs intensified they sometimes merited prolonged contracts (Murrell, 2015, 125). But their presence remained largely absent in prevalent discussions of the war's coverage.

The prevailing insistence on journalism's singularity was similarly diminished as journalism's boundaries were blurred in two directions: on the one hand toward blogs and online journalism, on the other toward satirical comedy. From the beginning, bloggers actively and systematically told the story of the war in their own words. Calling themselves "personal journalists" – as contrasted with either "professional" or "amateur" reporters (Allan, 2004, 357) – these online diarists linked information, opinion and intimate detail in ways thought to supplement the stories provided by recognized news outlets. They tended not to provide breaking news as much as to focus attention on news reported but buried by conventional journalistic practice. Many saw the war in Iraq as their "breakthrough." In *Newsweek* reporter Steven Levy's words, the blogs "finally found their moment" as bombs struck Baghdad, when they were able to provide "an easy-to-parse overview for news junkies who wanted information from all sides, and a personal insight that bypassed the sanitizing Cuisinart of big-media news" (cited in Allan, 2004, 358).

Prominent here was Salaam Pax, an invented *nom de guerre* for a 29-year-old architect in Baghdad, who posted English-language warblogs from September 2002. Ranging in scope, his postings included humorous accounts of everyday life and angry responses to the events unfolding around him. Critically, via this "embedded reporting of a different order" (Allan, 2004, 361), bloggers saw themselves doing what journalists were not accomplishing. In Salaam Pax's words, "I was telling everybody who was reading the web log ... what the streets looked like ... It is just somebody should be telling this because journalists weren't" (cited in Allan, 2004, 361).

Similarly, online journalism sites run by marginal members of the journalistic community provided continual access to information elsewhere deemed inappropriate. When a furor erupted over the display of pictures of flag-draped coffins of US soldiers in April 2004 and mainstream news outlets were prohibited from showing the photos, hundreds of images, secured through a Freedom of Information Act request, instead appeared on a website run by Russ Kick, www.memoryhole.org. When grisly photographs of the charred corpses of American contractors in Fallujah, Iraq, appeared that same April and non-US news outlets published footage of the bodies being beaten, dragged and hanging from a bridge, the *Wall Street Journal* pondered the different levels of graphic display: in a front-page rejoinder separated from the surrounding text in bold type, it admitted that US television had shown "unusual restraint" in airing the images but that "graphic photos and video were widely available on the Web, on sites owned by traditional media. The ready availability of a raw material has altered decision-making" (A Complex Picture, 2004). Later, the paper offered the view that "viewers now can seek out controversial images on the Internet even if mainstream news outlets avoid them" (Angwin & Rose, 2004, B1). It was not long before professional trade forums began publishing guidelines on "how to introduce truly disturbing images online" (Outing, 2004).

The war also drew significant attention from satirists, comedians and late-night talk-show hosts, where during much of 2003 it remained the leading topic of jokes from Jay Leno, David Letterman and Conan O'Brien (Media Monitor, 2003). Jon Stewart lampooned the war's prosecution on *The Daily Show*, just as his following reached significant proportions among US youth, with as many people aged 18–29 receiving their news from TV comedy programs as from the nightly news ([Poll], 2004).

A similar case could be made, though on predictably debatable grounds, about the amateur photographers who took digital photographs of the atrocities committed in Abu Ghraib prison while serving in the US military. Though the display of these images in the media was more serendipitous than intentional, it nonetheless raised the question of trophy pictures of all kinds in the news and extended the boundaries of news providers. As Sontag (2004, 27) put it, "where once photographing war was the province of photojournalists, now the soldiers themselves are all photographers – recording their war, their fun, their observations of what they find picturesque, their atrocities – and swapping images among themselves and emailing them around the globe."

In each case, journalism changed by virtue of who inhabited its culture. It became, at least for a time, less authoritative, less reverent, more improvisory, in places more critical, more partisan and even ironic. And it became so in a way that spoke reams about the coverage of public events. The annual report of the Project for Excellence in Journalism noted at the time that, unlike in earlier years when growth was widespread, only three of eight media sectors saw audience growth in 2003 – ethnic media, alternative media and online media (*State of the Media*, 2004). It is no surprise, then, that during the 2004 US presidential campaign, three dozen bloggers were given full press credentials for the first time at the Democratic national convention in August, prompting reporters to call 2004 "the year of the blog" (Lee, 2004, 7). Such recipients of credentials have increased in the years since. If nothing else, this showed that when marginal members inhabit the culture of journalism, they expand its collective boundaries.

What is the Culture of Journalism For?

The most prevalent view of journalism focuses on its capacity to convey information. This view, which is primarily institutional in nature, sees journalism through its political effect, its role in maintaining an active and healthy body politic and its impact on the public good. Journalism is considered a power-rendering institution, and scholars look at its influence, prestige and authority in addressing what journalism is for. Much of this view has to do with notions of journalism being "for" a culture, with an emphasis on what journalism does "for" – and, in some views, "to" – the public.

By contrast, the culture of journalism sees journalists as being "in" a culture, viewing journalists not only as conveyors of information for others but also as producers of a cultural mindset for themselves. Seeing journalism as culture suggests that journalists themselves are part of the culture to which they report. How and to what degree journalism works for the people who create it are as important as the role it plays for its publics. In this regard, journalists impart preference statements about what is good and bad, moral and amoral and appropriate and inappropriate in the world, and their preference statements implicitly or explicitly shape the news. Journalists' positioning as the creators and conveyors of views about how the world works is linked with the positioning of their audiences, who make sense of the news in ways that reflect their own identity politics and that of institutions that grant them access and/ or protection (Zelizer, 1993a). Seeing journalism as culture thus goes beyond an emphasis on information relay, helping to keep journalism's study in step with some of the more contemporary news developments, which, as already mentioned, have expanded to the previously unlikely places of satirical comedy shows, blogs, talk shows, reality television and user-generated content.

In line with the prevalent prisms for thinking about journalism, the war's first draft of coverage rendered discussions of the public good somewhat unsatisfying, if for no other reason than that "good" journalism encountered obstacles. For instance, the most visible discussion of the 2003 war coverage hovered over the question of journalism's presumed public impact. Much of this institutionally driven discourse focused on the issue of patriotism, with journalism's performance evaluated as to whether or not it had worked for the public good. Despite the fact that, initially, readers' letters ran against the war (War and the Letters Page, 2003), the climate for reportorial judgment was nonetheless set: CNN's lead morning anchor, Paula Zahn, said on-air after hearing a familiar song, "If that rendition of the Star Spangled Banner doesn't stir you, I don't know what will," while an anxious observer saw "US newsrooms bewitched by the war" (Moscou, 2003). US flags temporarily appeared on reporters' lapels and permanently adorned the studios of Fox News and MSNBC. The words "we" and "us" cluttered US coverage, and professional organizations such as the Poynter Institute and the Project for Excellence in Journalism lobbied continual overviews of what to do about patriotism in the news.

While the question of how patriotic and impartial one could be was never fully resolved, it reduced the internal flux of covering Iraq into an overly coherent prism of patriotic behavior without accounting for what was fast becoming the forefront of its operation. Particularly egregious was the degree to which the media bought into the US administration's line on the war. In the *Columbia Journalism Review*'s view, "did the media fall for the Pentagon's spin? In a word, yes" (Smith, 2003, 28). But beyond the effect on information was its impact on journalistic performance itself: criticism by journalists that was seen as not explicitly supportive of the troops was labeled unpatriotic. The emergence of the so-called "Fox effect" (Rutenberg, 2003a), whereby commentators regularly skewered anyone who did not strut out his or her patriotism, established a different playing ground for journalists used to protected borders on the issue of national sentiment. It was the "cheerleading, can-do tone that infected too much of the reporting" (Smith, 2003, 8). And though charged with jingoism, Fox News remained the ratings leader in cable news.

This emphasis on patriotism diverted attention from what was a key aspect of journalistic coverage of Iraq that surfaces when thinking about journalistic culture – physical safety. What journalists were supposed to do reflected how well their capacity to report melded with their capacity to stay alive. These concerns over physical danger and well-being, however, rarely made it into the frenetic jockeying for coverage laid out initially by US news outlets. Given energized headlines like "TV's Battle Plan" (Storm, 2003), "Wire Services Deploy Their Own Troops" (Astor, 2003) and "Papers Say They're Ready" (Strupp, 2003a), news accounts reflected the parameters of upbeat industrial overviews, telling readers excitedly how many reporters were going to Iraq or how they were to be transported. Very little initial attention was paid to the question of physical danger, which was enhanced among freelance journalists who often lacked environmental training, institutional backing, financial support or health insurance. In one *Boston Globe* reporter's view, her preparation for entering a war was brief and non-comprehensive (personal conversation, March 2003). News executives admitted that they were also slow to provide counseling for reporters returning from combat, to say nothing of the lack of attention to those killed in combat or kidnapped (Strupp, 2003b). Although war correspondents remained at risk of developing severe mental problems from covering war, particularly post-traumatic stress disorder (PTSD), with one in four certain to develop some problem after returning to the homefront, many lacked health insurance (Feinstein, 2003). One 16-year employee of the *Christian Science Monitor*, who had no previous combat experience before Iraq, said she remained jittery once back from the front, and weeks later she had yet to begin reading the news again (Strupp, 2003b).

Danger's effect on journalistic practice quickly and consistently took its toll on coverage. In the war's initial stages, the proximity to danger enhanced journalists' dependence on the embedding arrangements provided by the US and coalition forces, even when doing so meant the provision of less satisfying news stories. But even embedding could not shield reporters from their environment, as the deaths of certain journalists attested. Later in the war, hotels housing journalists were strafed by coalition forces, a Wikileaks video showed Reuters' reporters being targeted and an Al Jazeera station was hit by US missiles, killing one of its reporters (Massing, 2003).

Concerns reached a high point by mid-2004, following an increase in instances of threat, abduction and murder, when reporters began to keep to their hotel rooms, locked down in the middle of Baghdad and reporting on places such as Sadr City and Fallujah from afar. Online reporter Dahr Jamail, writing for the website Electronic Iraq, pointed to a "horrendous disparity between what is really occurring on the ground and what the western corporate media chooses to report . . . Even stories that were on the front pages stateside are regularly being covered from the press room and not the field" (cited in Schechter, 2004). Ridiculed by US Deputy Defense Secretary Paul D. Wolfowitz in late June 2004 for being too scared to get out and tell the story of the war, US journalists vied with the impression, created largely by obsequious video cameras manned by Iraqi nationals, that "anyone can go anywhere in Iraq, even if it isn't true" (Fisher, 2004, 2). Also not reported was a reliance on fixers, minders, drivers, translators and stringers, who began increasingly to do the job that conventional reporters could not accomplish. This in turn produced new journalistic conventions, such as separating internal from external credit for a news story. Members of journalism's precarious labor force shied away from the latter, because "it was too dangerous to have their work's authorship assigned to their name" (Murrell, 2015, 130).

Discussion of journalism's war coverage neglected these cues and others. Calling the war coverage an "experiment in war journalism," seen through the eyes of "an Iraqi housewife, a college student and a veteran of the Iran–Iraq war" and others who could go anywhere more freely than reporters, the *New York Times* admitted that it remained still too early to evaluate the strengths – and weaknesses – of its coverage (Fisher, 2004, 2). But the fact that the paper offered such a view 16 months into the war belied how ill prepared much of the western media had been for the physical dangers that awaited reporters. As Hassan Fattah, the founding editor of the English-language newspaper *Iraq Today*, commented, "perhaps the most important – and difficult – decision any journalist in a war zone has to make is when to get out" (Fattah, 2004, 62). There is little room in conventional thinking about journalism that makes such a decision a natural option in providing coverage. And when the question of "what journalism is for" is decided in conjunction with its impact on the public, opting out of coverage is not viable.

The question of what journalism is for thus generated a narrow set of assumptions for evaluating journalistic practice in wartime. When such evaluations move decidedly in the direction of the public good, as they do during war, the welfare of reporters themselves tends to fade in importance. The often-compromised positions that ensue for reporters in wartime thus require greater focus, a focus that emerges when thinking about journalism as culture. Seeing journalism through a cultural lens helps make journalists part of the culture on which, to which and for which they report – rather than maintaining them as vessels for a public good that lies beyond them.

The Culture of Journalism

In covering the 2003 war in Iraq, whole communities of journalists and their practices escaped public attention, largely because the prisms for evaluating them favored narrow views of their activity. Deprived of nuanced discussion were journalists who wrestled with their patriotism, who worked for online or alternative news media, who were hired locally or worked as independents, who learned new practices from marginal members of the community, who cringed under the limitations created by technology and who worried over their physical safety.

With no clear or universal answer to any of the dilemmas these populations created, seeing journalism as a culture accommodates their presence more fully. The lens of culture facilitates the examination of facets of journalism that go under the radar of conventional prisms. In working around the contradictions between what journalists hope to do and what they actually can do, it keeps tabs on the fluctuating definitions, boundaries, conventions and practices of implementing journalism, particularly in crisis situations such as wartime. Doing so from the bottom up bypasses the insistence that journalism conform to predetermined, normative notions associated with its value as a profession, industry, institution or craft.

All of this suggests that seeing journalism through a cultural lens creates and proceeds from its own strategic dissonance. Despite the prevalence of arguments for journalism's unitary nature, the culture of journalism presupposes that journalistic conventions, routines and practices are dynamic and contingent on situational and historical circumstance. It offers a view of journalism that is porous, relative, less judgmental and more flexible. Given the troubling, uncontrollable and unclear horizons that contemporary journalists continue to face, adopting a prism that necessarily accommodates its flux is a useful step toward more fully understanding its ever-evolving trappings.

11

When 21st-Century War and Conflict Are Reduced to a Photograph

Journalism's images of war and conflict disturb. Among the most powerful visuals known to humankind, they are haunted by the stubborn inevitability and proximity of death. Combining the cool mechanics of the camera with the hot passions of battle, they offer visual statements about circumstances much of the world prefers not to see: mangled bodies and shattered buildings, triumphant soldierly gestures, hopes and broken spirits nestled inside devastation somehow too deep for the camera to record. Journalism's images of war and conflict both show what has been and offer glimpses of what might be. And for those who have never experienced them firsthand, journalism's images provide what may be the only depiction of what sadly has become one of the reigning circumstances of the contemporary age.

But journalism's images of war and conflict do not emerge from a vacuum. They are shaped through a turn to the visual – a journalistic emphasis on images that typically takes place during times of crisis. Crafted through a maze of practices and standards, both explicit and implicit, by which those involved with news pictures decide how war and conflict can be reduced to a photograph, journalism's images have come to represent an elaborated template for imagining and assessing the battles of the twenty-first century. Such images reflect what the camera sees by projecting onto that vision a set of broader assumptions about how the world works. The ways in which this happens, however, raise questions about how images, particularly photographs, shape public encounters with war and conflict.

When war and conflict are reduced to a photograph, the camera provides images that show far more than just the scene at hand. These images tend to be composite, more schematic than detailed, conventionalized and simplified. Used as pegs not to specific events but to stories larger than can be told in a simple news story, they become a key tool for interpreting in ways consonant with persistent understandings about how war and conflict are supposed to be waged – notions about patriotism, dignity, heroism, human rights, sacrifice, humanity, the nation-state and fairness that come as much from outside journalism as from within it. War and conflict are often presented in a clean and at times antiseptic fashion, suggesting efforts made for a greater good. Whether or not this actually reflects how combat is waged is beyond the mission of these images. A range of visual cues, or familiar templates for using images, helps journalists depict circumstances that are fraught with unpredictability, stressful judgment, emotionalism, inconsistency and high stakes, facilitating journalism's depictions but not necessarily in ways that support the images' workings as tools of news relay. Relying on cues that have proven themselves over time, journalism's images of war and conflict gravitate toward the memorable – as established through frequently depicted, aesthetically appealing and familiar images – as much as toward the newsworthy.

And yet it is images that the public tends to rely on to understand what transpires in otherwise invisible and far-away conflict zones. How much do we recognize about that dependency? Do expectations that journalism delivers a certain kind of information through images need to be altered? In what follows, I examine that question in conjunction with US journalism's depiction of some of the widely covered wars and conflicts of the twenty-first century, both tracing the characteristic attributes of pictures of combat writ large and reflecting on their changing contemporary role in the news.

Why Do War and Conflict Turn to the Visual?

How journalism depicts war and conflict has always been considered against a more complicated set of assumptions about the ways in which images, particularly photographs, work. The photograph's specific attributes – its materiality, ease of access, frozen capture of time, an affective and often gestalt-driven view of the world that is thought to bypass the intellect and communicate directly with the emotions – highlight its power and durability. Photographs are thought to work through a twinning of denotative and connotative forces, by which the ability to depict the world as "it is" is matched with notions about what "it means" – the interpretive power to couch what is being depicted in a broader, generalizable frame that helps us recognize the image as consonant with broader understandings of the world. These two forces—the first associated with photographic verisimilitude, realism, indexicality and referentiality, the second with universality, generalizability and symbolism (Hall, 1973; Sekula, 1975) – are rarely presumed to work equally in journalism, where the former is privileged over the latter. Denotation and the truth-value of the photograph, more than connotation, are thought to be critical, because journalism needs photographic realism to enhance its ability to vouch for events in the real world. Leaning on photography's own reliance on realism – evident in terms like "video," "frame," "capture," "point" and "shoot" – thus fits journalism's rhetoric about itself. In reality, however, connotation is as important as denotation, if not more so.

Connotation emerges in journalism's visual coverage of combat in multiple ways. The coverage of war and conflict tends to produce more pictures, more varied pictures and pictures whose display is justified on a wide range of attributes, such as drama or vividness. A picture's use depends not so much on explicit and articulated standards as on informal strategies among journalists about how best to use them (Zelizer, 1993a; Glaser, 2003; Rosenstiel, 2003). Thus, journalists – in their roles as reporters, editors, photo-editors and photographers – negotiate decisions about what can be depicted and in which ways. Reflecting the larger environment in which pictures are displayed, these negotiations often accommodate the agendas and interests of those beyond journalism – politicians, human rights workers, military officials, news executives and family members, among them. They also take into account the bystanders, citizen journalists and even perpetrators – Islamic State and its reliance on videos being the most recent example – who take and display images beyond news outlets on digital platforms. From within this environment, journalism orients toward the visual during times of combat.

This turn to the visual has always been historically complicated, for it occurs against the backdrop of a wide-ranging journalistic inattention to images. For most journalists, news images occupy a backseat to words. Since the photograph's inception in the mid-1800s, pictures have long been seen as the fluff of journalism, the stuff that illustrates but is adjunct to verbal description. Early on, journalism thus gravitated backward from visual detail because its presence was not seen as necessary (Zelizer, 1995a). The extensive captions that arrived over the wires with pictures of the liberation of the concentration camps in 1945, for instance, were summarily shortened to brief, generalized phrases like "Nazi Icon" (Zelizer, 1998). The slippery captions, absent credits and unclear relationship with words continue even today, despite an array of imaging technologies like television, cable, cinema and the interactive displays of the digital environment. There still remain insufficient standards for how to use an image in news, where to put an image, whether to credit an image, how to title an image or how to connect images and texts (Zelizer, 1998). Though the current wealth of images circulating in the online environment as GIFs, Vines, webTV, video and other modes of digital depiction is driving efforts to verify and authenticate images from unconventional news outlets (Wardle, 2013), they are not yet producing systematic documentation about images across the board of their display.

Remarkably, the slide away from denotation and toward connotation tends to occur when the need for definitive information is greatest. When the magnitude or scale of bloodshed is too large for any one photo to depict, when the strategies involved in war and conflict are too complicated to visualize, when the competing contexts are too embedded or invisible to track: these are circumstances in which journalism exhibits less of an orientation to detail, favoring images that reflect less information than is available but that paradoxically seem to make hostilities more comprehensible. Engagement thus comes at the expense of fuller understanding.

Three main attributes characterize journalism's turn to the visual, each of which caters to a picture's memorability: when tasked with depicting combat, journalism displays more images, images function more like non-journalistic modes of visual representation and images gravitate more toward familiar depictions of the past. Each of these attributes – frequency, aesthetic appeal and familiarity – builds upon the picture's connotative force, downplaying its referential detail. That unevenness makes visual imagery a significant player in creating a record of war and conflict with singular attributes.

By and large, journalism has crafted its orientation to frequency, aesthetic appeal and familiarity in varying ways since the news image's earliest appearance. Frequency – the sheer burst of multiple news pictures in times of combat – should raise no eyebrows, for images have always taken over the spaces available to them when hostilities rear their head, in ratios disproportionate to how journalists cover the world in more peaceful times.

This was evident already in early artistic renditions of wartime. The illustrated newspapers, for instance, devoted multiple issues to images of the US Civil War, with the battle of Antietam covered in scores of pictures that were later re-circulated for private use (Goldberg, 1991). The Spanish–American War was "the first war in which photojournalism had a significant presence in the media" (Moeller, 1989, 48). World War II, documented by more photographers than any previous military conflict, produced special illustrated supplements in newspapers that relayed combat's far-reaching scope via the rapid transmission of wire photos, making a 1940s public feel "far closer to events on the battlefield than his [sic] grandfather, regardless of the actual distance he might be removed from active fighting" (Mathews, 1957, 193). By the time the concentration camps were liberated in 1945, their depiction – groups of five, ten and twenty images in a single newspaper – ruled the news media for weeks on end, with some photographs reproduced and blown up into sidewalk exhibits (Zelizer, 1998). Even the eventual introduction of more sophisticated imaging technologies – in particular, the moving image and its subsequent platforms of documentary, television, cable and digitization – did not undo the importance of the still image and its relevance to combat's visualization. Though accounts of newsgathering practices widely hold, for instance, that the Korean War was the first war covered by television or the Vietnam War introduced graphic televised images of combat, both sets of hostilities relied on photography as an integral part of coverage.

That is not to say that all wars and conflicts receive extensive visual documentation. One need only consider the uneven visual documentation surrounding US domestic racial conflicts in Ferguson, Baltimore or other US cities or the total absence of visual documentation of US conflict with Puerto Rico, despite the "warlike" behavior attributed to the relationship between the US and its subordinate state (Denis, 2015). For journalism's turn to the visual rests on an agreement, not readily articulated, that news photographs depict certain aspects of bloodshed, but not all. And, in fact, only certain aspects of certain hostilities have ever been seen in the news. The trench warfare and heavy press control of World War I so undermined the capacity to witness and record events that, visually, "the war never showed up" (Moeller, 1989, 124). Photographic coverage of the Korean War was hampered by extensive nighttime fighting that made capturing the full spectrum of battle difficult (289). Depiction of the Falklands War totaled a meager 200 individual photographic shots, mostly cleansed portrayals of antiseptic warfare and virtually no human corpses, creating an "illusion of a clean war" (Taylor, 1991, 112–13), while the Gulf War of 1991 was depicted primarily by television cameras that showed shaky settings accommodating incoming SCUD missiles and helmeted television reporters hopping before live cameras as they tried to dodge fire (Zelizer, 1992c). Photographs were "censored into invisibility, void of images of real violence and suffering" (Robins, 1993, 325), and when they did appear – such as a much-discussed shot of an Iraqi soldier immolated in his vehicle published in the *Observer* of London – US editors refused to publish them.

Selective depiction is particularly prevalent when it concerns areas of the world that lay beyond the presumed western sphere of interest. Conflicts in both Africa and Asia generated little attention because, in one view, the "bone-thin men behind barbed wire in the Balkans, on the doorstep of the West, resonate[d] more deeply . . . than the many horrors of Asia and Africa" (Lane, 1992, 27). Pictures that did appear of conflicts in Rwanda and Burundi showed the public a "dark continent, where nothing happens except coups, massacres, famines, disease and drought" (Douglas, 1994, 15). The Balkan violence of the 1990s was so unevenly visualized that it paradoxically earned both the status of "Europe's first television war" (Marshall, 1994, A16) and the title "the war that can't be seen" (Cohen, 1994, E4). By and large, its stories and pictures were "lost in the fog of second-hand reporting" by journalists who "were unable to get there" (Rohde, 1995, A1). At the same time, observers claimed that the stream of photographs depicting people who looked like "one's neighbors" was responsible for generating support for the war (Douglas, 1994, 15).

Lacking depiction, then, have always been those sides of war and conflict that do not fit the prevailing interpretive assumptions about how combat is to be waged. In most cases, there are few or no images of human gore, one's own war dead or POWs, military operations gone badly or the effect of one's own activity on civilians of the other side. There also tend to be few images of conflict in regions that are marginal to the presumed public self-interest.

Similar tensions surround journalism's longstanding orientation toward a picture's aesthetic appeal in times of combat. Exemplified by images that look less like typical news relays and more like non-journalistic images, combat images tend to be typically bigger, bolder, more colorful, more dramatic, prettier, shocking and more aesthetically pleasing or noteworthy than the relays received otherwise. For instance, photographer Patrick Baz's (Baz, 2003) famous photo of a bloodied camera in the Iraq War of 2003 remains the icon of friendly fire launched on Baghdad's Hotel Palestine, not the journalists who were killed there that April.

The sway toward pictures with dramatic appeal has long impacted the shifting value that journalists attribute to verisimilitude. In the early years of the illustrated press, artists "had little compunction about distorting the real facts of the event," whose battles they rarely saw (Voss, 1994, 136). The US Civil War brought with it a stark realism associated with photography and moved away from the romanticized tenor of drawings, introducing what came to be known as the "first living room war" (Goldberg, 1991, 20). Combat's representation was then couched in terms of realist discourse and authenticity rather than imagination and interpretation.

How the draw of aesthetic appeal plays out has been dependent on the larger environment in which images are crafted, which changes with each war and conflict. In one view, "the first [world] war photographers really didn't photograph war at all. Because of the bulk of their equipment and the length of time it took to make an exposure, they were limited to battleground landscapes, posed pictures of fighters, simulated combat, and portraits of soldiers prior to battle" (Howe, 2002, 14). An early emphasis on distant battlefields, exemplified in the Spanish–American War, gave way by the Korean War to large numbers of close-ups of individual soldiers. Parts of the aesthetic cycled irregularly over time: Vietnam displayed a return to studio portraits of the dead, as favored during the Spanish–American War (Moeller, 1989), while pastoral landscapes, also common to the Spanish American War, re-emerged in areas known for breathtaking physical terrain, like the 2001 war in Afghanistan. But, by and large, combat tends to be framed at least in part via dramatic, pleasing or shocking images. Though the play to aesthetic appeal has been criticized as legitimating war and conflict (Chouliaraki, 2006), its invocation nonetheless offers images that draw engagement for aspects of combat that otherwise might go unnoticed.

Similar patterning can be found across journalism's orientation to familiar visual cues and themes. Because pictures of combat are tasked with making the strange understandable, a play to familiarity – using pictures that recall depictions of earlier hostilities either implicitly or explicitly – makes sense. The interpretive assumptions guiding picture display thus often have to do with images that withstand the test of time, and journalists play to this convention by weaving memorable scenes from the past into pictures of the present. With photographs, then, historical precedent offers an accessible context for combat in need of visual definition.

Familiar photographic themes include the wasteland caused by hostilities, large-scale battle scenes and close-ups of specific instances of combat, the dead and the wounded, surviving civilians. Many memorable photos draw upon frequently visited themes: struggles for human rights, heroism in the face of diminishing odds or the draw of the frontier. Thus, Robert Capa's iconic tribute to Republican Spain (Capa, 1936), hailed as a death-in-action shot which depicted a soldier of the Spanish Civil War at the moment he was impacted by a bullet, in fact thematically recycled an image taken at the siege of Verdun in 1916 during World War I. That earlier shot, taken from film footage by an anonymous cameraman, showed a French officer being shot to death as he led a counter-attack straight into the field of a German machine-gun (Stepan, 2000). Reminiscent of a longstanding tradition in which soldiers ran directly into the field of fire, the photograph not only portrayed the trench warfare of Verdun but also became emblematic of the collision of "nineteenth century notions of courage" with "modern reality" (Stepan, 2000, 30). Though its authenticity has since been questioned (Rohter, 2009), it continues to be widely recalled in the broad context of combat images that followed.

Sometimes the familiarity of earlier news images helps offset the discomfort that accompanies the display of cruelty characterizing current war and conflict. In such a light, the atrocity images of World War II were recycled into the later depiction of atrocities in the Balkans, Rwanda and

Africa, cueing later publics into a visual template that had been set in place decades earlier (Zelizer, 1998). Coverage of the Balkan war crimes tribunal in the mid-1990s was thereby illustrated with a photo from the Nuremburg trials forty years earlier (Van Der Deen, 1995).

All of this suggests that journalism's turn to the visual in times of war and conflict has long rested upon a systematic but generally unarticulated orientation to image frequency, image aesthetics and image familiarity, all of which establish an image's power and memorability regardless of whether or not it is newsworthy. Together, they offer a compelling template through which to consider news images of the wars and conflicts of the twenty-first century.

Visualizing Twenty-first Century Combat

The play to connotation over denotation, as embodied by an orientation to image frequency, aesthetics and familiarity, is particularly useful in the combat of the twenty-first century because warfare itself has changed. War and conflict today combine what have been labeled "wars of iron" and "wars in the shadows" (Barno, 2013) – the hybrid warfare of places like Iran, Iraq, Syria, North Korea and Russia which uses both traditional state-driven tactics and irregular, cyber- and unconventional tactics, versus the shadow warfare unfolding in primarily civilian spaces in Gaza, Yemen and Ukraine, as well as the non-state capabilities embodied by Al Qaeda and Islamic State. Information warfare has been strengthened and leveraged in multiple ways. These circumstances complicate journalism's reliance on traditional visual responses to the conventional state-to-state warfare of earlier times.

Journalism is thereby tasked with depicting warfare that involves widespread subterfuge and subversion, civilian areas and casualties, high-tech weaponry, an asymmetrical employment of power, covert backing from established nations and the employment of masked fighters acting without conventional state attribution. These activities constitute difficult scenes for journalists to record – to say nothing of today's widespread targeting of journalists themselves. Less a clear-cut defined set of practices and more a residual term for a vast array of differential activities involving death and destruction, contemporary instances of war and conflict are thus difficult to identify, classify and categorize. Depicted with the help of bystanders and citizen journalists who use mobile phones and digital technology to circulate their own images, and navigating around perpetrators who display their own images, combat of the twenty-first century seems less able to accommodate, and perhaps needs less of, journalism's intervention than in previous eras. As Reporters Without Borders noted in 2013 about Syria, its journalistic coverage had become "one of the war's collateral victims" (Journalism in Syria, 2013). Coverage comes with a price.

No surprise, then, that coverage itself has changed too. Those responsible for reporting hostilities comprise a vast and often motley crew of reporters and camera-personnel, activists and members of a precarious labor force – drivers, translators, fixers, guides, stringers and freelancers. Covering war and conflict is no longer the aspired-to high ground of journalism but tends to result instead from making do in the face of high stakes, danger, unpredictability and uneven resources. Often, coverage involves assigning risky gambles to relatively unprepared personnel, which produces huge disparities between what happens and what is reported.

In these uneven circumstances, connotation is a more achievable aim than the careful detailing of current hostilities. Three examples illustrate. Pictures of the shooting of 12-year-old Mohammad Aldura in Gaza (Abu-Rahma, 2000), an event which sparked the second Intifada between Israel and Palestine in 2000, carried a message about the futility of hostilities, limits of paternal protection, cruelty of military conflict and strength of resistance but spawned no agreement about the definitive details of how the boy had died. Even today 15 years later, both sides continue to debate the particulars of what happened, despite the availability of the France 2 video of the event from which frame grabs were taken. The lack of definitive information, however, was the point. This "about-to-die" photograph called on the viewing public to complete the information not provided by imagining what had happened, rather than offering them definitive proof of the death of the boy. In so doing it captured their attention and led to engagement with the image (Zelizer, 2010).

Similarly, images of the dismantling of a statue of Saddam Hussein in Baghdad's Firdos Square in 2003 – in which US armed forces took down the statue in front of a small crowd, refuting Iraqi claims that they were winning the war – were called by the *Boston Globe* a depiction of "the first feel-good moment of the war" (Gilbert & Ryan, 2003, 1). Likened to Eastern European revolts of the 1950s, the event was seen as a sign of impending democracy for the region. This was despite the fact that the square was closed to the public, the gathering limited to journalists and US military, the statue removal organized by occupying US troops and the photographic opportunity staged (Fisk, 2003; Lichfield, 2003; Brown, 2003). And yet the photos continued to circulate, said even today to document "the iconic moment of the American invasion," "the symbolic end of the combat phase of operations" and "one of the war's most iconic images" (Axelrod, 2013; Gompert, Binnendijk & Lin, 2014; Frey & Mallin, 2015).

More recently, the Syrian conflict in 2012 was depicted by *Time* with a cover photo from Homs, titled *Escape from Syria* (Daniels, 2012). Eerily prescient, given the numerous images of masses of Syrian refugees from 2014 onward, the photo was inanimate, showing no humans among the city's destroyed infrastructure and underscoring a supposed escape already in progress. Elsewhere, however, scores of photos documented the transformation of Homs into an urban battlefield during that same time period, focusing on the incongruous attempts to maintain semblances of daily life in 2011 and 2012 alongside the rubble of human and physical devastation: multiple photos appearing, often taken by activists, stringers and freelancers, showed shattered buildings, families rent asunder, corpses of children in plastic bags, wounded left in the streets to die, massive demonstrations and burial processions.

In each incident, connotation – and the completion work it required of the public – was everything. Though on each occasion, more detail was available than was shared by any given image, the decision to step backward in degree of detail reflected a paradoxical act that used images to engage rather than to more fully inform the public.

The central role played by connotation in journalism's turn to the visual and the engagement it forces on audiences may, however, approximate the best that can be offered in current situations of combat. As the capacity to gain access, verify and corroborate information and remain safe comes stridently under question, the role of news outlets in providing detailed information about hostilities becomes all the more difficult. By conveying implication over evidentiary fact, images provide enough detail to let viewers know they are looking at war and conflict but not so much detail that the image remains stuck in a particular time and place. In this regard, it may be that the wars and conflicts of the twenty-first century are showing cracks in a well-worn but always problematic alliance between news norms and news pictures. Images may be playing a different kind of role in documenting bloodshed because they now reflect the incomplete degree of detail journalism has always been able to provide. In this regard, it is useful to consider what image frequency, image aesthetics and image familiarity look like in the hostilities of the new century.

Image Frequency

As conventional warfare has given way to situations of blended combat – forcing journalists to attend equally to "wars of iron" and "wars in the shadows" – the relationship between combat and photography has changed. Fueled in part by a simultaneously expanding visual culture beyond the news and in part by a diminishing journalistic capacity to document distant combat, a turn toward frequently displayed images manifests visibly in the sheer numbers of images that surface.

Following the events of 9/11, newspapers and news-magazines doubled the number of photographs over that published in non-crisis times (Zelizer, 2002). This continued to be the case in the two wars that followed – Afghanistan and Iraq. The war in Afghanistan was visualized through numerous images that implied a certain romanticized nostalgia for a reclaimed civilization, with shots of newly unveiled women or women appearing for the first time in public places (Nalkur, 2002), liberated crowds and breathtaking colorful landscapes topping the coverage. Coverage of the 2003 war in Iraq became equally visual as it embraced broadband Internet and its associated digital devices – websites containing live video, photography collections, audio reports, animated weaponry displays and interactive maps. Said to offer a "more intimate and multifaceted view of the war than . . . possible ever before" (Harmon, 2003, C4), newspapers turned over whole pages and sections to prominently displayed images that were larger, bolder and more colorful – likened by Tom Brokaw to "drinking from a fire hydrant" and by Dan Rather to a "literal flood of live pictures from the battlefield" (cited in Hilbrand & Shister 2003, A1, A20). During the first few months of the invasion, twice the number of images that usually appeared in the *New York Times* was displayed – 40 or 50 images rather than 20. Newspapers featured double-page photographic spreads and quarter-, half- and full-page photographs; television networks displayed galleries of still photographs to background music while tracking the experiences of single war photographers as part of their nightly line-up. Margins of photographs were lined up across news outlets' websites, offering updated visual digests of that day's events on the battlefield. In the early combat of the twenty-first century, then, the message seemed clear: photographs matter.

But how did these photographs matter? On the face of things, the move toward more visual relays fits what the news is supposed to do in times of hostilities – give the public more information when more information is needed. Images, however, often instead provided what was already known and failed to append detail that might distinguish one picture from another. For instance, images of the 9/11 attack, which showed initial visual documentation of victims falling or jumping to their deaths from the World Trade Center, were soon pulled from view and replaced with scores of pictures of unnamed individuals making their way to safety (Zelizer, 2002). During the war in Iraq, one *New York Times* article showed not one but three pictures of Iraqis (see figure 1) uncovering the graves of their relatives (Fisher, 2003, A10). A different image focused on the horror on the face of an American servicewoman as she watched Al Jazeera images of captured and killed soldiers – which significantly were not shown. Audiences were instead forced to supply the context against which to explain the image (An American Servicewoman, 2003, B6). The *Philadelphia Inquirer* published a full-page spread of five images under the joint title *Portraits of War: Conflict, Capitulation.* The captions appended to each picture were broad and lacking in discrete detail, as in "Iraqis welcome members of Britain's Second Royal Tank Regiment,"

A10   N   THE NEW YORK TIMES, FRIDAY, APRIL 25, 2003

AFTEREFFECTS: Bundles of Cash, and Countless Questions

PRISON GRAVEYARD

Iraqis Dig To Retrieve Executed Relatives

Continued From Page A1

Iraqis. But now a new organization, the Committee for Free Prisoners, says it has received millions of documents from the custodians of the nation's graveyards for executed political prisoners. The numbers are contained in these documents.

The head of the group, Ibrahim Raouf Idrisi, who says he spent 6 of his 35 years in prisons because he joined a Muslim party, has opened the records to family members to find what happened to their loved ones, and they are coming here every day.

Sitting today in the abandoned house in Baghdad of a Hussein general, whose rooms are now piled with fat green record books of torture and execution, Mr. Idrisi mused at the hundreds of millions of dollars Mr. Hussein spent jailing and killing his enemies. "If he had spent only half that money on the people, they would have loved him," he said. "He is a terrorist, the only terrorist in the universe."

The documents represent only a small part of what existed on cemeteries around Iraq, he said, before the government went on a spree of paper shredding in its last hours.

Much survived. Mr. Hani, for example, now has the death certificate of his brother, which states plainly that on Aug. 23, 1997 he was "executed by hanging."

A slightly broader picture of what happened has emerged from the chief gravedigger, just 21 years old. He is Muhammad Muslim Muhammad and he said he began digging graves here when he was 14 to fulfill his military service.

He said he received the bodies every Wednesday at about 11 a.m. after the weekly hangings at around 5 a.m. There were never fewer than nine bodies to bury. During one especially bad time in 2001, he said, the numbers rose. One day he buried 18 people. He said he had never told anyone the details of his job.

"I didn't open my mouth, or I would have ended up with these poor people here," he said.

The oldest graves in the cemetery, he said, date to 1983, four years after Mr. Hussein took power. The most recent, he said, was from six months ago, about the time that Mr. Hussein declared an amnesty for prisoners at Abu Ghraib as the threat of an attack by the United States rose.

He said he personally helped bury 700 people, but he has no idea how many bodies are in the cemetery, a walled-off part of the large Islamic cemetery here. The area is sizable, measuring about 120 graves by 25 graves, which if full might hold more than 2,000 bodies.

Slowly, the area is emptying of corpses. In the two weeks since the government fell, the families have been coming, but they were not able to find their relatives until the documents were recovered. So far, Mr. Muhammad said, 86 bodies have been removed.

It is not easy, even for families who have the numbers. Today, a 40-year-old caller named Russian Jassim arrived with a scrap of paper scrawled with the number 848, which was supposed to mark the grave of his brother, Selim.

A student in the Hawza, the Shiite

religious school in Najaf, about 85 miles south of Baghdad, Selim was arrested in 1998 at the family's home in Baghdad. The military then destroyed the house.

What Mr. Jassim wanted was to provide his brother with a proper Islamic burial, at which the body is ritually washed and wrapped in white linen. But he could not find the grave: The numbers ran from 847 to 848, then skipped up to 853.

They decided to dig anyway. "Do

you want me to dig up everything or just the head," the gravedigger asked. Mr. Jassim decided just to see the head, because he believed he could identify his brother by his two missing buck teeth.

"There are so many graves that don't have numbers," he said. "We don't know what to do."

The dirt was dry and easily dug and soon the gravedigger held up a skull. "It's not him," Mr. Jassim said. "The teeth are complete."

At grave No. 444, a large family worked together to unearth Hamid Omran, who was 31 when he was arrested in 1994. As the family carefully lifted the bones onto fresh linen, his cousin, Farhan Jassim, 47, exploded in anger.

"I don't think there was a regime in the world that treated political prisoners the way Saddam did," he said. "You can't imagine such exaggerated injustice."

The jaw surfaced. Mr. Hussein, the

cousin said, "hated every Iraqi. Believe me, he hated all Iraqis."

Then the family found the skull, which showed a crack in a temple. A guard kicked him when he was arrested, the family said.

Another cousin, Thaer Ghaws, 27, wept as he smoked a cigarette once the bones were out of the grave. "We are just people who opposed the regime," he said. "Why couldn't he just put political prisoners in prison?"

Mr. Hani, the man whose brother

disappeared in 1995, spent three hours picking through the grave of his brother. It was laborious. After the teeth, a few small bones, perhaps from the feet or hands, were found. Finally, Mr. Hani had found enough to fill a small coffin. He did not find the skull.

"It is enough for me," he said as he loaded the coffin onto a truck. "I feel relieved. What worried me before was I didn't know if he was alive or dead. Now I know."

A relative of an executed prisoner discovers his grave in a cemetery near Abu Ghraib prison. Thousands were identified by numbers until a new group found the names with the numbers.

Ghirayer Ali kisses the skull of his son Rahim as his remains are unearthed in a cemetery in Abu Ghraib. The family says Rahim was 32 in 2000 when government authorities took him away without giving a reason.

Relatives began exhuming the bodies of executed political prisoners for an Islamic burial. More than 1,000 were executed, mostly by hanging.

Figure 1 Photographs taken by Taylor Hicks and Brennan Linsley / Associated Press, April 25, 2003.

Credit: From the *New York Times*, April 25, 2003 © 2003 The New York Times. All rights reserved. Used by permission and protected by the copyright laws of the United States. the printing, copying, redistribution, or retransmission of this content without express written permission is prohibited.

with no names, locations or times at which the photographs had been taken (Portraits of War, 2003, A21).

The absence of detail in images has prevailed across the pictures of more recent combat, regardless of how many pictures are displayed. In 2015, an outpouring of Syrian refugees following the five-year war in that country, for instance, produced scores of pictures across news platforms, showing groups of anonymous bedraggled individuals crowding transport halls, sleeping in public places, clutching meager possessions, frantically trying to secure passage to safety. Few were given names or identities or ways to tell their own stories. Only in September 2015 when the subject of one of a series of photographs (Demir, 2015) was given a name – toddler Aylan Kurdi, who died with his mother and brother on the Turkish shore (see figure 2) – did people visibly respond. Though the public outcry over the boy's death did not sustain itself across the refugee crisis (EJO Research, 2015; Zelizer, 2015b), it is telling how long it took for the myriad of refugee images to be given identities, however fleeting and partial. What this suggests is that, though more photographs tend to appear during contemporary situations of discord, they do not necessarily bring with them more information.

But it may be that news images offer something other than information, for the assist they provide in facilitating public engagement is clear. One need only consider what happens when an orientation toward numerous pictures does not manifest. Multiple hostilities have in fact escaped visual coverage altogether, with current combat in Pakistan,

Figure 2 Photograph taken by N. Demir / DHA, September 2, 2015.
Credit: Associated Press.

Somalia and Chechnya among those missing from most western news coverage. Thus, while the frequency of news photos is not an automatic channel to fuller understanding of war and conflict, it does help ensure the engagement that is a necessary first step in that direction.

Image Aesthetics

Images of discord in the twenty-first century continue to accommodate the aesthetically appealing news photograph. Colorful, dramatic and alternately shocking or beautiful, these photos display current hostilities in ways that focus on the power of war and conflict and their strong hold on public sentiment. Massoud Hossaini's Pulitzer Prize-winning photo of a young girl draped in bright green fabric, depicted screaming after a 2011 suicide bombing in Kabul, is a case in point (Hossaini, 2011).

Connected here is a long tradition of altering photographic images – dramatizing a look of menace by darkening skin or shifting the position of figures and structures so as to enhance overall composition – so that the image's aesthetic appeal can help secure a "better" picture. The decision in March 2004, for instance, to delete clearly visible body parts in UK newspaper pictures of the terrorist bombings in Madrid (Luckhurst, 2004) exemplified the underside of the urge to publish only those pictures that accommodated the simmering moral outrage over gruesome pictures. By contrast, in 2006 freelance photographer Adnan Hajj lost his job with Reuters when he deepened the color of the smoke spirals over Beirut in one shot and added flares to another to enhance the dramatic effect of events (Aspan, 2006). The value accorded aesthetic appeal thus shifts according to the larger environment at hand.

At the same time, accommodating the aesthetic draw of an image produces images that are not always clear or focused, as one might expect from a news photograph. At the beginning of the 2003 war in Iraq, the *Chicago Tribune* ran a story titled "As Sandstorm Rages, Iraqis Seized" alongside an AP photograph of Iraqis being detained (Bouju, 2003, 3). While the photograph's caption noted that the detention was taking place "in the glare of Humvee headlights," it did not clarify that the headlights' glare obscured the detainees from public vision. Nor did that faulty vision stop the newspaper from printing the photograph as the largest, most prominent image on the page.

Color has become a central way of signaling aesthetic appeal. Photographs of the 2001 war in Afghanistan in particular played to the colorful vividness of the fabrics swathing dispossessed women and children as well as to the stunning landscapes pitching voluminous mountain-caps against bright blue skies. No wonder, then, that readers' letters celebrated the photographs in positive terms: one reader of the

Los Angeles Times hailed them as "not sensational or sentimental, just beautiful. (They get) right in the middle of things and shoot at the precise moment when reality unfolds. Nothing in (the) images is mere background" (Coonradt, 2001, B12). Another noted that the photographs of Afghani children were "a glorious testament to the timeless beauty of innocence and to the common admiration of this human condition among Earth's inhabitants" (Takase, 2001, A12). At a time in which the incursion into Afghanistan was already a month or so under way and thousands of refugees had gone homeless, hungry or lost their lives, lauding photography's aesthetic appeal gives pause to the image's role in documenting combat.

During the 2003 war in Iraq, color was at the forefront of the photograph's aesthetic appeal. As the US forces moved across Basra in April of 2003, the *New York Times* featured a half-page portrayal (see figure 3) of women carrying potable water (Hauling Water, 2003, B1). The picture, striking for a peculiar orange haze that characterized many images from the region owing to the impact of dense sand in the air, lacked definitive detail: *The Times* mentioned nothing about where precisely the photograph had been taken other than on the outskirts of Basra, nothing about the women other than that they carried potable water and nothing about what lurked behind the orange haze. In fact, the orange haze appeared to be the striking reason for choosing the photograph and others like it, as is

Figure 3 Photograph taken by Yannis Behrakis / Reuters, April 17, 2003.
Credit: Reuters.

evident when looking at a black-and-white version of the image, pictured here. On a day in which accompanying news stories documented attacks against Iranian opposition groups in Iraq, exchanges of fire in Mosul and the plundering of the Iraqi National Museum, this artistic choice to lead the section on the war displaced an informationally rich one. In the words of the *Chicago Tribune*'s art critic: "If you have the capacity to dazzle in newsprint, you make pictures to take advantage of it [and] color rescues [these photographs]. It is bright, upbeat, conveying an atmosphere of Operation Happy Trails even when the content of the shots is dark, treating death . . . Eye-popping color draws us from the truth" (Artner, 2003, 4). As news, the aesthetic appeal of images thus often works against the information that news depictions can provide.

Similarly, aesthetic appeal often means not seeing the journalistic target of depiction. One particularly illustrative example was the much-discussed photo *The Situation Room* (Souza, 2011), that depicted US leaders and top security personnel watching a live feed of the killing of Osama bin Laden in 2011 (see figure 4). Called by CNN "a photo for the ages" (Silverleib, 2011), the image did not depict the footage but instead focused on a dozen officials watching in deep concentration scenes provided by an unmanned drone that the public could not see. Borrowing from a highly prevalent trope in depictions of the liberation of the Nazi concentration camps in 1945 (Zelizer, 1998), the picture made

Figure 4 Photograph taken by White House photographer Pete Souza, May 1, 2011.
Credit: Wikimedia Commons.

its aesthetic mark by pulling viewers into a position in which they had to complete what the picture did not show, thus strengthening their engagement. Though afterward the photo, taken by a White House photographer and circulated widely across US and international news outlets, was critiqued on multiple counts including its staging, its symbolic standing as a portrait of US politics and attitudes toward bin Laden was telling as an aesthetic, but not particularly newsworthy, image.

At times, the aesthetic appeal of war and conflict images favors explicitly non-journalistic modes of visual representation over those more fully conforming to news norms. Though such images do not conform to modes of journalistic depiction, they reflect broader visual sensibilities in the surrounding culture. Thus, a *Philadelphia Inquirer* article in March 2003 about the false surrender of Iraqi troops was illustrated by a reprint of the Goya painting *The Third of May 1808*, which depicted the execution of Madrid residents at the hands of Napoleonic forces (Lubrano, 2003, Cl). With the decision to include it came another decision not to include a photograph that depicted more directly what was happening in Iraq, suggesting how aesthetic values can offset newsworthiness.

The aesthetic draw of images, then, is deeply embedded in the pictures of contemporary war and conflict. Given that publics today can, by and large, retrieve more images than at any other time in journalism's history, the orientation to pleasing or shocking pictures with lasting aesthetic appeal is a choice that may have little informative value but can be instrumental in crafting public engagement.

Image Familiarity

Journalism's images of war and conflict in the twenty-first century continue to offer pictures that are consonant with already existing notions of what combat is. As media critic Frank Rich said of the initial coverage from Iraq, audiences knew what was coming: "Iraqis are the better seen-than-heard dress extras in this drama, alternately pictured as sobbing, snarling or cheering" (Rich, 2003, 15). While such displays suit editors' desire to keep newspapers "family friendly" and offset their fears of advertiser backlash, news photography nonetheless offers what becomes a default visual setting for many current hostilities. The turn to the visual, then, accommodates familiar images that couch combat's representation in already resonant ways. As one column in the *Chicago Tribune* phrased it, "it's as though all wars become, at some level, the same war; all reaction that of a common humanity" (Leroux, 2003, 1).

In that journalists only have so much space in which to present their coverage, each decision to incorporate the past is accompanied by one to incorporate the present to a lesser degree. In other words, war and conflict coverage often hinges on a vehicle that works against the grain of "good" journalism yet adheres precisely to the grain of "good" memory work. For instance, depictions of both September 11 (Franklin, 2001) and the war in Afghanistan (Chenelly, 2001) relied on images that recalled a World War II photograph of the flag-raising atop Mount Suribachi (Rosenthal, 1945). Though neither photo relayed much about the later circumstances, the parallel instantiated the message of heroism, patriotism, human sacrifice and the importance of the nation-state that accompanied the earlier photograph. This suggests that, even if the associations are irrelevant to later hostilities, the use of images as parallel depictions establishes a connection that lasts. In one media critic's view, the "heroic, often unrepresentative images" are useful in that they "deliberately recall [other] photographs and famous cinematic sequences" (Kakutani, 2003, E1, E5). Much of the power of depicting new hostilities thus comes from earlier times.

Journalism's journey to the past in times of combat is somewhat uncharted territory. There are no standards, guidelines or explicit directives about what in the past best works in the present, for whom and to which ends. Simply stated, who is to say which past makes sense? Should the 2003 war in Iraq be seen against the First Gulf War, Somalia or Vietnam? Should the conflicts that began in 2011 across the Middle East be seen against the 1848 springtime of nations, as the contested title of "Arab Spring" implies, the Eastern European revolutions of 1989 or internal conflict between secular and fundamentalist forces? Should Islamic State be contextualized against the centuries-old notion of the caliphate, the Cold War or US actions in Iraq? And yet journalists look to the past, in all of its forms, as one way to reinstate the normal. This means that hostilities not necessarily alike can receive a similar visual treatment in the news simply because the form of their coverage is rendered similar. The past thus intrudes into the present of news photographs by acting as a carrier for symbolism and connotative force. Bringing recycled associations that help show why a current conflict matters, new hostilities are linked with earlier experiences involving nationalism, human rights, patriotism, civic or ethnic pride and heroic sacrifice, among others. Photographs are used to drive these associations home. Thus, connecting backward in time is signified by a visual trajectory of journalism's images that extend across combat in different times and places.

There are multiple ways in which journalists cue links between an image of combat and the past. Three are particularly relevant here: cueing a linkage through words, through parallel pictures and through substitutional depictions (Zelizer, 1998).

Words function as carriers of meaning that direct interpretations of the images at their side (Barthes, 1967, 1977, 1981; Hall, 1973), and they offer a way to definitively connect what is depicted with the intention for which it is shown. The parallel between contemporary hostilities and those of earlier times is here enunciated primarily in words and only secondarily in the image itself. Articulation is generally found in the words surrounding the photograph – captions, titles, headlines and accompanying bodies of text – that guide audiences in the image's interpretation. A *New York Post* cover photo of the 2005 London subway bombing was titled *Blitz* (Blitz, 2005) in a simple nod to World War II, while the *Sun*'s depiction of a 2011 massacre outside of Oslo (see figure 5) was called *Norway's 9/11* (Norway's 9/11, 2011). Using words as directed cues for interpretation is part of how journalists invoke familiar standards for describing combat to the public. In a column titled "The Real Echoes from Vietnam" alongside an image of Saigon, *Newsweek* addressed the circumstances of war-torn Iraq in 2003 by discussing the implications of having "a moment early last week [when] it felt like 1967" (Alter, 2003, 41). Some images are contextualized against an unspecific past, couched in broad terms, such as a 2014 *Time* magazine cover on Vladimir Putin titled *Cold War II* (Cold War II, 2014). Other times the past is invoked more specifically, as when the Boston Marathon bombing in 2013 was likened to that of the 1996 Olympics (Boston Bombing Compared, 2013).

Figure 5 Cover page published on July 24, 2011.
Credit: The *Sun* / News Syndication.

Yet other parallels are struck by recalling the circumstances of a photograph's taking, as in likening the 2000 image of the impending death of Mohammad Aldura (Abu-Rahma, 2000) to Eddie Adams' iconic shot (Adams, 1968) of the shooting of a presumed Vietcong soldier in 1968 (Roskis, 2000). Parallels are also shaped by region or locality. On March 31, in its first issue after the 2003 war in Iraq began, *Time* magazine titled its cover photograph *Gulf War II*. In each case, the implication that earlier wars could offer an appropriate backdrop against which to interpret contemporary battles sets up an associative framework by which more recent situations of discord could be seen through the filter of earlier ones. The use of words as guides, then, pushes the public to engage with hostilities that came before while dealing with more recent military conflicts. As *Time* put it, "the shock of recognition is acute . . . Surely these pictures . . . come from another time" (Walsh, 1995, 46–7).

A second way of cueing the past through images is by repeating the thematic portrayal of earlier combat, visually marking the past but offering no verbal cues. Ranging from the predictable impulses embodied in the heroic gestures of soldiers to the grotesque ones represented by the stark display of human corpses, journalism's images of combat rework recognizable and familiar themes of representation in visually depicting new hostilities. Pictures are used as parallels in ways that mark the associations surrounding certain hostilities as antecedents to later ones. Malcolm Browne's much-celebrated image of a Buddhist monk immolating himself in the streets of Saigon of 1963 to protest the Vietnam War (Browne, 1963) resurfaced later in photographs of an Indian national who set himself on fire in front of the state legislature to protest against police harassment (India Suicide, 2000), and a Tibetan exile who set himself alight to protest Chinese government repression (Swarup, 2012). And though the self-immolation of Tunisian Mohamed Boazizi, said to have sparked the Jasmine Revolution and then the Arab Spring, was not depicted at the time, its image circulated widely in discussions of the conflict afterward (Suicide Protest, 2011). Combat is signified via the simple depiction of large piles of devices of torture and death, evident in photographs of RPGs, car bombs and spent cartridges from Sudan, Pakistan and Syria (Felt, 2007; Desta, 2010; Mustafa, 2012). A World War II image taken by W. Eugene Smith of a US soldier holding a fly-covered baby removed from a cave of corpses (Smith, 1944) – hailed by *Life* magazine as one of the score of photographs that "people most readily remember" ("Moments Remembered," 1960, 91) – was recycled in 2003 into a much-publicized photograph (see figure 6) of a US soldier holding an Iraqi child (Sagolj, 2003), when it was proclaimed by the *Detroit Free Press* to be an image that would be "embedded in history" (Hinds, 2003, H1). The opposite circumstance – when children cannot be saved despite the efforts

Figure 6 Photograph taken by Damir Sagolj / Reuters, April 11, 2003.
Credit: Reuters.

of aid personnel – works from the same impulse, embodied in a series of 2015 pictures of a drowned Aylan Kurdi, one of which depicted the boy being held by a distressed Turkish rescue worker (Demir, 2015).

A third kind of stopover in the past employs an image of previous hostilities that is both articulated and visible. This kind of image implies a direct connection between different instances of combat by substituting photographs of recent events with earlier ones. These acts of substitutional representation extend a broader disjunction, often evident in news, between the place of the news-text and the place of the image at its side. The editorial decision to use photographs from the past comes at the expense of the hostilities being covered and establishes a definitive visual corollary between the combat of then and now.

Pictures are used often in the task of partial substitution, with pictures of the past positioned alongside images of current hostilities. Following September 11, the *Philadelphia Inquirer* displayed a pair of images – one depicting the collapsed World Trade Center towers, the other the 1941 assault on Pearl Harbor – which drew a visual parallel between the two events despite the fact that other historical parallels might have been more suitable (Infield, 2001, A11). A *Time* column on the so-called "victory in Afghanistan" was accompanied by two photographs – one of Afghanistan and one of Somalia (Krauthammer, 2001, 60). A *Boston*

Globe article about the toppling of the statue of Saddam Hussein in Baghdad in 2003 was illustrated with additional photographs depicting other seemingly similar moments from earlier points in time – the razing of the Berlin Wall, a lone protester in Tiananmen Square and workers jumping off a statue of Lenin in Riga before Latvia seceded from the Soviet Union (Gilbert & Ryan, 2003, D1). The *New York Times* ran an essay titled "Watching Iraq, and Seeing Vietnam," in which pictures of Saigon and Baghdad were positioned side by side (Whitney 2003).

Sometimes the photograph of the past completely displaces visualization of the contemporary one, with pictures of the past used in place of any image of contemporary hostilities. *US News & World Report*'s reassessment of the impact of 9/11 two years later reused a photo (see figure 7) from 2001 showing people in the street watching the attack, which remained undepicted (Never Again?, 2003). A *New York Times* piece about civilian casualties, written at the onset of the 2003 Iraq War, was illustrated with photos of dead civilians and structural devastation in Kosovo and Kabul from 1999 and 2001, but no image of combat in Iraq (Eviatar, 2003, D7, D9). *Newsweek* featured an image of Saigon in a column on Iraq (Alter, 2003, 41). A *US News & World Report* cover article on the parameters of

Figure 7 Cover page published on September 11, 2003.
Credit: US News and World Report.

wartime experience used a cover photo of a World War II GI from over half a century earlier (Real Stories of Wartime, 2007). A story driven by the self-immolation of Tunisian Mohamed Boazizi and its effect on the Arab Spring was depicted by a different immolation from the Vietnam War (Worth, 2011). In all of these cases, the distance between the discord of today and that of earlier times is collapsed via its visual representation. The image of then is used as a substitute for the image of today.

When War and Conflict Are Reduced to a Photograph

What does the turn to the visual in times of combat show? Coverage of war and conflict involves making quick decisions under fraught circumstances. In that regard, the availability of memorable visual cues – whether they have to do with frequency, aesthetic appeal or familiarity – helps journalists make judgments about which photographs should depict a given circumstance of bloodshed. All of this matters because it is not the photograph's referentiality – its ability to present the world as is – that endures in journalism's turn to the visual. Despite the fact that news codes have long suggested that the referential force matters in news photographs, it is the photograph's symbolic or connotative force – its ability to contextualize the discrete details of a setting in a broader frame – that facilitates the durability and memorability of a news image. The turn to the visual thus makes sense as a way of nurturing public engagement with the news via its images, even if what is depicted in images is rarely all – or even much – of what has transpired in combat.

Today, perhaps more than ever, the capacity to offer even a partial view matters. To be sure, journalism's images of war and conflict provide their own way of documenting the battlefield. Rather than facilitate fuller understanding, as news stories are expected to do, they also activate the emotions, the imagination and much of what is contingent about a news depiction. This means that journalism's visualization of the battlefield does not necessarily follow longstanding codes of newsworthiness and that it regularly offsets many normative expectations about documenting war and conflict in the news.

Instead, when a news photograph is deemed "memorable," modes of appraisal in addition to newsworthiness are invoked. This suggests that journalism works actively along trajectories that are not emphasized by traditional understandings of the news. These trajectories reflect a larger mindset among journalists about how the world works than that offered by conventional notions of journalistic practice.

The contours of the dissonance between news norms and news images are intuited by most of those who work with pictures in journalism.

On the one hand, visual coverage drives a bare-bones engagement with war and conflict that flattens and neutralizes their complicating circumstances, circumstances often verbally described in ways that end up distancing or polarizing publics. Visual coverage puts differences aside so as to target core issues related to survival and dignity that can draw dissenting publics together. It provides close visual evidence of the particularities of combat. On the other hand, visual coverage allows journalists to strike parallels between hostilities for no better reason than that the surrounding mandates for interpreting them resemble each other. Lost in the depictions tracked here are important visual aspects of individual hostilities and the socio-political differences that distinguish them from each other. Is it any surprise, then, that images facilitate the accomplishment of political and military ends, mobilizing public support for strategic action in times of combat?

But given the difficult circumstances under which war, conflict and their coverage today unfold, that is no mean feat. For it suggests that images may be a particularly useful vehicle for providing the degree and kind of detail that is attainable in current hostilities. And in that regard, the wars and conflicts of the twenty-first century may be revealing what has long been an unfulfilled linkage between news norms and news pictures – that existing news norms have never really taken into account the exigencies by which war and conflict are depicted or by which news pictures are crafted. Against the much-curtailed ability to depict what happens in current situations of discord, the pictures that do surface may constitute an optimum kind of documentation that reflects current circumstances of newsgathering even if it reflects less the existing normative notions of what news should look like.

Visual coverage in the news may therefore follow the beat of a different drummer, but the ends it attains may be particularly useful for promoting public engagement with war and conflict. These circumstances are not new. Nor are they limited to the depiction of war and conflict. Rather, they are the fallout of excessive years of not privileging images for what they do differently from words in the journalistic environment.

Two options remain for figuring out how news images and words can come together more productively as alternative platforms of information provision. One is to make images more like words – developing and accommodating the detail that is in their captions and credits, affixing images in a more precise relation with news stories, treating each image as a document in and of itself, applying standards of image presentation that are consonant with surrounding news spaces. Most of these practices do not involve photographers per se but members of the larger journalistic community in which they work as well as the public. Though new digital platforms like Vine or Snapchat offer moves in the right direction – the captions provided on Instagram, for instance, were recently labeled "the new blogging" (Chayka, 2015) – they do not always provide the extensive documentation that news pictures are capable of providing regardless of a shared app. Without that documentation, there is scant chance of recognizing images and words as two platforms engaged equally in the common mission of providing the news.

The second option is to recognize images for their differences from words – developing and accommodating visual imagery as it flows across the information environment. This means recognizing the power and memorability of a picture regardless of the detail in its surrounding text, privileging images in news presentation not only in times of war and conflict but as part of an increasingly ocular-centric world, accepting that publics need to care about issues and events before they can incorporate the information at journalism's core and recognizing more fully the images that came from non-conventional journalists and non-journalists. In this regard, images may offer a fruitful entry point for prompting public understanding from sources other than visuals.

When war and conflict are reduced to a photograph, journalism ends up being less journalistic than it would like to be. The question, however, is whether the deficit is with images or with long-held expectations of journalism. Because both strategies cannot be accommodated simultaneously, one or the other has to prevail.

Endings

12

Thinking Temporally about Journalism's Future

Addressing the future is symptomatic of a more general push to forecast what is yet to come – in financial markets, political regimes, weather and conflict situations. Orientation to the future directs us, in the historian Reinhart Kosellek's view (2004 [1985], 259), to the "not-yet, to the non-experienced, to that which is to be revealed." Journalism is not immune to this temporal focus. Indeed, its future seems to be on everyone's mind these days. A Google search produces over 52 million hits for the phrase "future of journalism," alongside links to conferences, roundtables, blogs, books and websites on the topic.

Why does journalism's future raise such concern? In what follows, I consider what this emphasis means, why it has become such a central contour of discussions about the news and what might be done to allay the anxieties it contains.

Predicting the Future

Addressing the future of anything requires a degree of redress to the other temporalities that neighbor it – the present and the past. George Orwell, who reminded us long ago that those who control the past control the future, also observed that those who control the present control the past. Such temporal interdependence – which positions past, present and future on unequal footing, giving the present a significant head-start on the others – directly influences how we position ourselves temporally. Orientation to the future – often alongside an orientation to the past – comes to the forefront in challenging times, when the search for certain trajectories is difficult to sustain. In that light, futures studies – also called forecasting studies, futurology and futures research – was launched in the United States during the 1940s and 1950s as a Cold War platform to forecast military and economic potential under the threat of nuclear war. Offering a useful reliance on prediction as part and parcel of grappling with the challenges of late modernity, the project of assessing the future became a productive tool for sustaining an array of political, economic, social and cultural institutional settings in times of uncertainty and risk.

What do predictions of the future involve? The consideration of "options, possibilities for change, different entry points into understanding a particular long-term problem . . . probabilities, ideas, desires and hopes as well as fears" (Moll, 2001) is central to a future orientation, and it tends to require the consideration of alternatives, some act of prognosis or prediction, a scenario of desired pragmatic action and the involvement of normative thinking. Significantly, "*the* future, as something that can be analyzed, observed and studied in the academic sense, does not exist: it is yet to come" (Moll, 2001). Addressing it is thereby predicated on the internally contradictory exercise of erasing or minimizing uncertainty about an enterprise that remains inherently – and insistently – uncertain.

And yet, enterprises orienting to some sense of the future abound in the current environment, where the "thirst for certainty" (Moll, 2001) often produces less than satisfying results. Notions of transitional justice, for instance, are dependent on a future orientation, while the opinion polls and predictive discourse that accompany political campaigns have become a naturalized part of the political environment in many parts of the world.

So too with journalism, where current discourse about the news is rife with future-oriented contemplations. The frequently voiced aims in the West, for instance, of using journalism to bolster democracy, enhance civic engagement and foster public involvement are largely driven by concerns for the future. The Huffington Post hosts a vertical under the name "Future of Journalism," while news outlets as varied as the *Washington Post*, the *New York Times*, the *Guardian*, the *London Financial Times* and the Nieman Journalism Lab ran discussions of the topic within a few months of each other in 2015. And yet there are so many disconnects about journalism's many pasts and presents that no agreement orients the future moves of the multiple forms of journalism that exist. Thinking about journalism's future, then, has many sides, many voices and many suggested paths to resolution.

In large part, this is because considerations of journalism's future have been eclipsed by an unstable present, in which current notions of crisis are aplenty. Journalism, it is repeatedly said, is on its way out (Shirky, 2009; McChesney & Nichols, 2010). Newspapers are dying, audiences are uninterested, business concerns kill public interest and journalists lag behind the documentary efforts of bystanders and private individuals.

In fact, a panoply of complicated economic, political, technological, social, occupational and moral impulses under which journalists currently labor facilitates different evaluations of what is to transpire next, despite rhetorical claims of a shared destiny of diminished expectation (Zelizer, 2015b). For instance, Nielsen (2015) identified three modalities of crisis characterizing journalism in different geographic regions: an economic crisis tends to predominate in Southern European countries such as Italy and France; a professional crisis drives journalism's instability in the United States and United Kingdom; and a crisis of confidence rattles public sentiments about the news in Northern European countries such as Finland and Germany. Technology features unevenly in most places, and even more diversity exists in locations where the free flow of information is not guaranteed, such as China or Russia. Such variations, which reflect the complexity under which journalism operates and underscore multiple ways of experiencing current conditions, leave many questions unresolved: why, for instance, has the newspaper survived almost a full century past the earliest predictions of its demise that accompanied the arrival of radio? How can one assume the primacy of the Internet when so many regions of the world have yet to experience it in reliable or systematic ways? Despite the lingering resonance of the idea of one future for all, circumstances on the ground unmoor the capacity to view any kind of future as a shared enterprise for journalists everywhere.

Why do predictions of a dire future for journalism persist? In large part, they are typical of a broader tendency to assert more certainty in discourse than is possible to realize in reality. Much of this is related to how institutions deal with uncertainty. Modernity and its accouterments, institutions central among them, were long tasked with holding the uncertainty that modernity wrought. Among the first to note that the very quest for knowledge depended on certainty, Dewey (1929, 85) argued that the anchoring of any enterprise – politics, art and science, among others – requires unifying the "settled and the unsettled, the stable and the hazardous." Giddens (1991b, 3) maintained how "under conditions of modernity, the future is continually drawn into the present by means of the reflexive organization of knowledge environments." Elster (1993, 175) said that institutions provide a "certainty [which] enables the citizen to form long-term plans [and to] count on the basic institutional framework remaining in place over reasonably long periods." Pushing a unitary notion of crisis, then, has allowed those invested in the future to imagine closure, a solution, another side where circumstances might settle – in short, a landscape of certainty (Zelizer, 2015a).

To an extent, identifying and articulating certainty has always been at least the rhetorical purview of journalism. That is because, in the *Washington Post*'s view, journalism

is based on a fundamental belief that the reporters tasked with covering a beat know that beat so well that they are able to judge for you what matters and what doesn't, what to pay attention to and what to ignore. It's why journalism has clung so tightly to certainty for all these years; if we aren't the authoritative voice, what good are we? Certainty functions as job security.

(Cillizza, 2014)

Yet such claims to certainty are more malleable and less linear than they might appear. Particularly with journalism, the dialectics connecting certainty and uncertainty are ongoing. Keeping a news story alive often means highlighting its uncertain aspects, as Tenenboim-Weinblatt (2008, 2013b) showed in conjunction with coverage of both the Israeli–Palestinian conflict and instances of kidnapping and captivity around the world. At times, journalism voluntarily accommodates an uncertain stance even when certainty is available. Particularly in coverage of death, accommodating certainty might be so difficult that news outlets opt for less certain representations, displaying pictures of individuals about to die rather than those already dead (Zelizer, 2010).

Today's widely shared emphasis on journalism's diminished future, however, suggests that the capacity to discern in nuanced ways what lies ahead has been somewhat derailed. There is need, then, to entertain other modes of engaging with the future.

On Knowledge Transfer and Time

Thinking about time itself and what it does to knowledge becomes relevant in the context just described. Though it might seem counterintuitive to look to the past or present in order to imagine journalism's future, in fact looking backward and sideways is a necessary step to moving forward. In Alistair MacIntyre's (1981, 223) words, "an adequate sense of tradition manifests itself in a grasp of those future possibilities which the past has made available to the present." Thus, a temporal understanding of action necessarily draws from neighboring temporal alternatives so as to compare, contrast, evaluate and predict across the past, present and future. This distribution not only makes visible how difficult it is to maintain temporal binaries between now and then, but also underscores the fact that temporal engagement helps situate enterprises of all kinds in the world. In this regard, using the prism of time to consider journalism can help offset the current misunderstanding of its many pasts and reluctance to account for the differences in its many presents.

Not surprisingly, the connection between past, present and future can take multiple shapes. Alternative notions of the future, for instance, are invoked by embracing different kinds of temporal strategies: whether time is thought to progress or recycle, to move in a zig-zagged or straightforward fashion, or to be continuous – as implied by bridges – or discontinuous – as implied by periodization – sets up a fundamentally different temporal expectation of the future (Zerubavel, 2003). In each case, temporal engagement necessarily builds from juxtaposing different temporalities with each other, but it draws too from adopting strategies that accommodate certain ways of thinking about time while minimizing others.

This is important, because time is a central determinant of the successful transfer of knowledge among group members, which in turn is instrumental to the consolidation of group identity. Key to how knowledge transfer operates, temporal strategies help shape the role that knowledge plays in generating and sustaining action among those invested in the future of any enterprise. To be sure, scholars interested in the production and flow of knowledge have long focused on the fact that knowledge arises from strategies of knowledge creation (Brown, 2007; Vosniadou, 2007). Specifically, knowledge flow depends on the carriers by which people come to know themselves, for they provide cues on how to orient to new conditions, engage with what seems relevant and lend meaning to unfolding experience. These carriers are widespread and varied, involving symbolic structures like representations, stories, narratives and images; routines and habits embedding tacit understandings of what is important to the group; the interpersonal interactions that informally support notions of value; and material objects and artifacts. Often they involve what Pollitt and Hupe (2011) called "magic concepts," whereby the promise of a challenge's resolution is crafted through a broadly abstract, normatively charged, near-universally applicable and transportable idea. Taken together, these different routes for transmitting information, beliefs, values and preference statements comprise what is typically seen as a group's collective knowledge base.

When transported onward, knowledge can take on contours that become formalized, even ossified, over time. Recognizable under the label of groupthink, where what we know relies upon how we know and with whom, this now somewhat fundamental notion, intimated long ago by Kuhn (1962), maintains that knowledge depends on consensus building and that developing shared paradigms – naming and characterizing problems and procedures in ways recognized by the group – is a necessary step for knowledge spread. Shared knowledge is central too to the idea of interpretive communities (Fish, 1982; Zelizer, 1993a), whereby the group uses shared interpretive strategies to guide collective action. The transfer of knowledge thereby moves forward in systematic, shared and recognizable ways, reinforcing knowledge creation that privileges community, solidarity and power as much as cognitive cues.

Time plays a central role in this scenario. Anthropologists have long maintained that the time/space dimensions of knowledge creation generate contours by which knowledge circulates (Massey, 1999). Among those interested in the mechanics of knowledge transfer, time has long been seen as the source of codified knowledge, while space has been thought to introduce variety. In such views, the more temporally oriented the knowledge, the less oriented to space it will be. Conversely, if knowledge is more diffuse and tacit than codified, its spatial parameters become more central (Von Krough, Ichijo & Nonaka, 2000).

For journalism, focusing on temporality and the temporal aspects of knowledge transfer is useful because it offsets what is most entrenched in journalists' sense of themselves. Journalists engage more readily with the unarticulated, tacit, mimetic and informal aspects of embedded knowledge than they do with formal and explicit codification. Journalists, it has been maintained from the earliest days of journalism's study, learn by osmosis (Breed, 1955; Sigelman, 1973). Their conventions and collective lore are embedded in routines that for the most part remain unarticulated and are informally and ritually passed among group members (Roshco, 1975; Tuchman, 1978a; Gans, 1979).

Though reticence about codification raises the question of what to do with codified knowledge in collectives that do not value it, it also underscores one of the basic roadblocks for understanding how journalism works. Introducing a temporal riff to the longstanding characterization of journalists as so-called "failed professionals" – those who are "in the profession but not of it" (Weaver & Wilhoit, 1986) – it suggests that in eschewing codification, those involved with journalism have obscured the capacity to discern what we know about journalism and where it has come from. This is even more the case because accessing core knowledge remains a different exercise across the groups invested in thinking about journalism: journalism scholars, for instance, engage with journalism's future as a way to address their own research interests as much as to resolve the existential concerns of practitioners. Thus, as argued over a decade ago (Zelizer, 2004b), journalists, journalism educators, journalism students and journalism scholars, as well as the public, continue to function within the boundaries (and confines) of their own interpretive communities. Their still persistent demarcation from each other underscores both that journalism has not yet codified its own core understanding and that its lack of codification now impacts its capacity to navigate the future.

Temporality constitutes a relevant intervention, because it helps to shape a group's core knowledge by advancing collective understanding in ways that make sense to group members. Relevant to the translation work that takes place in moving from experience to abstract ideas or from individual reflections to those of the collective are the given default temporal beliefs and shared temporal logic that underlie collective action. Thus, there might be value in forcing codified knowledge – and its reliance on temporality – to the forefront of discussions about journalism, even if doing so means understanding journalism against its own rhetoric of what matters – that is, reading journalism against its own grain.

Tools of Temporal Engagement

Journalism's relationship with time has tended to be rhetorically unidimensional. In the popular eye, journalists are seen as largely if not exclusively situated in the present, driven by the organizing concepts of immediacy, timeliness, speed and liveness. As Patterson (1998, 55) put it, "the news is deliberately short-sighted, is rooted in novelty rather than precision, and focuses on fastbreaking events rather than enduring issues." Thought to be responsible for the here-and-now rather than the there-and-then, and despite periodic lapses toward long-form journalism, commentary and analytical pieces, journalists are primarily expected to offer a record of action that is wedged firmly and definitively between past and future. Furthermore, that record is expected to change markedly from day to day, justifying the novelty of the news and counteracting its ensuing perishability.

How realistic is it, however, to assume that the temporal nature of any kind of practice can be so clearly delineated? General experience of time suggests that action in the present is always conducted with a sense of the past and an orientation to the future. From the changing rhythms introduced by a newborn to the truncated future promoted by terminal illness, from truisms like speeding up time when having fun to slowing it down when in pain, we readily accept time's fundamentally mutable nature. How we live in time, then, depends on our emotions, personality, connections and the political, social, economic and cultural circumstances around us. Producing an experience of time that is non-linear, subjective and constructed, the forms that it takes depend on multiple variables.

Journalism is no exception to these circumstances. In fact, the practical displays of journalists' core knowledge – not what is said about journalism but what journalists do – exhibit a far more complicated interweaving of multiple temporalities than just an adherence to the present. "As time passes," wrote Schudson (1986, 89), "the story grows, the ripples spread out into the past and future, the reverberations to past and future become the new context for the story." The very acts of evaluating, comparing, analogizing and measuring, so central to the news, are imbued with orientations to both past and future. As Lang and Lang (1989, 126) argued, even cursory perusal reveals many references to events no longer new and hence not news in the journalistic sense. This past and future together frame the reporting of current events. Just what part of the past and what kind of future are brought into play depends on what editors and journalists believe legitimately belongs within the public domain, on journalistic conventions, and of course on personal ideologies.

The discursive proclamation of journalism's orientation to the present, then, is a limited assessment that is not borne out in practice. Practically speaking, journalists display a rich and complex engagement with temporal positions of many kinds.

Scholarship already bears this out. For instance, journalists' mastery of time – what Schlesinger (1977) famously called journalism's "time-machine" – facilitates their ability to claim professionalism. The news accommodates its embrace of the "continuous present" by encouraging journalists to routinely involve themselves across a wide span of temporalities (Schudson, 1986). Journalists regularly inhabit "double time," revisiting the coverage of earlier events at will (Zelizer 1993a). In orienting to context, news itself broadens temporality beyond the present (Barnhurst & Mutz, 1997), and journalists regularly use past and future time to situate news events regardless of medium (Barnhurst, 2011). Live news accommodates repair work in real time, as audiences navigate between their own time and that of what is being reported (Scannell, 2014), while different cultures develop different temporal practices in the news (Neiger & Tenenboim-Weinblatt, 2016). Even the move toward digital platforms and their accommodation of immediacy and speed does not affect journalists' temporal sensibilities in predictable ways: Tenenboim-Weinblatt and Neiger (2015) showed how, contrary to intuition, digital news outlets reveal more attention to the past than do print newspapers, while Bodker (2016) demonstrated how news websites exhibit what he called "accumulated contemporaneity": the para-doxical combination of chronicling and archiving – or, looking sideways and backwards – in crafting news events.

Similar degrees of temporal nuance characterize ongoing discussions of journalism itself, even though they are not readily admitted as such. Three tools of temporal engagement drive the complicated temporality in which journalism exists. They include:

- engaging with journalism's past via the tool of reflexivity
- engaging with journalism's present via the tool of transparency
- engaging with journalism's future via the tool of proactivity.

Each tool – reflexivity, transparency and proactivity – constitutes an example of a "magic concept (Pollitt & Hupe, 2011), notions which practitioners and academics use to orient themselves to magically resolving existing dilemmas. In offering an abstract, normative, universal and portable frame for resolution, such tools are critical to discussions of journalism's imagined durability. Though offered here as a heuristic exercise that presumes more temporal separation than is the case, these temporal positions – all magic concepts for those invested in journalism – are useful in identifying the kind of codified knowledge that might help more fully contemplate what lies ahead.

The Past and Reflexivity

The notion of reflexivity – being thoughtful, self-aware and reflective about oneself and one's collective – draws necessarily from the past, where journalism's capacity to learn from past mistakes and triumphs is a necessary precondition for present and future survival. Reflexivity has always been central to theories of learning, which have long postulated that experience, past mistakes and trial and error provide some of the most useful mechanisms for adapting to change, accommodating growth and sustaining viability (Dyke, 2009). Reflexive enterprises of all kinds are expected to engage in self-conscious and self-critical ways with their pasts. Part of what has been called a "memory imperative" (Levy & Sznaider, 2005), expectations are marshaled together to evaluate and repair past performance so as to adjudicate the tenor of present and future action.

And yet discourse about journalism – as shaped by practitioners, educators, students, scholars and the public – suggests that those involved with journalism have not easily recognized lessons from the past. As a placard alongside the exhibits at the US Newseum in Washington, DC explains, "News is history in the making. Journalists provide the first draft of history." For as long as journalism has been around, the popular assumption has been that it provides a first, rather than final, draft of the past, leaving to historians the final processing of journalism's raw events with presumably more distance, objectivity and permanence. This has rendered journalism into a temporally interim platform suspended between past and future, entrenching the news in what often seems like a fundamentally ahistoric space.

Expectations of ahistoricism have had direct effect on the value of learning through reflexivity. They have helped justify journalism's often facile engagement with issues, particularly in times of crisis. "From Pol Pot to ISIS: The Blood Never Dried," proclaimed one headline about the absence of memory in considering human rights violations (Pilger, 2015). Another header admonished institutions of all kinds for not regularly confronting their pasts, for "short memory leads to repeating mistakes" (Waterford, 2015). As Edy (1999, 74) succinctly stated, "the fact that news media make use of historical events at all is somewhat counterintuitive." Not surprisingly, then, despite complicated temporalities that emerge in practice, in discussions about journalism the past continues to be seen as largely beyond the parameters of journalists' responsibility.

But despite a discursive insistence on the present, evidence of journalism's reflexive involvement in the past is extensive. Invoking the past helps those concerned with journalism regularly make sense of a rapidly evolving present, build connections, suggest inferences, create story pegs, find yardsticks for gauging an event's magnitude and impact, offer analogies and provide short-hand explanations (Lang & Lang, 1989). And although much has been made of journalists' so-called "reliance on the commandment questions of news" – the who, what, where, when and how of journalism, with not enough emphasis on the "why" (Carey, 1986a) – a necessary attachment to the explanatory paradigms underlying current events is always there for the taking in journalism. The past thus remains one of the richest repositories available to those invested in journalism for appraising and explaining current events and issues.

It is therefore not surprising that a reflexive orientation to the past permeates the full spectrum of journalistic practice. One of the key lessons of contemporary memory studies is that vast and intricate memory work is being accomplished all the time in settings having little to do with memory per se, like politics, law, religion and education (Schudson, 1992, 1995; Zelizer, 1992b, 1993a, 1995a). Journalism is no exception, though journalists do not necessarily recognize its presence (Zelizer, 1998, 2001; Meyers, Neiger & Zandberg, 2011; Zelizer & Tenenboim-Weinblatt, 2014). Via practices such as rewrites, revisits to old events, commemorative or anniversary journalism and even investigations of seemingly "historical" events and happenings (Huxford, 2001; Meyers, 2002; Kitch, 2005, 2006; Wardle, 2007; Szpunar, 2012), journalists find themselves squarely in the realm of memory's work, producing a patterned treatment of the past that rarely appears in discourse about how journalism works. Invoking the past accommodates reflexivity by helping journalists reconfigure the past to suit present-day aims, suggesting that journalists regularly look to the past but not in ways that clearly demarcate it from either the present or the future. Rather, journalists engage the past – and the tool of reflexivity it promotes – via a nuanced intertwining of temporal positions.

Seen in this fashion, a reflexive past should permeate discussions of journalism as much as it characterizes journalistic practice. Instead, those invested in journalism's discussion ignore the past, in some cases, and invoke it in naturalized ways, in others. Neither strategy encourages productive learning from it.

Discourse on journalism tends to avoid the fact that models of news-making are nearly always framed in conjunction with that which came before and often in not very novel ways. And yet, because it relentlessly repeats itself, the past offers valuable patterns for perusal: at least five "new journalisms" surfaced between the 1860s and 1990s in the United States and United Kingdom – the criticism of Mathew Arnold in 1860, yellow journalism of the late 1880s, jazz journalism of the 1920s, the literary journalism of the 1960s and stretching all the way to the present reinstatement of so-called "narrative journalism." Similarly, certain particularly fertile time periods in US journalism produced multiple and often contradictory platforms for thinking anew about what journalism could be: the first two decades of the 1900s generated the opposite alternatives of jazz journalism and muckraking; the 1960s gave birth to renewed forms of neutral, advocacy and literary journalism; and the 1990s/2000s generated public journalism, citizen journalism and a revival of literary/narrative journalism. Additionally, change in journalism is almost always accompanied by change outside of journalism: the journalistic embrace of objectivity, for instance, was accompanied by the rise of the scientific method, a move toward realism in novels and the development of the telegraph (Schudson, 1978; Carey, 1986a; Armstrong, 1999), suggesting that change is always broader than the platform on which it surfaces. Reflexive discourse about the past could help clarify these patterns, and others.

Furthermore, many of those invested in journalism continue to invoke outdated discursive cues in their discussions, revealing how much the lessons of the past have not been widely applied to the present. Journalists are among the worst offenders in this regard, trotting out old (and increasingly irrelevant) definitions of what journalism is and who journalists are. Examples include repairing to narrowed definitions of hard news that constitute a small portion of journalism's universe or favoring non-inclusive rosters of who counts as a journalist. Currently, the latter case excludes the precarious labor force quietly referenced as journalism's "last dirty secret" because it is increasingly responsible for what journalists used to do on their own (Schachter, 2014). These dated discursive cues suggest that while journalistic practices and those who act as journalists have expanded, journalists have not exhibited similar expansion in their discussions of themselves.

Outdated cues are also prevalent among many journalism educators, and by extension the journalism students subject to their curricula. Many still separate themselves and their curricular sequences by medium, applying irrelevant demarcations between print and television, while reifying digital media as if they exist in their own isolated bubble. This pattern has surfaced before: in the US, it characterized the radio press

wars of the 1920s (Jackaway, 1995) and the resistance to television in the
1950s and 1960s (Watson, 1990; Zelizer, 1992b). Today, these outdated
modes of demarcation prevail despite the fundamental blending of the
current multi-media world, where multi-skilling and multi-tasking force
journalists to create multiple platforms for each news story they produce.

Similarly, many journalism scholars remain non-reflexively entrenched
in academic bubbles, continuing to inhabit largely isolated disciplinary
pockets that have not fully benefited from insights of the past (Zelizer,
2004b). As different kinds of academics continue to splinter their notions
of the journalistic environment, they privilege the narrowed mindsets
on which their disciplinary vantage points took form. Many remain
unmindful of the fact that journalism's study is today even more part of
a multi-faceted inquiry across the university curriculum than it was in
earlier years. For instance, engineering and computer science are today
centrally relevant to journalism's existence. Yet, because no productive
academic intersection embraces the multiple offerings of different kinds
of academic knowledge about journalism, there persists an ahistoric
understanding of the multiple technologies that preceded the digital
environment but continue to drive parts of journalism.

Moreover, much journalism scholarship keeps alive the discussion
of multiple news practices that are no longer pertinent to journalism.
These include overused notions of neutral, objective and impartial
journalism; breathless identification with so-called "new modes of participation," whether this be advocacy journalism, public journalism or
citizen journalism; a repeated regard for journalism as autonomous and
revolutionary rather than as a phenomenon that works incrementally
and slowly with other forces in its environment; and the somewhat tired
epistemological prism of organizational logic – which sees news work as
routinized, fosters expectations of journalism as a predictable and man-
ageable phenomenon, regards newsrooms as central parts of everyday
work life, and treats multi-platform stories and multi-media journalism
as curiosities rather than evolutionary necessities. Journalists here are
seen as the backbone of news outlets, even while multi-media journalists,
video journalists and the variously named solo journalists, mobile journalists and backpack journalists all suggest an uptick in an evolving form
of solitary – not organizational – journalistic practice, to say nothing
of non-journalists or non-conventional journalists producing content.
While such forms may be both democratizing journalistic practice and
legitimating the logic of the network, they undercut the centrality of
formal organizational logic for understanding how journalism works.

The public too, even when it is invested in journalism, often lobs critiques from ahistoric and unreflexive positions. Each time journalists
fare less than satisfactorily in covering the latest act of terrorism, war or

natural disaster, public voices loom large in disapproval but reveal little recognition of the structural changes in the journalistic environment – fewer full time reporters, more multiskilling, more parachute journalists, more dangerous ground conditions – that might affect the ensuing coverage. As more of the public become producers of user-generated content on their own – what Rottwilm (2014) characterized as a move from news recipients to news sources – the general understanding of the conditions under which news is made will no doubt be enriched. But this requires an understanding of what has come before.

Though there are nuances and exceptions to each of these points, the absence of a reflexive look backwards still prevails. All of this suggests that, though the journalistic practices of engaging with the world include being reflexive about the past, discourse about journalism has not been as temporally expansive. The failure to learn from the past impedes journalism moving forward.

The Present and Transparency

A second tool for journalism's future is transparency: how those invested in journalism engage with the present by identifying and articulating the how and why of journalistic decision-making at the time of its unfolding. Paralleling a push for greater transparency in venues as diverse as global politics and the corporate financial world (Schudson, 2015), transparency in journalism embeds "a sense of how the story came to be and why it was presented as it was" (Kovach & Rosenstiel, 2001, 83). Though, in other domains, transparency has been seen as an offset to corruption, for western journalism it is largely expected to repair problems, foibles and mistakes associated with bias and faulty decision-making (Wasserman, 2006). In this regard, learning from the present constitutes as rich a platform for those concerned with journalism's future as does learning from the past. Accommodating a capacity to share information itself as well as its mode of disclosure (Craft & Heim, 2008, 219), transparency gives news outlets a way to admit and correct errors, clarify process and engage with the public.

Significantly, transparency offers a platform for explaining and justifying decisions at the time they are taken. This is critical because journalism's temporal positioning in the present can have brutal repercussions: because journalists cannot be late for events or they will occur without them, cannot dally with coverage or they will have no audience and cannot stay with a story beyond its first recounting or they will encroach on historians, they have little opportunity for reflection. As Edy (1999, 74) noted:

Journalists have traditionally placed a high value on being the first to publicize new information. Extra editions, news flashes, and program interruptions for important new information all testify to a desire to present the latest information to audiences. Many stories go out of date and cannot be used if there is not space in the news product for them on the day that they occur.

Transparency thus counterbalances the risks that ensue from newsmaking's rapid pace and its investment in topicality, novelty, proximity, deadlines, exclusives and scoops. It provides a momentary time-out for journalists to reflect on what they do, facilitating openness about a frenetically changing journalistic environment.

It is thus no surprise that the spectrum of journalistic practice often involves a nod to transparency. Though not part of the US political heritage (Schudson, 2013), it nonetheless constitutes a standard-bearer in the United States for best practices in journalism (Bowles, Hamilton & Levy, 2013). Today, transparency resides in a slew of unevenly used practices, including public editors, correction boxes, published correction policies, virtual newsroom tours and explanation alongside anonymous sources. It also finds its way into media talk shows, journalistic forums, professional conferences and the trade media. In the words of the *American Journalism Review*, such efforts provide the "panacea for sullied reputations, the antidote to ... [cheating] ... and the tonic to arrogance" (Smolkin, 2006). Seen as a platform for journalistic integrity, transparency is widely thought to give journalists a way to maintain public trust and reestablish it when it goes awry (Craft & Heim, 2008).

Given how central transparency is to the current environment, new platforms that facilitate transparent engagement are continually surfacing. For instance, ProPublica's "Explore Sources" or the BBC's UCG Hub – which utilize tools such as TinEye, Topsy and GeoFeedia – allow readers to scrutinize the source material underlying news stories or to correct news articles themselves. The radio platform Hearken invites the public to assign stories while reporters share their work in progress. Multiple tools for fact-checking and verification in the digital environment, such as checking timestamps or establishing a chain of custody (Wardle, 2013), are driven by aspirations toward transparency.

But there is need for greater nuance in its celebration. To be sure, the time-out that transparency introduces is a useful antidote to the linearity and sure-footedness implied by conventional understandings of journalism. Debates over open source documentation, for instance, mean accommodating as strengths the skepticism, doubt and uncertainty that are so central to the current moment, rather than disregarding them as obstructions in journalism's rush to judgment.

Thus, it might be worth admitting that even as a widely applauded standard for journalistic practice, transparency remains slippery. Though it is practiced, by and large, across the board, most journalists are reluctant to correct news that has already circulated. Fewer than 2 percent of factual errors committed by news outlets are actually corrected (Maier, 2007), while instances of self-correcting mistakes from the far past are rare. Exceptions include the *Lexington Herald-Leader*, which ran a clarification in 2004 that repaired an error from decades earlier: "It has come to our attention," read the editorial, "that the Herald-Leader neglected to cover the Civil Rights movement. We regret the omission." In 1969 the *New York Times* retracted a 1920 editorial that had pronounced space flight as impossible, correcting it on the day after Apollo 11 launched (Tenore, 2011). Similarly, the 2011 phone hacking scandal at News International exemplified how an absence of transparency produced collusion across multiple institutional settings, including journalism. The fact that all of the violations associated with the scandal – paying for information, the use of deception and impersonation to secure information, cozying up to officials, disregarding privacy – had been around for some time suggested a failure to learn from the past, but it also underscored how institutional complicity could magnify exponentially when not treated transparently in the present (Zelizer, 2012).

It might be worth admitting too that transparency is not invoked consistently among journalists for the same ends: Phillips (2010), for instance, suggested using transparency to counter "news cannibalization," instances in which digital material is taken without attribution. Nor is transparency evenly applied in journalism: while the *New York Times* dedicated two full pages of its newspaper in 2003 to exposing the misdeeds of errant reporter Jayson Blair, one year later it delayed for over a year its report of the NSA's illegal eavesdropping practices. Similarly, NBCUniversal chose to sideline NBC anchor Brian Williams in 2015 after his sharing of fabricated exploits and then quietly reinstate him six months later at the smaller MSNBC platform. Transparency is also unequally relevant across journalism's many locations: highly western, it remains largely inoperative in regimes where the free flow of information is not guaranteed. In such cases, where full transparency may not be possible or advisable, it might be worth admitting that even some is better than none. Each of these examples attests to transparency's uneven texture, underscoring that it tends to surface as a performative assessment when the gains are great, the losses few.

How has transparency fared in discussions of journalism among educators, students and scholars? Here too, a more nuanced approach might be in order. In large part, the call for transparency has recuperated long-standing criticism of trends toward journalistic navel-gazing. Though the self-orientation of journalists was long seen as an intrusion in the news environment – where "the press's ability to tell itself how it has done often interferes with our capacity, as publics, to reach evaluations of our own that may differ" (Zelizer, 1997) – today it has become a catch-all for adjudicating journalism's foibles.

Among many journalism educators and the students they teach, transparency is now akin to a public good. The SPJ's current Code of Ethics includes a section titled "Be Accountable, Be Transparent," and the last two decades have been driven by an institutional desire to wear transparency as a badge of honor. Already in 2005, an Aspen Institute conference on journalism and transparency called for "a presumption of openness through which journalists, media executives and the public can come together to rebuild trust in the media" (Ziomek, 2005, 5). Jeff Jarvis noted that "there's no such thing as too much explanation," making media criticism the best possible answer to the public demand for transparency (cited in Smolkin, 2006). In 2013, both the Reuters Institute for the Study of Journalism and the Knight Center for Journalism in the Americas published books on transparency in journalism (Bowles, Hamilton & Levy, 2013; Knight Center for Journalism in the Americas, 2013). That same year, the Poynter Institute's ongoing ethical guidelines for journalists replaced the dictum of "Be Independent" with "Be Transparent" (Rosenstiel, 2013): what transparency offers, it argued, is an orientation toward "intellectual independence," that builds upon acknowledging one's intentions and showing "how the reporting was done and why people should believe it."

Many journalism scholars applaud transparency as a sure-fire safety-guard for journalism's conduct in the present. Related to and often substituted for terms like accountability, responsibility and sincerity, transparency constitutes "the new objectivity [that] brings us to accept ideas as credible the way the claim of objectivity used to" (Weinberger, 2009). This is even more the case in a digital environment where independent voices, bystanders and citizen journalists remain ready to pounce if they catch the mistake before journalists do (Anderson, 2011; Revers, 2014).

Much of the celebration of transparency stems from a broadly accepted understanding of its centrality in the news that aligns it with contemporary events. Many discussions of transparency in US journalism place its origin alongside events that occurred in 2000, when the *New York Times* sparked controversy for its over-zealous coverage of a nuclear scientist suspected of espionage with China and subsequently admitted the need for "a public accounting" of its actions (*The Times* and Wen Ho Lee, 2000). Four years later, a similar admission followed its coverage of the debacle surrounding Weapons of Mass Destruction (Okrent, 2004), giving way to what Jay Rosen (2004) called "the transparency era of the *New York Times*."

In fact, however, transparency has been a resident of journalism for longer than discussions suggest and thus deserves a more complicated reception. Evident already in the 1950s and 1960s (Schudson, 2015) when it was journalistically associated with both letters to the editor and ombudsmen positions while displaying a consonance with the broader ascent of reform-oriented politics, social movements and watchdog groups, it instead emblematizes a wide-ranging recognition of the public's "right to know" and the rise of openness in US institutions. Yet problems in its practice remain. For instance, what precisely needs to be transparent? As Craft and Heim queried (2008, 219), "is it the methods used to gather and verify information, how newsroom resources affect editorial choices, why certain stories are pursued and others aren't?" Complications also ensue, for, as Ward argued (2013), even when practiced, transparency may "lead to a risk-averse culture of management. The fact that everything is public, or potentially public, changes how people act on many levels – and not always for the better." Many discussions meld journalistic practice with journalistic discourse about practice, encouraging journalists to articulate an investment in transparency even when it might not necessarily undergird their coverage.

Thus, transparency – as a platform for learning about the present – could be more thoughtfully invoked. Other vantage points exist, for example, from which those invested in journalism could learn about the present. Journalism educators are well poised to remind journalists and journalism students of the complicated contexts in which journalism operates – of the many institutional, social, cultural, political, technological and economic impulses that are awash in its environments. They can help journalists and students recognize that it is worth being transparent not only about proximate issues but about distant ones too. In such a light, journalists might be persuaded not to overgeneralize from a small number of cases, to consider events and issues incrementally and to read widely. Looking more closely at the present makes it easier to explain why there are no easy answers to financial meltdown, global warming and disease, thereby adjusting the widely embraced notion among journalists that the public does not understand complexity.

The public too in its many forms can orient toward more transparency. Reflected in part in discussions of the "algorithmic audience," which suggests that audiences are knowable through their data (Anderson, 2011), the digital environment creates multiple positions through which public transparency can be considered. Though being transparent is often seen as a goal for the public good, the digital environment complicates in whose name the public good is being invoked. Moreover, as the boundaries between conventional journalists, non-journalists, private citizens, bystanders, citizen journalists and activists become harder to identify and easier to cross, attempting to maintain some semblance of transparency for one's postings, tweets and blogs, whenever possible, becomes all the more relevant. Though transparency about one's identity, agenda, backers or opponents in many parts of the world may bring harm or inflict damage (Han, 2016), the notion that public involvement with the news brings with it the aim of being transparent about that involvement is worth considering.

Journalism scholars also have a particular role to play in reimagining the contours of transparency. Because they too need to be upfront about process, they might use transparency to address why certain aspects of journalism get studied or not; which kinds of pressure coax journalism scholars to follow certain modes of inquiry; how the seemingly unrelated practices of tenure, promotion, book publishing and job security impact decision-making about one's research direction; how access, proximity and availability limit the research choices that are made. Being transparent about the politics of inquiry might help establish different ground rules for the authority attached to journalism scholarship. This is particularly important because journalism scholarship's center no longer sufficiently reflects the spread of the practices it tracks. As journalism thrives in multiple forms around the world, specifically in locations where transparency might have negative or dangerous effects, scholars need to be more thoughtful and upfront about what transparency looks like under different conditions.

Using transparency to consider current lingering questions could change the default assumptions that persist about journalism. Some possible examples include:

- The newspaper has not died, as widely claimed, but has only diminished in the US and western Europe. More than half the world's adult population still reads a newspaper daily, and 93 percent of newspaper company revenue globally still comes from print (WAN-IFRA World Press Trends Report, 2014).
- The government/media link has not softened, as repeatedly argued, but has just moved to multiple kinds of non-democratic regimes. It exists in manifold forms in transitional states, regimes of soft authoritarianism and governments different from the democracy/journalism nexus originally envisioned in the West. They in turn affect journalists' fears about their own security and that of their sources (Han, 2016).
- The government/market/media intersection has not diminished the efforts of other invested parties, as widely assumed, but has given

way to new kinds of actors. NGOs, for instance, entrench asymmetrical power relations and facilitate powerful influence over the kinds of journalism that journalists produce (Conrad, 2015).

- The news media have not lost their audience, as frequently declared, but new technological opportunities have shifted the nexus of engagement. Legacy media populate all but two of the major US news websites, while radio and broadcast news are drawing larger audiences than in previous years (*State of the News Media*, 2015).
- The business of journalism has not been wiped out, as often stated, but has just changed form. One example is the pro-am model that pairs professional reporters with amateurs in producing news stories (Leadbeater & Miller, 2004).

The point here should be clear: were transparency to extend across the board of current journalistic practice, education and study instead of being invoked for a small subset of issues, the resulting picture for understanding journalism might look very different from how it does today.

Finally, transparency might help all those involved with journalism to be more open to criticism. In real terms this means exhibiting an increased orientation toward transparency not only about journalistic practice but also about professional school curricula and academic politics. Adopting more transparency might lead to an increased recognition that non-journalists may be better able to critique journalism because they can look at it from the margins. Implicit here is the fact that journalists might profit from listening more to educators, students and academics and minimizing their sensitivity to the criticism that arises. At the same time, educators, students and scholars could be more available to journalists – to write in terms they can understand and to craft arguments consonant with journalists' experience. The public, in having a bigger voice, might twin it with a fuller understanding of how journalism works, while the real world of journalism ought to be more firmly grounded in scholarly work. If a fuller aim of transparency is to be achieved, all of these correctives can help.

The Future and Proactivity

The third temporal tool, the one that orients journalism most overtly toward its own future, is proactivity. Difficult to see and incremental in its effect, proactivity refers to anticipatory action that those invested in journalism might take to impact what lies ahead. Though two conceptions of futurist thought guide activity into the temporally unknown – notions of rational progress versus a more philosophical engagement with historical process (Koselleck, 2004 [1985], 18) – in fact the engagement with the future often melds with the institutional imperatives at hand. Thus, the capacity to entertain the future as an abstract entity independent of one's circumstances of evaluation is minimal. Rather, it accommodates the larger institutional environment in which it resides.

Proactivity, however, is generally unrealized in journalism, where reactivity tends to be more the rule than the exception. Journalists' reticence about proactivity has many sources. It has to do first with the temporal conditions of newswork, which unfolds so quickly that journalists end up often chasing events. These circumstances reduce journalists to "time machines" (Schlesinger, 1977), who expend much effort trying to keep pace with events unfolding faster than they can account for them. In content, journalists react to crisis, rapidly changing news events and carefully dropped pieces of information from those in power. In form, they react to challenges to their authority and dips or spikes in public trust.

Reticence about proactivity also has to do with journalists' structural conditions that make anticipating action difficult. Economic pressures responsible for cutting available funds and staff render any kind of anticipatory organization inconvenient and cumbersome. When added to the occupational and organizational conditions that make journalists less inclined to engage in collective action, and the political and technological changes that keep journalism lagging behind unstable and often unpredictable circumstances, it is no surprise that journalists cannot easily foresee the complexities of their surrounding environments.

And, third, the reluctance to be proactive also derives from journalism's ambivalence about identifying a patterned treatment of the news before it happens: journalists report the news, not make it, goes the widely repeated refrain. Because a proactive orientation to the news signifies a particular kind of a priori journalistic involvement – the kind of investment typical of advocacy platforms like peace journalism or human rights reporting, for instance – it tends to be associated most readily with journalism that sees itself as fundamentally oriented toward enhancing or facilitating future action. Conversely, it tends not to be discussed among journalists who do not have that kind of investment in the events and issues they cover.

Being prone to reactive impulses is exacerbated by the fact that journalists themselves have generally not been receptive to attempts to closely examine what they do. As Rosenberg (2010) noted in a column titled "Why Can't Journalists Handle Public Criticism?," the public repeatedly encounters "the sorry spectacle of distinguished reporters losing it when their work is publicly attacked or columnists sneering at the feedback they get." Doing so, however, keeps journalists in a reactive relationship with their critics, analysts and even enthusiasts. This tends to produce either inertia or delayed struggles with looming challenges to their environment. Significantly, it also generates tension with the populations that should be their closest neighbors – those already invested in thinking about journalism, as educators, students, scholars and members of the public.

No surprise, then, that proactivity and journalism do not readily surface together. Journalism's future orientation remains the least likely temporal positioning to develop among journalists. And yet it is the most directed temporal tool for sustaining journalism's future.

On closer examination, much about journalism is in fact fundamentally proactive, even if it is not readily admitted. Journalists cannot do their work without being proactive. Regardless of their capacity to do so, journalists are expected to orient forward, anticipating events before they occur. They need to predict ahead of time what they need, or they will not secure the necessary resources for coverage. They need to be proactive both in pitching stories before their outcomes are clear and in seeking feedback before a story goes into the final stages of production.

Because proactivity suggests a mode of engagement that replaces reactivity with anticipatory action to ongoing stimuli, it assumes that a set of already organized dynamics shapes practice. Cobbled together before any particular stimulus – a war, a financial meltdown, a juicy piece of information – is dropped into the picture, the proactive nature of journalistic work tends to remain understated. Though journalists themselves tend to avoid the articulation of predictable patterns or the establishment of so-called "standards of action" in advance of the development of a news issue or event, identifying them has long been the investment of journalism scholars, educators and students. Looking to their efforts, then, could offset journalism's fundamental reactivity and promote a fuller collective orientation to the future.

Journalism educators, for instance, and by extension their students, are heavily invested in articulating best practices, shared guidelines and aspired standards of action for journalists, providing substantive future-oriented cues about what journalists ought to do when certain kinds of situations arise. The Poynter Institute is one of many professional forums that compile updated lists of best practices for journalists and journalism students (Tenore, 2012), while platforms like Twitter and Facebook offer social media guidelines for proactively shaping journalistic presence in the digital era (Luckie, 2012; Lavrusik, 2013). The Online News Organization (ONA) offers a "build your own ethics project," that recognizes that "no simple ethics code can reflect the needs of everyone in our widely varied profession" (Kent, 2015). Such cues, which circulate widely in journalism even if they are not automatically followed, depend on a proactive stance toward future action. Without it, they are unusable.

Similarly, scholarship on the news provides evidence that journalists are widely proactive in practice: the time *of* newsmaking is often oriented to the future. Work in ethics argues that there is an ongoing tension between proactive and restraining principles of action, by which journalists piece together how they will respond to news events (Ward, 2011). Scholarship on news routines substantiates how heavily the production of news relies on anticipating what will happen, as Tuchman (1978a) specified long ago in her discussion of news typifications: the notion of "developing" or "continuing" news, for example, forces journalistic attention beyond the daily news cycle (Tuchman, 1978a), while the "what a story" or what Gans (1979) called the "gee whiz story" signifies news routines that cannot be readily anticipated. Moreover, the ongoing demands of change force constant adaptation: Tsui (2010), for instance, argued for a proactive journalism oriented to conversation, listening and hospitality after analyzing the new production environment that emerged when both legacy and alternative news organizations migrated online. Prediction and speculation are thus systematically and regularly used in the news (Jaworski, Fitzgerald & Morris, 2003).

Proactivity can also be found in how journalists signify time in their reports: the time *in* journalism is often future-oriented. Time can be narratively managed in ways that make the future seem more proximate, with the majority of news headlines dealing with an event's future, and its future orientation signaled via multiple narrative cues of speculation (Neiger, 2007). A tendency to premediate the future surfaces in the aftermath of traumatic events (Grusin, 2010). Journalism orients to the future in order to serve as society's prospective memory of what collectively needs to be done (Tenenboim-Weinblatt, 2013a). Though differences remain – commentary tends to be more future-oriented than reports, for instance (Barnhurst, 2013) – what emerges across the board is a clear orientation to the future, in which, in Neiger's (2007, 310) words, "news items deal with questions such as 'what will happen?' or 'what is likely to happen?' rather than 'what happened?'"

And yet proactivity tends not to be invoked widely in discourse about the news, largely because it signals too much of an independent investment ahead of an event or issue's unfolding. But what if the proactivity of news practice were applied more systematically to discourse about journalism? How might a proactive stance help stead journalism with more resolve toward its future?

First, incorporating a greater degree of proactivity might help stabilize journalists as they consider what lies ahead. Though the multiple transformations in journalism have prompted many to argue for more adaptability and an intensified willingness to embrace change among practitioners, little has been said about how to do so or about what should remain the stable ground underlying impending transformation. Proactivity offers one way to accommodate change without losing current footing. It can help identify the challenges that lead the way to adaptability while counterbalancing the ensuing heightened state of vulnerability to more powerful forces in the environment. In other words, being proactive about change could help those involved in journalism change from a community that struggles to sidestep blows as they are launched into one that anticipates as much as it responds. Proactively fielding emergent developments in the larger environment can delay, blunt or even alter the landing of such blows on journalism. And in this regard it is instrumental for securing a mindset that can help journalists work more effectively toward their own future.

Second, proactivity might help tweak existing understandings of journalism through patterned and predictable outcomes that build more directly from journalism's contours on the ground: what would journalism look like, for instance, if crisis were seen less as an exception and more as the rule? What kinds of anticipatory activity or planning would it involve? And how would that activity impact journalism's future practice, education and study? Other "what-ifs" include how notions of journalism might change if:

- the inevitability of working from the bottom up rather than the top down were admitted;
- journalism were seen as activity taking place across porous boundaries rather than within tightly contained units;
- journalism were known to invite a multiplicity of practices rather than accommodating just one preferred set of dynamics;
- journalism's symbiosis with, rather than autonomy from, other institutional settings were accepted;
- public engagement with journalism were expanded from information retention to different modes of interactivity, using the news as a platform for artistic expression and gaming.

Without being proactive on each of these points, journalism is continually aspiring to standards of practice that it has little hope of reaching. No wonder, then, that its future continues to seem so uncertain.

All of this indicates that there is much to gain by adopting more actively a stance of proactivity among those involved with journalism. Time is running out. For if journalists do not pause long enough to think proactively about where journalism is heading, others may do so on their behalf.

Toward Journalism's Future

Nearly a century ago, John Dewey (1929, 85) noted that "there is no such thing as fulfillment when there is no risk of failure." In this regard, it is precisely the magical status of temporal tools – that belief that they can somehow resolve the dilemmas facing journalism – that can be put to good use. Because magic concepts "do not easily admit 'opposites,' certainly not ones which most people want to support," they necessarily call forth a rich spectrum of possible paths of action, embodying "the capacity to mobilize" by multiple means (Pollitt & Hupe, 2011, 643, 652).

Thus, the sense of magic in the concepts discussed here may be what is needed to move those invested in journalism beyond their current entrenchment. I have argued that the tools for journalism's future, all temporal in nature, are preliminary to orienting journalism forward. If those invested in journalism are to more confidently and productively navigate what lies ahead, we need discourse about journalistic engagement that decisively understands itself across time. This means a more reflexive, transparent and proactive discussion of journalism that accounts for the complex temporalities at play as a pre-condition for the news to work more fully, wherever and whenever it unfolds.

Temporality, then, has much to offer, even if practice, education and scholarship have not yet taken it in its stride. Central to the effective transfer of knowledge among those invested in journalism's future, these tools of temporality orient us to the margins of the journalistic landscape, so named because until now they have tended to elude attention.

Too much current conversation about journalism rides on its latest failing, deficiency or scandal. This may be the moment to change all that, for journalism is too important for developments to go in any other direction. Journalism, in all its forms, needs to face up to its future, and those who are invested in thinking about it, in all their forms, need to help secure its journey.

References

Abu-Fadil, M. (2015, December 17). Lebanon: Media Put Humanity in the Picture as Refugee Crisis Takes Hold. *Huffington Post.com.*

Abu-Rahma, T. (2000, September 30). [Video Frame Grab] Shooting of Mohammad Aldura. *France 2 TV.*

Adam, G. S. (1976). *The Journalistic Imagination.* In *Journalism, Communication, and the Law.* Scarborough: Prentice-Hall, 3–22.

Adam, G. S. (1989). Journalism Knowledge and Journalism Practice: The Problems of Curriculum and Research in University Schools of Journalism. *Canadian Journal of Communication,* 14, 70–80.

Adam, G. S. (1993). *Notes Toward a Definition of Journalism.* St. Petersburg, FL: Poynter Institute.

Adamo, S. J. (1973, September 8). Watergate Honeymoon. *America,* 152.

Adams, E. (1968, February 2). [Photo] General Loan Shooting of Vietcong Soldier. Saigon, Vietnam: AP / World Wide Photos.

Adorno, T. (1976 [1969]). Introduction in T. Adorno et al., *The Positivist Dispute in German Ideology.* London: Heinemann, 1–67.

Ainley, B. (1998). *Black Journalists, White Media.* Stoke on Trent: Trent Books.

Al-Ghazzi, O. (2014, November). "Citizen Journalism" in the Syrian Uprising: Problematizing Western Narratives in a Local Context. *Communication Theory,* 24(4), 435–54.

Al-Hasani, A. (2010). Teaching Journalism in Oman. In B. Josephi (ed.) *Journalism Education in Countries with Limited Media Freedom.* New York: Peter Lang, 95–114.

Alan Henning "Killed by Islamic State." (2014, October 4). *BBC News.*

Aldridge, M. & Evetts, J. (2003, December). Rethinking the Concept of Professionalism. *British Journal of Sociology* 54(4), 547–64.

All the President's Men – and Two of Journalism's Finest (1976, January 13). *Senior Scholastic,* 14–17.

Allan, S. (1999). *News Culture.* Buckingham, UK, and Philadelphia, PA: Open University Press.

Allan, S. (2004). The Culture of Distance: Online Reporting of the Iraq War. In S. Allan & B. Zelizer (eds.), *Reporting War: Journalism in Wartime*. London: Routledge, 347–65.

Allan, S. (2006). *Online News*. New York: Open University Press.

Allan, S. & Zelizer, B. (eds.) (2004). *Reporting War: Journalism in Wartime*. London: Routledge.

Alter, J. (2003, April 14). The Real Echoes from Vietnam. *Newsweek*, 41.

American Heritage Dictionary (2000). *American Heritage Dictionary of the English Language*. New York: Houghton Mifflin.

An American Servicewoman Watched Images from AI-Jazeera ... (2003, March 24). [Photo] *The New York Times* via Getty Images, B6.

Anden-Papadopoulos, K. & Pantti, M. (eds.) (2011). *Amateur Images and Global News*. Bristol: Intellect.

Anderson, B. (1983). *Imagined Communities*. New York: Schocken Books.

Anderson, C. W. (2011). Deliberative, Agonistic, and Algorithmic Audiences: Journalism's Vision of its Public in an Age of Audience Transparency. *International Journal of Communication*, 5, 529–47.

Anderson, C. W. (2013). *Rebuilding the News: Metropolitan Journalism in the Digital Age*. Philadelphia, PA: Temple University Press.

Anderson, M. & Perrin, A. (2015, July 28). 15% of Americans Don't Use the Internet: Who Are They? Pew Research Center.

Andrejevich, M. (2003). *Reality TV: The Work of Being Watched*. Lanham, MD: Rowman & Littlefield.

Andrews, J. C. (1955). *The North Reports the Civil War*. Pittsburgh, PA: University of Pittsburgh Press.

Anees, M. (2015, July 27). Neo-Orientalist Islamophobia is Maligning the Reputation of the Prophet Muhammad (PBUH) Like Never Before. *Pakistan Today*.

Angwin, J. & Rose, M. (2004, April 1). When the News is Gruesome, What's Too Graphic? *Wall Street Journal*, B1.

Appadurai, A. (1996). *Modernity at Large*. Minneapolis, MN: University of Minnesota Press.

Arango, T. (2015, July 21). ISIS Transforming into Functioning State that Uses Terror as Tool. *The New York Times*, A1.

Armstrong, N. (1999). *Fiction in the Age of Photography*. Cambridge, MA: Harvard University Press.

Armstrong, S. (1990, May/June). Iran-Contra: Was the Press Any Match for All the President's Men? *Columbia Journalism Review*, 27–35.

Artner, A. G. (2003, April 10). The War, in Color. *Chicago Tribune*, sect. 5, 1, 4.

Asante, M. K. (2005). *Race, Rhetoric and Identity*. New York: Humanity Books.

Aspan, M. (2006, August 14). Ease of Alteration Creates Woes for Picture Editors. *The New York Times*, C4.

Astor, D. (2003, February 27). Wire Services Deploy Their Own Troops. *Editor and Publisher*.

Atton, C. (2002). *Alternative Media*. London: Sage.

Axelrod, J. (2013, April 9). A Decade After Saddam Hussein's Statue Falls. *CBS News*.

Awtry, J. (2003, October 15). There Just Isn't a Story There. www. poynter.org.

Ayish, M. (2003). Beyond Western-Oriented Communication Theories: A Normative Arab-Islamic Perspective. *Javnost*, 10(2), 79–92.

Ayres, D. (1972, November 20). Editors' Parley Focuses on Concern for the Reporter's Freedom to Protect Sources. *The New York Times*, 42.

Bagdikian, B. H. (1997). *The Media Monopoly* (5th edn.). Boston, MA: Beacon.

Baker, Jr., H. A., Diawara, M. & Lindeborg, R. H. (eds.) (1996). *Black British Cultural Studies: A Reader*. Chicago, IL: University of Chicago Press.

Banker, S. (1991, June). In Bob We Trust. *Washington Journalism Review*, 33.

Barker, C. (2000). *Cultural Studies: Theory and Practice* (rev. edn.). London: Sage.

Barnard, A. (2015, December 28). Syrian Family's Tragedy Goes Beyond Iconic Image of Boy on Beach. *The New York Times*.

Barnhurst, K. (2011). The Problem of Modern Time in American Journalism. *KronoScope*, 11(1–2), 98–123.

Barnhurst, K. (2013). Newspapers Experiment Online: Story Content After a Decade on the Web. *Journalism: Theory, Practice and Criticism*, 14, 3–21.

Barnhurst, K. & Mutz, D. (1997). American Journalism and the Decline in Event-Centered Reporting. *Journal of Communication*, 47(4), 27–53.

Barnhurst, K. & Nerone, J. (2001). *The Form of News: A History*. New York: Guilford.

Barno, D. (2013, March 19). Silicon, Iron and Shadow. *Foreign Policy*.

Barratt, E. & Berger, G. (eds.) (2007). *50 Years of Journalism: African Media Since Ghana's Independence*. Johannesburg: African Editors' Forum.

Barthel, M. (2015, January 6). Around Half of Newspaper Readers Rely Only on Print Edition. Pew Research Center. www.pewresearch.org/ fact-tank/2016/01/06/around-half-of-newspaper-readers-rely-only-on-print-edition.

Barthes, R. (1967). *Elements of Semiology*. London: Cape.

Barthes, R. (1977). The Rhetoric of the Image. In *Image/Music/Text*. London: Hill and Wang, 32–51.

Barthes, R. (1981). *Camera Lucida*. London: Hill and Wang.

Battle of the Files (1950, 20 March). *Time*, 16.

Batty, D. (2011, December 29). Arab Spring Leads Surge of Events Captured on Cameraphones. *The Guardian*.

Bayley, E. R. (1981). *Joe McCarthy and the Press*. Madison: University of Wisconsin Press.

Baym, G. (2009). *From Cronkite to Colbert: The Evolution of Broadcast News*. Oxford University Press.

Baz, P. (2003, April 8). [Photo] Bloodied Camera of a Photographer. Patrick Baz / AFP / Getty Images.

Becker, H. (1984). *Art Worlds*. Berkeley, CA: University of California Press.

Becker, H. (1986). Culture: A Sociological View. In *Doing Things Together*. Evanston, IL: Northwestern University Press, 11–24.

Becker, L., Fruit, J. L. & Caudill, S. (1987). *The Training and Hiring of Journalists*. Norwood, NJ: Ablex.

Beckerman, G. (2004, March/April). In Their Skin. *Columbia Journalism Review*, 40–3.

Becquet, N. (2015, December 21). Mobile Reporting Has Great Potential, But Where Are the Journalists? https://www.journalism.co.uk/news/mobile-journalism-has-great-potential-but-where-are-the-journalists-/s2/a594525.

Behrakis, Y. (2003, April 17). [Photo] Iraqi Women Carried Nonpotable Water. Behrakis / Reuters.

Behrens, J. C. (1977). *The Typewriter Guerrillas*. Chicago, IL: Nelson-Hall.

Bell, A. (1991). *The Language of News Media*. Oxford: Blackwell.

Bell, M. (1995). *In Harm's Way: Reflections of a War Zone Thug*. London: Hamish Hamilton.

Bell, M. & Flock, E. (2011, June 12). A "Gay Girl in Damascus" Comes Clean. *Washington Post*.

Bellah, R., Madsen, R., Sullivan, W., Swidler, A., & Tipton, S. (1985). *Habits of the Heart*. Berkeley, CA: University of California Press.

Beltran, L. R. (2004 [1993]). *Communication for Development in Latin America: A Forty Year Appraisal*. Penang, Malaysia: Southbound.

Bennett, T. (1998). *Culture: A Reformer's Science*. London: Sage.

Bennett, T., Grossberg, L. & Morris, M. (2005). *New Keywords: A Revised Vocabulary of Culture and Society*. Malden, MA, and Oxford: Blackwell.

Bennett, W. L. (1988). *News: The Politics of Illusion* (2nd edn.). New York: Longman.

Benson, R. (2006). News Media as a Journalistic Field. *Political Communication*, 23, 187–202.

Benson, R. (2009). Shaping the Public Sphere: Habermas and Beyond. *American Sociology*, 40, 175–97.

Benson, R. (2013). *Shaping Immigration News*. New York: Cambridge University Press.

Benson, R. & Neveu, E. (eds.) (2005). *Bourdieu and the Journalistic Field*. Malden, MA, and Cambridge: Polity.

Benson, T. W. (ed.). (1985). *Speech Communication in the 20th Century*. Carbondale, IL: Southern Illinois University Press.

Berger, J. M. & Morgan, J. (2015, March). The ISIS Twitter Census: Defining and Describing the Population of ISIS Supporters on Twitter. Brookings Institution. www.brookings.edu/research/papers/2015/03/isis-twitter-census-berger-morgan.

Berger, P. (1963). *Invitation to Sociology: A Humanistic Perspective*. Garden City, NY: Doubleday.

Berger, P. & Luckmann, T. (1966). *The Social Construction of Reality*. Garden City, NJ: Anchor Books.

Berkhead, D. (2015, November 2). Q & A with Zaina Erhaim: Teaching Citizen Journalists to Survive in Syria. *International Journalists Network*. http://ijnet.org/en/blog/qa-zaina-erhaim-teaching-citizen-journalists-survive-syria.

Berkowitz, D. (2000). Doing Double Duty. *Journalism: Theory, Practice and Criticism*, 1(2), 125–43.

Berkowitz, D. & TerKeurst, J. V. (1999, September). Community as Interpretive Community: Rethinking the Journalist–Source Relationship. *Journal of Communication*, 49(3), 125–36.

Berman, S. (2001). Ideas, Norms and Culture in Political Analysis. *Journal of Comparative Politics*, 33(2), 231–50.

Bernstein, C. (1973, June). Watergate: Tracking It Down. *The Quill*, 45–8.

Berryhill, M. (1983, March). The Lede and the Swan. *The Quill*, 13–16.

Berube, M. (2009, September 14). What's the Matter with Cultural Studies? *Chronicle for Higher Education*.

Bhabha, H. K. (1990). DissemiNation: Time, Narrative and the Margins of the Modern Nation. In *Nation and Narration*. London: Routledge, 291–322.

Biernatzki, W. (2003). War and Media. *Communication Research Trends*, 22(3), 2–31.

Bird, S. E. (1992). *For Enquiring Minds: A Cultural Study of Supermarket Tabloids*. Knoxville: University of Tennessee Press.

Bird, S. E. (ed.) (2009). *The Anthropology of News and Journalism*. Bloomington: Indiana University Press.

Bird, S. E. & Dardenne, K. W. (1988). Myth, Chronicle and Story: Exploring the Narrative Qualities of News. In J. W. Carey (ed.), *Media, Myths and Narratives: Television and the Press.* Beverly Hills, CA: Sage, 67–87.

Black, J. & Barney, R. D. (1985). The Case against Mass Media Codes of Ethics. *Journal of Mass Media Ethics*, 1(1), 27–36.

Black, J. & Whitney, F. C. (1983). *Introduction to Mass Communications.* Dubuque, IA: Wm. C. Brown.

Blanchard, M. (1986). *Exporting the First Amendment: The Press–Government Crusade of 1945–1952.* New York: Longman.

Blau, P. & Meyer, M. (1956). *Bureaucracy in Modern Society.* New York: Random House.

Blitz (2005, July 8). [Cover photo] *New York Post*, front cover.

Blumenthal, R. & Rutenberg, J. (2003, February 18). Journalists are Assigned to Accompany Troops. *The New York Times*, A12.

Blumer, H. (1969). *Symbolic Interactionism: Perspective and Method.* Englewood Cliffs, NJ: Prentice Hall.

Blumler, J. G. & Gurevitch, M. (1995). *The Crisis of Public Communication.* London and New York: Routledge.

Boafo, S. & George, N. (eds.) (1992). *Communication Research in Africa.* Nairobi, Kenya: ACCE.

Boczkowski, P. (2004). *Digitizing the News.* Chicago, IL: University of Chicago Press.

Boczkowski, P. (2010). *News at Work: Imitation in an Age of Information Abundance.* Chicago, IL: University of Chicago Press.

Bodker, H. (2016). The Times(s) of News Websites. In B. Franklin & S. Eldridge II (eds), *The Routledge Companion to Digital Journalism Studies.* Abingdon, UK: Routledge, 55–63.

Border News: Third Annual Report about Media Coverage of Migrations (2015). Rome, Italy: Cartadiroma.org (ECPMF: European Center for Press and Media Freedom). www.rcmediafreedom.eu/Publications/Reports/Border-news-Third-annual-report-about-media-coverage-of-migrations.

Boston Bombing Compared to 1996 Olympics. (2013, April 16). WXIA TV.

Bouju, J. (2003, March 27). [Photo] Iraqis Detained. *Chicago Tribune*, 3.

Bowles, N., Hamilton, J. T. & Levy, D. (eds.) (2013). *Transparency in Politics and the Media.* London: I. B. Tauris.

Boycott ISIS's Videos [Editorial] (2015, February 10). *Asharq Alawsat* (English edn.).

Boyd-Barrett, O. (2004). Understanding: The Second Casualty. In S. Allan & B. Zelizer (eds.), *Reporting War: Journalism in Wartime.* London and New York: Routledge, 25–42.

Boylan, J. (1986, November/December). In Our Time: The Changing World of American Journalism. *Columbia Journalism Review*, 11–45.

Boyle, D. (1992). From Portpak to Camcorder: A Brief History of Guerrilla Television. *Journal of Film and Video*, 44(1/2), 67–79.

Bradshaw, P. (2015, July 20). In the Wake of Ashley Madison, Towards a Journalism Ethics of Using Hacked Documents. *Online Journalism Blog*. http://onlinejournalismblog.com/2015/07/20/ashley-madison-ethics-journalism-hacked-documents.

Branch, T. (1976, November). Gagging on Deep Throat. *Esquire*, 10–12, 62.

Brandsma, J. (ed.) (1998). *The Impossibilities and Perspectives for Life Long Learning. "New Knowledge Frontiers: The Didactic Scaffolding of the Network University."* www.netuni.nl/pulse/didactics/collaborative_based.htm.

Brantlinger, P. (1990). *Crusoe's Footprints: Cultural Studies in Britain and America.* New York: Routledge.

Brants, K., Hermes, J. & van Zoonen, L. (eds.) (1998). *The Media in Question: Popular Cultures and Public Interests.* London: Sage.

Breed, W. (1955). Social Control in the Newsroom. *Social Forces*, 33, 326–35.

Britannia Waves the Rules (1946, July 15). *Broadcasting*, 52.

Brock, G. (2010). Road to Regaining the High Ground. *British Journalism Review*, 21(4), 19.

Broder, D. S. (1987). *Behind the Front Page.* New York: Touchstone Books.

Bromley, M. (1997). The End of Journalism? Changes in Workplace Practices in the Press and Broadcasting in the 1990s. In M. Bromley & T. O'Malley (eds.), *A Journalism Reader.* London: Routledge, 330–50.

Bromley, M. (2003). Objectivity and the Other Orwell. *Media History*, 9(2), 123–35.

Bromley, M. (2006). One Journalism or Many? Confronting the Contradictions in the Education and Training of Journalists in the United Kingdom. In K. W. Y. Leung, J. Kenny & P. S. N. Lee (eds.) *Global Trends in Communication Education and Research.* Cresskill, NJ: Hampton Press, 53–72.

Bromley, M. (2009a). Introduction. In G. Terziz (ed.), *European Journalism Education.* Chicago, IL: Intellect, 27–34.

Bromley, M. (2009b). The United Kingdom Journalism Education Landscape. In G. Terziz (ed.), *European Journalism Education.* Chicago, IL: Intellect, 49–66.

Bromley, M. & O'Malley, T. (eds.) (1997). *A Journalism Reader.* London: Routledge.

Bromley, M. & Stephenson, H. (eds.) (1998). *Sex, Lies and Democracy: The Press and the Public*. Reading, MA: Addison-Wesley.

Brooker, P. (1999). *A Concise Glossary of Cultural Theory*. London: Arnold.

Brothers, C. (1997). *War and Photography*. London and New York: Routledge.

Brown, H. (2007). *Knowledge and Innovation: A Comparative Study of the USA, the UK and Japan*. London: Routledge.

Brown, J. (2003, April 12). "They Got It Down": The Toppling of the Saddam Statue, *Counterpunch*. www.counterpunch.org/brown04122003.html.

Browne, M. (1963, June 12). [Photo] Reverend Quang Duc in Flames. AP / World Wide Photos.

Brunsdon, C. & Morley, D. (1978). *Everyday Television: "Nationwide."* London: BFI.

Bruns, A. & Highfield, T. (2012). Blogs, Twitter and Breaking News: The Produsage of Citizen Journalism. In R. A. Lind (ed.), *Produsing Theory in a Digital World*. New York: Peter Lang.

Buchanan, R. T. (2015, September 3). VICE News Journalists Released by Turkish Authorities – But Local Fixer Still in Custody. *The Independent*.

Buck-Morss, S. (2009). *Hegel, Haiti and Universal History*. University of Pittsburgh Press.

Bunyan, T. (2015). The View from Brussels: Missed Opportunities to Call the European Union to Account. In A. White (ed.), *Moving Stories: International Review of How Media Cover Migration*. London: Ethical Journalism Network, 10–17.

Burgett, B. & Hendler, G. (2014). *Keywords to American Cultural Studies* (2nd edn.). New York University Press.

Burke, P. (2001). *Eyewitnessing: The Uses of Images as Historical Evidence*. Ithaca, NY: Cornell University Press.

Busy Man (1951, October 8). *Time*, 26.

Buttry, S. (2011). 21st Century Journalism Requires 21st Century Code. *Quill*, 99(2), 16–19.

Cain Offers Ethics Reminder to Reporters in Pushback over Sex Harassment Allegations (2011, November 6). *Fox News*. www.foxnews.com/politics/2011/11/06/cain-offers-ethics-reminder-to-reporters-in-pushback-over-sex-harassment.

Cameron, J. (1997 [1967]). Journalism: A Trade. In M. Bromley & T. O'Malley (eds.), *A Journalism Reader*. London: Routledge, 170–3 (reprinted from *Point of Departure*. London: Arthur Barker).

Campbell, R. (1991). *60 Minutes and the News: A Mythology for Middle America*. Urbana, IL: University of Illinois Press.

Cannon, L. (2015, July 31). Echoes of Joe McCarthy in Donald Trump's Rise. *Real Clear Politics.com.* www.realclearpolitics.com/articles/2015/07/31/echoes_of_joe_mccarthy_in_donald_trumps_rise_127597.html.

Capa, R. (1936, September 15). [Photo] Death of a Loyalist Soldier. *Vu.*

Carey, J. (ed.) (1987). *Eyewitness to History.* New York: Avon Books.

Carey, J. W. (1969). The Communications Revolution and the Professional Communicator. *Sociological Review Monographs*, 13, 23–38.

Carey, J. W. (1974, Spring). The Problem of Journalism History. *Journalism History*, 1(1), 3–5, 27.

Carey, J. W. (1975). A Cultural Approach to Communication. *Communication*, 2(1), 1–22.

Carey, J. W. (1978). A Plea for the University Tradition. *Journalism Quarterly*, 55(4), 846–55.

Carey, J. W. (1986a). The Dark Continent of American Journalism. In R. Manoff & M. Schudson (eds.) *Reading the News.* New York: Pantheon, 146–96.

Carey, J. W. (1986b). Journalists Just Leave: The Ethics of an Anomalous Profession. In M. G. Sagan (ed.), *Ethics and the Media.* Iowa Humanities Board, 5–19.

Carey, J. W. (1989a). The Press and Public Discourse. *Center Magazine*, 20(2), 4–32.

Carey, J. W. (1989b). Overcoming Resistance to Cultural Studies. In *Communication as Culture.* London: Unwin-Hyman, 89–112.

Carey, J. W. (1995). The Press, Public Opinion and Public Discourse. In T. L. Glasser & C. L. Salmon (eds.), *Public Opinion and the Communication of Consent.* New York: Guilford, 373–402.

Carey, J. W. (1996). The Chicago School and Mass Communication Research. In E. Dennis & E. Wartella (eds.), *American Communication Research: The Remembered History.* Mahwah, NJ: Erlbaum, 21–38.

Carey, J. W. (1997a). Reflections on the Project of (American) Cultural Studies. In M. Ferguson & P. Golding (eds.), *Cultural Studies in Question.* London, UK: Sage, 1–24.

Carey, J. W. (1997b). Afterword: The Culture in Question. In E. Munson & C. Warren (eds.), *James Carey: A Critical Reader.* Minneapolis: University of Minnesota Press, 308–35.

Carey, J. W. (2000). Some Personal Notes on Journalism Education. *Journalism: Theory, Practice, and Criticism*, 1(1), 12–23.

Carlebach, M. L. (1992). *The Origins of Photojournalism in America.* Washington, DC: Smithsonian.

Carlson, M. (2006). War Journalism and the "KIA Journalist": The Cases of David Bloom and Michael Kelly. *Critical Studies in Media Communication*, 23(2), 91–111.

Carlson, M. (2011). *On the Condition of Anonymity*. Urbana: University of Illinois Press.

Carlyle, T. (1974 [1905]). *The French Revolution*. New York: AMS Press.

Carruthers, S. (2011). *The Media at War* (2nd edn.). London: Palgrave.

Carter, C., Branston, G. & Allan, S. (eds.) (1998). *News, Gender and Power*. London: Routledge.

Carvin, A. (2013). *Distant Witness: Social Media, the Arab Spring and a Journalism Revolution*. New York: CUNY Journalism Press.

Cassidy, T. (2014, February 10). The New Public-Interest Journalism. *The New Yorker*.

Chalaby, J. (1996). Journalism as an Anglo-American Invention. *European Journal of Communication*, 11(3), 303–26.

Charity, A. (1995). *Doing Public Journalism*. New York: Guilford.

Charon, J. M. (2003). Journalist Training in France. In R. Frohlich & C. Holtz-Bacha (eds.), *Journalism Education in Europe and North America*. Cresskill, NJ: Hampton Press, 139–68.

Chayka, K. (2015, November 11). Why Instagram Captions are the New Blogging. *New York Magazine*.

Chen, G. M. (2006, October). Asian Communication Studies: What and Where to Now. *The Review of Communication*, 6(4), 295–311.

Chenelly, J. (2001, December 24). [Photo] New Way. *Time*, 61.

Cherbonnier, A. (2003, January 8). The *Sun* Shows No Nose for News. *Baltimore Chronicle & Sentinel*. www.baltimorechronicle.com/media-joblessrptjan03.html.

Cheung, N. (2011, April 20). ABC Seeks Publicity Director with a Nose for News. www.adweek.com/prnewser/abc-seeks-publicity-director-with-a-nose-for-news/20531.

Chinese Journalists Criticize News of the World in Light of Hacking Scandal (2011, August 1). Xinghua News Agency.

Chittum, R. (2012, March 2). Checkbook Journalism's Slippery Slope. *Columbia Journalism Review*.

Chouliaraki, L. (2006). The Aestheticization of Suffering on Television. *Visual Communication*, 5(3), 261–88.

Chouliaraki, L. (2012). *The Ironic Spectator*. Cambridge: Polity.

Christians, C., Ferre, J. P. & Fackler, M. (2003). *Good News: Social Ethics and the Press*. New York: Oxford University Press.

Christopherson, F. (1953, January 1). Are We Being Objective in Reporting the Cold War? *ASNE Bulletin*, 1.

Cillizza, C. (2014, November 18). Certainty Is Dead in Political Journalism: That's a Good Thing. *The Washington Post*. www.washingtonpost.com/blogs/the-fix/wp/2014/11/18/certainty-is-dead-in-political-journalism-thats-a-good-thing.

Ciobanu, M. (2015, December 8). Report: Technology Trends Journalists Should Watch in 2016. *Journalism.co.uk*. https://www.journalism.co.uk/news/report-technology-trends-journalists-should-watch-in-2016/s2/a590651.

CJR Comment (2004, July/August). Out of Sight, Out of Mind. *Columbia Journalism Review*, 6.

Cohen, E. (June 1906). With a Camera in San Francisco. *Camera Craft*, 12(5), 183–94.

Cohen, R. (1994). In Bosnia, the War That Can't Be Seen. *The New York Times*, E4.

Cohen, S. & Young, J. (eds.) (1973). *The Manufacture of News: A Reader*. Beverly Hills, CA: Sage.

Cold War II (2014, August 4) [Cover Photo]. *Time*.

Complex Picture, A (2004, April 1). *The Wall Street Journal*, A1.

Conboy, M. (2004). *Journalism: A Critical History*. London: Sage.

Conboy, M. (2013). *The Language of the News*. Abingdon, Oxon: Routledge.

Connerton, P. (2009). *How Modernity Forgets*. New York: Cambridge University Press.

Connery, T. (ed.) (1992). *A Sourcebook of American Literary Journalism*. New York: Greenwood.

Conrad, D. (2015). "The Freelancer–NGO Alliance: What a Story of Kenyan Waste Reveals about Contemporary Foreign News Production." *Journalism Studies*, 16(2), 275–88.

Cook, J. (2009, December 29). Checkbook Journalism: A User's Guide. *Gawker Media*.

Cook, J. (2012, June 18). The De-Watergating of American Journalism. *Gawker Media*.

Cook, T. (1998). *Governing with the News*. University of Chicago Press.

Cooke, K. & White, A. (2015). Introduction. In A. White (ed.), *Moving Stories: International Review of How Media Cover Migration*. London: Ethical Journalism Network, 5–7.

Coonradt, P. (2001, November 22). Afghan Coverage (Letter to the Editor). *Los Angeles Times*, B12.

Cotter, C. (2010). *News Talk: Investigating the Language of Journalism*. Cambridge and New York: Cambridge University Press.

Cottle, S. (1993). *TV News, Urban Conflict and the Inner City*. Leicester University Press.

Cottle, S. (1997). *Television and Ethnic Minorities*. Aldershot, UK: Avebury.

Cottle, S. (2000a). New(s) Times: Towards a "Second Wave" of News Ethnography. *Communications*, 25(1), 19–41.

Couldry, N. (2000). *Inside Culture: Re-Imagining the Method of Cultural Studies*. London: Sage.

Couldry, N., Livingstone, S., & Markham, T. (2007). *Media Consumption and Public Engagement: Beyond the Presumption of Attention.* Basingstoke: Palgrave MacMillan.

Coyle, K. & Lindlof, T. (1988, May). Exploring the Universe of Science Fiction: Interpretive Communities and Reader Genres. Paper presented at the International Communication Association, New Orleans, LA.

Craft, S. & Heim, K. (2008). Transparency in Journalism: Meanings, Merits and Risks. In L. Wilkins & C. Christians (eds), *The Handbook of Mass Media Ethics.* New York: Routledge, 217–28.

Craig, R. (1989). Communication as a Practical Discipline. In B. Dervin, G. Grossberg, B. O'Keefe, & E. Wartella (eds.), *Rethinking Communication: Paradigm Issues* (Vol. I). Newbury Park, CA: Sage, 97–122.

Craig, R. (1999). Communication Theory as a Field. *Communication Research,* 9(2), 119–61.

Cunningham, B. (2004, May/June). Across the Great Divide: Class. *Columbia Journalism Review.*

Cuomo, C. (2011, June 12). ABC's Chris Cuomo Defends Checkbook Journalism: "It Is the State of Play Right Now." Poynter Institute. www.poynter.org/2011/abcs-cuomo-defends-checkbook-journalism-it-is-the-state-of-play-right-now/135609/.

Curran, J., & Park, M.-J. (eds.) (2000). *De-westernizing Media Studies.* London: Routledge.

Curran, J. & Seaton, J. (1985). *Power without Responsibility.* London: Fontana.

Curry Jansen, S. (2010). Forgotten Histories: Another Road Not Taken – The Charles Merriam – Walter Lippman Correspondence. *Communication Theory,* 20, 127–46.

Czitrom, D. (1982). *Media and the American Mind.* Chapel Hill: University of North Carolina.

Dahlgren, P. (1992). Introduction. In P. Dahlgren & C. Sparks (eds.), *Journalism and Popular Culture.* London: Sage, 1–23.

Dahlgren, P. (1995). *Television and the Public Sphere.* London: Sage.

Dahlgren, P. & Sparks, C. (1991). *Communication and Citizenship: Journalism and the Public Sphere.* London and New York: Routledge.

Dahlgren, P., & Sparks, C. (eds.) (1992). *Journalism and Popular Culture.* London: Sage.

Dana, C. A. (1895). News and Reporting. In *The Art of Newspapermaking.* New York: D. Appleton & Company (reprinted in F. L. Mott (ed.) (1937). *Interpretations of Journalism.* New York: F. L. Crofts & Co.).

D'Angelo, P. & Kuypers, J. (2010). *Doing News Framing Analysis: Empirical and Theoretical Perspectives.* New York: Routledge.

Daniels, W. (2012, March 8). [Cover Photo] Escape from Syria. *Time*.

Darnton, R. (1975). Writing News and Telling Stories. *Daedalus*, 120(2), 175–94.

Daston, L. (1994). Marvelous Facts and Miraculous Evidence in Early Modern Europe. In T. Chandler, A. I. Davidson & H. D. Harootunian (eds.), *Questions of Evidence*. University of Chicago Press, 243–74.

Davies, N. (2014, June 25). Phone-Hacking Trial was Officially About Crime; But in Reality It Was About Power. *The Guardian*.

Day, J. & Johnston, C. (2005, July 8). Public Provides New Dimension to Media Coverage. *TheGuardian.com*. http://media.guardian.co.uk/site/story0,14173,1524154,00.html.

De Certeau, M. (1978). *The Writing of History*. New York: Columbia University Press.

De Tocqueville, A. (1900). *Democracy in America*. New York: Colonial Press.

De Zuniga, H., Jung, S. & Valenzuela, S. (2012, April). Social Media Use for News and Individuals' Social Capital, Civic Engagement and Political Participation. *Journal of Computer-Mediated Communication*, 17(3), 319–36.

Deans, J. (2003, March 27). Fox Challenges CNN's US Ratings Dominance. *The Guardian*.

Degh, L. (1972). Folk Narrative. In R. M. Dorson (ed.), *Folklore and Folklife*. University of Chicago Press, 53–83.

Delia, J. (1987). Communication Research: A History. In C. Berger & S. Chaffee (eds.), *Handbook of Communication Science*. Newbury Park, CA: Sage, 20–98.

Demir, N. (2015, September 2). [Photo] Aylan Kurdi. DHA.

Denis, N. (2015). *War Against All Puerto Ricans: Revolution and Terror in America's Colony*. New York: Nation Books.

Dennis, E. (1984). *Planning for Curricular Change: A Report on the Future of Journalism and Mass Communication Education*. Eugene: School of Journalism, University of Oregon.

Dennis, E. & Wartella, E. (eds.) (1996). *American Communication Research: The Remembered History*. Mahwah, NJ: Erlbaum.

Desmond, R. W. (1984). *Tides of War: World News Reporting, 1940–1945*. University of Iowa Press.

Desta, S. (2010, September 8). [Photo] Eighteen Killed, 33 Hurt in Pakistani Suicide Blast. CNN.

Deuze, M. (2005). What is Journalism? *Journalism: Theory, Practice and Criticism*, 6(4), 442–64.

Deuze, M. (2007). *Media Work*. Cambridge: Polity.

Deuze, M. & Marjoribanks, T. (2009). Newswork. *Journalism: Theory, Practice and Criticism*, 10(5), 555–61.

Dewey, J. (1918, January 21). The New Paternalism. *The New Republic*, 17, 216.

Dewey, J. (1929). *The Quest for Certainty: A Study of the Relevance of Knowledge*. New York: Minton, Balch & Company.

Dewey, J. (1954 [1927]). *The Public and Its Problems*. Columbus: Ohio State University Press.

Dicken-Garcia, H. (1989). *Journalistic Standards in Nineteenth Century America*. Madison: University of Wisconsin Press.

Dipsy-doodle Ball (1951, August 13). *Time*, 21.

Doctor, K. (2015, July 28). Newsonomics: The Halving of America's Daily Newsrooms. *NiemanJournalismLab*. www.niemanlab.org/2015/07/newsonomics-the-halving-of-americas-daily-newsrooms.

Doherty, T. (1993). *Projections of War: Hollywood, American Culture, and World War II*. New York: Columbia University Press.

Domingo, D. & Paterson, C. (2011). *Making Online News: Volume II*. New York: Peter Lang.

Donaldson, S. (1987). *Hold On, Mr. President*. New York: Fawcett Crest.

Donvan, J. (2003, May/June). For the Unilaterals, No Neutral Ground. *Columbia Journalism Review*, 35–6.

Douglas, M. (1986). *How Institutions Think*. Syracuse University Press.

Douglas, S. (1994, July). A Three Way Failure. *Progressive*, 15.

Doward, J. (2003, April 6). Sky Wins Battle for Rolling News Audience. *The Observer*.

Downing, J. (1996). *Internationalizing Media Theory*. London: Sage.

Dugan, A. (2014, June 19). American Confidence in News Media Remains Low. Gallup Poll.

Durham, M. G. & Kellner, D. M. (eds.) (2001). *Media and Cultural Studies: Keyworks*. Malden, MA: Blackwell.

During, S. (ed.) (1993). *The Cultural Studies Reader*. London: Routledge, 1993.

Durkheim, E. (1965 [1912]). *The Elementary Forms of the Religious Life*. New York: Free Press.

Dyke, M. (2009). An Enabling Framework for Reflexive Learning: Experiential Learning and Reflexivity in Contemporary Modernity. *International Journal of Lifelong Education*, 28(3), 289–310.

Eagleton, T. (1995). *The Crisis of Contemporary Culture*. London: Oxford University Press.

Eason, D. L. (1984). The New Journalism and the Image-World: Two Modes of Organizing Experience. *Critical Studies in Mass Communication*, 1(1), 51–65.

Eason, D. L. (1986). On Journalistic Authority: The Janet Cooke Scandal. *Critical Studies in Mass Communication*, 3, 429–47.

Edelman, M. (1985 [1967]). *The Symbolic Uses of Politics*. Urbana: University of Illinois Press.

Edgar, A. & Sedgwick, P. (eds.) (2002). *Cultural Theory: The Key Concepts*. London: Routledge. (Revised edn. 2007).

Editors, The. (2015. April 8). Do Scandals Like *Rolling Stone*'s Do Lasting Damage to Journalism? *Columbia Journalism Review*.

Edy, J. (1999). Journalistic Uses of Collective Memory. *Journal of Communication*, 49(2), 71–85.

Edy, J. (2006). *Troubled Pasts: News and the Collective Memory of Social Unrest*. Philadelphia, PA: Temple University Press.

Edy, J. A. & Daradanova, M. (2006). Reporting the Present Through the Lens of the Past: From Challenger to Columbia. *Journalism: Theory, Practice and Criticism*, 7(2), 131–51.

Ehrlich, M. (1997). The Journalism of Outrageousness: Tabloid Television News Versus Investigative News. *Journalism and Mass Communication Monographs*, 155, 3–27.

Eisendorf, R. J. (2004, July 19). Are Terrorists Hijacking the News? *San Francisco Chronicle*, B7.

EJO Research: How Europe's Newspapers Reported the Migration Crisis (2015, November 9). European Journalism Observatory. http://en.ejo.ch/research/research-how-europes-newspapers-reported-the-migration-crisis.

Elber, L. (1994, June 5). Commemorating D-Day. *Philadelphia Inquirer TV Week*, 6.

Eliasoph, N. (1988). Routines and the Making of Oppositional News. *Critical Studies in Mass Communication*, 313–34.

Ellis, J. (2000). *Seeing Things: Television in the Age of Uncertainty*. London: I. B. Tauris.

Elster, J. (1993). Constitution-Making in Eastern Europe. *Public Administration*, 71, 169–217.

Embedded Reporters: What Are Americans Getting? (2003). Washington, DC: Project for Excellence in Journalism.

Emery, M. & Emery, E. (1996). *The American Press*. New York: Allyn & Bacon.

Entman, R. (1989). *Democracy Without Citizens*. New York: Oxford University Press.

Entman, R. (1993). Framing: Towards Clarification of a Fractured Paradigm. *Journal of Communication*, 43(4), 51–8.

Epstein, E. J. (1973). *News from Nowhere: Television and the News*. New York: Random House.

Epstein, E. J. (1974, July). Did the Press Uncover Watergate? *Commentary*, 21–24.

Eribo, F. & Tanjong, E. (eds.) (2002). *Journalism and Mass Communication in Africa: Cameroon.* Lanham, MD: Lexington Books.

Erni, J. N. (2001). Media Studies and Cultural Studies: A Symbiotic Convergence. In T. Miller (ed.), *A Companion to Cultural Studies.* London: Blackwell, 187–213.

Ernie Pyle is Killed on Ie Island (1945, April 19). *The New York Times,* 1, 14.

Escobar, A. (1995). *Encountering Development: The Making and Unmaking of the Third World.* Princeton University Press.

Ettema, J. S. & Glasser, T. L. (1998). *Custodians of Conscience: Investigative Journalism and Public Virtue.* New York: Columbia University Press.

Europe or Die (2015). Vice News.

Evans, H. (1991, March). Who Has the Last Word? *Quill,* 28–9.

Eviatar, D. (2003, March 22). Civilian Toll: A Moral and Legal Bog. *The New York Times,* D7, D9.

Failure of IPSO, The (2015, September). London: Hacked Off. http://hackinginquiry.org/wp-content/uploads/2015/09/FailureOfIPSO.pdf.

Faiola, A. (2011, August 15). British Phone Hacking Scandal: Whittamore Case Underscores Past Failures. *Washington Post.*

Fairclough, N. (2013 [1989]). *Language and Power.* Abingdon, UK, and New York: Routledge.

Farhi, P. (2007, April/May). A New Portfolio. *American Journalism Review.*

Farhi, P. (2009, July 1). TMZ.com Earns Newfound Respect after Scoop on Michael Jackson's Death. *Washington Post.*

Farhi, P. (2010, November 17). Up for Audit: "Checkbook Journalism" and the News Groups That Buy Big Stories. *Washington Post.*

Fattah, H. (2004, July/August). Goodbye, Baghdad. *Columbia Journalism Review,* 62.

Feinstein, A. (2003). *Journalists Under Fire: The Psychological Hazards of Covering War.* Baltimore, MD: Johns Hopkins University Press.

Feldstein, M. (2004, August/September). Watergate Revisited. *American Journalism Review.*

Felman, S. & Laub, D. (1992). *Testimony: Crises of Witnessing in Literature, Psychoanalysis and History.* New York: Routledge.

Felt, C. [2007]. [Photo] Darfur, Sudan. Reuters.

Fialka, J. (1991). *Hotel Warriors: Covering the Gulf.* Washington, DC: Woodrow Wilson Center.

Fish, S. (1982). *Is There a Text in This Class? The Authority of Interpretive Communities.* Cambridge, MA: Harvard University Press.

Fisher, I. (2003, April 25). Threat Gone, Iraqis Unearth Hussein's Nameless Victims. *The New York Times,* A1, A10.

Fisher, I. (2004, July 18). Reporting, and Surviving, Iraq's Dangers. *The New York Times*, Sect. 4, 1–2.

Fishkin, S. (1985). *From Fact to Fiction*. Baltimore, MD: Johns Hopkins University Press.

Fishman, M. (1980). *Manufacturing the News*. Austin: University of Texas Press.

Fisk, R. (2003, April 11). Baghdad: The Day After. *The Independent*, 1.

Fiske, J. (1988). *Television Culture*. London: Methuen.

Fiske, J. (1992a). British Cultural Studies and Television. In R. Allen (ed.), *Channels of Discourse, Reassembled*. New York: Routledge, 284–326.

Fiske, J. (1992b). Popularity and the Politics of Information. In P. Dahlgren & C. Sparks (eds.), *Journalism and Popular Culture*. London: Sage, 45–63.

Fiske, J. (1996). *Media Matters*. Minneapolis: University of Minnesota Press.

Fiske, J. & Hartley, J. (1978). *Reading Television*. London: Methuen.

Foremski, T. (2010, May 25). The Rise of Pay View Journalism. *ZDNet*.

Foucault, M. (1972). *The Archaeology of Knowledge*. London: Tavistock.

Fowler, R. (1991). *Language in the News: Discourse and Ideology in the Press*. London and New York: Routledge.

Fox, E. (1988). *Media and Politics in Latin America: The Struggle for Democracy*. Newbury Park, CA: Sage.

Fox, E. & Waisbord, S. (eds.) (2002). *Latin Politics / Global Media*. Austin: University of Texas Press.

Fox's Tucker Carlson Dismisses Jorge Ramos as "An Activist" (2015, August 26). *Media Matters*. mediamatters.org/video/2015/08/26/foxs-tucker-carlson-dismisses-jorge-ramos-as-an/205205.

Franceschi-Bicchierai, L. (2014, August 20). Twitter is Suspending Accounts That Post Journalist's Beheading. *Mashable*. mashable.com/2014/08/20/twitter-suspends-accounts-james-foley-beheading-execution.

Franklin, T. E. (2001, September 11). [Photo] Flag Raising after September 11. *The Record*.

Fraser, N. (1990). Rethinking the Public Sphere. *Social Text*, 25/26, 56–80.

Freedom of the Press (2014). New York: Freedom House.

Freidson, E. (1986). *Professional Powers: A Study of the Institutionalization of Formal Knowledge*. University of Chicago Press.

Frey, K. & Mallin, A. (2015, March 19). Iraq Invasion 12 Years Later: See How Much Has Changed. *ABC News*.

Friedman, J. (2002). *Reality Squared: Televisual Discourse on the Real*. New Brunswick, NJ: Rutgers University Press.

Friedman, P. (2003, May/June). TV: A Missed Opportunity. *Columbia Journalism Review*, 29–31.

Frohlich, R. & Holtz-Bacha, C. (2003). Journalism Education in Germany: A Wide Range of Different Ways. In R. Frohlich & C. Holtz-Bacha (eds.), *Journalism Education in Europe and North America*. Cresskill, NJ: Hampton Press, 187–208.

Frohlich, R. & Holtz-Bacha, C. (2009). The German Journalism Education Landscape. In G. Terzis (ed.), *European Journalism Education*. Chicago, IL: Intellect, 133–47.

Frow, J. (1995). *Cultural Studies and Cultural Value*. Oxford: Clarendon Press.

Full Text: Beijng Declaration of the BRICS Media Summit (2015, December 1). www.globalpost.com/article/6697270/2015/12/01/full-text-beijing-declaration-brics-media-summit.

Fukuyama, F. (1992). *The End of History and the Last Man*. New York: Free Press.

Fulton, H., Husiman, R. & Murphet, J. (eds.) (2006). *Narrative and Media*. Cambridge University Press.

Further Proofs of Rebel Inhumanity (1864, June 18). *Harper's Weekly*, 387.

Gabriel, J. (1998). *Whitewash: Racialized Politics and the Media*. London: Routledge.

Gammage, J. (2016, January 12). Lenfest Donates Newspapers, Website to New Media Institute. *Philadelphia Inquirer*. http://mobile.philly.com/beta?wss=/philly/business&id=364939631.

Gamson, W. (1989). News as Framing. *American Behavioral Scientist*, 33(2), 157–61.

Gandy, O. H., Jr. (1982). *Beyond Agenda Setting: Information Subsidies and Public Policy*. Norwood, NJ: Ablex.

Gans, H. (1979). *Deciding What's News*. New York: Pantheon.

Garber, M. (2015, May 28). How Comedians Became Public Intellectuals. *The Atlantic*.

Garcia, M. (2014, September). Financial Times: A Classic Redesign for the Digital Age. www.poynter.org/news/mediawire/269613/financial-times-a-classic-redesign-for-the-digital-age.

Garcia-Canclini, N. (1995). *Hybrid Cultures: Strategies for Entering and Leaving Modernity*. Minneapolis: University of Minnesota Press.

Garret, G. & Weingast, B. R. (1993). Ideas, Interests and Institutions: Constructing the European Community's Internal Market. In J. Goldstein & R. Keohane (eds.) *Ideas and Foreign Policy: Beliefs, Institutions and Political Change*. Ithaca, NY: Cornell University Press, 173–206.

Gates, G. P. (1978). *Airtime: The Inside Story of CBS News*. New York: Harper and Row.

Geertz, C. (1973). *The Interpretation of Cultures*. New York: Basic Books.

Getler, M. (1991, March 17). View from the Newsroom. *Washington Post*.

Gibson, S. W. (1998, February 15). Entrepreneur Must Have a Sixth Sense. *Deseret News*.

Giddens, A. (1991). *The Consequences of Modernity*. Cambridge: Polity.

Giddens, A. (1991b). *Modernity and Self Identity*. Stanford University Press.

Giddens, A. (2001). *Sociology* (4th edn.). Cambridge: Polity.

Gilbert, M. & Ryan, S. C. (2003, April 10). Snap Judgments: Did Iconic Images from Baghdad Reveal More About the Media Than Iraq? *Boston Globe*, D1.

Giles, J. & Middleton, T. (1999). *Studying Culture: A Practical Introduction*. Malden, MA: Blackwell.

Gilewicz, N. (2013). "The Living Heart of Memory": The Retro Report Project and Mediatized Maintenance of the Baby Boomers. (Unpublished manuscript.)

Gilewicz, N. (2015). To Embody and Embalm: The Uses of Collective Memory in the Final Editions of Failed Newspapers. *Journalism: Theory, Practice & Criticism*, 16(5), 672–87.

Gillmor, D. (2006). *We the Media: Grassroots Journalism by the People for the People*. New York: O'Reilly Media.

Gitlin, T. (1980). *The Whole World is Watching*. Berkeley: University of California Press.

Glander, T. (2000). *Origins of Mass Communications Research During the American Cold War*. Mahwah, NJ: Lawrence Erlbaum.

Glaser, M. (2003, August 7). Photojournalism Gets Boost Online. *Online Journalism Review*. www.ojr.org/ojr/glaser/1060300231.ph.

Glasgow University Media Group (1976). *Bad News*. London: Routledge and Kegan Paul.

Glasgow University Media Group (1980). *More Bad News*. London: Routledge and Kegan Paul.

Glasser, T. L. & Ettema, J. (1989a). Investigative Journalism and the Moral Order. *Critical Studies in Mass Communication*, 6(1), 1–20.

Glasser, T. L. & Ettema, J. (1989b, Summer). Common Sense and the Education of Young Journalists. *Journalism Educator*, 44.

Glasser, T. L. & Ettema, J. (1993). When The Facts Don't Speak for Themselves: A Study of the Use of Irony in Daily Journalism. *Critical Studies in Mass Communication*, 320–38.

Glasser, T. L. & Ettema, J. (1998). *Custodians of Conscience*. New York: Columbia University Press.

Glasser, T.L. & Ettema, J. (2008). Ethics and Eloquence in Journalism:

An Approach to Press Accountability. *Journalism Studies*, 9(4), 512–34.

Glynn, K. (2000). *Tabloid Culture: Trash Taste, Popular Power and the Transformation of American Television*. Durham, NC: Duke University Press.

Goldberg, V. (1986). *Margaret Bourke-White: A Biography*. New York: Harper and Row.

Goldberg, V. (1981). *The Power of Photography*. New York: Abbeville Press.

Golding, P. & Murdock, G. (1991). Culture, Communications and Political Economy. In J. Curran & M. Gurevitch (eds.), *Mass Media and Society*. London and New York: Edward Arnold, 70–92.

Goldstein, T. (1985). *The News at Any Cost: How Journalists Compromise Their Ethics to Shape the News*. New York: Simon and Schuster.

Gompert, D. C., Binnendijk, H. & Lin, B. (2014, December 25). The Iraq War: Bush's Biggest Blunder. *Newsweek*.

Goodenough, W. (1981). *Culture, Language, and Society*. Reading, MA: Addison-Wesley.

Goodman, N. (1978). *Ways of Worldmaking*. Indianapolis, IN: Hackett.

Gore, W. (2014, August 26). The Only Way is Ethics: To Censor the Atrocities of ISIS Would Dishonor James Foley and His Work. *The Independent*.

Gouldner, A. (1979). *The Future of Intellectuals and the Rise of the New Class*. London: MacMillan Press.

Gourarie, C. (2015, July 30). "Structured Journalism" Offers Readers a Different Kind of Story Experience. *Columbia Journalism Review*.

Grabe, M. & Bucy, E. (2009). *Image Bite Politics: News and the Visual Framing of Elections*. New York: Oxford University Press.

Graber, D., McQuail, D. & Norris, P. (eds.) (1998). *The Politics of News: The News of Politics*. Washington, DC: CQ Press.

Graham, T. (2003, April 1). No Honest Eyewitness. *National Review*. www.nationalreview.com/comment/comment-graham040103.asp.

Greatbatch, D. (1988). A Turn-Taking System for British News Interviews. *Language in Society*, 17(3), 401–30.

Greenhouse, J. (2015, July 24). Is It Ever Acceptable for the Media to "Out" Someone? *HuffingtonPostLive*. www.huffingtonpost.com/entry/is-it-ever-okay-for-a-media-publication-to-out-somebody_55b0f640e4b08f57d5d3c2b7.

Greenslade, R. (2015, November 9). Images of Drowned Boy Made Only a Fleeting Change to Refugee Reporting. *The Guardian*.

Gross, L. (2002). *Up from Invisibility*. New York: Columbia University Press.

Grossberg, L. (1997). *Bringing It All Back Home: Essays on Cultural Studies*. Chapel Hill, NC: Duke University Press.

Grossberg, L., Nelson, C. & Treichler, P. (eds.) (1992). *Cultural Studies.* New York: Routledge.

Grossman, L. J. (2003, May/June). War and the Balance Sheet. *Columbia Journalism Review*, 6.

Grueskin, B. (2013, April 22). In Defense of Scoops. *Columbia Journalism Review.*

Grusin, R. (2010). *Premediation: Affect and Mediality after 9/11.* New York: Palgrave MacMillan.

Gunaratne, S. (1998). Old Wine in a New Bottle: Public Journalism, Developmental Journalism and Social Responsibility. In M. E. Roloff (ed.), *Communication Yearbook 21.* Thousand Oaks, CA: Sage, 276–321.

Gunaratne, S. A. (2005). *The Dao of the Press: A Humanocentric Theory.* Cresskill, NJ: Hampton Press.

Gunnison, R. A. (1942). Manila Eyewitness. *Collier's*, 13, 43–5.

Gunter, B. (2003). *News and the Net.* Mahwah, NJ: Lawrence Erlbaum.

Gunther, R. & Mughan, A. (2000). *Democracy and Media: A Comparative Perspective.* Cambridge: Cambridge University Press.

Guo, Z. (2010). Through Barbed Wires: Context, Content and Constraints for Journalism Education in China. In B. Josephi (ed.), *Journalism Education in Countries with Limited Media Freedom.* New York: Peter Lang, 15–32.

Habermas, J. (1974, Autumn). The Public Sphere: An Encyclopedia Article (1964). *New German Critique*, 3, 49–55.

Hagen, C. (1994, June 3). The Essence of the Invasion in Just a Few Frames. *The New York Times*, C26.

Halabi, N. (2016). Recreating Syria Between Physical Places and online Spaces: Nostalgia and Home-Building in Sarouja Restaurant. Paper presented at the International Association of Media Communication Research Leicester, UK.

Halbwachs, M. (1992 [1925]). *On Collective Memory* (ed., trans., L. A. Coser). University of Chicago Press.

Hall, S. (1972). The Social Eye of *Picture Post. Working Papers in Cultural Studies, 2.* Birmingham, UK: CCCS University of Birmingham.

Hall, S. (1973). The Determinations of News Photographs. In S. Cohen & J. Young (eds.), *The Manufacture of News.* London: Sage, 226–43.

Hall, S. (1980). Encoding and Decoding in the Television Discourse. In S. Hall, D. Hobson, A. Lowe & P. Willis (eds.), *Culture, Media, Language.* London: Hutchinson, 128–39.

Hall, S., Connell, I. & Curti, L. (1976). The "Unity" of Current Affairs Television. *Working Papers in Cultural Studies 9.* Birmingham, UK: CCCS University of Birmingham.

Hall, S., Critcher, C., Jefferson, T., Clarke, J. & Roberts, B. (1978). *Policing the Crisis.* London: Macmillan.

Hallin, D. (1986). *The "Uncensored War": The Media and Vietnam.* Oxford University Press.

Hallin, D. & Mancini, P. (2004). *Comparing Media Systems.* Cambridge University Press.

Hallin, D. & Mancini, P. (2011). *Comparing Media Systems Beyond the Western World.* Cambridge University Press.

Hallock, S. (2015, August 5). Journalism Takes a Hit with Return of Williams. *Philadelphia Inquirer.*

Halloran, J. D. (1970). *Demonstrations and Communication: A Case Study.* Harmondsworth: Penguin.

Hamill, P. (1998). *News Is a Verb: Journalism at the End of the Twentieth Century.* New York: Ballantine.

Hamilton, C. H. (1954, September 1). Call it Objective, Interpretive or 3-D Reporting. *ASNE Bulletin,* 6–7.

Hamilton, J. M. (2011). *Journalism's Roving Eye: A History of American Foreign Reporting.* Baton Rouge, LA: LSU Press.

Han, E. L. (2016). *Micro-Blogging Memories: Weibo and Collective Remembering in Contemporary China.* London: Palgrave MacMillan.

Hanitzsch, T. (2007, November). Deconstructing Journalism Culture: Toward a Universal Theory. *Communication Theory,* 17(4), 367–85.

Hanitzsch, T. & Mellado, C. (2011). What Shapes the News around the World? How Journalists in 18 Countries Perceive Influences on Their Work. *International Journal of Press/Politics,* 16, 404–26.

Hannerz, U. (2004). *Foreign News: Exploring the World of Foreign Correspondents.* University of Chicago Press.

Hanusch, F. (2013). Journalists in Times of Change: Evidence from a New Survey of Australia's Journalistic Workforce. *Australian Journalism Review,* 35(1), 27–40.

Hanusch, F. (2014, November). Dimensions of Indigenous Journalism Culture. *Journalism: Theory, Practice and Criticism,* 15(8), 951–67.

Hardt, H. (1986). British Cultural Studies and the Return of the "Critical" in American Mass Communication Research: Accommodation or Radical Change? *Journal of Communication Inquiry,* 10(2), 117–24.

Hardt, H. (1990). Newsworkers, Technology, and Journalism History. *Critical Studies in Mass Communication,* 7, 346–65.

Hardt, H. (1992). *Critical Communication Studies: Communication, History and Theory in America.* New York: Routledge.

Hardt, H. (2002). Rereading the Russian Revolution: International Communication Research and the Journalism of Lippman and Merz. *Mass Communication and Society,* 5(1), 25–39.

Hardt, H. & Brennen, B. (eds.) (1995). *Newsworkers: Toward a History of the Rank and File.* Minneapolis: University of Minnesota Press.

Hardy, A. (1946, December 7). [Photo] Winecoff Hotel Death. Associated Press.

Harmon, A. (2003, March 24). Improved Tools Turn Journalists into a Quick Strike Force. *The New York Times*, C1, C4.

Harper, C. (2014, September 3). Media Ethics in the Gruesome Age of the Islamic State. *Washington Times*.

Harrington, S. (2012, August). Australian Journalism Studies after "Journalism": Breaking Down the Disciplinary Boundaries (For Good). *Media International Australia Incorporating Culture and Policy*, 144, 156–62.

Hartley, J. (1982). *Understanding News*. London: Methuen.

Hartley, J. (1992). *The Politics of Pictures: The Creation of the Public in the Age of Popular Media*. London: Routledge.

Hartley, J. (1996). *Popular Reality: Journalism, Modernity, Popular Culture*. New York: Arnold.

Hartley, J. (1999). What Is Journalism? The View from Under a Stubbie Cap. *Media International Australia Incorporating Culture and Policy*, 90.

Hartley, J. (2002). *Communication, Cultural and Media Studies: The Key Concepts*. London: Routledge.

Hartley, J. (2003). *A Short History of Cultural Studies*. London: Sage.

Has ISIS Found a Base on African Soil? [Editorial] (2015, May 4). *Swazi Observer*.

Hauling Water (2003, April 17). [Photo] *The New York Times*, B1.

Hebdige, D. (1979). *Subculture: The Meaning of Style*. London: Methuen.

Hebdige, D. (1988). *Hiding in the Light*. London: Comedia.

Henningham, J. (1985). Journalism as a Profession: A Reexamination. *Australian Journal of Communication*, 8, 1–17.

Henrichsen, J., Betz, M. & Lisosky, J. (2015). *Building Digital Safety for Journalists: A Survey of Selected Issues*. New York: UNESCO.

Hermida, A. (2010). Twittering the News: The Emergence of Ambient Journalism. *Journalism Practice* 4(3), 343–56.

Hermida, A., Fletcher, F., Korell, D. & Logan, D. (2012). Share, Like, Recommend: Decoding the Social Media News Consumer. *Journalism Studies*, 13(5/6).

Hiebert, R. & Gross, P. (2003). Remedial Education: The Remaking of Eastern European Journalists. In R. Frohlich & C. Holtz-Bacha (eds.), *Journalism Education in Europe and North America*. Cresskill, NJ: Hampton Press, 257–84.

Higham, S. & Nakashima, E. (2015, July 16). Why The Islamic State Leaves Tech Companies Torn Between Free Speech and Security. *Washington Post*.

Hilbrand, D. & Shister, G. (2003, March 27). A Flood of Images into Homes. *Philadelphia Inquirer*, A1, A20.

Hill, A. (2011, May 2). Osama bin Laden Killed – How a Live Blogger Captured the Raid. *The Guardian.*

Hill, E. (1933, March 1). Radio Journalism on the Job at Miami. *Broadcasting*, 12.

Himmelman, J. (2012, April 29). The Red Flag in the Flowerpot. *New York Magazine.*

Hinds, J. (2003, April 11). Photographic Memory. *Detroit Free Press*, pp. H1, H4.

Hobsbawm, E. & Ranger, T. (eds.) (1985). *The Invention of Tradition.* Cambridge University Press.

Horkheimer, M. & Adorno, T. (1972). *Dialectic of Enlightenment.* Palo Alto, CA: Stanford University Press.

Hossaini, M. (2011, December 6). [Photo] Girl in Green. Massoud Hossaini / AFP / Getty Images.

Hounshell, B. (2011, June 20). The Revolution Will Be Tweeted. *Foreign Policy Magazine.*

Howe, P. (2002). *Shooting Under Fire: The World of the War Photographer.* New York: Artisan.

Hoyt, P. (1943, May 9). Obligation to Extend Free Press Around World. *Editor and Publisher*, 22.

Hughes, E. C. (1958). *Men and Their Work.* Glencoe, IL: Free Press.

Hughes, H. M. (1940). *News and the Human Interest Story.* University of Chicago Press.

Huxford, J. (2001). Beyond the Referential: Uses of Visual Symbolism in the Press. *Journalism: Theory, Practice and Criticism*, 2(1), 45–72.

Hymes, D. H. (1980). Functions of Speech. In D. H. Hymes (ed.), *Language in Education.* Washington, DC: Center for Applied Linguistics, 1–18.

Ignatius, D. (2011, July 13). The World According to Rupert Murdoch. *Washington Post.*

India Suicide (2000, January 11). [Photo] Associated Press / Press Trust of India.

Infield, T. (2001, September 13). Tuesday's Terror Evoked Echoes of Pearl Harbor. *Philadelphia Inquirer*, A11.

Ip, C. (2015, July/August). The Cult of Vice. *Columbia Journalism Review.*

Irwin, W. (1906, June). San Francisco, A Month Ago. *Everybody's Magazine*, 753–60.

ISIS Runs a Dark Media Campaign on Social Media (2014, September 6). NPR.

Iyengar, S. & Reeves, R. (1997). *Do the Media Govern?* Thousand Oaks, CA: Sage.

Jackaway, G. (1995). *Media at War.* Westport, CT: Praeger.

Jacobsen, J. K. (1995). Much Ado about Ideas. *World Politics*, 47, 283–310.

Jacubowicz, K. (2007). *Rude Awakening: Social and Media Change in Central and Eastern Europe*. Cresskill, NJ: Hampton Press.

Janowitz, M. (1975). Professional Models in Journalism: The Gatekeeper and the Advocate. *Journalism Quarterly*, 52(4), 618–26.

Jarvis, J. (2011). *Public Parts: How Sharing in the Digital Age Improves the Way We Work and Live*. New York: Simon & Schuster.

Jaworski, A., Fitzgerald, R. & Morris, D. (2003). Certainty and Speculation in News Reporting of the Future: The Execution of Timothy McVeigh. *Discourse Studies*, 5 (1), 33–49.

Jebril, N., Stetka, V. & Loveless, M. (2013, September). *Media and Democratization: What Is Known about the Role of Mass Media in Transitions to Democracy*. Oxford: Reuters Institute for the Study of Journalism.

Jelin, E. (2011). Models of Transnational Scholarly "Cooperation": A Site of Geopolitical Struggles? In Zelizer, B. (ed.), *Making the University Matter*. London: Routledge, 219–27.

Jensen, J. (1990). *Redeeming Modernity: Contradictions in Media Criticism*. Thousand Oaks, CA: Sage.

Jensen, J. & Pauly, J. J. (1997). Imagining the Audience: Losses and Gains in Cultural Studies. In M. Ferguson & P. Golding (eds.), *Cultural Studies in Question*. London: Sage, 155–69.

Johnson, S. & Harris, J. (1942). *The Complete Reporter: A General Text in News Writing and Editing Complete with Exercises*. New York: Macmillan.

Johnson, T. (1977). *Professions and Power*. London: MacMillan.

Johnson-Cartee, K. (2004). *News Narratives and News Framing*. Lanham, MD: Rowman & Littlefield.

Johnstone, J. W. C., Slawski, E. J. & Bowman, W. W. (1976). *The News People*. Urbana: University of Illinois Press.

Jones, A. (2009). *Losing the News*. New York: Oxford University Press.

Jones, E. L. (1945, October). The Care and Feeding of Correspondents. *Atlantic Monthly*, 46.

Jones, J. (2009). *Satire TV: Politics and Comedy in the Post-Network Era*. NYU Press.

Josephi, B. (2009). Journalism Education. In T. Hanitzsch & K. Wahl-Jorgensen (eds.), *Handbook of Journalism Studies*. London and New York: Routledge, 42–58.

Journalism in Syria, Impossible Job? (2013, November 6). *Reporters Without Borders*.

Kakutani, M. (2003, March 25). Shock, Awe and Razzmatazz in the Sequel. *The New York Times*, E1, E5.

Kalyango, Y., Jr., & Eckler, P. (2010). Media Performance, Agenda

Building and Democratization in East Africa. *Communication Yearbook*, 34, 355–90.

Kang, H. D. (1991). *Media Culture in Korea*. Seoul National University Press.

Kannis, P. (1991). *Making Local News*. University of Chicago Press.

Kant, I. (1885). An Answer to the Question: What is Enlightenment? In H. Riess (ed.) (1970). *Kant: Political Writings*. Cambridge University Press, 54–60.

Keeble, R. (2007). Introduction: On Journalism, Creativity and the Imagination. In R. Keeble & S. Wheeler (eds.), *The Journalistic Imagination*. New York: Routledge, 1–14.

Kelliher, L. (2004, May/June). Brits vs. Yanks: Who Does Journalism Right? *Columbia Journalism Review*.

Kellner, D. (1992). *The Persian Gulf TV War*. Boulder, CO: Westview.

Kenner, H. (1985, September 15). The Politics of the Plain Style. *The New York Times Book Review*.

Kent, T. (2015). A Customized Ethics Code for Every Organization. *Online News Association*. http://ethics.journalists.org.

Kern, J. (2008). *Sound Reporting: The NPR Guide to Audio Journalism and Production*. University of Chicago Press.

Khamis, S. & Sisler, V. (2010). The New Arab "Cyberscape": Redefining Boundaries and Reconstructing Public Spheres. In C. Salmon (ed.), *Communication Yearbook*, 34. New York: Routledge, 277–316.

Khan, I. (2012, July 13). A Nose for News: Analytics Inspired Journalism. *ITworld.com*.

Khiabany, G. (2007). Is There an Islamic Communication? The Persistence of "Tradition" and the Lure of Modernity. *Critical Arts*, 21(1), 106–24.

Khiabany, G. (2010). *Iranian Media: A Paradox in Modernity*. London: Routledge.

Kitch, C. (2003). Mourning in America: Ritual, Redemption, and Recovery in News Narrative After September 11. *Journalism Studies*, 4(2), 213–24.

Kitch, C. (2005). *Pages from the Past: History and Memory in American Magazines*. Chapel Hill: University of North Carolina Press.

Kitch, C. (2006). "Useful Memory" in Time Inc Magazines. *Journalism Studies*, 7(1), 94–110.

Knight Center for Journalism in the Americas (2013). *Transparency and Accountability*. Austin, TX: Knight Center for Journalism in the Americas at UT Austin.

Knightley, P. (1975). *The First Casualty*. London and New York: Harcourt Brace and Jovanovitch.

Kosellek, R. (2004 [1985]). *Futures Past: On the Semantics of Historical Time*. New York: Columbia University Press.

Kovach, B. & Rosenstiel, T. (2001). *The Elements of Journalism*. New York: Crown.

Krasner, S. (1993). Westphalia and All That. In J. Goldstein & R. Keohane (eds.), *Ideas and Foreign Policy: Beliefs, Institutions and Political Change*. Ithaca, NY: Cornell University Press, 235–64.

Krasnoboka, N. (2010). Between the Rejected Past and Uncertain Future: What Have We Learned about Media in Russia and What Do We Do Next? *Communication Yearbook*, 34, 317–54.

Krauthammer, C. (2001, December 24). Only in Their Dreams. *Time*, 60–1.

Kreiling, A. (1993). The Commercialization of the Black Press and the Rise of Race News in Chicago. In W. S. Solomon & R. W. McChesney (eds.), *Ruthless Criticism: New Perspectives in US Communication History*. Minneapolis: University of Minnesota Press, 176–203.

Kress, G. & Van Leeuwen, T. (1996). *Reading Images*. Oxon, UK: Routledge.

Kroll, J. (1994, January 10). Eyewitness to the 20th Century. *Newsweek*, 66.

Kuhn, R. (1995). *The Media in France*. London: Routledge.

Kuhn, R. & Neveu, E. (eds.) (2002). *Political Communication: New Challenges, New Practices*. London and New York: Routledge.

Kuhn, R. & Nielsen, R. (eds.) (2013). *Political Journalism in Transition*. London and New York: I. B. Taurus (Reuters Institute for the Study of Journalism).

Kuhn, T. (1962). *The Structure of Scientific Revolutions*. University of Chicago Press.

Kumar, K. (1995). *From Post-Industrial to Post-Modern Society*. Oxford: Blackwell.

Lacey, N. (1998). *Image and Representation: Key Concepts in Media Studies*. New York: St. Martin's Press.

Lago, C. & Romancini, R. (2010). Aspects of Journalism Education in Brazil. In B. Josephi (ed.), *Journalism Education in Countries with Limited Media Freedom*. New York: Peter Lang, 175–98.

Lakoff, G. & Johnson, M. (1980). *Metaphors We Live By*. University of Chicago Press.

Lane, C. (1992, August 17). When Is It Genocide? *Newsweek*, 27.

Lang, K. (1996). The European Roots. In E. Dennis & E. Wartella (eds.), *American Communication Research: The Remembered History*. Mahwah, NJ: Erlbaum, 1–20.

Lang, K. & Lang, E. (1953). The Unique Perspective of Television and Its Effect. *American Sociological Review*, 18(1), 103–12.

Lang, K. & Lang, G. E. (1989). Collective Memory and the News. *Communication*, 11, 123–39.

Langer, J. (1998). *Tabloid Television: Popular Journalism and the "Other News."* London: Routledge.

Langley, M. & Levine, L. (1988, July/August). Broken Promises. *Columbia Journalism Review*, 21–4.

Larson, M. S. (1977). *The Rise of Professionalism: A Sociological Analysis.* Berkeley: University of California Press.

Lasorsa, D., Lewis, S. & Holton, A. (2012). Normalizing Twitter. *Journalism Studies*, 13(1), 19–36.

Lauter, D. (2015, December 21). Polls May Actually Underestimate Trump's Support, Study Finds. *Los Angeles Times*.

Lavrusik, V. (2013, May 2). Best Practices for Journalists on Facebook. https://www.facebook.com/notes/journalists-on-facebook/best-practices-for-journalists-on-facebook/593586440653374.

Lawler, A. (2003, November/December). Lifting the Fog of the Bias War. *Columbia Journalism Review*, 68–9.

Leadbeater, C. & Miller, P. (2004). *The Pro-Am Revolution: How Enthusiasts Are Changing Our Society and Economy.* New York: Demos.

Lee, C. C. (ed.) (2000). *Power, Money and Media: Communication Patterns and Bureaucratic Control in Cultural China.* Evanston, IL: Northwestern University Press.

Lee, C. C. (2001). Beyond Orientalist Discourses: Media and Democracy in Asia. *Javnost: The Public*, 8(2), 7–20.

Lee, J. (2004, July 26). Year of the Blog? Web Diarists Are Now Official Members of Convention Press Corps. *The New York Times*, P7.

Lee, K. (2015). *The Rise of Brand Journalism: Understanding the Discursive Dimensions of Collectivity in the Age of Convergence.* (Unpublished doctoral dissertation.) Annenberg School for Communication at the University of Pennsylvania, Philadelphia.

Lee, P. & Thomas, P. (2012). *Public Memory, Public Media and the Politics of Justice.* London: Palgrave MacMillan.

Leroux, C. (2003, March 27). Still Images, Moving Words. *Chicago Tribune*, sect. 2, 1.

Leslie, J. (1986, September). The Anonymous Source: Second Thoughts on "Deep Throat." *Washington Journalism Review*, 33–5.

Leung, K. W. Y., Kenny, J. & Lee, P. S. N. (eds.) (2006). *Global Trends in Communication Education and Research.* Cresskill, NJ: Hampton Press.

Levi-Strauss, C. (1966). *The Savage Mind.* University of Chicago Press.

Levy, D. & Sznaider, N. (2005). *The Holocaust and Memory in a Global Age.* Philadelphia, PA: Temple University Press.

Lewis, J. (2002). *Cultural Studies: The Basics.* London: Sage.

Lewis, S. (2012). The Tension Between Professional Control and

Open Participation: Journalism and Its Boundaries. *Information, Communication and Society*, 15(6), 836–66.

Lewis, S. & Carlson, M. (2015). *Boundaries of Journalism: Professionalism, Practices and Participation*. London: Routledge.

Liao, K.-H., Chang, C.-C., Liang, C.-T. & Liang, C. (2016). In Search of the Journalistic Imagination. *Thinking Skills and Creativity*, 19, 9–20.

Liberation and Revenge [Editorial] (2001, November 14). *Chicago Tribune*, 22.

Libin, S. (2006, October 9). Late-Breaking News about Live, Local Coverage. *Poynteronline.com*. www.poynter.org/column.asp?id=34& aid=111941.

Lichfield, J. (203, April 10). Single Pictures that Capture History's Turning Points. *The Independent*, 10.

Lichterman, J. (2014, May 14). Why Aren't Local Newsrooms Innovating Digitally? Because the Goat Must Be Fed. *NiemanLab*.

Lilly, W. S. (1889). The Ethics of Journalism. *The Forum*, 503–12.

Lindlof, T. (ed.) (1987). *Natural Audiences*. Norwood, NJ: Ablex.

Lindstrom, C. (1953, January 1). By What Right Do We Interpret or Explain? (Address to APME, Boston). *ASNE Bulletin*, 2–3.

Lippman, W. (1914). *Drift and Mastery*. New York: Mitchell Kennedy.

Lippman, W. (1925). *The Phantom Public*. New York: MacMillan.

Lippman, W. (1960 [1922]). *Public Opinion*. New York: Harcourt Brace.

Lipschultz, J. H. & Hilt, M. (2002). *Crime and Local News: Dramatic, Breaking and Live from the Scene*. Mahwah, NJ: Lawrence Erlbaum.

Loftus, E. (1980). *Eyewitness Testimony*. Cambridge, MA: Harvard University Press.

Logiurato, B. (2013, April 19). Jon Stewart Destroys CNN over Boston Marathon Blunder. *Business Insider*.

Lowrey, W. & Mackay, J. (2008). Journalism and Blogging. *Journalism Practice* 2(1), 64–81.

Lowry, B. & Jensen, E. (2003, March 28). The "Gee Whiz" War. *The Los Angeles Times*, E1.

Lubrano, A. (2003, March 30). Even War Has Rules. *Philadelphia Inquirer*, sect. C, 1.

Luckhurst, T. (2004, March 16). Altered Images. *The Independent*.

Luckie, M. (2012, September 20). Best Practices for Journalists. https://blog.twitter.com/2012/best-practices-for-journalists.

Lukes, S. (1975). Political Ritual and Social Integration. *Sociology*, 9(2), 289–308.

Lumby, C. (1999). *Gotcha: Life in a Tabloid World*. Sydney: Allen and Unwin.

MacDougall, C. D. & Reid, R. D. (1987). *Interpretative Reporting* (9th edn.). New York: Macmillan.

MacIntyre, A. (1981). *After Virtue: A Study in Moral Theory.* University of Notre Dame Press.

MacVane, J. (1979). *On the Air in World War II.* New York: Morrow.

Maier, S. (2007). Setting the Record Straight. *Journalism Practice,* 1(1), 33–43.

Malik, A. (2004, December 30). Can CNN, BBC Get Away with This Corpse Show? *The Indian Express.*

Malone, B. (2015, August 20). Why Al Jazeera Will Not Say Mediterranean "Migrants." *Al Jazeera.*

Mander, M. (1987). Narrative Dimensions of the News: Omniscience, Prophecy, and Morality. *Communication,* 10, 51–70.

Manjoo (2013, April 19). Breaking News Is Broken. *Slate.* www.slate.com /articles/technology/technology/2013/04/boston_bombing_breaking_ news_don_t_watch_cable_shut_off_twitter_you_d_be.html.

Manoff, R. K. & Schudson, M. (eds.) (1986). *Reading the News.* New York: Pantheon.

March, A. (2014, October 1). Is Vice's Documentary on ISIS Illegal? *Atlantic Monthly.*

Marcus, R. (2011, November 7). "Herman Cain Harassment Story Was Good Journalism." *Washington Post.*

Mariscal, J. (2001). Can Cultural Studies Speak Şpanish? In T. Miller (ed.), *A Companion to Cultural Studies.* London: Blackwell, 232–45.

Markel, L. (1953, April 1). The Case for "Interpretation." ASNE *Bulletin,* 1–2.

Marques de Melo, J. (2009). Journalistic Thinking: Brazil's Modern Tradition. *Journalism: Theory, Practice and Criticism,* 10(1), 11–27.

Marshall, T. (1994, March 19). Faced with a TV War, Europeans Switch Off. *Los Angeles Times,* A16.

Martinez, M. (2014, September 16). Fixer Recounts How ISIS Abducted Him and Steven Sotloff. *CNN.* www.cnn.com/2014/09/16/world/steven-sotloff-fixer-isis-interview.

Martz. L. (1992, June 22). For the Media, a Pyrrhic Victory. *Newsweek,* 32.

Marvin, C. (1983). Space, Time and Captive Communications. In M. Mander (ed.), *Communications in Transition.* New York: Praeger, 20–38.

Marvin, C. (1988). *When Old Technologies Were New.* New York: Oxford University Press.

Massey, D. (1999). Space–Time, Science and the Relationship Between Physical Geography and Human Geography. *Transactions of the Institute of British Geographers,* 24, 261–76.

Massing, M. (2003, May/June). The High Price of an Unforgiving War. *Columbia Journalism Review,* 33–5.

Mathews, J. J. (1957). *Reporting the Wars*. Minneapolis: University of Minnesota Press.

Mattelart, A. (2006). Toward the End of the French Exception in Communication Research? In K. W. Y. Leung, J. Kenny & P. S. N. Lee (eds.), *Global Trends in Communication Education and Research*. Cresskill, NJ: Hampton Press, 73–96.

Maurantonio, N. (2012). Standing By: Police Paralysis, Race and the 1964 Philadelphia Riots. *Journalism History*, 38(2), 110–21.

Mauro, T. (1987, September). The Name of the Source. *Washington Journalism Review*, 36–8.

May, R. (1953, April 20). Is the Press Unfair to McCarthy? *New Republic*, 128, 10–12.

Mayer, H. (1964). *The Press in Australia*. Melbourne: Lansdowne.

McBride, K. (2015, June 9). When It's O.K. to Pay for a Story. *The New York Times*, A23.

McCarthy, J. (2014, September 17). Trust in Mass Media Returns to All Time Low. Gallup Poll. www.gallup.com/poll/176042/trust-mass-media-returns-time-low.aspx?version=print.

McChesney, R. & Nichols, J. (2010). *The Death and Life of American Journalism*. New York: Nation Books.

McChesney, R. & Pickard, V. (2011). *Will The Last Reporter Please Turn Out the Lights? The Collapse of US Journalism and What Can Be Done to Fix It*. New York: The New Press.

McCollam, D. (2004, July/August). The List: How Chalabi Played the Press. *Columbia Journalism Review*, 31–7.

McConnell, P. & Becker, L. (2002, July). The Role of the Media in Democratization. Paper presented to the International Association of Media Communication Research, Barcelona, Spain.

McCullin, D. (1987). Notes by a Photographer. In E. Meijer & J. Swart (eds.), *The Photographic Memory: Press Photography – Twelve Insights*. London: Quiller Press, 11–26.

McDonough, J. (1994). The Longest Night: Broadcasting's First Invasion. *American Scholar,* Spring, 193–211.

McGrory, M. (1973. December 8). A Time Not to Be Away. *America*, 437.

McGuigan, J. (1992). *Cultural Populism*. London: Routledge.

McKenzie, V. (1938, December). We Saw It with Our Own Eyes. *Quill*, 5.

McManus, J. (1994). *Market-Driven Journalism: Let the Citizen Beware*. Thousand Oaks, CA: Sage.

McNair, B. (2000). *Journalism and Democracy*. London: Routledge.

McNamara, K. R. (1998). *The Currency of Ideas*. Ithaca, NY: Cornell University Press.

McQuail, D. (2000). Some Reflections on the Western Bias of Media Theory. *Asian Journal of Communication*, 10(2), 1–13.

Media Monitor (2003). *The Media Go to War*. Washington, DC: Center for Media and Public Affairs.

Meerbach, G. (2003). The Development of Journalism in the Netherlands. In R. Frohlich & C. Holtz-Bacha (eds.), *Journalism Education in Europe and North America*. Cresskill, NJ: Hampton Press, 105–20.

Mellado, C., Moreira, S., Lagos, C. & Hernandez, M. (2012). Comparing Journalism Cultures in Latin America. *International Communication Gazette*, 74(1), 60–77.

Meltzer, K. (2010). *TV News Anchors and Journalistic Tradition*. New York: Peter Lang.

Merrill, J. & Nerone, J. (2002). *The Four Theories of the Press* Four and a Half Decades Later: A Retrospective. *Journalism Studies*, 3(1), 133–6.

Merritt, D. (1997). *Public Journalism and Public Life: Why Telling the News is Not Enough*. Hillsdale, NJ: Lawrence Erlbaum.

Meyer, E. L. (2011). *Media Codes of Ethics: The Difficulty of Defining Standards*. Washington, DC: Center for International Media Assistance and National Endowment for Democracy.

Meyers, A. M. (1943, June). The Camera: A Silent Witness. *American Photography*, 20–2.

Meyers, M. (2013). African American Women in the News: Gender, Race and Class in Journalism. Abingdon, Oxon, and New York: Routledge.

Meyers, O. (2002). Still Photographs, Dynamic Memories: An Analysis of the Visual Presentation of Israel's History in Commemorative Newspaper Supplements. *Communication Review*, 5(3), 179–205.

Meyers, O., Neiger, M. & Zandberg, E. (2011). *On Media Memory: Collective Memory in a New Media Age*. London: Palgrave MacMillan.

Miike, Y. (2006). Non-Western Theory in Western Research? An Asiacentric Agenda for Asian Communication Studies. *The Review of Communication*, 6(1–2), 4–31.

Mikula, M. (2008). *Key Concepts in Cultural Studies*. London: Palgrave MacMillan.

Mill, J. S. (2008 [1869]). *On Liberty*. New York: Oxford University Press.

Miller, T. (1998). *Technologies of Truth: Cultural Citizenship and the Popular Media*. Minneapolis: University of Minnesota Press.

Miller, T. (ed.) (2006). *A Companion to Cultural Studies*. London: Blackwell.

Mirkinson, J. (2012, July 4). Phone Hacking: A Year after Milly Dowler Scandal, There Is No End in Sight to Crisis. *Huffington Post*.

Mitchell, A. Gottfried, J. & Matsa, K. (2015, June 1). Millenials and Political News. Pew Research Center. www.journalism.org/2015/06/01/millennials-political-news.

Mitchell, G. (2004, May 13). Where Was Press When 1st Iraq Prison Allegations Arose? *Editor and Publisher*.

Moeller, S. D. (1989). *Shooting War: Photography and the American Experience of Combat.* New York: Basic Books.

Moll, P. (2001). The Thirst for Certainty: Futures Studies in Europe and the United States. In R. A. Slaughter (ed.), *Knowledge Base of Futures Studies.* Millennium Edition CD-ROM. Queensland: The Futures Study Centre.

"Moments Remembered" (1960, December 26). *Life*, 91–102.

Montopoli, B. (2011, May 5). Obama: I Won't Release bin Laden Death Photos. *CBS News.*

Mooney, C. (2004, March/April). The Editorial Pages and the Case for War. *Columbia Journalism Review*, 28–34.

Moore, M. (2015, July). *Election Unspun: Political Parties, the Press and Twitter During the 2015 UK Election Campaign.* London: Media Standards Trust and the Policy Institute at Kings College London.

Moore, W. (1970). *The Professions: Roles and Rules.* New York: Russell Sage Foundation.

Moreira, S. & Helal, C. (2009). Notes on Media, Journalism Education and News Organizations in Brazil. *Journalism: Theory, Practice and Criticism*, 10(1), 91–107.

Morgenthau, H. (1985[1948]). *Politics Among Nations: The Struggle for Power and Peace.* New York: Alfred A Knopf.

Morley, D. (1980). *The "Nationwide" Audience: Structure and Decoding.* London: BFI.

Morris, M. (1988). The Banality of Cultural Studies. *Discourse*, 10, 3–29.

Morris, N. & Waisbord, S. (eds.) (2001). *Media and Globalization: Why the State Matters.* Lanham, MD: Rowman and Littlefield.

Morrison, D. & Tumber, H. (1988). *Journalists at War: The Dynamics of News Reporting During the Falklands War.* London: Sage.

Mortensen, M. (2014). *Journalism and Eyewitness Images.* London and New York: Routledge.

Moscou, J. (2003, January 30). Newsrooms Bewitched by Iraq War. *Editor and Publisher.*

Moses, L. (2003, March 5). How Would Iraq War Affect Advertising? *Editor and Publisher.*

Mott, F. L. (ed.). (1937). *Interpretations of Journalism.* New York: F. L. Crofts & Co.

Mowlana, H. (1996). *Global Communication in Transition.* Thousand Oaks, CA: Sage.

Muhlmann, G. (2010). *Journalism for Democracy.* Cambridge: Polity.

Murdoch's Malign Influence Must Die with the News of the World [Editorial] (2011, July 9). *The Guardian.*

Murdock, G. (1993). Communications and the Constitution of Modernity. *Media, Culture and Society*, 15, 521–39.

Murdock, G. (2010). Journeys to the West: The Making of Asian Modernities. In G. Wang (ed.), *De-westernizing Communication Research*. London: Routledge.

Murrell, C. (2015). *Foreign Correspondents and International Newsgathering: The Role of Fixers*. London and New York: Routledge.

Mustafa, T. (2012). [Photo] Aleppo, Syria. AFP / Getty Images.

Myers, S. (2011, July 20). Phone Hacking Scandal a Corruption Story, Like Enron and Countless Others. *Poynter.org*. www.poynter.org/latest-news/top-stories/139853/phone-hacking_scandal-a-corruption-story-like-enron-and-countless-others.

Nalkur, S. (2002). Images of Liberation in the Coverage of Afghan Women. (Unpublished Master's thesis.) Annenberg School for Communication at the University of Pennsylvania, Philadelphia.

Naughton, J. (2015, June 13). "Undemocratic, Unnecessary, Intolerable" . . . The Official Verdict on Britain's State Snoopers. *The Guardian*.

Neal, R. M. (1933). *Newspaper Desk Work*. London and New York: D. Appleton.

Neiger, M. (2007). Media Oracles: The Cultural Significance and Political Import of News Referring to Future Events. *Journalism: Theory, Practice and Criticism*, 8(3), 309–21.

Neiger, M. & Tenenboim-Weinblatt, T. (2016, February). Understanding Journalism through a Nuanced Deconstruction of Temporal Layers in News Narratives. *Journal of Communication*, 66(1), 139–60.

Nelson, C. & Gaonkar, D. P. (eds.) (1996). *Disciplinarity and Dissent in Cultural Studies*. New York: Routledge.

Nelson, C. & Grossberg, L. (eds.) (1988). *Marxism and the Interpretation of Culture*. Urbana: University of Illinois Press.

Nerone, J. (1994). *Violence Against the Press*. New York: Oxford University Press.

Nerone, J. (ed.) (1995). *Last Rights: Revisiting "Four Theories of the Press."* Urbana: University of Illinois Press.

Nerone, J. (2013). Why Journalism History Matters to Journalism Studies. *American Journalism*, 30(1), 15–28.

Nerone, J. (2015). *The Media and Public Life: A History*. Cambridge, UK, and Malden, MA: Polity.

Never Again? (2003, September 11). [Cover Photo] *US News & World Report*.

Neveu, E. (1998). Media and Politics in French Political Science. *European Journal of Political Research*, 33(4), 439–58.

"News of the World" Closes Due to Public Pressure (2011, July 8). Islamic Republic of Iran News Network Television (IRINN).

Newsmen Hailed over Watergate (1973, May 1). *The New York Times*, 28.

Newton, E. (ed.) (1999). *Crusaders, Scoundrels, Journalists: The Newseum's Most Intriguing Newspeople.* New York: Times Books.

Nguyen, K. (2015, December 18). Bigotry, Panic Reflected in Media Coverage of Migrants and Refugees. Reuters and Thomson Reuters Foundation. www.reuters.com/article/us-refugees-media-idUSKBN0U129620151218.

Nielsen, R. (2012). *Ground Wars: Personalized Communication in Political Campaigns.* Princeton University Press.

Nielsen, R. (2015). The Many Crises of Western Journalism: A Comparative Analysis of Economic Crises, Professional Crises and Crises of Confidence. In J. Alexander, E. B. Breese & M. Luengo (eds.), *The Crisis of Journalism Reconsidered.* Cambridge University Press.

Nimmo, D. & Combs, J. (1983). *Mediated Political Realities.* New York: Longman.

Noguchi, Y. (2005, July 8). Camera Phones Lend Immediacy to Images of Disaster. *Washington Post*, A16.

Nora, P. (1996). *Realms of Memory* (Vols. I–III). New York: Columbia University Press.

Nordland, R. (2015, February 1). ISIS Tactics Questioned as Hostages Dwindle. *The New York Times*, A6.

Norris, B. (2000). Media Ethics at the Sharp End. In D. Berry (ed.), *Ethics and Media Culture: Practices and Representations.* Waltham, MA: Focal Press, 325–38.

Norway's 9/11 (2015, July 24). *The Sun*, front cover.

Nussbaum, E. (2015, May 11). The Little Tramp. *The New Yorker.*

Nyamnjoh, F. B. (2005, November). Journalism in Africa: Modernity, Africanity. *Rhodes Journalism Review*, 25, 3–6.

Okrent, D. (2004, May 30). The Public Editor: Weapons of Mass Destruction? Or Mass Distraction? *The New York Times*, 30.

Orme, B. (2015). United States: The Trump Card: How US News Media Dealt with a Migrant Hate Manifesto. In A. White (ed.), *Moving Stories: International Review of How Media Cover Migration.* London: Ethical Journalism Network, 101–5.

Ornebring, H. (2009). *The Two Professionalisms of Journalism: Updating Journalism Research for the 21st Century.* Oxford: Reuters Institute for the Study of Journalism.

Orwell, G. (1946). Why I Write. *Gangrel*, Summer.

Orwell, G. (1999 [1946]). *Smothered Under Journalism: 1946.* London: Martin Secker and Warburg, Ltd.

O'Sullivan, T., Hartley, J., Saunders, D. & Fiske, J. (1983). *Key Concepts in Communication.* London: Methuen.

O'Sullivan, T., Hartley, J., Saunders, D., Montgomery, M. & Fiske, J.

(1994). *Key Concepts in Communication and Cultural Studies*. London: Routledge.

Oswell, D. (2006). *Culture and Society: An Introduction to Cultural Studies*. London and Thousand Oaks, CA: Sage.

Ouellette, L. (2002). *Viewers Like You?* New York: Columbia University Press.

Outing, S. (2003, March 26). War: A Defining Moment for Net News. *Editor and Publisher*.

Outing, S. (2004, April 1). How to Introduce Truly Disturbing Images Online. *The Poynter Institute*. www.poynteronline.org.

Overholser, G. (2001). Our Nose for News Fails Us When the Smell Is Close to Home. *Columbia Journalism Review*.

Owen, L. (2015a, October 26). Instant Articles Get Shared More Than Old-Fashioned Links, Plus More Details from Facebook's News Push. *NiemanJournalismLabs*. www.niemanlab.org/2015/10/instant-articles-get-shared-more-than-old-fashioned-links-plus-more-details-from-facebooks-news-push.

Owen, L. (2015b, November 24). Jeff Bezos Says the Washington Post's Goal is to Become the "New Paper of Record." *Nieman JournalismLabs*. www.niemanlab.org/2015/11/spacesuit-wearing-jeff-bezos-says-the-washington-posts-goal-is-to-become-the-new-paper-of-record.

Pantti, M. & Bakker, P. (2009, September). Misfortunes, Memories and Sunsets: Non-Professional Images in Dutch News Media. *International Journal of Cultural Studies*, 12(5), 471–89.

Parenti, M. (1986). *Inventing Reality: The Politics of the Mass Media*. New York: St. Martin's.

Park, D. W. & Pooley, J. (2008). *The History of Media and Communication Research: Contested Memories*. New York: Peter Lang.

Park, R. E. (1925). The Natural History of the Newspaper. In R. E. Park, E. W. Burgess & R. D. McKenzie (eds.), *The City*. University of Chicago Press, 80–98.

Park, R. E. (1940, March). News as a Form of Knowledge. *American Journal of Sociology*, 45, 669–86.

Paterson, C. & Domingo, D. (eds.) (2008). *Making Online News*. New York: Peter Lang.

Patterson, T. E. (1993). *Out of Order:* New York: Knopf.

Patterson, T. E. (1998). Time and News: The Media's Limitations as an Instrument of Democracy. *International Political Science Review*, 19(1), 55–67.

Pauly, J. J. (1988). Rupert Murdoch and the Demonology of Professional Journalism. In J. W. Carey (ed.), *Media, Myths and Narratives*. Beverly Hills, CA: Sage.

Pause for Hindsight, A [Editorial] (2004, July 16). *The New York Times*, A20.

Pearson, R. & Hartley, J. (eds.) (2000). *American Cultural Studies: A Reader.* New York: Oxford University Press.

Pedelty, M. (1995). *War Stories: The Culture of Foreign Correspondence.* London and New York: Routledge.

Perlman, D. (1946, May 11). French Editors Favor Press Control Clause. *Editor and Publisher,* 59.

Perry, R. B. (1935). *The Thought and Character of William James.* Nashville, TN: Vanderbilt University Press.

Peters, C. & Broersma, M. (2012). *Rethinking Journalism: Trust and Participation in a Transformed News Landscape.* London and New York: Routledge.

Peters, J. D. (1986). Institutional Sources of Intellectual Poverty in Communication Research. *Communication Research,* 13, 527–59.

Peters, J. D. (1999). *Speaking into the Air: A History of the Idea of Communication* University of Chicago Press.

Peters, J. D. (2001). Witnessing. *Media, Culture & Society,* 23, 707–23.

Peters, J. W. (2011, August 6). Paying for News? It's Nothing New. *The New York Times,* SR4.

Phillips, A. (2010). Transparency and the New Ethics of Journalism. *Journalism Practice,* 4(3), 373–82.

Picard, R. G. (2002). *The Economics and Financing of Media Companies.* New York: Fordham University Press.

Picard, R. G. (2015, May). *Journalists' Perceptions of the Future of Journalistic Work.* Oxford: Reuters Institute for the Study of Journalism.

Pickard, V. (2014). *America's Battle for Media Democracy.* New York: Cambridge University Press.

Pickard, V. & Torres, J. (2009, July 4). Saving America's Democracy-Sustaining Journalism. *Seattle Times.*

Pietila, V. (2008). How Does a Discipline Become Institutionalized? In D. W. Park & J. Pooley (eds.), *The History of Media and Communication Research: Contested Memories.* New York: Peter Lang, 205–24.

Pilger, J. (2015, November 17). From Pol Pot to ISIS: The Blood Never Dried. *Counterpunch.*

Pincus, W. (1973, October 20). Unidentified News Sources and Their Motives: The Usable Press. *New Republic,* 17–18.

[Poll] (2004, April 5). Pew Research Center for the People and the Press.

Pollitt, C. & Hupe, P. (2011, June). Talking about Government: The Role of Magic Concepts. *Public Management Review,* 13(5), 641–58.

Pooley, J. & Park, D. W. (2008). Introduction. In D. W. Park & J. Pooley (eds.), *The History of Media and Communication Research: Contested Memories.* New York: Peter Lang, 1–15.

Portraits of War: Conflict, Capitulation (2003, March 23). *Philadelphia Inquirer,* A21.

Powers, R. (1973, June). The Essential Cronkite. *Quill*, 32–6.

Press after Nixon, The (1974, November/December). *ASNE Bulletin*, 6–11.

Press and Watergate: Intervening in History (Views of the Editors) (1974, September/October). *Columbia Journalism Review*, 1.

Preston, P. (2012, November 17). Journalism Once Had Woodward and Bernstein: Now It's Guns for Hire. *The Guardian.*

Price, M. & Rozumilowicz, B. (2002). *Media Reform: Democratizing the Media, Democratizing the State.* London: Routledge.

Price, V. & Tewksbury, D. (1997). News Values and Public Opinion: A Theoretical Account of Media Priming and Framing. In G. Barnett & F. J. Boser (eds.), *Progress in the Communication Sciences.* Norwood, NJ: Ablex.

Radway, J. (1984). *Reading the Romance.* Chapel Hill: University of North Carolina Press.

Rather, D. (1977). *The Camera Never Blinks.* New York: Ballantine Books.

Real Stories of Wartime (2007, September 24). [Cover Photo] *US News & World Report.*

Reese, S. D. (1990). The News Paradigm and the Ideology of Objectivity. *Critical Studies in Mass Communication*, 190–409.

Reese, S. D., Gandy, Jr., O. & Grant, A. (eds.) (2001). *Framing Public Life.* Mahwah, NJ: Erlbaum.

Reporting A New Kind of War (1991, March). *Washington Journalism Review*, 12–33.

Reston, J. (1991). *Deadline.* New York: Random House.

Revers, M. (2014, October). The Twitterization of Newsmaking: Transparency and Journalistic Professionalism. *Journal of Communication*, 64(5), 806–26.

Rich, F. (2003, April 13). The Spoils of War Coverage. *The New York Times*, sect. 2, 1, 15.

Richards, I. (2009). Uneasy Bedfellows: Ethics Committees and Journalism Research. *Australian Journalism Review*, 31(2), 35–46.

Richardson, J. (2007). *Analyzing Newspapers: An Approach from Critical Discourse Analysis.* London: Palgrave MacMillan.

Riddell, G. (1932). The Psychology of the Journalist. In M. Bromley & T. O'Malley (eds.) (1997). *A Journalism Reader.* London and New York: Routledge.

Rieder, R. (2011, July 8). *News of the World* Scandal: US Journalism Shrugs. *BBC.com.*

Riess, C. (1944). *They Were There: The Story of World War II and How It Came About by America's Foremost Correspondents.* New York: G. P. Putnam's Sons.

Risse-Kappen, T. (1994). Ideas Do Not Float Freely: Transnational Coalitions, Domestic Structures, and the End of the Cold War. *International Organization*, 48, 185–214.

Ristovska, S. (2016). Strategic Witnessing in an Age of Video Activism. *Media, Culture & Society*, 38(7), 1034–47.

Robins, K. (1993). The War, The Screen, The Crazy Dog, and Poor Mankind. *Media, Culture and Society*, 15.

Robinson, G. (1988). "Here Be Dragons": Problems in Charting the US History of Communication Studies. *Communication*, 10, 97–119.

Robinson, S. (2011). Journalism as Process: The Labor Implications of Participatory Content in News Organizations. *Journalism & Communication Monographs*, 13(3), 138–210.

Robinson, S. & DeShano, C. (2011). "Anyone Can Know": Citizen Journalism and the Interpretive Community of the Mainstream Press. *Journalism: Theory, Practice and Criticism*, 12(8), 963–82.

Rodgers, R. (2007) Journalism Is a Loose-Jointed Thing: A Content Analysis of *Editor and Publisher*'s Discussion of Journalistic Conduct Prior to the Canons of Journalism, 1901–1922. *Journal of Mass Media Ethics*, 22(10), 66–82.

Rodman, G. (2014). *Why Cultural Studies?* New York: Wiley-Blackwell.

Roeh, I., Katz, E., Cohen, A. A. & Zelizer, B. (1980). *Almost Midnight: Reforming the Late-Night News*. Beverly Hills, CA: Sage.

Rogers, E. (1994). *A History of Communication Study*. New York: Free Press.

Rogers, E. & Chaffee, S. (1994, December). Communication and Journalism from "Daddy" Bleyer to Wilbur Schramm. *Journalism Monographs*, 148.

Rohde, D. (1995, August 18). Evidence Indicates Bosnia Massacre. *Christian Science Monitor*, AI.

Rohter, L. (2009, August 17). New Doubts Raised Over War Photo. *The New York Times*.

Roig-Franzia, M., Higham, S. & Grittain, A. (2015, February 14). Storytelling Ability Connected Brian Williams with Reviewers But Also Led to His Downfall. *Washington Post*.

Romano, A. & Bromley, B. (eds.) (2005). *Journalism and Democracy in Asia*. London: Routledge.

Root, M. A. (1864). *The Camera and the Pencil*. Philadelphia, PA: J. B. Lippincott.

Rose, S. (2014, October 7). The ISIS Propaganda War: A High-Tech Media Jihad. *The Guardian*.

Rosen, J. (1999). *What are Journalists For?* New Haven, CT: Yale University Press.

Rosen, J. (2004, May 29). From Wen Ho Lee to Judy Miller: The Transparency Era at *The New York Times*. *Press Think*.

Rosenberg, S. (2010, June 17). Why Can't Journalists Handle Public Criticism? *Mediashift.org*. http://mediashift.org/idealab/2010/06/why-cant-journalists-handle-public-criticism167.

Rosenstiel, T. (2003, April 10). War in Iraq: Covering the News. *Washington Post*. www.washingtonpost.com/wp-srv/liveonline/03/special/iraq/sp_iraq_rosenstiel041003.htm.

Rosenstiel, T. (2013, September 16). Why "Be Transparent" Has Replaced "Act Independently" as a Guiding Journalism Principle. *Poynter.com*. www.poynter.org/news/media-innovation/223657/why-be-transparent-is-now-a-better-ethical-principle-than-act-independently.

Rosenthal, J. (1945, February 23). [Photo] Flag Raising Atop Mount Suribachi.

Rosenthal, M. (2001, December 3). Just Massacres? *The Progressive*.

Roshco. B. (1975). *Newsmaking*. University of Chicago Press.

Roskis, E. (2000, December). Replaying the Pictures. *Le monde diplomatique*.

Rosoff, M. (2011, May 2). CNN Just Had Its CNN Moment. *Business Insider*.

Rottwilm, P. (2014, August). *The Future of Journalistic Work: Its Changing Nature and Implications*. Oxford: Reuters Institute for the Study of Journalism.

Rovere, R. (1984). *Final Reports*. Middletown, CT: Wesleyan University Press.

Rowe, D. (1999). *Sport, Culture and the Media*. Buckingham, UK: Open University Press.

Rubin, B. (1978). *Questioning Media Ethics*. New York: Praeger Publications.

Russell, R. (2012, September 14). David Carr's Golden Age of Journalism. *J-Source.ca (The Canadian Journalism Project)*. http://j-source.ca/article/david-carrs-golden-age-journalism#sthash.3C1tlUa7.dpuf.

Rutenberg, J. (2003a, April 16). Cable's War Coverage Suggests a New "Fox Effect" on Television. *The New York Times*, B9.

Rutenberg, J. (2003b, May 5). From Cable Star to Face in the Crowd. *The New York Times*, C1.

Ryan, M. (2010). *Cultural Studies: A Practical Introduction*. Alden, MA, and Oxford: Wiley-Blackwell.

Ryfe, D. (2012). *Can Journalism Survive: An Inside Look at American Newsrooms*. Cambridge: Polity.

Sagolj, D. (2003, April 11). [Photo] US Marine Doctor with Iraqi Girl. *Detroit Free Press*, H1.

Sakka, I. (2015, February 5). Slaying, Slaughtering and Burning: ISIS, The Cinematic Caliphate. *Al Akhbar* (English edn.).

Saldivar, J. (1997). *Border Matters: Remapping American Cultural Studies.* Berkeley and Los Angeles: University of California Press.

Samuels, R. (2015, September 22). As Hostility Flares, Hungary's Muslim Community Mobilizes to Aid Refugees. *Washington Post.*

Samyn, P; (2015, March 20). Free Press Rolling Out New Digital Platform. *Winnipeg Free Press.*

Sandler, L. (2003, March 24). Magazine War Coverage: Time is the Enemy. *The Los Angeles Times.*

Scanlan, C. (2003, July 28). Writing for Your Nose. www.poynter.org.

Scannell, P. (1996). *Radio, Television, and Modern Life: A Phenomenological Approach.* Oxford, UK, and Cambridge, MA: Blackwell.

Scannell, P. (2002). History, Media and Communication. In K. B. Jensen (ed.), *A Handbook of Media and Communication Research.* London: Routledge, 191–205.

Scannell, P. (2014). *Television and the Meaning of "Live."* Cambridge: Polity.

Schachter, A. (2014, October 27). Fixers Are a Foreign Reporter's Best Friend – and Often Their Lifeline. *PRI.* www.pri.org/stories/2014-10-27/fixers-are-foreign-reporters-best-friend-and-often-their-lifeline.

Schecter, D. (2003). *Embedded: Weapons of Mass Deception: How the Media Failed to Cover the War in Iraq.* New York: News Dissector.

Schecter, D. (2004, April 8). Misreporting the Iraqi Uprising. *Media Channel.* www.mediachannel.org.

Schell, O. (2004). "Preface." In M. Massing (ed.), *Now They Tell Us: The American Press and Iraq.* New York Review of Books, ii–xviii.

Schiller, D. (1981). *Objectivity and the News.* Philadelphia: University of Pennsylvania Press.

Schiller, D. (1996). *Theorizing Communication.* New York: Oxford University Press.

Schlesinger, P. (1977, September). Newsmen and Their Time-Machine. *British Journal of Sociology*, 28(3), 336–50.

Schlesinger, P. (1987). *Putting Reality Together.* London: Methuen.

Schlesinger, P. & Tumber, H. (1995). *Reporting Crime.* London: Oxford University Press.

Schorr, D. (1977). *Clearing the Air.* Boston, MA: Houghton Mifflin.

Schramm, W. (1957). Twenty Years of Journalism Research. *Public Opinion Quarterly*, 21(1), 91–107.

Schramm, W. (1959). *One Day in the World's Press.* Stanford University Press.

Schudson, M. (1978). *Discovering the News: A Social History of American Newspapers.* New York: Basic Books.

Schudson, M. (1982). The Politics of Narrative Form: The Emergence of News Conventions in Print and Television. *Daedalus*, 3(4), 97–112.

Schudson, M. (1986). Deadlines, Dateline and History. In R. K. Manoff & M Schudson (eds.), *Reading the News*. New York: Pantheon, 79–108.

Schudson, M. (1988). What is a Reporter? In J. W. Carey (ed.), *Media, Myths and Narratives*. Newbury Park, CA: Sage, 228–45.

Schudson, M. (1991). The Sociology of News Production, Revisited. In J. Curran & M. Gurevitch (eds.), *Mass Media and Society*. London: Arnold, 141–59.

Schudson, M. (1992). *Watergate in American Memory: How We Remember, Forget and Reconstruct the Past*. New York: Basic Books.

Schudson, M. (1995). Dynamics of Distortion in Collective Memory. In D. Schacter (ed.), *Memory Distortion: How Minds, Brains and Societies Reconstruct the Past*. Cambridge, MA: Harvard University Press, 346–64.

Schudson, M. (1996). *The Power of News*. Cambridge, MA: Harvard University Press.

Schudson, M. (2002). *The Sociology of News*. New York: W. W. Norton and Company.

Schudson, M. (2008). The "Lippmann–Dewey Debate" and the Invention of Walter Lippmann as an Anti-Democrat, 1986–1996. *International Journal of Communication*, 2, 1–20.

Schudson, M. (2013). Origins of the Freedom of Information Act in the United States. In N. Bowles, J. T. Hamilton & D. Levy (eds.), *Transparency in Politics and the Media*. London: I. B. Tauris, 1–18.

Schudson, M. (2015). *The Rise of the Right to Know*. New York: Belknap Press.

Schulte-Sasse, J. (1986, Winter). Imagination and Modernity: Or the Taming of the Human Mind. *Cultural Critique*, 5, 23–48.

Schwartz, D. (1992). To Tell the Truth: Codes of Objectivity in Photojournalism. *Communication*, 13, 95–109.

Schwartz, S. (2004, March 9). [Photo] Suicide. *New York Post*, front cover.

Schwarzlose, R. A. (1989). *The Nation's Newsbrokers* (Vol. I): *The Formative Years, From Pretelegraph to 1865*. Evanston, IL: Northwestern University Press.

Scott, C. (2015, September 22). Covering the Refugee Crisis on Snapchat and Periscope as a "Day by Day Documentary." Journalism.co.uk.

Second-guessing. (1955, January 1). *ASNE Bulletin*, 1–2.

Selfies and Public Perception of the Syrian Refugee Crisis [Blog] (2015, September 16). *Digital Journalism*. http://digitaljournalism.blogs.wm.edu/2015/09/16/selfies-and-public-perception-of-the-syrian-refugee-crisis.

Sekula, A. (1975, January). On the Invention of Photographic Meaning. *Artforum*, 13(5), 36–45.

Sender, K. (2012). *The Makeover: Reality Television and Reflexive Audiences*. New York: NYU Press.

Sella, M. (2014, October 19). The Making of the World's Scariest Terror Brand. *Matter*. https://medium.com/matter/the-making-of-the-worlds-most-effective-terrorist-brand-92620f91bc9d.

Sesser, S. N. (1973, December). The Press after Watergate. *Chicago Journalism Review*, 14–20.

Shaaber, M. S. (1929). *Some Forerunners of the Newspaper in England, 1476–1622*. Philadelphia, PA: Octagon Books.

Shattuc, J. M. (1997). *The Talking Cure: TV Talk Shows and Women*. London: Routledge.

Shiach, M. (ed.) (1999). *Feminism and Cultural Studies*. London: Oxford University Press.

Shirer, W. (1941). *Berlin Diary: The Journal of a Foreign Correspondent, 1934–1941*. New York: Hamish Hamilton.

Shirky, C. (2008). *Here Comes Everybody: The Power of Organizing without Organizations*. New York: Penguin.

Shirky, C. (2009). Newspapers and Thinking the Unthinkable. www.shirky.com/weblog/2009/03/newspapers-and-thinking-the-unthinkable.

Short, K. R. M. (1985). *World War II through the American Newsreels, 1942–1945*. New York: Oxford University Press.

Should Tass Reporters Be Curbed? (1951, October 1). *ASNE Bulletin*, 1–2.

Siebert, F., Peterson, T. & Schramm, W. (1956). *Four Theories of the Press*. Urbana: University of Illinois Press.

Sigal, L. (1973). *Reporters and Officials*. Lexington, MA: D. C. Heath.

Sigelman, L. (1973, July). Reporting the News: An Organizational Analysis. *American Journal of Sociology*, 79(1), 132–51.

Silverleib, A. (2011, May 3). Obama on Sunday: A Photo for the Ages? CNN.

Simon, J. & Libby, S. (2015, April 27). Broadcasting Murder – Militants Use Media for Deadly Purpose. New York: Committee to Protect Journalists.

Simonson, P. (2010). *Refiguring Mass Communication: A History*. Urbana: University of Illinois Press.

Simpson, C. (1999). *Science of Coercion*. New York: Oxford University Press.

Sims, A. C. (2003, February 25). Music Channels are "N-Synch" with War Coverage. *Fox News*.

Sims, N. (1984). *The Literary Journalists*. New York: Ballantine.

Singer, J. (2003). Who Are These Guys? The Online Challenge to the

Notion of Journalistic Professionalism. *Journalism: Theory, Practice and Criticism*, 4(2), 139–63.

Singer, J. (2005). The Political J-Blogger: Normalizing a New Media Form to Fit Old Norms and Practices. *Journalism: Theory, Practice and Criticism*, 6(2), 173–98.

Singer, J., D. Domingo, A. Heinonen et al. (2011). *Participatory Journalism: Guarding Open Gates at Online Newspapers*. New York: Wiley Blackwell.

Skjerdal, T. (2010). Research on Brown Envelope Journalism in the African Media. *African Communication Research*, 3(3), 357–406.

Smerconish, M. (2010, January 26). The Curious Tale of Obama's Biggest Defender. *The Daily Beast*. www.thedailybeast.com/articles/2010/01/27/the-curious-tale-of-obamas-biggest-defender.html.

Smith, E. W. (1944, August 28). [Photo] Baby Found in Cave. *Life*.

Smith, S. (2014, December 24). Top 10 Media Ethics Issues of 2014. *Imediaethics.org*, http://imediaethics.org/top-10-media-ethics-issues-of-2014.

Smith, T. (2003, May/June). The Real-Time War: Hard Lessons. *Columbia Journalism Review*, 26–31.

Smolkin, R. (2006, April/May). Too Transparent? *American Journalism Review*. http://ajrarchive.org/Article.asp?id=4073.

Snyder, L. I. (ed.) (1962). *Masterpieces of War Reporting*. New York: Julian Messner.

Soloski, J. (1989). News Reporting and Professionalism: Some Constraints on the Reporting of the News. *Media, Culture and Society*, 11(2), 207–28.

Sontag, S. (2004, May 23). Regarding the Torture of Others. *The New York Times Magazine*, 24–9, 42.

Souza, P. (2011, May 1). [Photo] The Situation Room.

Sparks, C. (1992). Popular Journalism: Theories and Practice. In P. Dahlgren & C. Sparks (eds.), *Journalism and Popular Culture*. London: Sage, 24–44.

Sparks, C. & Tulloch, J. (eds.) (2000). *Tabloid Tales*. Lantham, MD: Rowan and Littlefield.

Sparrow, B. H. (1999). *Uncertain Guardians: The News Media as a Political Institution*. Baltimore, MD: Johns Hopkins University Press.

Splichal, S. & Sparks, C. (1994). *Journalists for the 21st Century*. Norwood, NJ: Ablex.

Sproule, J. M. (2008). "Communication": From Concept to Field to Discipline. In D. W. Park & J. Pooley (eds.), *The History of Media and Communication Research: Contested Memories*. New York: Peter Lang, 163–78.

Stabile, C. (2006). *White Victims, Black Villains: Gender, Race and Crime News in US Culture*. London and New York: Routledge.

Stahl, J. (2013, April 15). Thou Shalt Not Stoop to Political Point-Scoring. *Slate*. www.slate.com/articles/technology/technology/2013/04/boston_marathon_bombing_all_the_mistakes_journalists_make_during_a_crisis.html.

State of the News Media (2004, March 15). Washington, DC: Pew Project for Excellence in Journalism.

State of the News Media (2007, March 12). Washington, DC: Pew Project for Excellence in Journalism.

State of the News Media (2015, April 29). Washington, DC: Pew Project for Excellence in Journalism.

Steffens, L. (1931). *The Autobiography of Lincoln Steffens*. New York: Harcourt Brace.

Steinberg, D. (2015, July 17). "Trainwreck" and a Brief History of Journalists Who Sleep with Their Subjects in Film. *Wall Street Journal*.

Steiner, L. (1992, October). Construction of Gender in Newsreporting Textbooks: 1890–1990. *Journalism Monographs*, 135, 1–48.

Stepan, P. (ed.) (2000). *Photos that Changed the World: The 20th Century*. Munich, London and New York: Prestel.

Stephens, M. (1988). *A History of News*. New York: Viking.

Stephens, M. (1998). *The Rise of the Image, The Fall of the Word*. New York: Oxford University Press.

Stokes, J. (2012). *How To Do Media and Cultural Studies* (2nd edn.). Newbury Park, CA, and London: Sage.

Stone, M. (1921). *Fifty Years a Journalist*. Garden City, NJ: Doubleday.

Storey, J. (1993). *An Introductory Guide to Cultural Theory and Popular Culture*. Athens, GA: University of Georgia Press.

Storey, J. (1996). *Cultural Studies and the Study of Popular Culture: Theories and Methods*. Athens, GA: University of Georgia Press.

Storey, J. (2003). *Inventing Popular Culture*. Malden, MA: Blackwell.

Storm, J. (2003, March 11). TV's Battle Plan. *Philadelphia Inquirer*.

Stratton, J. & Ang, I. (1996). On the Impossibility of a Global Cultural Studies: "British" Cultural Studies in an "International" Frame. In D. Morley & K. Chen (eds.), *Stuart Hall: Critical Dialogues in Cultural Studies*. London: Routledge, 361–91.

Striphas, T. (1998). The Long March: Cultural Studies and Its Institutionalization. *Cultural Studies*, 12(4), 453–75.

Strupp, J. (2003a, February 27). Papers Say They're Ready to Cover Iraq War. *Editor and Publisher*.

Strupp, J. (2003b, April 24). Out of Embed, But Facing Trauma? *Editor and Publisher*.

Su, A. (2014, January 31). Post Arab Spring, Citizen Journalists Struggle. *Columbia Journalism Review.*

Suffee, Z. (2015). United Kingdom: How Journalism Plays Follow-My-Leader with Rhetoric of Negativity. In A. White (ed.), *Moving Stories: International Review of How Media Cover Migration.* London: Ethical Journalism Network, 39–43.

Suicide of Alice Blanche Oswald (1872, September 20). [Photo] *Illustrated Police News.*

Suicide Protest Helped Topple Tunisian Regime (2011, January 14). *Toronto Star.*

Sutcliffe, C. (2015, December 15). Prediction Rankings: The Most Likely Media and Tech Developments in 2016. *TheMediaBriefing.* www.themediabriefing.com/article/prediction-rankings-the-most-likely-media-and-tech-developments-in-2016.

Swartz, J. (2003, March 19). Iraq War Could Herald a New Age of Web Based News Coverage. *USA Today.*

Swarup, N. (2012, March 27). [Photo] Tibetan Exile. Associated Press.

Swidler, A. (1986). Culture in Action: Symbols and Strategies. *American Sociological Review*, 273–86.

Szpunar, P. (2012). Western Journalism's "Other": The Legacy of the Cold War in the Study of Media Systems. *Journalism: Theory, Practice & Criticism*, 13(1), 3–20.

Takase, R. M. (2001, November 26). Refugee Children (Letter to the Editor). *Los Angeles Times*, A12.

Talev, M. (2015, November 18). Bloomberg Politics Poll: Most Americans Oppose Syrian Refugee Resettlement. Bloomberg News. www.bloomberg.com/politics/articles/2015-11-18/bloomberg-poll-most-americans-oppose-syrian-refugee-resettlement.

Tarde, G. (1969 [1901]). *On Communication and Social Influence.* University of Chicago Press.

Taylor, C. (2002). Modern Social Imaginaries. *Public Culture*, 14(1), 91–124.

Taylor, J. (1991). *War Photography: Realism in the British Press.* London: Routledge.

Taylor, P. (1990). *See How They Run: Electing the President in an Age of Mediocracy.* New York: Alfred A. Knopf.

Tenenboim-Weinblatt, K. (2008). Fighting for the Story's Life: Non-Closure in Journalistic Narrative. *Journalism*, 9(1), 31–51.

Tenenboim-Weinblatt, K. (2013a). Bridging Collective Memories and Public Agendas: Toward a Theory of Mediated Prospective Memory. *Communication Theory*, 23(2), 91–111.

Tenenboim-Weinblatt, K. (2013b). The Management of Visibility: Media

Coverage of Kidnapping and Captivity Cases Around the World. *Media, Culture & Society*, 35(7), 791–808.

Tenenboim-Weinblatt, K. & Neiger, M. (2015). Print is Future, Online is Past: Cross-Media Analysis of Temporal Orientations in the News. *Communication Research*, 42(8), 1047–67.

Tenore, M. (2011, March 4). Why Journalists Make Mistakes and What We Can Do About Them. *Poynter.org.* www.poynter.org/news/ mediawire/104195/why-journalists-make-mistakes-what-we-can-do-about-them.

Tenore, M. (2012, October 8). Best Practices: Journalism Education. *Poynter.org.* www.poynter.org/tag/best-practices-journalism-education.

The Times and Iraq [Editorial] (2004, May 26). *The New York Times.*

The Times and Wen Ho Lee (2000, September 26). *The New York Times.*

Thompkins, A. (2004, March 10). Eyewitness Mistakes. *Poynteronline. com.* www.poynter.org/column.asp?id=2&aid=62228.

Thompson, H. (1972). *Fear and Loathing in Las Vegas.* New York: Random House.

Thompson, J. B. (1984). *Studies in the Theory of Ideology.* Berkeley and Los Angeles: University of California Press.

Thompson, J. B. (1996). *The Media and Modernity.* Palo Alto, CA: Stanford University Press.

Thurman, N. & Walters, A. (2013). Live Blogging – Digital Journalism's Pivotal Platform? *Digital Journalism*, 1(1), 82–101.

Thussu, D. (ed.) (2007). *Media on the Move.* London: Routledge.

Tomalin, N. (1969, October 26). Stop the Press, I Want to Get On. *The Sunday Times Magazine.* Reprinted in M. Bromley & T. O'Malley (eds.) (1997). *A Journalism Reader.* London: Routledge.

Tomaselli, K. (2002). Journalism Education: Bridging Media and Cultural Studies. *Communication*, 28(1), 22–8.

Tomaselli, K. (2003). "Our Culture" vs "Foreign Culture": An Essay on Ontological and Professional Issues in African Journalism. *Gazette*, 65(6), 427–41.

Tomlinson, J. (1999). *Globalization and Culture.* Cambridge: Polity.

Tönnies, F. (1971 [1923]). The Power and Value of Public Opinion. In W. J. Cahnman & R. Heberle (eds.), *Ferdinand Tönnies on Sociology.* University of Chicago Press, 261–75.

Tregaskis, R. (1942, September 7). Guadalcanal Landing. International News Service Dispatch.

Tregaskis, R. (1943). *Guadalcanal Diary.* New York: Random House.

Tregaskis, R. (2004). *Invasion Diary.* Lincoln: University of Nebraska Press.

Tremblay, J. (2010, June 14). Twitter: Can It Be a Reliable Source of News? *Nieman Reports.*

Truong, E. (2015, August 5). Telling Stories Visually. *Poynter.org*. www.poynter.org/news/mediawire/362763/telling-stories-visually-5-designers-and-their-advice-for-writers.

Tsetsura, K. & Kruckeberg, D. (2014). *Transparency, Public Relations and the Mass Media: Combating Media Bribery Worldwide*. New York: Routledge.

Tsui, Lokman. (2010). A Journalism of Hospitality. (Unpublished Ph.D. dissertation.) Annenberg School for Communication at the University of Pennsylvania, Philadelphia.

Tuchman, G. (1972). Objectivity as a Strategic Ritual. *American Journal of Sociology*, 77, 660–79.

Tuchman, G. (1978a). *Making News: A Study of the Construction of Reality*. New York: Free Press.

Tuchman, G. (1978b). Professionalism as an Agent of Legitimation. *Journal of Communication*, 28(2), 106–13.

Tudor, A. (1999). *Decoding Culture: Theory and Method in Cultural Studies*. London: Sage.

Tumber, H. & Palmer, J. (2004). *The Media at War: The Iraq Crisis*. London and New York: Sage.

Tumber, H. & Prentoulis, M. (2005). Journalism and the Making of a Profession. In H. De Burg (ed.), T*he Making of Journalists*. London: Routledge, 58–73.

Tumber, H. & Webster, F. (2006). *Journalists Under Fire*. London: Sage.

Tunstall, J. (1970). *The Westminster Lobby Correspondents; A Sociological Study of National Political Journalism*. London: Routledge and Kegan Paul.

Tunstall, J. (1971). *Journalists at Work*. Beverly Hills, CA: Sage.

Turner, G. (1990). *British Cultural Studies: An Introduction*. London: Unwin and Hyman.

Turner, G. (2000, December). Media Wars: Journalism, Cultural and Media Studies in Australia. *Journalism: Theory, Practice and Criticism*, 1(3), 353–65.

Turner, G. (2011). *What's Become of Cultural Studies?* London: Sage.

Udupa, S. (2015). *Making News in Global India*. Cambridge University Press.

UK Phone Hacking Scandal Undermines Individual Privacy [Editorial] (2011, July 10). *The Asian Age Online*.

Ungar, S. J. (1990). The Role of a Free Press in Strengthening Democracy. In J. Lichtenberg (ed.), *Democracy and the Mass Media*. New York: Cambridge University Press, 368–98.

Usher, N. (2014). *Making News at the New York Times*. Ann Arbor, MI: University of Michigan Press.

Valeriani, R. (1991, March/April). Covering the Gulf War: Talking Back to the Tube. *Columbia Journalism Review*, 24–8.

van der Deen, D. (1995, November 12). [Photo] Watching for a Judgment of Real Evil. *The New York Times*.

Van Dijk, T. (1987). *News as Discourse*. Hillsdale, NJ: Erlbaum.

Volkmer, I. (ed.) (2006). *News in Public Memory*. New York: Peter Lang.

Von Krough, G., Ichijo, K. & Nonaka, I. (2000). *Enabling Knowledge Creation*. New York: Oxford University Press.

Vos, T. (2012) "Homo Journalisticus": Journalism Education's Role in Articulating the Objectivity Norm. *Journalism: Theory, Practice and Criticism*, 13(4), 435–49.

Vosniadou, S. (2007). The Cognitive–Situative Divide and the Problem of Conceptual Change. *Educational Psychologist*, 42(1), 55–66.

Voss, F. S. (1994). *Reporting the War*. Washington, DC: Smithsonian.

Vulliamy, E. (ed.) (1994). *Seasons in Hell: Understanding Bosnia's War*. New York: St. Martin's Press.

Wagner, K. (2016, January 5). Twitter CEO Jack Dorsey Shows Users Why 10,000-Character Tweets Aren't So Crazy. *Re/Code.net*. http://recode.net/2016/01/05/twitter-ceo-jack-dorsey-shows-users-why-10000-character-tweets-arent-so-crazy.

Wahl-Jorgensen, K. (2000). Rebellion and Ritual in Disciplinary Histories of U.S. Mass Communication Study: Looking for "the Reflexive Turn." *Mass Communication and Society*, 3(1), 87–115.

Wahl-Jorgensen, K. (2002, August). The Construction of the Public in Letters to the Editor: Deliberative Democracy and the Idiom of Insanity. *Journalism: Theory, Practice and Criticism*, 3, 183–204.

Wahl-Jorgensen, K. (2004, September). How Not to Found a Field: New Evidence on the Origins of Mass Communication Research. *Journal of Communication*, 547–64.

Waisbord, S. (2000). *Watchdog Journalism in South America*. New York: Columbia University Press.

Waisbord, S. (2013). *Reinventing Professionalism*. Cambridge: Polity.

Waisbord, S. (ed.) (2014). *Media Sociology: A Reappraisal*. Cambridge: Polity.

Waldman, P. (2013, April 16). The Trouble with Scoops. *The American Prospect*.

Waldman, S. (2015, June 15). Report for America: A Community-Based Service Model for Saving Local Journalism. *Columbia Journalism Review*.

Walker, L. (2003, March 20). A Medium Meets Its War. *The Washington Post*.

Walsh, J. (1995, January 29). Unearthing Evil. *Time*, 46–7.

WAN-IFRA World Press Trends Report (2014). www.wan-ifra.org/reports/2014/10/07/world-press-trends-report-2014.

WAN-IFRA World Press Trends in Newsrooms (2015, May 26). https://www.google.com/search?q=wan-ifra+trends+in+newsroom+2015&ie=utf-8&oe=utf-8.

Wang, G. (ed.) (2010). *De-Westernizing Communication Research.* London: Routledge.

War and the Letters Page: Who's Counting? (2003, May/June). *Columbia Journalism Review*, 10.

War in the Living Room: Radio Gives Public the News – and the Jitters (1939, September 11). *Newsweek*, 42–3.

War Photographers' Stories (1944, June 26). *Life*, 13–14.

Ward, S. (2010). *Global Journalism Ethics.* Toronto: McGill Queens University Press.

Ward, S. (2011). *Ethics and the Media.* New York: Cambridge University Press.

Ward, S. (2013, November 4). Why Hyping Transparency Distorts Journalism Ethics. *Media Shift.* http://mediashift.org/2013/11/why-hyping-transparency-distorts-journalism-ethics.

Ward, S. (2015). *Radical Media Ethics.* Malden, MA, and Oxford: Wiley-Blackwell.

Wardle, C. (2007). Monsters and Angels: Visual Press Coverage of Child Murders in the US and UK, 1930–1990. *Journalism: Theory, Practice and Criticism*, 8(4), 263–84.

Wardle, C. (2013). Verifying User-Generated Content. In C. Silverman (ed.), *Verification Handbook.* Maastricht, The Netherlands: European Journalism Centre.

Wark, M. (1997). *The Virtual Republic: Australia's Culture Wars of the 1990s.* London: Allen and Unwin.

Wasserman, E. (2006, Fall). Plagiarism and Prejudice. *Media Ethics*, 18(1).

Wasserman, H. (2010). *Tabloid Journalism in South Africa.* Bloomington: Indiana University Press.

Waterford, J. (2015, November 14). Political Amnesia Affects Politics, Bureaucracy and Journalism. *The Age.*

Watergate Bacchanal: Letter to Editor (1973, September). *Quill*, 6.

Watson, M. (1990). *The Expanding Vista.* New York: Oxford University Press.

Weaver, D., R. Beam, B. Brownless, P. Voakes & C. L. Wilhoit (2007). *The American Journalist in the 21st Century.* New York: Lawrence Erlbaum.

Weaver, D. & Wilhoit, G. C. (1986). *The American Journalist: A Portrait of U.S. News People and Their Work.* Bloomington: Indiana University Press.

Weaver, D. & Wilnat, L. (2012). *The Global Journalist in the 21st Century.* New York and Abingdon, Oxon: Routledge.

Webb, J. M. (1974). Historical Perspective on the New Journalism. *Journalism History*, 1, 38–42, 60.

Weber, M. (1958 [1913]). The Social Psychology of the World's Religions. In H. H. Gerth & C. W. Mills (eds.), *From Max Weber: Essays in Sociology.* New York: Oxford University Press, 267–301.

Weibull, L. (2009). Introduction. In G. Terzis (ed.), *European Journalism Education.* Chicago, IL: Intellect, 69–79

Weimer, R. (1992). *Live from Ground Zero.* New York: Doubleday.

Weinberger, D. (2009, August 28). Transparency: The New Objectivity. www.kmworld.com/Articles/Column/David-Weinberger/Transparen cy-the-new-objectivity-55785.aspx.

White, A. (2015). *Moving Stories: International Review of How Media Cover Migration.* London: Ethical Journalism Network.

White, G. B. (2015, July 24). Where Are All the Minority Journalists? *The Atlantic.*

Whitney, C. R. (2003, November 9). Tunnel Vision: Watching Iraq, Seeing Vietnam. *The New York Times*, sect. 4, 1.

Whorf, B. L. (1956). *Language, Thought and Reality.* Reprinted as B. L. Whorf & J. B. Carroll (eds.), *Language, Thought and Reality: Selected Writings of Benjamin Lee Whorf.* New York: Wiley and MIT Press.

Wilkins, L. & Brennen, B. (2004). Conflicted Interests, Contested Terrain: Journalism Ethics Codes Then and Now. *Journalism Studies*, 5(3), 297–309.

Williams, B. & Delli-Carpini, M. (2011). *After Broadcast News: Media Regimes, Democracy, and the New Information Environment.* New York: Cambridge University Press.

Williams, M. (2014, May 14). *Times* Journalists Escape after Kidnapping in Northern Syria. *The Guardian.*

Williams, R. (1978). The Press and Popular Culture: An Historical Perspective. In C. Boyce, J. Curran & P. Wingate (eds.), *Newspaper History from the Seventeenth Century to the Present Day.* Beverly Hills, CA: Sage, 41–50.

Williams, R. (1982). *The Sociology of Culture.* New York: Schocken.

Williams, R. (1983). *Keywords.* New York: Oxford University Press.

Windshuttle, K. (1998). Cultural Studies versus Journalism. In M. Breen (ed.), *Journalism: Theory and Practice.* Paddington, New South Wales: Macleay Press, 17–36.

Withnall, S. (2015, December 15). Aylan Kurdi Images Were Seen by "20 Million People in 12 Hours." *The Independent.*

Wodak, R. & Meyer, M. (2002). *Methods of Critical Discourse Analysis.* London and Thousand Oaks, CA: Sage.

Woodward, B. & Bernstein, C. (1974). *All the President's Men.* New York: Simon and Schuster.

Woodward, B. & Bernstein, C. (1976). *The Final Days.* New York: Avon.

Woodward, O. L. (1945, August 18). From a Soldier in Europe on V-E Day. *Gospel Messenger,* 11.

Worth, R. F. (2011, January 21). How A Single Match Can Ignite a Revolution. *The New York Times.*

Wright, C. & Fayle, C. E. (1928). *A History of Lloyd's.* London: Macmillan & Co.

Wright, H. (1998). Dare We Decentre Birmingham? *European Journal of Cultural Studies,* 1(1), 33–56.

Wright Mills, C. (1959). *The Sociological Imagination.* Oxford and New York: Oxford University Press.

Wu, T. (2006). Journalism Education in China: A Historical Perspective. In K. W. Y. Leung, J. Kenny & P. S. N. Lee (eds.), *Global Trends in Communication Education and Research.* Cresskill, NJ: Hampton Press, 133–58.

Yazbeck, N. (2015, October). Behind the Byline: What Coverage of the Syrian Crisis Reveals About War Reporting in the Digital Age. Presentation to Negotiating Culture: Integrating Legacy and Digital Cultures in News Media. Reuters Institute for the Study of Journalism, Oxford, UK.

Yu, X., Chu, L. & Guo, Z. (2000). Reform and Challenge: An Analysis of China's Journalism Education Under Social Transition. *Gazette,* 64(1), 577–97.

Yu-His, L. E. (2015, December 17). 10 Numbers That Prove 2015 Was the Year of the Refugee. *ThinkProgress.org.* http://thinkprogress.org/immigration/2015/12/17/3731094/year-of-the-refugee.

Yudice, G. (2001). Comparative Cultural Studies Traditions: Latin America and the US. In T. Miller (ed.), *A Companion to Cultural Studies.* London: Blackwell, 217–23.

Zaller, J. (1992). *The Nature and Origins of Mass Opinion.* New York: Cambridge University Press.

Zelizer, B. (1990). Where is the Author in American TV News: On the Construction and Presentation of Proximity, Authorship, and Journalistic Authority. *Semiotica,* 80(1/2), 37–48.

Zelizer, B. (1992a). On Communicative Practice: The "Other Worlds" of Journalism and Shamanism. *Southern Folklore,* 49, 19–36.

Zelizer, B. (1992b). *Covering the Body: The Kennedy Assassination, the Media, and the Shaping of Collective Memory.* University of Chicago Press.

Zelizer, B. (1992c). CNN, the Gulf War, and Journalistic Practice. *Journal of Communication,* 42(1), 68–81.

Zelizer, B. (1993a). Journalists as Interpretive Communities. *Critical Studies in Mass Communication*, 10, 219–37.

Zelizer, B. (1993b). News: First or Final Draft of History? *Mosaic*, 2, 2–3.

Zelizer, B. (1995a, Spring). Journalism's "Last" Stand: Wirephoto and the Discourse of Resistance. *Journal of Communication*, 45(2), 78–92.

Zelizer, B. (1995b). Reading the Past Against the Grain: The Shape of Memory Studies. *Critical Studies in Mass Communication*, 12(2), 215–39.

Zelizer, B. (1997, February 7). Journalism in the Mirror. *The Nation*.

Zelizer, B. (1998). *Remembering to Forget: Holocaust Memory Through the Camera's Eye*. University of Chicago Press.

Zelizer, B. (2001). Collective Memory as "Time-out": Repairing the Time-Community Link. In G. J. Shepherd & E. Rothenbuhler (eds.), *Communication and Community*. New York: Lawrence Erlbaum, 181–9.

Zelizer, B. (2002). Photography, Journalism, and Trauma. In B. Zelizer & S. Allan (eds.), *Journalism after September 11*. London and New York: Routledge, 48–68.

Zelizer, B. (2004a). When War Is Reduced to a Photograph. In S. Allan & B. Zelizer (eds.), *Reporting War: Journalism and Wartime*. London: Routledge, 115–35.

Zelizer, B. (2004b). *Taking Journalism Seriously: News and the Academy*. Thousand Oaks, CA: Sage.

Zelizer, B. (2004c). The Voice of the Visual in Memory. In K. Phillips (ed.), *Framing Public Memory*. Birmingham: University of Alabama Press, 157–86.

Zelizer, B. (2007). On Having Been There: On "Eyewitnessing" as a Journalistic Key Word. *Critical Studies in Media Communication*, 24(5), 408–28.

Zelizer, B. (2010). *About to Die: How News Images Move the Public*. New York: Oxford University Press.

Zelizer, B. (2011a). Journalism in the Service of Communication. *Journal of Communication*, 61(1), 1–21.

Zelizer, B. (ed.) (2011b). *Making the University Matter*. London: Routledge.

Zelizer, B. (2012). How to Give Meaning to the Hand-Wringing After Scandal. *Media, Culture and Society*, 34(5), 625–30.

Zelizer, B. (2015a, October). Terms of Choice: Uncertainty, Journalism and Crisis. *Journal of Communication*, 65(5), 888–908.

Zelizer, B. (2015b, September 8). The Heartbreaking Image of the Syrian Boy Will Not Necessarily Lead to Action. *Huffington Post*.

Zelizer, B. (2016a, August). Communication in the Fan of Disciplines. *Communication Theory*, 26(3), 213–35.

Zelizer, B. (2016b, June 3). McCarthy Revisited? *Huffington Post*. www.

huffingtonpost.com/barbie-zelizer/mccarthy-revisited_b_10262546.
html.

Zelize, B. (2016c, July 4). Kept in the Dark: By Decree or By Choice. *Philadelphia Inquirer*.

Zelizer, B. (2016d). Journalism's Deep Memory: Cold War Mindedness and Coverage of Islamic State. Plenary presented to International Association of Media Communication Research, Leicester, UK.

Zelizer, B. (2017 in press). Order in Baltimore? On Place-Frames in US Journalism. In L. Steiner & S. Waisbord (eds.), *Race, News and the City: Uncovering Baltimore*. New York: Routledge.

Zelizer, B. & Tenenboim-Weinblatt, K. L. (eds.), (2014). *Journalism and Memory*. London: Palgrave MacMillan.

Zerubavel, E. (2003). *Time Maps*. University of Chicago Press.

Zhang, G. L. (2006). The Rise, Development and Trends of the Chinese Communication Studies. *China Media Research*, 2(2), 103–11.

Zhao, Y. (1998). *Media, Market and Democracy in China*. Champaign-Urbana: University of Illinois Press.

Ziomek, J. (2005). *Journalism, Transparency and the Public Trust*. Washington, DC: The Aspen Institute.

Index

9/11 6, 55, 118, 173, 229, 233
World Trade Center 92, 95, 222, 232
19 Million Project 78

ABC *see* American Broadcasting
Company
ABC Australia 53
Aboubaker, Yosef 98
Abu Ghraib 58, 92, 201, 207
Abyssinian War (1895-6) 45
academy
blended inquiry / future correctives
128–31
China 120
cultural analysis 127–8
educators/students 118–21
historical inquiry 124–5
interpretive communities 113–28
journalists 114–18
language studies 125–6
Latin America 119–20
link with journalism 107–9, 111
northern Europe 119
political science 126–7
proactive stance 259–60
publics 121
scholars 122–3
shape/study of journalism 111–13
sociology 123–4
United Kingdom 119
Accelerated Mobile Pages 116
Adam, G. S. 2, 4, 114, 157
Adams, E. 231
Adorno, T. 3, 143
Afghanistan War (2001) 56, 92, 173,
199, 225–6, 229, 232
Al-Ghazzi, O. 58

al-Hayyat Media Center 101
Al Jazeera 53, 57, 75, 199, 201, 209, 222
al-Kasasbeh, Moaz 93
Al Qaeda 219
Aldridge, M. 25
Aldura, Mohammad 220, 231
All the President's Men (film, 1976) 185,
186
Allan, S. 160
AlterNet 22
Amanpour, Christiane 204
American Broadcasting Company
(ABC) 90, 184
American Civil War (1861-5) 45, 46, 86,
215, 217
American Journalism Review 26, 252
American Press Institute 120
American Prospect 15
American Revolution (1775-83) 44
American Society of Newspaper Editors
(ASNE) 86, 188
Anderson, B. 3
Anderson, C. W. 31
Andrejevich, M. 162
AP *see* Associated Press
Appadurai, A. 3, 81, 82
Arab Spring (2011) 6, 57, 58, 59, 173,
229, 234
Aristotle 84, 103
Arnett, Peter 205
Arnold, Matthew 249
Ashley Madison (casual sex website) 85
Asian Age 94
Asian tsunami (2004) 57, 92, 95
Ask.fm 101
ASNE Bulletin 186, 188
Assange, Julian 58, 193

Associated Press (AP) 47, 50, 52, 58, 93, 184
   Freedom of Information Committee 184
Athar, Sohaib 57
The Atlantic 19, 22
Atlantic Monthly 93, 186
Attack: The Battle for New Britain (newsreel, 1944) 50
Australian Journalism Review 85
Aziz, Tariq 201

Baker Jr, H. A. 161
Balkan conflict 216–17, 219
Banfield, Ashleigh 205
Barney, R. 103
Barnhurst, K. 125, 158
Barnicle, Mike 20
Barthes, R. 159
Baym, G. 162
BBC 57, 99, 102, 143, 252
BBC World 53
Beacon 41
Bell, M. 52
Benson, R. 27
Berger, P. 113
Berkowitz, D. 113
Berlin Wall (1989) 55, 233
Berman, S. 64
Bernstein, C. 185, 186
Bezos, Jeff 5
Bhabha, H. K. 181, 183
bin Laden, Osama 6, 57, 92, 173, 199
Bird, S. E. 19, 157
Birmingham Centre for Contemporary Cultural Studies 142
Black, J. 103
Black Lives Matter 6, 7, 22, 57, 58
Black Standard of Islam 93
Black Twitter 108, 115
Blair, Jayson 20, 117, 253
Blair, Sandra 41
blogs, blogging 28, 42, 57, 58, 205–6
Boazizi, Mohammed 234
Boczkowski, P. 31
Bodker, H. 246
Boko Haram 92
Bordenave, Diaz 138
Boston Globe 209, 220, 232
Boston Marathon bombing (2013) 15, 58, 118, 230

Bourdieu, P. 124
Bourke-White, Margaret 46–7
Bradlee, Ben 14
Brady, Matthew 46
Bragg, Rick 117
Branston, G. 160
Brants, K. 166
Brennen, B. 125, 158
BRICs 79, 80
Broder, D. 183, 187, 189–90
Brokaw, Tom 222
Bromley, M. 25, 160
Brown, John 45
Browne, M. 231
Brunsdon, C. 159
Brussels attacks (2016) 118
Buecher, Karl 137
Build Your Own Ethics Code project 87
Burundi 216
BuzzFeed 15, 16, 108, 115

Cain, Herman 91
Calley, William 91
Cameron, J. 129
Campbell, R. 157
Cannon, L. 190
Capa, Robert 17, 49, 218
Carey, J.W. 19, 25, 41, 67, 120, 127, 155, 156, 157, 158, 162, 180
Carlson, M. 113
Carnegie-Knight Initiative on the Future of Journalism Education 120, 130
Carney, Jim 92
Carr, David 115
Carter, C. 160
Carvin, A. 57, 153
Casey, 136
CBS 17, 185
Ceasefire Map 77
censorship 52, 70, 88–9, 94, 140, 147, 162, 173
Center for Public Integrity 22
Certeau, M. de 180
Chalaby, Ahmed 201
Chechnya 225
checkbook journalism 90–2, 94–5, 96–7, 99–100
Chen, G. M. 144
Chicago Fire (1871) 45–6
Chicago School of Sociology 136

Chicago Tribune 225, 227
China 70, 74, 94, 117, 137, 138, 140, 142, 241, 254
Cleveland, G. 29
Clifford, Alexander Graeme 47–8
Closeup (TV program) 184
CNN 15, 51, 53, 58, 91, 182, 198, 199, 204
Colbert, Stephen 116
Cold War 66, 69, 190, 229, 239
Collier's 49
Columbia Journalism Review 15, 21, 26, 29, 91, 97, 117, 187, 208
Columbus, Christopher 43
Comedy Central 116, 143, 146
Committee for Public Information 136
The Committee to Protect Journalists 92
communication/journalism nexus 12, 105
  assumptions challenged 143–7
  challenges to notions of modernity 145–6
  contemporary form 134
  and culture 142–3
  either/or stance 143–4
  geographic nearsightedness 144–5
  historiography of 132–3
  Ivory Tower perspective 144
  journalism as center of communication 134–9, 147–9
  marginalization of journalism 139–43
  and politics 140–1
  reconsidering 132–4
  rethinking existing theories of 147
  and technology 141–2
  uneven exchange of knowledge 144
  worldwide education programs 137–8
concentration camps 92, 125, 227
Conde Nast 85
Connerton, P. 81, 145
Connery, T. 157
Control Room (film, 2004) 205
Cooke, Janet 20, 183
Cottle, S. 160
Craft, S. 255
Craig, R. 146
Crimean War (1853-6) 45
Cronkite, Walter 17, 185
crowd-sourcing 57
Cryptocat 109
cultural studies / journalism nexus

American/British scholarship 156–61
  analytical perspective 151–2
  broadening of study 166–7
  center/margin distinction 152
  challenges 155–6
  complications surrounding facts, truth, reality 154–6, 165
  digital challenges 154
  future of 167–8
  growth of 151–2
  as interdisciplinary/self-reflexive 151
  journalists as conveyors/producers of information 152
  key words / key concepts 161–2
  shared commitment to the real world 160–1
  uneven attention/interest in journalism 162–7
  uniting of journalist/non-journalist 152
  views on journalism 150–6
culture
  perspective on journalism 150–6
  scholarship in communication 142–3
culture of journalism 193–4
  blurring of boundaries in war reporting 204–6
  collective codes of knowledge / belief systems 194–5
  culture as construct 194–7
  description of 197–8
  industrial prism 195
  inhabitants of 202–7
  Iraq war as example 196, 198–202, 203–7, 208–10, 211
  journalism as craft 196, 201
  journalism as institution 195–6
  journalism as profession 195
  reasons for 207–11
  and technology 199–201
Cuomo, C. 90
Curran, J. 144

Dahlgren, P. 129, 154, 160, 193
Daily Mirror 205
The Daily Show (TV program) 116
Dana, Charles A. 41
Darnton, R. 28
Davis, Richard Harding 45
Deep Throat 184, 186
Democracy Now! 18

democracy/journalism nexus 36
  bolstered in World War II 66
  different kinds of links 68
  enabling retirement 82–3
  immunity of shelf life 79–82
  journalism's instrumentality for
    64–8
  and modernity 65, 68–9
  multiple dimensions 67
  not central for journalism 68–71
  philosophical arguments 64–5
  practical complications 69–70
  and the public sphere 65
  refugee crisis 71–8
  and rise of administrative research
    66–7
  shelf life metaphor 63–4
  as tenuous 70–1
  theoretical shortcomings 68–9
Dennis, E. 128
Detroit Free Press 231
Dewey, J. 8, 65, 136, 156, 241, 262
Dewey–Lippmann debate 65
Dickens, Charles 41, 112, 193
Didion, Joan 193
Digital Journalism 130
disciplinary matters 107–9
Domingo, D. 31
Donaldson, S. 183
Dos Passos, John 112
Douglas, M. 113
Dowler, Milly 99
Downing, J. 144
Drone Papers on The Intercept 192
Dropbox 108
Dunning, John P. 47
Durham, M. G. 166
During, S. 161
Durkheim, E. 113

Eason, D. L. 157
Eastlake, Lady Elizabeth 47
Editor & Publisher 26
Edy, J. 248, 251
Egeland, Jan 73
Einstein, Albert 1
Electronic Iraq 210
electronic news production system
  (ENPS) 56
Eliasoph, N. 158
Elster, J. 241

Embedded (play, 2005) 205
Epstein, E. J. 165
Erasmus Mundus program 130
Erdely, Sabrina Rubin 20
Erhaim, Zaina 77
Erni, J. N. 158
Escobar, A. 144
Esquire magazine 91, 186
Ethical Journalism Network 72, 75, 77,
  86
ethics 36–7, 259
  about-to-die images 88–9, 90, 92–3,
    95, 97–8, 101
  checkbook journalism 90–2, 94–5,
    96–7, 99–100
  codes of 87, 93, 98–9, 101–3
  geography and 94–6
  historical background 85–6
  impossibility of 102–3
  institutional culture and 96–9
  problem of 84–9
  public good / right to know 88, 98
  self-regulation 86–7
  standards of 84–5
  technology and 99–102
  temporality and 89–93
ethnic media 108
Ettema, J. 13, 86, 155, 158
Europe or Die (documentary, 2015) 72
Evernote 108
Evetts, J. 25
Eyewitness News (TV program) 41
eyewitnessing 36, 39
  deficiencies, limitations, reliability
    50–2, 58–60
  first-stage (report) 43–4
  fourth-stage (report/role/technology/
    aura) 53–9
  as good journalism 41
  and journalistic sense of self 41–2
  as key word 40–2
  metaphors for 52–3
  outsourcing of activity 55–6
  as professional/realistic 46–8
  resonance/adaptability across periods
    59–60
  romanticism of 44–5
  second-stage (report/role) 44–8
  subjective in tone 43–4
  third-stage (report/role/technology)
    48–53

use of drawings/photography 45–7
value of 42

Facebook 16, 23, 57, 101, 107, 108, 117, 259
  Instant Articles 116
Fahrenheit 9/11 (documentary, 2004) 205
Falklands War (1982) 51
Fallujah, Iraq 206, 210
Fattah, Hassan 210
Faulkner, William 19
Favre, Brett 99
Ferguson, M. 161
field theory 27
Financial Times 28, 240
First Look Media 22, 115
First World 80
Fish, S. 113, 179
Fiske, J. 159, 160
FiveThirtyEight 23
Fontaine, Felix Gregory de 45
Ford, Franklin 136
Ford, Rob 91
Foucault, M. 113
Fourth Estate 21, 70, 94
Fowler, R. 28
Fox News 93, 198, 199, 209
Franken, Al 200
Freedom of Information Act 206
Freire, Paulo 138
Frost, David 90
Fugger News-Letters 44
Fukuyama, F. 140
future
  knowledge transfer 242–5
  moving toward 262
  predicting 239–42
  and proactivity 257–61
  and reflexivity 247–51
  tools of temporal engagement 245–7
  and transparency 251–7

Gans, H. 30, 260
Garcia-Canclini, N. 69, 146
Gardner, Alexander 46
Garner, Eric 41
Gawker Media Deadspin 15, 85, 99–100
Gaza 219, 220
conflict (2008-9) 57
Gazan child of Intifada (2000) 90

Gellhorn, Martha 193
GeoFeedia 252
German Sociological Society 137
Giacom 115
Giddens, A. 2–3, 143, 241
Gitlin, T. 30, 165
Glander, T. 133
Glass, Stephen 20
Glasser, T. 13, 86, 155, 158
Global North 80, 82, 94, 95, 96, 144
Global South 80, 82, 88, 143, 144
Global Voices 17, 77
Golding, P. 161
Goodman, N. 113
Google 70, 140, 239
Google Cardboard 116
Google News Lab 116
GPG 109
Greenwald, Glenn 22, 58, 193
Grenada (1983) 51
Grossberg, L. 158, 161
Grossman, L.K. 200
Guantánamo Bay 93
Guardian 15, 58, 92, 99, 186, 240
Guo, Z. 117

Habermas, J. 65
Hacked Off 75
Halberstam, D. 28
Halbwachs, M. 133
Hall, S. 158–9
Hamill, P. 18
Hamilton, J. M. 125
Hannity, Sean 18
Hardt, H. 125, 136, 158
Harper's Weekly 45–6, 47
Hartley, J. 159, 160, 160–1, 161, 166
HBO 23
Heim, K. 255
Hemingway, Ernest 193
Herblock (Herbert Lawrence Block) 188
Hermes, J. 166
Hermida, A. 24
Hersey, John 112
Hersh, Seymour 14
Hicks, George 50
Hilton, Perez 12
Hindenburg disaster (1937) 42
Holt, Lester 12
Holton, A. 18
Homicide Watch 41

Horkheimer, M. 143
Hossaini, M. 225
Huffington Post 15, 240
Hughes, H. 28
Human Rights Watch 17, 78
Humans of New York (HONY) 78
Hupe, P. 243
Hurricane Katrina (2005) 22
Hussein, Saddam 58, 220, 232–3
Hutchins Commission (1947) 86
Hymes, D.H. 179

ICA *see* International Communication
    Association
imagination 2–3
Independent 93
Independent Press Standards
    Organization (IPSO) 86
Instagram 101, 235–6
Institute for War and Peace Reporting
    (IWPR) 77
The Intercept 22
International Communication
    Association (ICA) 139, 143
    Journalism Studies Interest Group
    (now Division) 130
interpretive community 179–80
    discourse and 191–2
    durational mode 182–4, 190–1
    journalists as 180–1
    local mode 181–2, 190
    McCarthyism example 187–90
    Watergate example 184–7
Intifada 90, 92, 173
IowaWatch 22
iPhone 99, 108
IPSO *see* Independent Press Standards
    Organization
Iran 146, 219
Iran TV 95
Iraq Today 210
Iraq War (2003) 6, 56, 57, 118, 172, 196,
    198–202, 203–7, 208–10, 211, 217,
    219, 222, 225, 226, 229, 231
Iraqi National Museum 201, 227
Iraqi TV 205
Islamic State 5, 7, 37, 71, 78, 88, 89, 90,
    92–3, 95, 97–8, 100–1, 130, 219, 229
Islamophobia 108
IWPR *see* Institute for War and Peace
    Reporting

Jackson, Michael 15
Jamail, Dahr 210
James, William 136
Jarvis, J. 162
Jebril, N. 67
Jelin, E. 144, 145
Jensen, J. 157
Johnson, Samuel 112, 193
Johnstone, J. W. 29
Jones, A. 162
journalism
    affiliation with professions 176
    anniversary 55
    brand 27
    as child 20–1
    as container 14–16
    craft of 4
    culture and 142–3, 203
    definitions 11, 31–2
    economic 5–6
    either/or categorizations 171–3
    as engagement 23–4
    gonzo 19
    imagining 1–8
    as institution 26–7
    journalists' explanations of 12–24
    marginalization of 139–40
    as mirror 16–18
    moral considerations 6–7
    online 206
    as people 29–30
    politics and 4–5, 140–1
    as practice 30–1
    presumed legitimacy 154
    as profession 25–6, 203
    realities of / official presentation of
        self 12
    rethinking 1
    reverence for facts, truth, reality
        154–5
    rooftop 52
    scholars' explanations of 24–31
    as service 21–3
    shape/study of 111–13
    as sixth sense 13–14
    as story 18–20
    team 56
    technology and 5, 141–2
    tensions in 35–7
    terminology associated with 11–12
    as text 27–9

trappings of professionalism 178
as world of contradiction/flux 193
Journalism: Theory, Practice, and Criticism 130
Journalism Practice 130
Journalism Studies 130
journalists 11
  competition over coverage 116–17
  effectiveness of 117–18
  engagement/sharing aspect 23–4
  exclusionary nature 202–3
  explanations/discussions of their craft 12–24
  informal networking among 177
  as interpretive community 179–84
  and journalistic depth 14–16
  moral scandals 117
  narrative/storytelling practice 2, 18–20, 29, 46, 49, 55, 125, 126, 154, 175, 177–8, 186, 249
  and news sense 13–14
  as objective/balanced reporters 177
  parental metaphor 20–1
  political attacks on performance 115–16
  professionalization of 129, 175–9
  relevance/challenges of eyewitnessing 54–9
  and serving the public 21–3
  technological challenges 116
  uncertainties concerning 115
  visual metaphors 16–18
Journohub 78

Kalb, Marvin 186
Kant, I. 64
Katz, E. 158
Katz, Jeffrey 16
Keeble, R. 2
Keller, Bill 23
Kellner, D. M. 166
Kelly, Jack 117
Kennedy, John F. 51, 55, 90, 125, 183
Kenner, H. 18
Khiabany, G. 144
Khmer Rouge 92
Kick, Russ 206
Kik 101
King, Rodney 41
Knight Center for Journalism in the Americas 254

Knight Foundation 120
Korean War (1950-3) 188, 216, 217–18
Kosellek, R. 239
Kracauer, Siegfried 137
Kreiling, A. 157
Kuhn, T. 61, 81, 113, 243
Kurdi, Aylan 72, 73, 224, 232

Lacey, N. 166
Lang, G. E. 245–6
Lang, K. 133, 245–6
Langer, J. 162
Lantern 41
Lasorsa, D. 18
Lasswell, Harold 136
Last Week Tonight (TV program) 116
Latvia 233
Lazarsfeld, Paul 136
Lee, C. C. 144
legacy media 56
Leno, Jay 206
Leslie's 46
Letterman, David 206
Leveson Report (2013) 75
Levi-Strauss, C. 180
Levy, Steven 205–6
Lewis, J. 166
Lewis, S. 18, 113
Lexington Herald-Leader 253
Life magazine 90, 231
LinkedIn 24
Lippmann, W. 29, 65, 136, 137–8
Lloyd, Anthony 98
Loebl, Herbert 137
London Underground bombing (2005) 57, 230
Los Angeles Times 91, 115, 226
Lou Grant 20
Lowrey, W. 26
Luckmann, T. 113
Lumby, C. 162
Lynch, Jessica 201

McAvoy, Will 20
McBride, K. 100
McCarthy, Joseph 188–90
McCarthyism 69, 173, 175, 184, 187–90
McCullin, D. 17
MacDougall, C. 14
McGrory, M. 185
MacIntyre, A. 242

Mackay, J. 26
McQuail, D. 144
MacVane, John 50
Malaysian Airlines 370 (2014) 42, 118
Malraux, André 112, 193
Mander, M. 157
Manning, Chelsea 201
Manoff, R. K. 157
Manti Te'o 15
The Marshall Project 23
Marvin, C. 141, 157, 158
Marx, Karl 137
Mashable 16, 24
Massing, M. 204
Matta, Fernando Reyes 138
May, R. 188
Media Standards Trust 75
MediaDiversified 77
Medium 24
Merz, Charles 137
Middle East 57, 58–9, 67, 71, 95, 183, 229
Mill, J. S. 64
Miller, Judith 201
Miller, T. 163
Mirror 41
Mirror/Mirror Productions 55
Morgenthau, H. J. 66
Morley, D. 159
Morris, M. 167
MSNBC 17, 205, 208, 253
Muhlmann, G. 65
Multeci 78
Murdoch, Rupert 5, 91, 117
Murdock, G. 144
Murrow, Edward R. 41, 188, 189
My Lai massacre (1968) 14, 90, 91

Napoleon III 46
National Magazine Award 22
National Public Radio (NPR) 19, 22, 101, 102
National Review 42
National Security Agency (NSA) 15, 22, 58, 70, 253
National Union of Broadcasters 49
NBC 14, 20, 50, 93, 178, 200, 253
NBCUniversal 253
Neiger, M. 63, 246, 260
Nelson, C. 161
Nerone, J. 125, 127, 158

New Republic 188
New World Information and Communication Order 70, 140
New York Evening Post 17
New York Post 14, 58, 230
New York Times 16, 48, 49, 55, 58, 72, 90, 91, 97, 115, 116, 118, 143, 201, 210, 222, 226, 233, 240, 253, 255
New York Tribune 45, 46
New Yorker 22
NewRepublic 115
news 11–12, 13
    binary opposites 171–2
    connectivity with its audience 23–4
    digital media 19–20
    explanation of 12–13
    hard/soft 18–19
    having a nose for 13–14
    multiple aspects of 14–15
    news hole 16
    nurturing 20–1
    public involvement in 54
    as public service 21–3
    as reflection of all that happens 16–18
    scoops 15
News Corps 97
News of the World 5, 15, 27, 37, 69, 70, 75, 84, 87-91, 94, 96, 97, 99, 117
newsreels 50, 55
The Newsroom 20
Newsvine 17
Newsweek 49, 205, 230, 233
Nielsen, R. 127, 241
Nieman Journalism Labs 6, 240
Nieman Reports 23
Nixon, Richard 90
North Korea 219
Norway's 9/11 massacre 230
Norwegian Refugee Council 73
NPR *see* National Public Radio
NSA *see* National Security Agency
NTV 205

Obama, Barack 92
O'Brien, C. 180, 206
Occupy movement 6, 57, 58
Oliver, John 12, 116
O'Malley, T. 160
ONA *see* Online News Association
One-Man Mobile Uplink caricature 200
The Onion 146

Online News Association (ONA) 37, 87, 259
Open Democracy! 77
Ornebring, H. 26
Orwell, G. 112, 193
Outfoxed (documentary, 2004) 205

Pakistan 224
parachute reporting 56, 138
Paris terrorist attack (2015) 53, 56, 118, 182
Park, M.-J. 144
Park, R. E. 13, 113, 136, 156, 194, 197
Paterson, C. 31
Patterson, T. E. 25, 245
Pauly, J. J. 157
Pax, Salaam (*nom-de-guerre*) 206
PBS 22
Pearson, Drew 188
Pearson, R. 166
People magazine 205
Periscope 56, 77
Persian Gulf War (1990-1) 51–2, 180, 183, 216, 229
    Operation Desert Storm (1991) 51
Peters, J. D. 146
Philadelphia Daily News 6
Philadelphia Inquirer 6, 223, 228, 232
Philadelphia Public Ledger 86
Phillips, A. 253
photography in war 17, 46–7, 212–13
    aesthetic appeal 215, 217–18, 225–8
    appraisal of 234–6
    combining words/images 235–6
    denotive/connotive forces 213–15, 220–1
    image familiarity 215, 218–19, 228–34
    image frequency/selectivity 215–17, 221–5
    problems concerning 214–15
    significance of 215
    and turn to the visual 212, 213–19, 221, 228, 234
    visualizing 21st-century combat 219–34
photojournalists 17, 202–3
Pickard, V. 125
Pliny the Younger 43
Politico 16, 22, 115
Pollitt, C. 243

post-traumatic stress disorder (PTSD) 209
Poynter Institute 13, 42, 96, 100, 208, 259
the press 12
    four theories of 66, 126–7
Price, M. 67
proactivity 257
    benefits of pursuing 261
    need for 259
    rational progress vs. historical process 258
    and reaction to criticism 258–9
    reticence concerning 258
    and scholarship 259–60
    and stabilization of journalists 260–1
    and time in journalism 260
    and tweaking understandings of journalism 261
    as unrealized 258
Project for Excellence in Journalism 200–1, 203–4, 207
Project Lightning 19
ProPublica 22, 252
Pulitzer Prize 21, 90, 184, 225
Putin, Vladimir 230
Pyle, Ernie 17, 48, 49

Quill 26, 186

radio 49–50, 166
Ramos, Jorge 76
Rather, D. 117, 185, 201, 222
Red Scare 69
reddit 24
Reese, S. D. 157
reflexivity 247–51
refugee crisis
    delayed coverage 73–4
    delegated coverage 76–8
    inflammatory rhetoric 76
    journalism/democracy link 71–8
    lack of coverage 71–2, 74
    negative 73–4
    prejudicial coverage 74–6
    problematic coverage 72–3
    shortcomings in coverage 78–9
    terminology used 74–5
The Refugee Project 78
Reporters Without Borders 219–20
Reston, J. 183, 188

Reuters 209, 225
Reuters Institute for the Study of
    Journalism 254
Rich, F. 228
Riddell, G. A. 14
Rieder, Rem 99
Riefenstahl, Leni 93
Rivera, Gerald 205
The Road 79
Rodman, G. 166
Rolling Stone 19, 26, 117, 178
Rosen, J. 255
Rosenberg, S. 258
Rottwilm, P. 6, 251
Rovere, R. 189
Rozumilowicz, B. 67
Russell, William Howard 45
Russia 36, 94, 137, 146, 219, 241
Rwanda 216, 218
Ryfe, D. 31

Salomon, Albert 137
Samoan hurricane (1889) 47
San Francisco Call 45
San Francisco earthquake (1906) 45
Sarnoff, David 136
Saturday Night Live 200
Schaeffler, Richard 137
Schell, Orville 56
Schlesinger, P. 160, 246
Schorr, D. 11, 17, 184, 190, 192
Schramm, W. 136, 138
Schudson, M. 18, 157, 180, 186, 190,
    245
Schumer, Amy 85, 116
Scott, Walter 41
See It Now (radio program) 41
Seid, Charles 189
shelf life
    definition 61
    and democracy/journalism nexus
        63–4
    dissemination of knowledge 61–2
    strategies associated with expiration
        of 62
Shiach, M. 161
Shirer, W. 48, 49
Silver, Nate 22, 193
Simonson, P. 136
Simpson, C. 133
Simpson, O. J. 42

Sims, N. 157
The Situation Room (photo) 227
Sky News 53
Skype 57
Small, William 185
Smith, W. Eugene 231
Snapchat 77, 235
Snowden, Edward 15, 58, 70
social media 5, 7, 16, 19, 23, 24, 56, 57,
    101, 107, 108, 115, 117, 259
Social Science Research Council 136
Society of Professional Journalists (SPJ)
    86, 91, 254
sociology 2–3, 123–4
Somalia 225, 229, 232
Sontag, S. 207
Sotloff, Steven 98
Soundcloud 101
Spanish American War (1898) 45, 86,
    215, 217
Spanish Civil War (1936-9) 46, 49, 92,
    218
Sparks, C. 160, 162
speak2tweet 153
SPJ *see* Society of Professional
    Journalists
St John, Robert 50
State of the News Media (2015) 121
Steele, John 189
Steffens, L. 17
Steiner, L. 157
Stephenson, H. 160
Stewart, Jon 206
Storey, J. 166
Storify 24
The Story of G. I. Joe (film, 1945) 49
Sun 75
Swidler, A. 80
Swinton, Ernest 46
Syria 6, 57, 58, 72, 73–4, 77–9, 98, 108,
    173, 183, 219, 220, 221

Tarde, G. 65, 137
Tass 188
Taylor, C. 3
Teapot Dome scandal 183
technology 142, 241
    centrality of 53–9
    culture of journalism in war 199–201
    effect on journalism 107–9, 141–2
    and ethics 99–102

mobile 19–20, 42, 56, 200–1
new platforms 48–53
television 51–2, 166
Tenenboim-Weinblatt, K. 63, 246
The Third of May 1808 (Goya painting)
228
Third World 80, 144
Thomas, Dylan 112
Thompson, H. S. 19
Thompson, J. B. 3, 143
Thought News 136
Tiananmen Square 233
Tiananmen Tank Man (1989) 90
time
and knowledge transfer 242–5
tools of temporal engagement 245–7
Time magazine 221, 230, 231, 232
The Times 226
TinEye 252
TMZ.com 15
Tocqueville, A. de 64–5, 137
Tolstoy, Leo 41
Tomlinson, J. 143
Tönnies, F. 65, 137
Topsy 252
Totenberg, Nina 19
Trainwreck (film, 2015) 85
Trans-Pacific Partnership 91
transparency
celebration of 252–5
centrality of 252
changing default assumptions about
journalism 256–7
and criticism 257
explaining/justifying decisions 251–2
failure of 253–4
inconsistency of use 253
link with the present 251–7
platforms for 252, 255
and the public 255–6
role of scholars 256
as slippery concept 253
Transphobia 108
Tregaskis, R. 49
Treichler, P. 161
Trump, Donald 76, 190
Tsui, L. 260
Tuchman, G. 30, 165
Tulloch, J. 162
Tumber, H. 160
Tumblr 101

Tunstall, J. 119
Turner, G. 159, 161
Twitter 16, 19, 57, 58, 101, 108, 115,
117, 259

UK Press Complaints Commission 86
Ukraine 219
UN High Commissioner on Human
Rights 75
UN Human Rights Committee 172
UN Security Resolutions 202
UNESCO 202
United Press International (UPI) 189
University of Chicago 136
University of Leipzig 119
Univision 76
UPI *see* United Press International
US News & Woirld Report 233

van Zoonen, L. 166
Veblen, T. 156
VICE News 14–15, 23, 72, 78, 93, 115
Vietnam War (1955-75) 14, 51, 90, 92,
180, 183, 216, 229, 231, 233, 234
Vine 235
Vos, T. 80
Vox 93, 115

Wahl-Jorgensen, K. 146
Waisbord, S. 176, 177
Wall Street Journal 85, 206
Wang, G. 144
war reportage 180, 196
amateur photographers 207
blogs / online journalism 205–6, 207
critiques of 201
embedded journalists 4, 52, 57, 172,
198, 200, 203–5
erroneous interpretations 201
eyewitnessing 49–52
informal activity 201–2
lampooning of war's prosecution 206
making sense of war 198
non-embedded positions 204–5
patriotic/impartial reporting 208–9
photography in 46–7
practice at the margins 199
professionalism of 46
subset of journalistic practitioners
205
and technology 49–52, 199–201

war reportage (*cont.*)
  threat, abduction, murder of
    reporters 209–10
  use of locally based individuals 56–7
Ward, S. 86
Warsaw Ghetto Boy (*c.*1945) 90
Washington, George 44
Washington Post 5, 14, 15, 52, 72, 91,
  97, 100, 101, 102, 184, 185, 240,
  241
Washington Star 189
Watergate (1972-4) 5, 15, 125, 173, 175,
  183, 184–7
Waugh, Evelyn 15
Weapons of Mass Destruction 192, 201,
  254
Weaver, D. 25, 29
Weber, Max 137
WhatsApp 101
White, Aidan 86
Whitman, Walt 44–5, 136
WikiLeaks 70, 91, 100, 193, 209
Wilhoit, G. C. 25, 29
Williams, Brian 14, 20, 26, 93, 117, 178,
  253
Williams, R. 40–1
Wilnat, L. 29

Witness 17, 41, 78
Wolfowitz, Paul D. 210
Woodward, B. 185, 186
World Editors Forum, *World Press
  Trends in Newsrooms* 116
The World Fixer Community 78
World War I 46, 135, 136, 144, 218
World War II 49, 50–1, 66, 125, 135,
  180, 204, 215, 218, 229, 231
  D-Day 50, 55
  Iwo Jima 50
  Pearl Harbor 50, 183, 232
Wright Mills, C. 2, 4

Xenophon 41
Xinhua news agency 95

Yahoo News 23
Yemen 219
Young Communist League 189
YouTube 14–15, 57, 101, 117

Zaatari refugee camp 79
Zahn, Paula 208
Zapruder, Abraham 90
Zelizer, B. 113, 158
Zola, Émile 41